Swimming and diving

to be much smaller when it is viewed above the surface than when it is viewed below the surface.

Comparative records are presented. The work schedules given are designed for summer swimming programs for high school and college men and women. Personalities have been intentionally omitted.

Crawl stroke techniques are evaluated, and information on conditioning, training, and refinements in technique of the back crawl, the dolphin butterfly stroke, and breast stroke are included. Topics on preparations for a swimming and diving meet, responsibilities of the various officials, and swimming pool design are presented.

As before, the side stroke and elementary back stroke have been included, and the newer stroke, called the resting back stroke, is presented again. The method of teaching beginners to swim, the all-stroke Armbruster method, employs the use of this new stroke to great advantage. The successful use of this system will eliminate the intermediate level in order that the swimmer can progress to an advanced level rapidly.

New dives, together with new techniques and hints in coaching have been added. Teaching methods for all strokes, as well as coaching the competitive strokes, have been added to this revision.

We are indeed grateful for the excellent contribution of a new chapter on skin and scuba diving by one of the outstanding West Coast authorities, Dr. George Q. Rich. He is an associate professor at San Fernando Valley State College, teaching exercise, physiology, and scuba diving. He also serves as Director of the Human Performance Laboratory at San Fernando Valley State College.

We also wish to express our gratitude to Dr. Leon E. Smith for his consultation on the new chapter. Dr. Smith is the head of the University of Iowa, Motor Performance Laboratory. An Australian, he is an outstanding expert and performer in skin and scuba diving.

We wish also to acknowledge the expert advice and consultation of Niel Fisher, M.S. Civil Engineering, Associate Professor of Preventive Medicine and Environmental Health. Professor Fisher filled the role of sanitary consultant on swimming pool water analysis and hygiene.

Unfortunately it is impossible to mention everyone to whom we owe a grateful debt of thanks for advice and encouragement. However, we wish to express additional thanks to the following:

Dr. W. W. Tuttle, Professor of Physiology, University of Iowa, and Dr. Laurence E. Morehouse, of the University of California at Los Angeles, for their inspiration and guidance throughout the preparation of the book and for their counsel pertaining to matters of a physiologic nature; the late Dr. C. H. McCloy, Professor of Physical Education, University of Iowa, for his inspiration and encouragement; Dr. Arthur

Preface

Source material in the field of swimming and diving is amazingly limited, and, mindful of this situation, the material in this book has been presented with the idea of aiding beginning instructors and coaches and beginning swimmers and competitors, in addition to improving the techniques, skills, and performances of advanced swimmers and divers. To this end, the technique of each stroke and dive is presented in some detail. Where technique and form are somewhat involved, we have attempted to present each phase in a clear, logical, and orderly sequence so that both the high school and college athlete can easily understand the discussion. We do not claim that the methods and techniques of swimming and diving and the styles and methods of teaching, learning, and coaching are to be taken as absolute. We merely present them as a means of more nearly approaching the basic fundamental principles of the ideal.

We recognize the differences of opinion as to what constitutes good form in swimming and the different methods of teaching beginners. Kinesiologic and physiologic principles as well as physical laws were the guiding factors in presenting the material. An attempt is made to fit the discussion to conform to practices that are recognized as being correct. Some new studies and techniques have been advanced as a result of experiments carried out at the University of Iowa. Where opinion was the only source material available, practices that are generally considered as being correct are given.

The diagrams presented in this book were drawn almost entirely from an underwater movie study of some of the world's greatest swimmers. These underwater motion picture studies, taken through underwater observation windows, have opened a new technique in the swimming world.

Our readers should bear in mind that this method is most accurate and desirable since it eliminates distortion of light upon surface refraction. For example, the range action of a swimmer's flutter kick appears

v

Fifth edition

Swimming and diving

David A. Armbruster, Sr., B.A., M.A.

*Associate Professor of Physical Education Emeritus
and Head Swimming Coach Emeritus,
University of Iowa, Iowa City, Iowa;
elected to Swimming Hall of Fame of Fort
Lauderdale, Florida, December, 1966*

Robert H. Allen, B.S., M.A.

*Head Swimming Coach, University of Iowa,
Iowa City, Iowa; President, American College
Swimming Coaches Association, 1966*

Hobert Sherwood Billingsley, B.S., M.S.

*Diving Coach, Indiana University,
Bloomington, Indiana*

With 35 illustrations

The C. V. Mosby Company

Saint Louis   1968

Wendler, Chairman of Undergraduate Major Students of Physical Education, University of Iowa, for his helpful guidance in pacing plans; Mrs. Paul J. Cilek, Iowa City AAU Secretary, for her contribution in the chapter pertaining to summer age-group swimming meets. Also, Dr. Donald Casady, Professor of Physical Education and former Diving Coach, University of Iowa, for guidance in diving; Mr. Lee Allen, Medical Illustrator, Department of Ophthalmology, University of Iowa Hospital, for the beautifully executed diagrams; Mr. Lee W. Cochran, Supervisor of Visual Instruction, University of Iowa, and his associate, Mr. John Hedges, for their patient and accurate services in filming the motion pictures used; the Dolphin, a national honorary swimming fraternity, for rendering invaluable service in the promotion of swimming studies at the University of Iowa and for supplying moving picture materials for the filming of underwater pictures; those champions who performed before the cameras and the many former and present members of the university swimming teams; and the leading swimming and diving coaches in the United States, for their suggestions and discussions throughout these many pleasant years for the advancement and improvement of swimming and diving.

David A. Armbruster
Robert H. Allen
Hobert S. Billingsley

Contents

1 Introduction—historical evolution of swimming and diving, 1

2 The all-stroke Armbruster method for teaching beginning swimming, 14

3 Teaching the resting back stroke, 27

4 Teaching the elementary back stroke, 31

5 Introduction to teaching the higher level skilled strokes, 33

6 Teaching the side stroke, 36

7 Advanced swimming, 43

8 Coaching the racing start, 46

9 Coaching the sprint crawl stroke, 61

10 Coaching the middle distance crawl stroke, 98

11 Coaching the distance crawl stroke, 106

12 Coaching the back crawl stroke, 118

13 Teaching and coaching the breast stroke, 142

14 Teaching and coaching the dolphin butterfly stroke, 161

15 Relay racing, 171

16 Conditioning, 175

17 Training, 192

18 Teaching and coaching springboard diving, 220

19 Teaching and coaching tower diving, 290

20 Teaching skin and scuba diving, 319

21 The swimming pool—its care and maintenance, 333

22 How to conduct dual, championship, and summer age-group meets, 343

Swimming and
diving

Chapter 1

Introduction—historical evolution of swimming and diving

The development of swimming techniques can be traced from writings dating to the sixteenth century. Prior to that time, accounts by the Greek, Roman, Anglo-Saxon, and Scandinavian classics dealt only with great feats of swimming prowess of the heroes of their day and left the type of swimming stroke used by these heroes to the reader's imagination. Other ancient narratives mentioned swimming in connection with religious rites, but these practices usually included dousing or bathing and not the art of moving progressively through the water.*

The first book on swimming was written by Nicolas Wynman, a German professor of languages, in 1538.† A more scientific treatise was later written by Thevenot, a Frenchman, in a book entitled *The art of swimming.*‡ The method Thevenot described resembles closely that which we now designate as the breast stroke. The arms stroked sideward like the oars in rowing a boat, except that they were recovered under the water. The legs also stroked sideward in unison in an action similar to the kick of a frog. Although the breast stroke was not adapted to speed swimming, it had many advantages which caused it to remain popular. The stroke gave the swimmer unobstructed forward vision and permitted more freedom for natural breathing. Stroking the arms under the surface prevented splashing the swimmer's face. The stroke thus gave the swimmer a feeling of stability, even in rough water. The pioneers constructed this stroke so well that it established the foundation of all strokes. Two and one half centuries after its origin, this method of swimming retains its original characteristics. It is still the most seaworthy of all our modern strokes.

*For a more complete account of historical swimming literature see Cureton, T. K.: How to teach swimming and diving, New York, 1934, Association Press, Chapter IV, p. 85.
†Wynman, Nicolas: Colymbetes, sive de arte natanli dialogus et festivus et incundus lectu (Dutch Copy), Bavana, 1538, Ingolstdt. The title of this book is translated literally as follows: "The diver, or a dialogue, concerning the art of swimming, both pleasant and joyful to read."
‡Thevenot, M.: L'art de nager, Paris, 1696.

SIDE UNDERARM STROKE

With the advance of swimming as a competitive sport, ways to speed up the breast stroke were sought. Some of its utilitarian values had to be sacrificed for the sake of speed. All of the foregoing strokes, that is, from the orthodox breast stroke era, have been originated and refined for speed in competition in less than one hundred years. European coaches began practical experiments to devise methods which would reduce the resistance of the arms and legs under water. It was found that if the swimmer swam on his side, he could lift one arm out over the water on the recovery of that arm and thereby speed the recovery as well as reduce the water resistance which impeded his forward motion. This shift to the side also necessitated an alteration of the leg action. A leg movement resembling that of the blades of scissors, in which the principles of the frog kick are employed in the horizontal position, was adopted. This stroke was called both the "side overarm" and the "English overarm," the names being descriptive of the arm action rather than the leg action. The best time recorded for swimming 100 yards with the English overarm stroke was 1:15.0, set by W. Cole of England at the first English championships in 1871. In the next twenty years this stroke was refined, and in 1895 J. H. Tyers of England reduced the time for swimming 100 yards to 1:02.5.

Experimenters in swimming then reasoned that, if by lifting one arm out of the water at the completion of its pull greater speed was obtained, then further speed might be expected from recovering both arms out of the water. The first practical use of this principle was made by J. Trudgeon. Each arm was permitted to recover out of the water by rolling the body from side to side. A kick resembling the action of scissors occurred following each arm stroke. The stroke was named after its originator, Trudgeon, but was sometimes called the "alternating overarm" stroke. The success of this innovation as a speed stroke was proved by further time reductions for swimming 100 yards. In 1901 F. V. C. Lane of England used the Trudgeon stroke and achieved the astounding time of one minute flat.

In thirty years the record for swimming the 100-yard crawl had been lowered 25 seconds. The first two eras in the history of speed swimming had produced considerable headway. During the English overarm era of twenty-three years, from 1871 to 1894, the swimming time for 100 yards improved 12.5 seconds. During the seven-year Trudgeon era from 1894 to 1901, there was a further improvement in time of 0:02.5.*

So far, attention had been given only to the arm action. The legs had been only a little more than just trailing members. An analysis of

*Note: Although other distances were also being swum, the 100-yard event is alluded to since records are most complete in this event. Also, this distance is excellent for measuring man's speed in water.

the leg action employed by swimmers using the Trudgeon stroke revealed three factors which had to be revised before the leg action could make a contribution to speed. First, the recovery phase of the Trudgeon kick involved too much resistance to forward progression. Doubling up the legs and their lateral spread preliminary to the drive of the scissors kick, presented an opposing force that materially discounted the drive of the power phase of the kick. This counterforce had to be reduced. Second, the Trudgeon kick had only one single unit of power for each arm cycle. A leg action that provided a continuous series of forward drives to each arm stroke was, therefore, sought. Third, the rhythm of the Trudgeon kick did not synchronize with the alternating overarm stroke. The body had to be rolled from side to side in order to deliver a good scissors kick. This rolling movement retarded the action of the arms and had to be eliminated before better timing could be attained.

The delivery of one kick with each arm stroke in the refined Trudgeon technique was an advance over the single kick for each arm cycle as employed by the side overarm swimmers. In order to double the number of leg kicks for each arm cycle, the width of the leg spread in the recovery phase was reduced. With this, the resistance to forward progression was also somewhat reduced.

The pause after each scissors kick in the side overarm stroke was eliminated in the Trudgeon stroke. Although the leg action in the latter stroke was slow and each kick was performed in an alternately different position, the kick was somewhat continuous and resembled a fluttering action. The increase in leg kicks from one to two beats for each arm cycle in the change from the side overarm to the Trudgeon stroke did not improve the timing, since the leg movement still had to be arrested in order to correspond with the recovery of the arms.

BEGINNING AND DEVELOPMENT OF THE CRAWL STROKE

In distant Australia, a man named Richard Cavill conducted an experiment which demonstrated the ineffectiveness of the Trudgeon kick when used with the alternating overarm stroke. Cavill observed a race between his brother, Tum, and a friend named Syd Davis. Both used the alternating overarm stroke, but Tum swam with his legs tied while Syd used the regular Trudgeon kick. Tum was able to beat Syd. When Tum's legs were untied and they raced over the same distance again, this time both of them using both arms and legs, Syd beat Tum. Here was a demonstration that the Trudgeon kick was a retarding rather than an advancing factor! Richard Cavill recalled a rapid, vertical action of the legs used by Alec Wickham of Colombo, Ceylon. He combined this leg action with the alternating overarm stroke and found that greater speed could thus be attained. This "Australian crawl" stroke was first introduced by Richard Cavill at the international championships in 1902. He lowered the world record for swimming 100 yards to 0:58.4 seconds. This new style immediately gained in popularity among the coaches of all nations, and soon the Australian crawl stroke was being swum in many parts of the world. The new leg action provided solutions to the three recognized drawbacks present in the Trudgeon stroke. The kick was called the "flutter" kick, its name being descriptive of the thrashing action of the legs. The recovery phase of this leg action offered only a small resistance to forward progression. It provided a continuous series of four power units for each arm cycle and was easily synchronized with the alternating overarm stroke. The reciprocal succession of acceleration and deceleration had been diminished, and now the forward progression was steady and more economically derived. The increased power from the legs in using the flutter kick permitted the body to maintain a position at the surface of the water which reduced the resistance of the water to the body considerably. The introduction of the flutter kick in 1902 established a new era in speed swimming.

There were still a few mechanical mysteries pertaining to the flutter kick that remained to be solved. The theory that the straightening of the bent leg at the knee pushed the water backward and provided the main propulsive force which drove the swimmer forward was still held. This propelling force was also thought to be supplemented by squeezing the water from between the legs as they came together. That phase of the leg action in which the legs are thrust vertically apart was considered to be a recovery phase only and, as such, provided no forward propelling force. The emphasis was therefore placed upon the extension of the knee and the closing of the legs.

The face was held down in the water, and the arms were moved in a crawling fashion. Because of the peculiar appearance of this stroke, it was first called the "creeping crawl" stroke.

American coaches sought to meet the keen competition by revising this new speed stroke. They increased the leg action from four to six beats to each arm cycle. An eight-beat kick was tried but was found to be too fatiguing and was soon abandoned. The crawl stroke was confined to use in short distances only since the swimmers were soon out of breath. A system of breath control was developed in which the swimmer raised his head forward for a gasp of air and then slowly bubbled it out under water. This so-called "underwater breathing" contributed to swimming performance over greater distances. Later it was found that breathing could be further improved by turning the face to the side for the inhalation.

A slightly "pigeon-toed" position of the feet was introduced in order to present a greater surface area to the water during the flutter kick. A further refinement by American coaches included a brief relaxation period for the arms. This occurred during the recovery phase while the arm was above the surface of the water. The coaches in the United States termed this revised edition of the Australian crawl stroke the "American crawl" stroke.

The results attained by the American coaches in perfecting the crawl stroke soon became evident. In 1906, Charles M. Daniels became the first United States speed swimming champion of the world. He lowered the 100-yard swimming record to 0:55.4 seconds. The crawl became so popular that it was the first stroke taught to beginners. "Duke" Kahanamoku, a Hawaiian, using the American crawl stroke, lowered Daniels' record to 0:54.6 seconds for 100 yards. This record was made in 1913 and remained unbroken until 1923. Kahanamoku's chief asset was a pair of long, broad feet which provided a large surface for propulsive action. He was tall and powerful and used a tremendous leg action. He was one of the first great swimmers to develop a purely vertical, full-measured, six-beat flutter kick to each arm cycle.

The leg action that was generally used at that time was the "trudge-crawl" kick, developed by Frank Sullivan of Chicago for distance swimmers. Six beats for each arm cycle were used. The first and the fourth beats were wide and scissorslike. These were called the major beats. The second, third, fifth, and sixth were narrow and faster. These were called the minor beats. The popular use of the trudge-crawl kick was gradually replaced by the faster, evenly measured, vertical flutter kick.

In 1923, Johnny Weissmuller, then 17 years old, lowered Kahanamoku's record to 0:52.8 seconds. In 1927, he lowered it again to 0:51.0 seconds. During this same year, Weissmuller, in a 20-yard course, swam 100 yards in 0:49.8 seconds. In seven years he established over fifty American and world records.

Weissmuller introduced four new and significant developments in the speed crawl stroke.*

1. The pull-and-push power arm stroke in which the pull starts from a straight arm action as soon as the arm enters the water. The arm is pressed down and slightly inward until it reaches a point just ahead of the shoulder. Here the arm is bent slightly at the elbow, resembling a boomerang, and from this point continues in a pushing delivery.

2. The turning of the head for breathing which was independent of the arm action.

3. A deep leg action for the flutter kick in order to obtain greater traction in the water.

*Weissmuller, John, and Bush, Clarence: Swimming the American crawl, Boston, 1930, Houghton Mifflin Co.

4.   The deeper leg action which allowed the chest and shoulders to be carried higher.

In the 1928 Olympic Games, Weissmuller captured nearly all of the sprint swimming championship titles. His style was generally accepted by American swimmers and coaches as the best speed swimming stroke in existence. The youth of this country set about to master this stroke with the aid of a special device which was soon to aid in again revolutionizing the speed swimming stroke. This special device was the slow-motion picture camera*. Many miles of film were being distributed which showed both out-of-the-water and underwater shots of Weissmuller's speed swimming style.

The use of these films was not limited to the Americans, however; Weissmuller and other American and European swimmers were photographed in action from all directions by the Japanese swimming technicians. These films were taken to Japan and were widely exhibited among the Japanese schools. These school children thus observed and were coached in the best styles from early youth, and through intensive training some of them were able to overcome all competition in speed swimming at the 1932 Olympic Games in Los Angeles. Four years before, in the 1928 Olympics, they won only the 200-meter breast stroke event. In 1932 they won every swimming event except the 400-meter free style.

The Japanese style contained nothing new but was essentially a combination of the best speed swimming mechanics used by previous champions. The essential features of the arm action were the quick recovery and long glide of each arm after it entered the water. This style was introduced by Buster Crabbe and his coach, "Dad" Center from Hawaii, at the 1928 United States Olympic tryouts.

A great portion of the success of the Japanese could be ascribed to their superb physical condition. This condition was due to a careful control of diet, exercise, and rest, as well as a rigorous training regime.

Although overshadowed by Japanese successes, two other styles of the crawl stroke were seen at the 1932 Olympics. Many European swimmers used a peculiar arm action in which the arms recovered with a low, lateral, straight arm sweep above the surface of the water. The arm action of this European crawl stroke resembled the sweep of a scythe. Another crawl style, used by the women's team from Holland, employed a high, straight arm recovery and smashed the arms into the water as the recovery was completed. This method is presently called op-position rhythm; that is, as the arm enters the water, it immediately

*In 1928 Armbruster introduced underwater movies of swimming strokes before the American College Swimming Coaches Association Forum in Fort Lauderdale, Florida. These movies were taken from the observation underwater windows of the then new University of Iowa fieldhouse swimming pool.

goes into its press, catch, and pull, thus eliminating the glide of the arm almost entirely.

American swimmers and their coaches returned from the 1932 games with a determination to develop their style and condition in order to recover the swimming crowns lost to the Japanese. Their efforts were rewarded at the 1936 games in Berlin where they were successful in winning the Olympic swimming and diving championships.

Again in Los Angeles in the summer of 1949 at the National Amateur Athletic Association Swimming Championships, the Japanese gained sweeping victories in the crawl stroke events. This time they had something new. Although underwater movies were not taken at this time, Furuhashi, whose performance was most outstanding, was watched very closely by keen-eyed observers. What was seen was a feature that Jam Handy, a Detroit producer of training films, had suggested at the coaches' meeting in Florida the winter before and what McCloy and Armbruster, working with hydraulics engineers, were learning from tedious research studies at the University of Iowa. It was this. Simply by shortening two of the beats of the six-beat flutter kick, some of the parasitic drag of the legs during the arm pull is reduced. Also, the slide of the supporting arm at the entry is eliminated so that the arm goes deeper for the catch and is thus more effective. This change in arm entry allows the shoulder of the pulling arm to be lowered, thus allowing the water to wash over it. This reduces the resistive bow wave ahead of the swimmer. However, the shoulder must remain on top of the hand and elbow as it goes down for the deeper catch.

Research studies of the arms and legs acting separately in swimming the crawl stroke have shown that the ratio of propulsive force between the arms and legs is approximately 70 to 30 in favor of the arms. At present this ratio is even greater in favor of the arms. It is obvious, then, that in coordinating the arm and leg action, when a compromise must be made, it should be in favor of the arm action.

In the 1956 Olympic Games at Melbourne, Australia, the Australian men's team won five of the nine gold medals, while the United States team won two. The Australian women's team, led by Dawn Frazer, won every freestyle event, including the 400-meter freestyle relay.

The outstanding success of the Australian swimmers became a challenge to the American coaches and swimmers. A study of the Australian swimming program indicated little differences in stroke technique. The training method was the big factor. The Australian was swimming more often, the total mileage of each workout was greater, and the stress placed upon the swimmer was more severe.

The desire on the part of the American coaches and swimmers to regain lost prestige led to the adoption of training methods used by track coaches and runners in breaking the 4-minute mile. The emphasis placed on training young swimmers, the popularity of the summer age group competitive program, and the application of new theories and techniques by swimming coaches were instrumental in the great success by the American swimmers in the 1960 and 1964 Olympic Games.

Champions have always had a large following. Some swimmers have become champions in spite of an arm stroke or leg kick that was mechanically unsound. A great many swimmers and some coaches have sought to copy the style of a champion on the theory that, if it was good for the champion, it was good enough for them. Others believed that certain styles should be adapted to athletes of a certain build. Many coaches contended that Weissmuller's style could be used by tall swimmers but that it was not suitable to those of less height.

The development of the technique of swimming the American crawl stroke has evolved from the trial-and-error method of experimentation, the criterion of the success of certain innovations being the increase in speed in swimming. The constant lowering of records is a good indication that the mechanics of the swimming strokes are still being improved.

In the development of speed swimming, attention has been focused on the crawl, the fastest of all strokes. Three other competitive strokes, the breast stroke, the dolphin butterfly breast stroke, and the back crawl stroke, were retained, and they have undergone a development which is also interesting to note.

BREAST STROKE

The breast stroke, outmoded as a speed stroke by the side over-arm stroke, was never eliminated from the international competitive swimming program. In fact, because of its utility it was placed on each program as a special event and was the only stroke in which a prescribed style was required.

ORIGIN AND DEVELOPMENT OF THE DOLPHIN BUTTERFLY STROKE

The underwater recovery of the arms and legs was the retarding factor in the breast stroke. The best time for swimming 100 yards using the breast stroke was 1:07.0 until in 1934 an arm stroke which complied with the rules and yet employed an out-of-the-water recovery was discovered. The recovery was a double overarm stroke in which the arms were simultaneously swung laterally and then forward. The swimmer resembled a butterfly in flight, and the name "butterfly" was given to this stroke.

Using the new butterfly breast stroke, 100 yards was swum in 1:05.0, a new record for the breast stroke. Although this stroke did not violate any of the rules pertaining to the breast stroke, it was a departure from the orthodox method, and it met with disapproval among many coaches and officials. The International Swimming Federation gave it sanction for universal use in 1937. Later the butterfly breast stroke was permitted only if used throughout the entire race. There was at this stage of development no interchange permitted between the butterfly and orthodox styles in international competition. In fact the F.I.N.A.* then went on record of dividing the breast stroke into two categories: the orthodox and the butterfly. In the butterfly style either the breast stroke kick or the dolphin fishtail kick may be employed, so long as they are executed in unison. For speed the dolphin butterfly stroke is now in second place to the sprint crawl stroke.

American records for the short course as established up to 1967 are as follows:

	N.C.A.A.
100 yards free style	0:45.6
100 yards butterfly	0:50.2
100 yards back	0:52.5
100 yards breast	0:58.5

The butterfly breast stroke was faster than the orthodox, but it still had a retarding factor to greater speed, the so-called frog kick, which had to recover under water and against forward progress.

With this new and faster arm action, the retarded recovery action of the legs became a matter of Armbruster's attention. In 1935, Jack Sieg, a University of Iowa swimmer, developed the skill of swimming on his side and beating his legs in unison similar to the action of a fish's tail. He was then asked to try the same leg action while swimming face down. With a little practice Sieg could perform the leg action just as efficiently in this position. Finally Armbruster and Sieg combined the butterfly arm action with this leg action and found that the two could be synchronized. Swimming with two leg beats to each butterfly arm action, Sieg swam 100 yards in 1:00.2. This kick was named the "dolphin fishtail" kick.†

The dolphin fishtail butterfly stroke has at present been so well refined that it now is in second place to the crawl stroke in speed.

It has taken rule makers approximately twenty years, after much debate, to legalize this stroke. It was used for the first time in Olympic competition in 1956 at Melbourne, Australia.

The dolphin kick was ruled illegal because the legs moved in a vertical plane; also the soles of the feet did not engage the water on the downbeat of the kick as was required of the orthodox breast stroke.

*Federation Internationale de Natation Amateur.
†Armbruster, David A.: The dolphin breast stroke, Journal of Health and Physical Education 6:23-26 (April), 1935.

Today, the dolphin kick is still the fastest of all kicks used by man in the water.

Originally, the butterfly arm action was combined with the orthodox breast stroke kick in order to give the stroke greater speed. However, later, this same butterfly arm action was combined with the newly discovered dolphin kick, giving the entire stroke surprisingly much greater speed, in fact, so much greater speed that the original butterfly breast stroke has at this writing become obsolete as a competitive stroke. For this reason the butterfly breast stroke will not be discussed in this writing.

ORIGIN AND DEVELOPMENT OF THE BACK CRAWL STROKE

The origin and development of the third competitive stroke, the back crawl, dates back to 1902, at about the time that Richard Cavill was combining the flutter kick with the Trudgeon crawl. The back crawl stroke, in fact, is a by-product of the crawl stroke. In its early form it was also a by-product of the breast stroke since the breast stroke kick and double overarm action were used. This inverted breast stroke was soon abandoned as a possible competitive stroke since it was too slow and served only to duplicate the regular breast stroke.

Previous to 1902, the back stroke had been considered to be nothing more than a stunt, combining a sculling action of the hands with a leg action similar to a flutter kick. Following an attempt to make the back stroke a speed swimming event by inverting the breast stroke, it was noticed that an inverted reverse alternating overarm crawl combined with the inverted flutter kick resulted in a stroke which gave more speed than the breast stroke. Jam Handy, then swimming at the Illinois Athletic Club of Chicago, and his coach did the foundation work in developing this style of swimming. In 1912 the back crawl stroke was established as a competitive swimming event and was gradually improved through the years by many refinements.

In 1935, a Chicago schoolboy, Adolph Kiefer, swam the back crawl stroke for 100 yards in 0:57.6. The technique developed by Kiefer contained three features that distinguished his back crawl stroke from the generally used form. First, the recovery of the arms was made in a very low, lateral fashion, with the arms held straight. Second, the arms entered the water just above a line opposite the shoulders instead of straight up from the shoulders, alongside the head. Third, the arms were drawn through the water just below the surface as contrasted with the deep pull then employed generally and were held straight. At present the current trend in the back crawl stroke is a high recovery of the arms followed by a slightly deeper purchase and pull of the arms. Two styles of pull, the straight arm and the bent elbow pull, are both being used to advantage. However, most champions of today are using the bent elbow pull-and-push drive.

The sensational performances of the American swimming team in the 1960 Olympic Games were largely due to the increased emphasis on conditioning and training since the 1952 games. The American coaches and swimmers generally followed a program of workouts consisting of a great number of sprint repetitions of distances from 400 meters to 25 yards, with predetermined rest intervals. This type of conditioning has replaced the longer distance, slower type of swimming of each workout. Then, too, champion swimmers work out two and three times a day, the year around. This type of conditioning has given the American swimmers nothing short of phenomenal performances at the 1964 games. At present, the American high school and summer age group swimmers are also responding to this type of conditioning. One need only look at their sensational performances from year to year. This holds very great promise for future Olympics.

The quest for speed has brought about revolutionary changes in swimming styles in the past two and one half centuries. It is expected that this advancement will be continued. Swimming and diving performance is gradually improving. This improvement is brought about mainly by refinement of techniques, more rigorous training, and better diet habits. The most important single factor that has put the United States out in front in the swimming world today is the great impetus given to this sport by the school, youth age swimming clubs, and groups actively engaged in competitive swimming and diving all over the country. The techniques used by swimmers and divers today are not to be considered an ultimate refinement.

DIVING

Competitive diving is an outgrowth of aerial acrobatics and tumbling. The first recorded diving competition took place in England in 1905. Since that time, diving has been an integral part of the competitive water sports program. Feats of diving have been recorded as early as 1871, when divers were reported to have plunged from London Bridge and other high places.

From the simple head-first and feet-first dives, there have been developed more than one hundred fancy dives. These are combinations of forward dives, backward dives, handstands and twists, somersaults, reverse dives, and jackknives and inward dives. They are performed in either a straight, pike, or tuck position. They are executed from either the low or high board or from a high platform.

The construction of new platform diving facilities and the increased interest in tower diving stimulated by the Pan-American and Olympic

ALL-STROKE ARMBRUSTER METHOD

PROGRESSIVE LEARNING PROCEDURE CHART FOR SCHOOL SWIMMING

ORIENTATION OF MAN IN WATER DISTURBS HIS BEHAVIOR AND ALTERS HIM

When exposed to water repeatedly, he learns to adjust to balance, buoyancy, stability, etc.

PHYSICALLY

PHYSIOLOGICALLY

By repeatedly exposing man to water, he accustoms self to physiologic disturbances, such as heat loss, irregular breathing, etc.

PSYCHOLOGICALLY (MENTALLY)
Response is tension, fear, unpleasantness, etc.

CONFIDENCE ESTABLISHED
When distress disappears from facial muscles, fear tensions are eliminated. Response becomes pleasant, relaxing, satisfying.

FURTHER ORIENTATION OF MAN IN WATER IN RELATION TO HIS MOVEMENT

UNSKILLED STROKES
Teach dog paddle method on face, sides, and back.

Moving on face, using alternating and simultaneous strokes

Push-and-pull strokes on left and right sides

Alternating and simultaneous strokes on back

Miscellaneous skills: sculling, finning, treading, elementary surface dive, dive from pool deck

SKILLED STROKES
Face and back crawl are taught. Side stroke on left and right side. Breast stroke on face and inverted and resting back stroke. This learning prevents "grooving" student into any one stroke, retarding learning. Student then fundamentally and basically grounded for future development.

Crawl strokes on face and back

Breast stroke on face and inverted and resting back stroke on back (dolphin)

Side stroke on left and right sides

Refining miscellaneous skills: finning, sculling, treading, surface dive, underwater swimming, both head and feet entry dives

AIMS
Student now swims as many strokes continuously and in succession as is possible with each style of stroke. All students can swim all strokes, but not all strokes are "naturals" for all students. Therefore, instructor cannot tell which stroke to teach to a beginner. Pupil finds it through distance orientation.

OBJECTIVES
Student should now swim his greatest possible distance daily, using all strokes, for at least 15 minutes or ¼ mile. His dominating stroke establishes itself as he shifts from one stroke to another. He reverts most often to stroke easiest for him. He acquires confidence, relaxation, and seaworthiness.

INTERMEDIATE SWIMMING ELIMINATED

STUDENT QUALIFIES FOR VARIOUS BRANCHES OF ADVANCED AQUATICS

ADVANCED COURSE Techniques in all strokes

COMPETITIVE Team and intramural

DIVING Team, scuba, or recreational

LIFESAVING Water safety camp course for training pool management

GAMES Informal and competitive

BALLET Synchronized swimming

Games competition has influenced the authors to include tower diving as an important addition to this revision.

The disciplines of the sciences of physics, physiology, and kinesiology are continually being applied in attempts to improve swimming and diving to greater performances. The application of the scientific method in testing new techniques is transforming swimming from an art to a science.

ALL-STROKE ARMBRUSTER METHOD
FOR TEACHING BEGINNING SWIMMING

The all-stroke Armbruster method not only teaches all of the skilled swimming strokes but is a new method of teaching beginners to swim. This method the authors call the all-stroke Armbruster method. Its aim and objective is to teach all of the skilled swimming strokes to the beginning student. He is thoroughly and basically grounded in all levels of aquatics. After completion of the course, should he not desire to enroll for more advanced classes in water training, he most certainly has been well grounded to be safe and able to manage himself adequately and satisfactorily in water.

This method has been used at the University of Iowa by the authors for the past twenty years with the younger-aged students, at the college age level, and in summer school with adult students to 60 years of age.

This method has produced tremendous results for students as a whole. If taught intensively, it creates tremendous interest. Discipline is no longer a problem because action creates interest.

This type of program speeds up the advancement of the student from the beginning level to the advanced levels. It eliminates the intermediate levels. It absorbs and stimulates the student's interest and is a challenging motivation for him to continue in the advanced areas. He now has acquired an urge to enter lifesaving, ballet, or varsity swimming.

The accompanying plan for an all-around school or college aquatic program is recommended.

Chapter 2

The all-stroke Armbruster method for teaching beginning swimming*

No instructor can truthfully stand in front of a class in beginning swimming and say, "We will teach you the crawl stroke or any other stroke in this course." All members of his class undoubtedly will swim the crawl, but it will not be a natural stroke for all members of the class.

Human beings differ physically in many respects—some having short or long necks, small or large hands or feet, a short or long torso, and short or long arms and legs. All of these physical characteristics may be a physical limitation to some students as they try to swim comfortably the crawl, back, side, or breast stroke. All persons can swim any one of the fundamental strokes, but not all swimmers can swim all strokes equally well and swim them with comfort and ease. Therefore, if the student is well grounded in the various categories of strokes and is well trained and orientated in a distance swimming program, somewhere within these categories of strokes (as he swims along) he finds one or two strokes that tire him least. He naturally resorts to them more often while learning in order to extend himself in distance swimming. For example, one need only look at any one of the top medley swimmers in the competitive field. Within the four styles that he swims, there will be one or two styles in which he is weakest, even though he swims the strokes well. One of the styles (usually the one he is least adept in) will be the one he likes least. This only proves that all students can swim all strokes, but not all students can swim all strokes equally well with ease and comfort.

It is then a problem for the student, not the instructor, to find his most pleasurable and satisfying stroke, or strokes, and to make these predominate through his orientation in distance swimming during his class instruction practices.

*Formerly called the all-stroke Iowa method for teaching beginning swimming.

If the all-stroke method is used, the instructor should have at least two class periods per week for one semester. Three periods are best. At the end of the course these beginners are fundamentally and basically grounded in all strokes. The student should be able to swim each of the fundamental strokes at least 50 yards before attempting distance orientation. He is easily beyond the intermediate level and can now enter an advanced class, a lifesaving class, or be promoted to the varsity swimming squad.

PREWATER CONDITIONING—MENTAL ATTITUDE

A nonswimmer's mental attitude will influence his progress considerably in the early stages of learning. A favorable mental attitude that depicts the desire to achieve the objective and the courage and willingness to follow instructions is highly desirable. The swimming instructor can establish a sound basis for proper mental attitude before taking a class into the water by means of a group discussion. The beginning swimmer should be aware of what to anticipate as he enters the water. When he enters into water at navel depth, the respiratory center is affected, resulting momentarily in irregular breathing. He may momentarily gasp for breath and have difficulty in exhaling. The muscles tense, and he may shiver as a result of the loss of body heat. This experience is quite comparable to that of standing under a cool shower, and, when it is explained in this manner, it becomes less frightening and more understandable. Standing in water chest deep, he may experience difficulty in maintaining balance due to buoyancy and loss of body weight. When he bobs up and down and moves about, he quickly learns to establish balance. His body gradually adjusts to unstableness in water, and he experiences a feeling of well-being and vitality.

In extreme cases because of this unstable feeling in water, some individuals may at first be reluctant to move from the end of the pool where they cling tightly to the scum gutter for support. It is advisable to allow these students to maintain this position for a short period, gradually dipping up and down until they develop the courage to move toward deeper water without support. The instructor may hold such a student by the arm and guide him as he bolsters his morale. Encouragement and praise help tremendously at this point.

When a student submerges his face beneath the surface, several new sensations are evident. Water irritates the nose, eyes, and ears. The typical reaction is to recover a standing position and rub the closed eyes. Rubbing the eyes can be eliminated if the eyes are squeezed shut and blinked several times. This procedure will minimize irritation to the eyes. The skill of submerging with the eyes open, which at first seems uncomfortable, becomes a very satisfying experience with repetition. One has only to observe a group of youngsters at play in the water to realize the pleasure they derive from underwater activity. They appear to be under the water more than they are above it. Fears and insecurity generally can be attributed to the unknown. When the pupil is informed as to what to anticipate and what his role must be to overcome the obstacles present, his chance of achieving the desired goal is greatly enhanced.

BASIC TECHNIQUES AND SKILLS IN ADJUSTING THE BEGINNER TO WATER

After the pupil has been mentally conditioned out of the water, he is now ready to learn elementary water skills designed to develop his confidence and to adjust him to the water. It is well at this point to have the class paired so that each student will have a partner. The advantages of using a partner relationship are numerous. From a safety viewpoint each partner is aware of the other's welfare. Psychologically, competition in performance is established. Each student acts as an instructor for his partner. He becomes more attentive to directions and, in the act of his performance as a teacher as well as student, acquires a better understanding of the skill being taught. With a large class, time usually does not permit the instructor to check each student individually on each progressive step. In the paired-pupil method, each swimmer is checked by his partner. The instructor can then survey the group and give his attention where it is most needed.

Most teachers of swimming are in accord in using some form of the Brink* word-picture system for adjusting the nonswimmer to the water. The following progressive procedure utilizes some of the basic steps of the Brink system, with supplementary material found to be of practical application.

Confidence drills

Water orientation. The following instructions are given to the members of the class.

1. Enter water and wade to waist-deep water.
2. Hold partner for support and bounce up and down.
3. Individually bounce around in circles to establish balance.
4. Cup water into hands and lower face to hands, simulating washing face.
5. Hold partner's hands for support, bend forward and lower face into the water, relax face muscles; repeat.
6. Hold partner for support and submerge entire body; repeat several times, holding breath.

*Cureton, Thomas K.: How to teach swimming and diving, New York, 1934, Associated Press.

7. Submerge individually; repeat several times, staying submerged longer with each repetition.

8. Place hands on knees, lower face into water, and open the eyes; reflex action may cause them to shut; immediately open them again and they soon adjust to the water.

9. Lower entire body, open eyes, and identify objects underwater; count partner's fingers, etc.

10. Do not rub the eyes; instead squeeze them together momentarily and blink them several times.

Breath control. Poor stroke technique is very often a result of improper breathing habits. Emphasis must be placed upon the importance of breathing correctly in the very early stages of learning. Patience on the part of the instructor is essential. He must be enthusiastic and original in creating interest through action. Action not only creates interest but also eliminates the problem of discipline. Most instructors of swimming advocate breathing through the mouth. The air can be exhaled more rapidly, and pressure needed to exhale through the nose is eliminated. Many skilled swimmers exhale primarily through the mouth, with some air passing through the nasal passages, keeping them clear of water droplets. The following instructions are now given to the members of the class.

1. In waist-deep water, cup hands together and scoop water from pool; inhale deeply through the mouth and blow the water from the hands by exhaling forcefully through the mouth.

2. Repeat step 1; exhale slowly, with a steady stream through the nose.

3. Repeat step 1, exhaling through the nose and mouth.

4. Place hands on spread knees, lower face into water, and exhale completely through the mouth.

5. Join hands with partner, facing each other; one partner submerges and exhales; as he comes up to inhale, the other partner submerges, etc.; start slowly and increase tempo gradually.

6. Place hands on spread knees, lower shoulders and head below surface and exhale, turn head only to the left, look over left shoulder and inhale; repeat 10 times; duplicate procedure, turning head to the right.

7. Line up at sides of pool, facing overflow gutter; take a deep breath, bend knees, and submerge with mouth wide open; retrieve and "ship" water out of mouth into overflow by squeezing mouth from the rear (Fig. 2-1). (This skill teaches student the reflex of "shipping" water rather than swallowing it which causes one to strangle.)

Fig. 2-1. Shipping water.

Fig. 2-2. A series of ideal form showing some methods of adjusting to water. **A,** Submerging to jackknife float position and recovery. **B** and **C,** Turtle float and recovery. **D** and **E,** Prone float position and recovery. **F,** Back float position and recovery.

Jackknife float. Give the following instructions to the members of the class.

1. In shoulder-deep water stand with feet spread well apart; inhale deeply, bend forward, slide hands downward along the legs toward the feet; lower the head and shoulders beneath the surface.

2. As the hands reach the ankle area, the feet will gradually rise from the bottom of the pool; hold this free-floating position momentarily (Fig. 2-2, *A*).

3. Slide the hands upward toward the hips, elevate the head, and plant the feet firmly on the bottom of the pool.

Standing up from a horizontal floating position. Give the following instructions to the members of the class.

1. Extend arms forward and lower head and upper body beneath the surface; as partner tows you forward, elevate your legs so that the body is in a horizontal position.

2. To recover to a standing position, bend the knees, moving them forward toward the chest; now press downward and backward with the arms and simultaneously elevate the head and shoulders; place the feet firmly on the bottom of the pool.

Jellyfish float. Give the following instructions to the members of the class.

1. In shoulder-deep water, inhale deeply and slowly lower head and upper body beneath the surface.

2. Lift the feet from the bottom, bend the knees, and draw them up to the chest; wrap the arms around the legs and keep the chin lowered to the chest. The body will now resemble a ball floating in the water (Fig. 2-2, *B* and *C*).

3. To recover, release the legs, straighten the knees and back, elevate the head, and stand up.

Front float. Give the following instructions to the members of the class.

1. Assume a jellyfish floating position.

2. From this position extend the arms and upper portion of the body forward, and simultaneously extend the legs and lower part of the body to the rear (Fig. 2-2, *D*).

3. To maintain this position, press forward and downward on the arms, head, and shoulders, and lift up on the legs.

4. Regain standing position as illustrated in Fig. 2-2, *D* and *E*.

Back float. Give the following instructions to the members of the class.

1. Bend knees and lower the back, shoulders, and head slowly until

the body is completely submerged except for the eyes, nose, mouth, and chin.

2. Extend the arms sideward and downward, hands reaching gently upward from the bottom (Fig. 2-2, *F*).

3. Lift the hips toward the surface, and push the feet gently upward from the bottom.

4. Recover standing position by dropping the hips to a sitting position, pressing the arms and hands downward, then forward and upward; lower the chin on the chest, plant the feet on the bottom, and stand up (Fig. 2-2, *F*).

Front glide with kick. Give the following instructions to the members of the class.

1. Start from a standing position in waist-deep water; bend forward and extend arms together and forward beneath the water surface.

2. Fall forward, submerge the head, and push off the bottom with the feet; lift the legs, and press the feet upward; glide.

3. Move legs up and down, keep the feet extended, and allow the knees to bend for relaxation.

4. Recover standing position as described for standing from a horizontal floating position.

Rear glide with kick. Give the following instructions to the members of the class.

1. Start from a back floating position.

2. Move the arms to the side of the body.

3. Initiate the kick from the hip joint, and emphasize the upbeat.

4. Move legs up and down slowly.

Body spin. The body spin teaches the pupil to appreciate the potentials of the arm action in swimming. It serves as a lead-up drill in teaching the arm action for the elementary and resting back strokes. Give the following instructions to the members of the class.

1. In breast-deep water, hold the feet together and bend the knees until only the head is above the surface; stand on toes, keeping knees together.

2. Position the left arm so that it is pressed across and held closely to the chest. Reach back with the right arm bending and leading with the elbow to a point as far to the rear as possible, without moving the trunk.

3. Pull forward with the right arm held straight and simultaneously twist and spin the body to the right; the resulting action should spin the body completely around.

4. Repeat action with the left arm.

5. Assume position of ball floating; bend right elbow, move well back, extend right arm, and pull forward with a straight elbow;

repeat action in a continuous series; resulting action should spin the body in circles.

6. Repeat, using left arm, and spin to the left.
7. Repeat, using both arms simultaneously, and move the body to the rear.

Sculling. Sculling is a basic skill required in treading water and various water ballet maneuvers. Give the following instructions to the members of the class.

1. Standing in waist-deep water, extend arms forward above surface of the water at shoulder level, with palms facing the water.
2. Elevate the little-finger side of the hands until the palms are at a 45-degree angle to the surface of the water; move the hands outward and slightly downward about 12 inches.
3. Reverse the position of the hands so that the thumb side is elevated, palm still facing downward at a 45-degree angle, and move hands and lower arm inward while pressing downward to original position.
4. Repeat the complete action in steps 2 and 3 several times, increasing the speed each time.
5. Continue action and lower arms and body into the water until water level reaches the chin.
6. As the hands engage the water, the legs are slowly eased off the bottom, and the body is supported by the sculling action of the arms.
7. Lower the head backward into the water until the ears are submerged, and gradually extend the body by lifting the chest and hips while the hands continue the sculling motion.

Motivating skills. The student is now sufficiently advanced in the basic fundamentals in water to proceed with motivating skills. These strokes are a natural or instinctive type and do not require highly skilled techniques. The purpose of this procedure is to condition the pupil so that he can make elementary progress through the water with the body in almost any position. It also teaches the student appreciation of the use of the hands and arms against the resistance of specific gravity, which is the constant upward pressure of the water. Give the following instructions to the members of the class.

1. In breast-deep water swim the elementary crawl stroke (dog paddle), keeping the head beneath the surface and the eyes open and using a slow, deep knee-bend kick.
2. Elevate the head until the mouth is just above the surface, and repeat step 1.
3. Start swimming as described in step 2, and turn over on right

side; reach farther forward with the right arm, shorten the action of the left arm, and keep arms recovering under water; turn head to the left, keeping the back of the head in the water.

4. Continue swimming, and turn over on the back; scull with the hands, and continue using deep, slow kick.

5. From the back position lower the left shoulder, bring the right arm across the body, and turn the head to the left (this action places the swimmer on his left side); reach well forward with the left arm, and shorten the right arm stroke; keep the arms under the surface throughout the stroke cycle while swimming on the left side.

6. Swim half the distance across the pool; turn around without touching bottom, and return to starting position.

DEEP WATER ORIENTATION

Fear of deep water is natural for a nonswimmer. This fear may be deeply seated if it has been caused by an unfortunate accident or experience in which the nonswimmer may have almost drowned. To overcome this fear, the progression from shallow water work to deep should be slow and well planned. A procedure which has been proved to be effective and is an integral part of the all-stroke Armbruster method is described on the following pages.

After the class has had instruction in the basic skills in adjusting to water and practice in the execution of the elementary and resting back stroke, deep water orientation is the next logical progression. The paired-pupil system is used as an added safety factor. The class is assembled on the deck of the pool at its deep end. The instructor enters the water with one of the class's weakest pupils and demonstrates submersion, bobbing, ball float, elongated float, bobbing float, treading water, and jumping from the deck into deep water.

Submersion. The instructor and the pupil hang on the scum gutter for support with their outside hand. They hold hands and the pupil is told to squeeze the instructor's hand should he want to be elevated to the surface at any time. The pupil then pulls himself upward, lets go of his support on the scum gutter, and submerges. The pupil squeezes the instructor's hand and is pulled to the surface. In most cases the student will have more difficulty in submerging than in raising to the surface due to his bouyancy. This procedure is repeated slowly until the pupil is acclimated.

Next, the procedure just described is repeated except this time the pupil is instructed to open his eyes, look around, and stay down longer.

Then, the pupil takes a deep breath and submerges alone to the bottom of the pool. The knees bend as the feet contact the bottom and then extend as the pupil pushes from the bottom to the surface. The instructor submerges his body but keeps one hand holding the scum gutter. His eyes are open, and his free arm is extended downward in a position to give assistance if needed. Repeat until the pupil is relaxed and confidence is established.

Bobbing. The pupil takes a deep breath and elevates the body by pressing down on the scum gutter. He then lets go and submerges, exhaling on the way down. Arms are stretched above the head. When he pushes up from the bottom, his body should angle toward the pool edge so that upon arrival at the surface he can grasp the scum gutter. Inhale and submerge again in one up-and-dowm movement without pause. This bobbing technique is repeated until the student can bob five times without stopping.

The instructor demonstrates the use of the arms in bobbing in deep water without the use of the side of the pool for support. The bobbing action is started by elevating the body as high above the surface as possible. A scissors kick accompanied by a downward sweep of the arms to the sides of the body will accomplish this elevated position. Now as the upward force is spent, the body will start to submerge, and the momentum will carry it downward about 4 feet. At this point the arms, which have been held close to the sides, sweep sideward and upward to an extended position above the head. This action of the arms will carry the body in a vertical position to the bottom of the pool. As the feet reach the bottom, the knees flex, then extend, moving the body upward. Half way to the surface the arms sweep sideward and downward from their extended position above the head to a resting position at the sides of the body. The arm action results in a drive which lifts the head well above the surface and permits adequate time to inhale without destroying the continuous up-and-down movement of the body. The pupil may practice this skill on the deck before executing it in the water. The instructor should stress the complete exhalation while the body is submerged so as to facilitate the timing of the inhalation.

Ball float. The instructor demonstrates the ball float. The pupil executes the ball float close to the side of the pool, always within reach of the instructor or partner.

Elongated float. The instructor demonstrates the elongated float. By taking a deep breath, he lowers the face into the water, keeping the body as relaxed as possible and in a vertical position with the arms extended downward and slightly forward. The pupil practices this within reach of his partner.

Bobbing float. The bobbing float is demonstrated by the instructor. A vertical float position is held until the need for air is experienced. At this point the legs kick using a verticle breast or side stroke kick. The arms, which have crossed beneath the face, press sideward and downward in a half sculling action simultaneous with the kick. The resulting upward force permits the head to be elevated to take in air. The exhalation is forceful through the mouth just prior to the inhalation to permit maximum bouyancy during the float phase.

After the air has been taken in, the kick and arm action is repeated to prevent the body from sinking. Once this skill has been acquired, the pupil can continue the action for an hour or more if necessary.

Treading water. The instructor reviews the sculling arm action and then demonstrates the leg action. The gutter is used as a support with one extended arm. The body is in a vertical position with the side of the body facing the pool edge. While one leg moves forward, the other moves to the rear in a scissors kick (Fig. 6-1). The legs do not reach as far forward and to the rear as they do in the side stroke, and the action is continuous, without pause.

When the pupil feels the support of his legs, he can then release his hold on the side of the pool and use his hands for support in the water sculling as previously taught and reviewed. A breast stroke kick may be used equally well in treading water (see Chapter 13). To learn this kick in a vertical position, use the gutter for support, grasping with both hands, body facing the side of the pool. Bend the knees slightly bringing the heels upward toward the buttocks. Execute a small breast stroke kick. Keep it moving without pause. When support is felt by the pupil, he releases the hands from the gutter and uses them in a sculling action for added support in the water.

Jumping from deck into deep water. A corner in the deep end of the pool is selected. The instructor stations himself in the water about 4 feet from the side of the pool and supports himself with one hand on the gutter at the end of the pool. The pupils are instructed to elevate both arms over their heads and keep them in that position as they step off the side of the deck, jumping feetfirst to the bottom of the pool. As the pupil enters the water, the instructor grasps the pupil's wrist with his free hand and maintains this contact as the pupil submerges to the bottom. Assistance in regaining the surface may thus be given by the instructor if he feels it necessary.

For his next jump, the instructor submerges in close proximity to the pupil but makes no contact unless it is needed. The pupil is then taught to jump in the water, bend his knees as the feet reach the bottom, and push off the bottom at an angle, so that it is in a horizontal position rather than a vertical position when he surfaces. This action places the body in a position to go immediately into a stroke and not be required to struggle from a vertical hole.

PROFESSIONAL AID FOR SUCCESSFUL TEACHING

The personality of the swimming instructor can be one of his greatest assets in effective teaching. He should have a thorough knowledge of the material he plans to use. His knowledge in the professional field should include an understanding of anatomy, kinesiology, physiology, psychology, and physics.

Personality of instructor:
1. Ability to inspire confidence
2. Good voice control (low and loud)
3. Natural sense of humor
4. Energy
5. Sympathetic understanding
6. Patience
7. Perseverance
8. Tact
9. Integrity

Knowledge of material:
1. Ability to detect errors in technique performance and to correct them
2. Invite questions and answer them with substance and meaning
3. Present material in a logical, progressive sequence
4. Take nothing for granted; repeat basic material
5. Remember that a solid foundation in elementary skills is a "must"; provide adequate time for learning; do not rush through basic fundamental skills

Ability to demonstrate:
1. Learning through imitation is highly recommended, provided the instructor has the ability to demonstrate accurately the skill he is demonstrating and concurrent with the demonstration explain the substance involved. The ability to demonstrate is essential. However, competitive swimmers, highly skilled in performance, do not always make the best instructors because they place too much emphasis on demonstration and often lack the ability to put into words what they are hoping to achieve through demonstration.

Understanding of anatomy, kinesiology, and body mechanics:
1. The instructor must be able to speak with authority. He should be a student of kinesiology, of anatomy, and of the mechanics involved in the skills being taught.
2. Technical training should be constantly supplemented by current theories and procedures. The instructor should have an open mind to new methods and evaluation of theories.

The lesson plan:
1. Discussion plan for the period
2. Warm-up drill exercise out of water; reaction to command discipline
3. Sufficient content to keep all members of class active at all times
4. Introduction of new skills and repetition of previous skills for practice

Chapter 3

Teaching the resting back stroke

The resting back stroke is the first coordinated stroke taught to the beginner in the all-stroke method. This stroke is unique in that the arm action in its recovery aids the less buoyant swimmer to maintain his hips well up in the surface of the water. The straight arm underwater recovery eliminates the possibility of the water being thrown over the face by recovery of the hands above the surface. Therefore, it is logical that this new resting back stroke precede the elementary back stroke in the sequence of learning. The Armed Forces in World War II stressed the use of this stroke in survival swimming.* It is an ideal stroke for restful swimming in an emergency. The shoulder action in the recovery is not restricted by clothing worn by the swimmer.

The kick is basic and provides a sound background for treading water as well as for the more highly skilled strokes. Towing techniques and specialized skills in lifesaving require perfection of the kick action of this stroke.

Coordination of arm and leg action is quickly learned. Arms and legs recover in unison and apply propulsive force at the same time (Fig. 3-1). Timing is further simplified by the pause or momentary glide between the propulsive action of the arms and legs and their recovery. Breathing is not restricted because the eyes, nose, and mouth are positioned above the surface throughout the stroke cycle.

The resting back stroke is highly motivating. The student progresses rapidly, and confidence in his ability is stimulated. He experiences the satisfaction of accomplishment at an early stage in his learning progression.

Kick. The recovery of the legs is executed by spreading the knees sideward while the heels, held together, are directed downward toward the buttocks. As the feet reach a position in which the lower leg is

*See F.M. 21-20, Physical training, The Department of the Army Field Manual (introduced by D. A. Armbruster and C. H. McCloy).

Fig. 3-1. A series of ideal form for performing the new beginner's resting back stroke, showing the arm and leg actions, position of the body and head, and breathing technique. **A**, The starting position. **B**, The arms and legs recover simultaneously, and air is inhaled. **C** and **D**, The arms and legs simultaneously start the propulsive drive, with the head well back. **E**, The stroke is completing its drive, and air is expelled. **F**, The arms and legs pause for the glide.

vertical to the water surface, the heels are separated and the feet and lower leg are rotated outward. The feet thrust outward beyond the knee, and the legs are extended, engaging the water with the soles of the feet. At a point prior to a full extension of the knee, the adductor muscles of the upper leg must squeeze the thighs together forcefully. The knee must remain relaxed and mobile so that the procedure just described will result in a strong whiplike action of the lower legs and feet. This is actually the inverted breast stroke kick.

Arm stroke. The arm recovery starts at the end of the glide in the stroke cycle. The palms are faced downward, with the little-finger side of the hand slightly elevated from the horizontal plane. The arms remain straight. Pressure is exerted downward and sideward as the arms move laterally under the surface to a point just beyond the shoulder. The position of the hand and the action of the arm in the recovery can be best described as an elongated sculling movement. The downward press of the arms against the upward pressure of specific gravity supports the body and eliminates hip sag.

The pull is executed by rotating the arms so that the palms are facing the feet, pulling with the elbows and wrists straight to the sides of the thighs.

Whole stroke. In the gliding phase of the stroke, the body is in a back floating position. The head is tilted backward, with the chin up. The hair and ears are submerged. The eyes are open and directed above the forehead. The hips and chest are pressed upward, while the shoulders lean backward and slightly downward. The above position streamlines the body and adds to the efficiency of the glide. The recovery of the arms and legs begins toward the end of the glide before the momentum is spent.

Breathing should be regular, with exhaling during the thrust and glide and inhaling during the recovery of the arms and legs.

Throughout the stroke the body, except the face, remains under water. The recovery is slow and smooth. The kick and pull are strong. The efficiency of the stroke is not measured in speed, but in the distance the body travels during the stroke cycle and in the ease of execution.

TEACHING AND LEARNING PROCEDURES

The following instructions and procedures are suggested in teaching the resting back stroke.

1. The student reviews and practices back float.
2. The instructor explains and demonstrates elongated sculling arm recovery and pull.
3. The student practices arm action in shoulder-deep water with toes on pool bottom, back arched, back of head in water, and chin up, pausing at the end of each pull.
4. The instructor demonstrates and explains kick.
5. The student practices kick, using side of pool for support.
6. The student practices kick with aid of free-floating device or support by partner.

7. The student practices whole stroke with support, using floating device or partner.
8. The student practices whole stroke alone, without aid.
9. The student works for efficiency, relaxation, coordination, breathing, etc.

Chapter 4

Teaching the elementary
back stroke

The leg action, coordination, and body position of the elementary back stroke are very similar to those of the resting back stroke. The arm action varies considerably. The elementary back stroke is one of the oldest strokes known to man. During its history it has gone through various changes in the arm and leg action. Primarily it is used as a resting stroke. It is relatively easy to learn once the student has mastered the skill of the resting back stroke. It is then simply a matter of recovering the arms in a bent position.

Arm stroke. The body is in a back, horizontal position, completely submerged except for the face. The arms are extended, with the palms pressing against the upper outer thigh just below the hip joint. The recovery is initiated by bending the elbow outward and downward. The palms slide along the side of the body until the finger tips are above the hip joint. From this position the hands rotate and face upward, while the arms extend laterally outward to a point just beyond the head. (See Fig. 4-1, *A-D*.) The arms are now positioned for the propulsive drive. The elbows are fully extended, and the palms are facing the feet (Fig. 4-1, *D* and *E*). The arms press and squeeze simultaneously toward the sides of the thighs to the starting position. The arms and legs now pause for the glide. When the momentum from this stroke is nearly spent, the next stroke is started. Care should be taken to make sure that the hands remain submerged throughout the arm stroke cycle in order to avoid splashing water over the face. In the transition from Fig. 4-1, *B*, to Fig. 4-1, *C* and *D*, some instructors favor planing the palms downward and moving the forearms laterally, thereby giving additional support to the face and hips. Pedagogically both methods are sound. The essential thing to remember in executing both the resting and elementary back strokes is that the arms and legs recover simultaneously, kick and pull simultaneously, and then pause for the glide. The breath-

Fig. 4-1. A series of ideal form for performing the elementary back stroke, an advanced stage of the resting back stroke. **A,** The starting position. **B** and **C,** The arms and legs recover simultaneously as air is inhaled. **D** and **E,** The propulsive phase. **F,** The arms and legs pause at the start of the glide.

ing in these two strokes is shown in Fig. 4-1, *B-D*. Inhalation is taken during the recovery, and exhalation is made during the propulsive phase.

The timing, breathing, and coordination of the resting and elementary back strokes are less complex than the more highly skilled strokes. For this reason, these strokes precede the more highly skilled strokes in teaching and learning progression.

Chapter 5

Introduction to teaching the higher level skilled strokes

The following instructions and procedures are suggested in teaching and learning the higher level skilled strokes, such as:

1. The side stroke on both left and right sides
2. The crawl strokes on both back and front sides
3. The breast stroke and the dolphin butterfly stroke

The instruction may be conducted with or without the aid of floating devices. This procedure will serve as a guide to conform to the all-stroke Armbruster method of teaching beginners in the area of the highly skilled swimming strokes.

The authors highly recommend the use of floating devices to facilitate the learning of these highly skilled strokes.

PREREQUISITE

A thorough schooling in the area of orientation and conditioning the student to water is necessary. This is accomplished by the learning of all the elementary skills as recommended in the chapter on the all-stroke method of teaching and learning requisites. Having accomplished these prerequisites, the student is then well adjusted to any situation or position in shallow water. He is then conditioned and in readiness to proceed in learning the various skilled strokes.

TEACHING AND LEARNING PROCEDURES FOR ALL SKILLED STROKES

Once the student has learned to motivate himself in the water with the resting and elementary back strokes, the instructor may proceed with any sequence of strokes. All of the skilled strokes can be learned by all pupils—just how well each stroke is mastered by each individual will depend upon his distance orientation, which procedure follows after each stroke has been coordinated into the whole stroke.

If there is a best sequence of learning the skilled strokes, the authors have found, through experimentation, a plan that has proved to be highly successful and it is hereby strongly recommended. To accomplish this, these strokes are grouped into three categories: (1) the crawl stroke, back and front; (2) the side stroke, both right and left sides; and (3) the breast stroke and dolphin butterfly stroke.

The crawl and back crawl strokes are learned in a combination sequence. Also, the side stroke is learned on both sides in sequence combination. Likewise, the breast stroke and dolphin butterfly are learned in combination sequence. The order of sequence of learning these group combinations is left to the discretion of the individual instructors.

Leg kicks. During the land and water drill practice of any one kick of any one stroke, the authors recommend that the fundamentals of all kicks of all the skilled strokes be taught and practiced during successive class sessions, until overlearned by the students. This method results in surprising and very rapid learning of the whole stroke in the future sessions. This phase of learning all the kicks of all the strokes is the heart and core of the beginner learning in the all-stroke Armbruster method. The kick is more difficult to different learning situations than are the arm strokes. The arms have smaller muscles and themselves react readily to complex movements, whereas the legs have larger muscles and react more slowly to learning situations. Therefore, the instructor should emphasize and stress the land and especially the water drill exercises. This work may be accomplished either with or without floating devices.

Arm and breathing skills. The arm and breathing skills can be practiced during rest intervals of the kicking exercises. Constant repetition of the various kicks in the water with adequate rest intervals is highly recommended to assure rapid improvement and achievement in learning all strokes in future weeks.

Whole stroke. Once the arm, breathing, and leg techniques have been individually learned during the water drills, the whole stroke is attempted. Here the instructor should emphasize the point of putting in sequence at least four consecutive whole strokes without a stop. Once four strokes are organized by the student, unhurriedly, and without a stop, he has mastered the coordination of that stroke. He can now motivate himself to almost any point or any given distance, providing he breathes regularly. At this point of learning, when the arms and legs have been coordinated, proper and regular breathing determine the distance he can swim the stroke. One must breathe to swim, not swim to breathe.

During the phase of learning the whole stroke, some students may have greater difficulty than others, in either the coordinations or breathing or both. Floating supports are recommended for these students. By the use of supports, he is able to concentrate upon the technique of his stroke as well as breathe more freely. As soon as he is able to motivate himself and breathe properly, the support is taken away.

DISTANCE ORIENTATION

Instructors will differ as to where and when to utilize distance orientation in the learning progression. Some will employ it as soon as a single stroke is coordinated. Others will delay its use until all strokes are learned and are swum only for short distances. The advantage to the latter plan is that the student can change from one stroke to another, without stopping when tiring, and thereby can learn to swim the other strokes while resting from the tiring one. This is sound pedagogy in learning; that is, by swimming longer distances without stopping, more strokes are practiced and greater ease of performance is experienced by the student.

As the student increases his distance on each stroke from class session to class session, he begins to unconsciously relax and breathe more freely and naturally. He is learning to give himself over to the water completely and rely upon the momentum of each stroke and the water to support him while swimming. Distance swimming now becomes a pleasurable and tireless experience. He has now gained water strength and self-assurance in his ability in water.

Chapter 6

Teaching the side stroke

The side stroke, an outgrowth of the breast stroke, was used in early competitive swimming. It was succeeded in the evolution of speed swimming by the overarm side stroke, the Trudgeon stroke, and the Trudgeon crawl stroke, all of which retained the scissors kick as an integral part of the stroke. All of these strokes in turn gave way to the faster Australian and American crawl strokes which eliminated the scissors kick, replacing it with a variation of the so-called flutter kick.

The side stroke is one of the most seaworthy strokes known to man. It is easy to learn and requires comparatively little effort to swim. It is preferred by women, whose natural buoyancy enables them to carry the head fairly high, keeping the hair and face out of the water. Many men favor the stroke because the head position, with the nose above the surface and directed to the rear, facilitates breathing.

Unless students are taught to use both sides of the body at once when learning the side stroke, the stroke should not be taught.

This stroke is the basis of two methods of rescue in lifesaving techniques. The cross-chest and hair-carry techniques utilize the strong scissors kick and the underarm pull of the side stroke to support and tow a drowning person to safety. The scissors kick may be used in treading water and is a foundation for numerous water ballet maneuvers.

Scissors kick. The scissors kick is so called because it resembles the action of the blades of a house shears. It is one of the most powerful of all kicks in the water. The pelvic girdle must remain in the vertical plane throughout the entire execution of the kick to give it effective, forceful, propulsive power.

The recovery of the legs starts from a side horizontal position of the body. The legs are extended one directly above the other, with the toes pointed. The knees are flexed, and the heels are drawn slowly backward. Both legs are held together and moved simultaneously. Drawing the heels backward gives just the proper amount of flexion at the hip joint.

In this position, if an imaginary line were passed through the midpoint of the shoulder and hip joints, it should project out over the legs at a midpoint between the knees and ankles when the legs are in full recovery position. The scissors are now opened by moving the under leg backward and the upper leg forward, while maintaining the flexed position of the knees. The foot of the top leg cocks itself, or flexes, toward the knee. The under foot remains extended. From this position the legs start the drive, reaching outward then forcefully together simultaneously by extending the knees and the foot of the top leg. The under leg is extended backward as far as anatomically possible, hooking the water and acting in the same manner as kicking a ball, while the top leg has a whip motion similar to the pawing of a horse. The legs meet together, are stretched straight and relaxed, and then pause long enough for momentum to be spent in the glide.

Arm stroke. During the glide the body is on the right side, with the shoulder girdle in a true vertical plane. The under right arm is extended forward directly under the head, with the palm facing down and hand just beneath the surface (Fig. 6-1, *A*). The upper left arm has completed its pull and is held close to the upper front part of the body, with the palm resting on the front side of the upper leg, never on top or behind. If it is held on top, the body will have a tendency to sink. If it is carried beyond and behind, it will cause the body to roll toward the back.

The student should have a clear mental picture of the pattern of the arm stroke from this starting position. Both arms move simultaneously along the longitudinal plane of the body. They meet just under the head, change direction, and simultaneously extend again to their starting position. The under arm moves forward, the upper arm moves backward. The swimmer can chant to himself "everything drawn in; everything thrust out." Therefore the upper arm moves forward during its recovery and the lower arm pulls diagonally downward and backward to a position directly beneath the head. Here it changes direction and starts its recovery movement, with hand and fingers pointed toward its starting position, while the upper arm pulls downward and backward to its starting position. Even though the hands move in and out together, the under arm is always pulling on the "in" movement, while the upper arm is always pulling on the "out" movement.

The upper arm is held close to the front upper part of the body, with the palm of the hand resting in front of the top thigh. The arm is held straight and submerged in this position. As the hand recovers, it slides away from the thigh, palm facing downward and slightly forward toward the face. The elbow bends but hugs close to the lower chest until the hand is well on its way forward to meet the under hand. There is a very special skilled technique that the beginner should learn at the very start of the upper arm recovery phase. If a slight pressure downward is brought to bear on the hand sliding forward, well under the surface,

Fig. 6-1. A series of ideal form for performing the side underarm stroke. **A,** The starting position. **B,** The stroke is initiated with the pull of the under arm. **B, C,** and **D,** Full recovery of the upper arm and the legs, while the under arm completes its propulsive phase. **D,** The hands are crossing under the head, while the legs have spread laterally on the horizontal plane, with the top ankle cocked toward the knee. The body is in position for the propulsive drive of the scissors kick and upper arm, while the under arm is in recovery position for the forward thrust. **E** clearly shows the action described in **D. F,** The final closing of the stroke and return to starting position, **A.**

close in front of chest, and moving on a horizontal plane, it will support the learner's face above the surface. The upper elbow and shoulder must be submerged as much as possible during the recovery phase to prevent the upper arm from pushing a wave over the face, causing choking and difficulty in breathing. The hand recovers about a hand's length beyond the face and passes above and beyond the under hand, just releasing the water and starting on its recovery. (See Fig. 6-1, *D*.) The upper hand now starts its pull by pressing downward and backward to its starting position in front of the thigh.

The planing effect of the upper hand and submergence of its elbow are very definitely factors in quick learning, even though it may be a resisting movement to forward progress.

Whole stroke. In the all-stroke method, the side stroke is taught on both sides. Most men prefer the right side, putting the strong arm underneath. However, if one side is dominant, it should be the left side because the upper arm, not the under arm, is the driving stroke. Then, too, in lifesaving techniques one usually reaches with the right arm in the approach, which results in a carry on the left side in which the right arm holds the person being towed and places the swimmer on his weak under arm in towing.

From a side-gliding position the stroke starts as the lower arm catches and begins its pull. The upper arm and legs recover. As the lower arm moves from its vertical position at the end of its pull directly under the shoulder to a doubled-up position, with the elbow bent and pressed against the chest wall and the hand in position ready to move forward, the legs have doubled-up and simultaneously spread in preparation for the kick. During the power or propulsive phase of the kick, the top arm pulls, and the lower arm extends forward. All movement comes to a halt as the body momentarily glides through the water. (See Fig. 6-1, *A*.) Breathing is not a hazard since the nose and mouth are turned to the rear and the water passes by the side of the face. Breathing should be regular and continuous throughout the stroke. Inhale through the mouth as the under arm pulls, and exhale during the pull of the top arm, again chanting "Everything in, arms, legs, and air; everything out, arms, legs, and air."

TEACHING PROCEDURE

The following instructions and procedures are used to teach the side stroke.

1. Demonstration and explanation of the kick by the instructor. Then the student is instructed to do the following:
2. Practice kick 50 times on each side, holding side of pool for support. (Daily drill strengthens the neuromuscular pattern.)

(a) Hold shoulder girdle and pelvic girdle in vertical position during the execution of the kick, since this will hold the legs in the correct horizontal plane.

(b) Prevent under knee from dropping down during recovery; hold it up against the upper leg.

(c) Emphasize under leg action by reaching as far back as possible at the beginning of the kick.

(d) Close legs at completion and hold there momentarily, simulating the glide. Do not permit the legs to cross each other.

3. Push from the side of the pool in glide position (face in the water). Repeat several times on each side until balance is established.

4. Learn coordination and timing of the side stroke using a four-step procedure or pattern as follows (learn one step at a time).

Step 1. Scissors kick only (Fig. 6-2, *A*). Take a deep breath and lie on right side floating position, with body straight and right under arm extended in line with body. Holding breath, turn face down into water on top of under arm. The left upper arm is in front of upper thigh. Take at least four kicks in succession, and pause between each stroke for glide. The upper hand is in front of the upper thigh, and remains on it during these kick exercises. This trains the upper arm to work in unison with the kick as it must in the whole stroke.

Step 2. Kick and upper arm (Fig. 6-2, *B*). The body is still on its extended right side, face under, as in Step 1. To execute Step 2, the upper hand and arm recover at the same time that the legs recover. The hand planes forward beyond the face, with the elbow and hand submerged to a point beyond the face. The arm pull starts at the same time as the kick. Here, again, as in the resting back stroke, the upper arm and legs recover at the same time and kick and pull at the same time.

Step 3. Kick, upper arm, and under arm (Fig. 6-2, *C*). Body with face under is still in the same position as in Step 1. To execute Step 3, press, do not pull, the under arm diagonally down and in a backward direction to a point under the face. At the same time that the under arm starts its press, the legs and upper arm are recovered. The hands meet, cross over, and repass as the hand of the under arm recovers and thrusts forward to guide the glide. At the same time as the under arm recovers, the upper arm and legs start the kick and pull, pause, and glide. Again chant the same singsong, "Everything in; everything out." Glide. This makes it simple to coordinate the arms and legs into the whole stroke. Take at least four stroke repetitions before stopping for air. If the student can coordinate four strokes in succession correctly, success is assured.

Step 4. Breathing (Fig. 6-2, *D*). Take one or two strokes in the Step 3 position, and then turn the face out of the water and face to the rear,

Fig. 6-2. A series of four learning steps of the side stroke, using the "part-whole" method. **A,** Skill 1, scissors kick only, with the face turned under. **B,** Skill 2, scissors kick and use of the upper arm. **C,** Skill 3, kick, upper arm and under arm. **D,** Skill 4, whole stroke, with the face turned out.

chin in line with the upper shoulder. Breathe in at the same time the arms and legs come in, breath out at the same time the arms and legs go out. "Everything in; everything out." In learning Steps 1, 2, and 3, the face is held under water in this position because the student is not likely to strangle. Once four or five strokes are correctly timed and coordinated, the student has learned the skill of coordinating the whole stroke. Now repeat the same four-step procedure on the right side. The water level should remain constant at the face, leveling at the corner of the lower eye and at the lower corner of the mouth.

For the teaching of crawl, back, and breast strokes see Chapters 9, 12, and 13.

Chapter 7

Advanced swimming

Since an intermediate level of swimming is eliminated from the all-stroke method of progressively learning to swim, an advanced course of swimming is offered. This course is recommended for those students who have successfully completed the beginners all-stroke course, and/or for those students who have never had instruction in swimming but swim some of the strokes quite well.

The aims and objectives of this course are as follows:

1. To teach proficiency in all-around watermanship and safety factors pertaining thereto
2. To teach the skill techniques in all of the strokes
3. To time the stroke movements correctly so that ease of performance is obtained, with added power and speed developed, thereby gaining greater confidence
4. To teach the miscellaneous skills, such as surface diving, treading water, underwater swimming, resting while tired in deep water, safety factors in outdoor wading, fishing, and boating
5. To swim 20 minutes safely
6. To accomplish a good racing start and turn
7. To teach the fundamentals of springboard diving
8. Demonstrate conservation of strength and energy over a longer distance while swimming
9. Be able to swim ¼ mile in 8 minutes or better

TEACHING AND LEARNING PROCEDURES

The instructor has the class review in shallow water the confidence skills as presented in the beginners course. The instructor will then demonstrate and have the class, in flights of four, swim one width or one length of the pool, with each style of stroke. This will adequately serve the instructor with a simple screen test. He rapidly grades them as they swim with a simple score; for example, very good 4, good 3, fair 2, very poor 1, cannot perform the stroke 0.

With the use of this simple screen test, the instructor can determine in which strokes the class as a whole is weak or deficient in stroke techniques. The instructor can in this way plan his future instruction sessions and stress those skills and strokes in which the class is most deficient. This will serve as an expedient method of teaching most effectively in the stroke and technique area most needed by the entire class.

In some of the class sessions it will be a question of teaching the entire stroke for those students who cannot swim the stroke or swim it very poorly. Those students who are most proficient can act as partner instructors. Throughout this area of learning, the basic fundamentals of all strokes and skills are reviewed and stressed. This is best accomplished by repetition type of swimming across the pool in flights. During the rest intervals, the instructor can best utilize the time by lecture or the practice of the miscellaneous skills, such as listed in the above objectives.

When the class as a whole has reached a point in the progress of learning that each member can swim 100 yards with each style of swimming, the instructor can now begin an advanced program of training.

Having followed this program, the class is thoroughly trained for further advanced swimming in various areas, such as varsity swimming, life saving, or merely recreational swimming.

DISTANCE ORIENTATION

When the class has been put through an intensive training period of about five to seven weeks in all the strokes and each member of the class can swim 100 yards, the class is now well conditioned for continually extending, during a four-week period of distance orientation, the distance each individual can swim.

At the very first class period in which distance orientation is started, the class is instructed to swim relaxed, slowly, and as easily as possible and to breathe naturally. This will be difficult at first. Members of the class are told to swim far enough that they extend themselves beyond comfort. They are also told that the first 150 to 250 yards will be the most difficult. In this range of distance it appears to the student that he is swimming up hill. However, once he is on the other side of the hill, it will suddenly be almost effortless. He has his "second wind." Once the student has experienced the sensations of going up and over this imaginary hill, the battle is won.

Again, the student is instructed that once he covers 300 yards, he can swim almost any distance. However, he must, in every class period, repeat and go several yards or lengths of the pool farther than he did the class period before.

In his first distance attempt he realizes that he has gone too fast and that fatigue has set in too soon. He now makes up his mind to go slower and take it easy. Here is one of the greatest lessons the beginner can learn. As he goes easier, he gradually gives himself over to the water and unconsciously learns to RELAX. As he relaxes he breathes more naturally. An instructor can repeatedly tell a student to relax, but without success. The student must learn to relax the hard way through a program of distance swimming.

Once he has acquired and tucked under his "belt," so to speak, several distance swims, he gains another great lesson in water that can seldom be gained any other way. This lesson is "water strength." This term includes many desirable traits which now begin to take place in the student. Some of these are confidence, self-assurance, relaxation, better breathing habits, and a respect for distance in water in distributing his effort in relation to his physical condition. Those desiring to go now into varsity swimming have received their first lesson in PACE. In other words, they are beginning to learn how to maintain an evenly distributed effort over a given distance.

All of the desired objectives and aims to be gained by the student are best derived through the all-stroke method. This method has been successfully tried with all age groups, ranging in ages from 9 to 60 years. The results have been amazing. It eliminates the intermediate level and takes the student into the various advanced fields of aquatics with a thorough grounding in the techniques of all the strokes.

Should students never come back for advanced instruction, they are now safely, adequately, and satisfactorily trained for participation in leisure-time hunting, fishing, boating, and outdoor sports in and around water.

Chapter 8

Coaching the racing start

The competitors with the fastest starting times have a significant advantage over those who are slow in leaving the marks. Likewise, a fast swimmer may see his efforts go for nought if for some reason he fails to leave his mark with precise, forceful, and well-timed movements. The mechanics of the start and the physiologic and psychologic factors entering into its performance are indeed complex.

The swimming start is defined as including the events which take place between the command, "Take your marks," and the beginning of the first swimming stroke.

The description of the start of a race in which the crawl stroke is used is presented in this chapter. The start of all distances of crawl swimming races is essentially the same, but the importance of having a good start is magnified as the swimming distance becomes shorter. The start of the breast and butterfly stroke races is the same as that of the crawl until the body enters the water. The events which take place in the breast stroke race after the entry into the water are described in Chapter 13.

Since the start of the back stroke race is altogether different from that of the crawl, dolphin butterfly, or breast stroke, it is discussed in detail in Chapter 12.

The take-off platform is 30 inches above the surface of the water. It is flat and parallel to the water's surface. At the signal, "Take your marks," the swimmer assumes his starting position with his toes gripped over the edge of the starting block. After he has held a steady balance in this position for an appreciable length of time, a pistol is fired. The swimmer throws his center of gravity in front of his base of support and then supplies the thrust which projects him forward from his mark with as much force as he can generate. He leaves the mark at the angle which will give him the greatest distance from his mark.

The start may be divided into the following components: (1) the preparatory position, (2) assuming the starting position, (3) leaving

Fig. 8-1, cont'd. H, Position of the body in the g of the body at the start of the stroke at the enc **J,** Position of the body as it swims to the surface.

Fig. 8-1. A-J, A series of ideal form for performing the standard crawl stroke start. **A,** The preliminary stance. **B,** On the mark in a position of momentary steadiness. **C,** Preliminary movements for executing the drop after the gun is fired. **D,** The position for the drive.

below the hip joints and places the leg mus for the drive. The feet are parallel to each the starting line. The force of the ankle anc over the toes which grip the edge of th advantage of the straight pull of the musc ished when the legs are overspread and the of the body rests mainly on the balls lightly on the platform to give support w himself balanced in the starting position a 8-1, *B*).

The grip of the toes is made with the flexed over the edge of the platform, the se The third, fourth, and fifth toes assist sl mainly lateral support. The grip of the to of balance.

The swimmer should never permit his If the body is swaying backward at the pis project his body forward until the body backward sway and has again recovered t accounts for some swimmers being caught

the mark, (4) the flight, (5) the entry, (6) the glide, and (7) the initial strokes.

Preparatory position. After the contestant is in his proper lane and starting station, adequate warning is given by the official starter that in a few moments the race will be underway. During this brief interval the swimmer can make preparation for the race. Stretching movements, such as lifting the legs, bending the trunk forward, swinging the arms in circles, and twisting the trunk, will improve the condition of the muscles. Loose shaking of the arms and legs is effective in reducing tension due to the excitement of the competitive situation. He then assumes the preparatory position standing erect, relaxed, and motionless, with both feet on the starting mark in readiness and alert for the starting command, "Take your marks." Two or three deep breaths, with emphasis on the expiration phase, taken just before taking the marks prepare the body for the violent exertion which is to follow and will ensure adequate ventilation at the beginning of the race.

Assuming the starting position. Upon the command, "Take your marks," the swimmer immediately assumes his starting position. A false start can be charged to a competitor if, in the opinion of the starter,

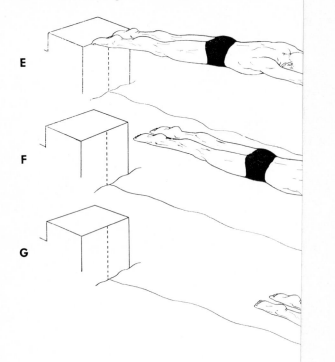

E

F

G

Fig. 8-1, cont'd. E, Position of the body as [...] body in flight. **G,** Position of the body as it [...]

he is too slow in moving to his startin[...]
be charged if the swimmer does not c[...]
movement before the starting pistol [...]
positions used by competitive swimr[...]
techniques.

Position of the trunk. The trunk [...]
forward to an angle approximating a[...]
sition (Fig. 8-1, *B*). The full-crouch s[...]
for the spring.

Position of the feet. The feet are [...]
right angles to the starting line (Fig. [...]
feet depends upon the width of the h[...]
of the legs. The foot position which [...]
the most stability is commonly one i[...]
inches apart. This position places th[...]

caught back on his heels when the pistol is fired, he may partially overcome it by suddenly lifting his toes and the balls of his feet. This action removes the forward point of support and allows the body to drop rapidly forward.

It has been the custom for swimmers to start from a flat-footed position on the edge of the pool. The success which sprint runners met with the use of inclined starting blocks on top of the track suggested that an inclined starting block might be of advantage to the swimmer. An investigation of the use of starting blocks in the swimming start showed quite conclusively that inclined starting blocks are a disadvantage to swimmers in leaving the mark, as far as starting time is concerned.* However, the inclined starting platform is still being used in international Olympic competition.

Position of the knees. The proper amount of flexion of the knees in the starting position is one in which a straight line passing from the tip of the shoulder to the ankle bone will pass just in front of the knee cap (Fig. 8-1, *B*). A greater knee flexion would cause the heels to be lifted and the center of weight to be shifted forward to a position over the toes. In this forward position the swimmer is less stable and is effecting too great a tension on his extensor muscles. The knees should be so bent that the heels can rest lightly on the platform and further flexion and extension can take place freely. In this position the swimmer is well poised and is ready to execute a powerful drive from his mark.

Position of the hips. The degree of flexion of the hips depends upon the choice of starting position. If the full-crouch position is used, the flexion is nearly complete, causing the trunk to be held in a horizontal plane, the hips held at about the same level as the shoulders (Fig. 8-1, *B*). If the semicrouch position is used, the shoulders are held above the level of the hips. In both positions the hips are held far enough behind the center of support so that that portion of the body in front of the base is counterbalanced.

Position of the head and eyes. In the starting position when the swimmer has placed the feet on the mark, he then looks down the course of the pool to a point near the water level at the end of his lane on the opposite side of the pool. The head should be raised high enough so that the swimmer can easily see this point (Fig. 8-1, *B*). In this position the eyes aid in holding a steady balance for an appreciable length of time and also aim the flight of the body when leaving the mark.

Position of the arms (Fig. 8-1, *B*). The arms are lifted backward as the swimmer comes onto the mark. While in the position of momentary steadiness, the swimmer holds the arms as far backward as comfort

*Tuttle, W. W., Morehouse, Laurence E., and Armbruster, David A.: Two studies in swimming starts. I. The use of starting blocks in swimming sprints, Research Quarterly 10:89-92 (March), 1939.

permits. This arm position should not be forced backward so far as to place a strain on the shoulder muscles.

From this position only a slight additional backward movement or hitch of the arms is needed to start the body forward. If the arms are held too low, the time required to swing them upward to the driving position (Fig. 8-1, *C*) will be too long, and the start will be delayed. If held too high, the force of the hitch is limited, and the forward momentum imparted to the body is lessened.

The legs cannot be brought into action until the body has been projected forward. The important feature of the arm action is the rapidity of the pitch forward, not the quantity of the momentum which is imparted. Force and speed which furnish momentum are the job of the legs; quickness of starting is the job of the arms. The elbows should be slightly flexed, which shortens the radius and decreases the range of movement. This increases the speed of the arms and allows greater speed in starting.

Now that the swimmer has assumed his starting position and is holding a steady balance, two further factors must be considered. They are, namely, breathing and attention.

Breathing. While the swimmer is awaiting the command, "Take your marks," he should take three or four deep breaths. During this period of increased ventilation, forceful expiration should be made in order to reduce the carbon dioxide content of the air in the lungs. When this is accomplished, the swimmer can hold his breath for a longer period of time, and thus breathing does not interfere with his arm mechanics in the early part of the race.

Deep breathing before a race can be overdone easily. Some swimmers are so sensitive to the changes in the blood due to hyperventilation that they become dizzy after taking six deep breaths. Such dizziness may reduce balance and coordination and spoil the start. Hyperventilation at the start should be used during practice before attempting it during competition. Only a few trials are needed to establish the number of deep breaths which can be taken without discomfort.

Some experimenters have demonstrated that a few deep breaths of oxygen before a race will increase the performance over short distances. This experiment met with the same success when regular air was substituted for the oxygen and the swimmers kept ignorant of the change. Deep breathing (washing out the excess carbon dioxide) plus a psychologic factor (faith in the beneficial effects of oxygen) were evidently the causes of increased performance.

Preliminary hyperventilation is especially important in races of short duration. It requires approximately 20 to 30 seconds to swim the 40-, 50-, or 60-yard dash. With adequate ventilation previous to the start, only a few breaths are required during the race. Some top-flight swimmers swim the entire 50 yards without taking a breath.

If conditions were such that forced respiration could be continued until the moment before the swimmer entered the water, the beneficial effects of hyperventilation would be augmented. However, in order to maintain his equilibrium in a delicately balanced starting position while awaiting the pistol shot, the swimmer must halt the heaving movements of his thorax which accompany forced respiration.

In addition to aiding the swimmer to maintain a steady balance in the "set" position, cessation of respiration also aids the swimmer to give maximum attention while waiting for the pistol shot.

If a swimmer frequently loses his balance while in the starting position or is a slow starter, the coach may check the swimmer's breathing habits to find if he is properly holding his breath in the starting position while awaiting the pistol shot.

A short and deep inhalation at the take-off acts to increase the swimmer's buoyancy and prevents him from sinking too deep during the plunge and glide. It also provides air which further aids him to hold his breath without distress during the glide and the first few strokes.

A study of the respiratory habits of trained swimmers during the start of a race supports the following conclusions*:

1.   Prior to the starter's command, "Take your marks," trained swimmers either use forced respiration or breathe normally. After the command, "Take your marks," as the swimmers assume the starting position and maintain a steady balance while awaiting the pistol shot, the breath is held at the end of a normal inspiration. After the pistol shot, as the swimmers prepare to leave their marks, a deep inspiration is made and is held.

2.   The respiratory habits of trained swimmers are similar to those of trained track runners. The adaptation of respiratory habits to race situations is, in most cases, so natural that the athlete acquires proper habits through practice and without advice from the coach.

Attention. When the contestant is behind his starting station awaiting the starter's instructions, he sets about the task in the following brief moments to prepare himself for the race at hand: The swimmer's attention becomes closely fixed on the words of the starter as the instructions are given. He then makes the bodily adjustments by placing his feet on the starting marks in preparation for the signal, "Take your marks." At this signal he carefully assumes his starting position, which he then holds for a period of momentary steadiness. It is during this period that

*Morehouse, Laurence E.: The respiratory habits of trained swimmers during the start of a race, Research Quarterly 12:186 (May), 1941.

attention must reach its peak. The swimmer is "set" for the gun; his breathing ceases, attention is diverted from the noises, movements of the spectators and other contestants are shut out, and his entire attention is centered upon the pistol shot.

Attention occurs in waves, reaching a peak and subsiding continuously. Thus, the length of time the starter holds the swimmers at a steady balance in the starting position will affect the start.

It is a well-known fact that the interval of time that a starter holds swimmers on their marks is subject to individual variation. Some starters allow only a short interval and start the swimmers before they are ready, and others prolong the holding time so that the swimmers have passed their peaks of attention and the initiation of performance is prolonged when the pistol is finally fired. The optimum interval of time that a swimmer should hold a steady balance in a starting position on his mark has been found to be 1.5 seconds.*

Practice in responding to the starting gun should be repeated frequently enough so that the swimmer's response is automatic. The swimmer should be so conditioned to the starting gun that any sharp noise will cause him to initiate the movements of the start. The official who is starting a race should be aware of this conditioned response and should not penalize swimmers who are disturbed by such an outside noise before the gun was fired.

Leaving the mark. The act of leaving the mark may be divided into two parts, the drop and the drive.

DROP. The drop may be defined as that portion of leaving the mark which is concerned with shifting the center of the body weight to a position in front of the base of support so that force applied behind the center of weight in this position will drive the body forward. A well-executed drop requires skillful and rapid movements of the arms and legs to overcome the inertia of the swimmer in the steady balanced position. At the pistol shot, the arms are flung backward and upward (Fig. 8-1, *C*). This action aids the body in moving forward. At the same time the body is continued forward by a slight extension of the knees and hips. At this moment a deep breath is taken and held.

The arms next reverse the swing from backward to forward. This is followed by a rapid body drop caused by a flexion at the hips, knees, and ankles. The heels now rest firmly on the platform until the body has almost reached the drive position and the ankles have been flexed.

DRIVE. The end of the drop occurs when the hips, knees, and ankles are flexed and the arms have been swung forward as far as the knees (Fig. 8-1, *D*). At this point the body is crouched and ready for a straight-

*Tuttle, W. W., Morehouse, Laurence E., and Armbruster, David A.: A further study of the optimum time for holding a swimmer on his mark, Research Quarterly 11:53-56 (March), 1940.

forward drive. If the arms are too far forward or too far backward at this point, much power will be lost.

The drive now commences with a powerful action of both the legs and arms. The legs propel the body forward by an extension of the knees and hips. The arms are swung forward from the knees until they reach a position slightly below eye level. At this point the swing is suddenly halted, transferring the forward momentum from the arms to the body.

The ankle is not extended until the arms are stopped. The ankles, being weaker joints than the knees or hips, are used to push the body forward only after it is well under way. At this advantageous moment they are snapped into extension, adding considerable force to the forward speed at the end of the drive.

One of the simplest starts has just been described. There are variations in this form of starting which have proved to be equally as successful and deserve consideration here. The swimmer would benefit

A   B   C   D

Fig. 8-2. A-G, A series of ideal form for performing the circular technique crawl stroke start. This start is also preferable for the dolphin butterfly and breast stroke events. **A,** The preliminary erect, relaxed, yet alert stance. **B,** On the mark in a position of momentary steadiness, with arms hanging below the shoulders in readiness for gun signal. **C,** Note the short, forward, preliminary movement of the arms after the gun is fired. The arms continue a lateral, upward, and backward sweep while the body continues to drop to the take-off position. **D,** The position for the drive.

by practicing all the good forms of starts and selecting the one which advances him to a 10-yard distance in the shortest interval of time. An experiment devised to seek the best start revealed that among expert swimmers the start which was regularly used by each proved to be the best for him and that variations in arm or leg action of the style he had learned tended only to inhibit him. A similar experiment with inexperienced swimmers showed that the start which contained the simplest movements was the most successful.*

Variations in the start. There are numerous variations in starting technique which are worthy of consideration.

Circular arm action. This start was designed to move the body for-

*Morehouse, Laurence E.: A comparison of the starting times of various forms of competitive swimming starts, Official aquatic guide, New York, 1941-42, A. S. Barnes & Co., p. 66.

Fig. 8-2, cont'd. E, Position of the body as it leaves the mark. Note the arms are driven forward and abruptly halted, just below the chin level. The head remains well upraised. **F,** The flight. The arms now line up with the body, and the head is lowered between the arms. **G,** The entry. For the underwater glide and initial strokes in surfacing, see Fig. 8-1, H-J.

ward from the balanced position with greater rapidity than the method previously described. This technique employs a circular arm action and in this manner adds power to the arms in both the drop and the drive portions of the start.

In this starting position the arms hang downward loosely from the shoulders, with the elbows slightly flexed. At the pistol shot, the knees and hips are extended slightly, lifting the body a little less than from a full-crouch type of start. At the same time the arms are moved in an outward circular movement to the rear, which assists the body to drop forward. The arms then continue their circular movement downward and forward as rapidly as possible. When the arms in their forward drive reach a point opposite the knees, the body starts to uncoil. The knees are forcefully extended, followed by the extension of the feet as they leave the starting block. The forward movement of the arms is abruptly halted at a point short of a straight alignment with the rest of the body. The angular momentum is thus transferred to the whole body. (See Fig. 8-2.) The remainder of this start is the same as described in the standard start (Fig. 8-1).

Knee extension technique. The swimmer using this technique fixes his hips and uses only his knees in the maneuver of the legs in the drop to the drive position. This start is suited for relay races since the head is held downward and the swimmer can see his teammate approach the finish mark under him.

The starting position of the swimmer employing the knee-action technique is similar to the full-crouch start. Following the pistol shot, the circular arm action is applied. The head is held low to keep the trunk from rising. At the instant the arms swing forward following the pistol shot, the knees straighten, and the body is extended forward. The knees are then rapidly flexed, and the forward speed of the body is increased due to the shortened radius. By the time the knees have dropped to a position of full flexion, the arms have completed their circular movement and have arrived opposite the knees. The body is now ready for the drive which is executed as described in the full-crouch start (Fig. 8-1, *D*).

The knee extension technique can also be accomplished using the standard arm swing.

Knee dip technique. Although this type of start considerably reduces stability in the starting position, it yields a very fast start when it is once mastered. Some swimmers with a slow response time but with good equilibrium find that their starting times are markedly improved using the knee dip technique.

In the starting position the knees are held straight, not hyper-extended, and the body is bent forward at the hips. The arms are held backward at a level slightly above that of the hips. The head is held well up.

In this stance the weight is carried further forward to a point at the front of the balls of the feet and just behind the toes. The body is held at a steady balance in this precarious position.

At the pistol shot the knees are promptly flexed, causing the body to drop forward toward the drive position. The arms are held backward as the body drops under them. When the body has nearly reached the drive position, the arms are swept downward. When the arms pass the knees, the drive is started and is carried out in the standard manner.

An additional speed-imparting skill can be added to this and other starts by those gifted with a high degree of equilibrium. While holding the steady balance awaiting the pistol shot, the swimmer can slowly lower the trunk so that, when the pistol is discharged, the body is already in motion. The force will be applied, then, in changing the direction of the motion instead of starting the motion from a position at rest. A steady balance must be held during this slow lowering of the body since the competitor will be charged with a false start if he has gained unfair advantage by being off balance in the direction of the start when the pistol is discharged.

Toe lift technique. The essential merit of this technique is its simplicity. The leg action is so fast, however, that the arm must react very fast in order to gather satisfactory momentum in so short a time as to be able to be coordinated with it.

This technique can be employed from the full-crouch position. The body is inclined forward, head up, arms back just below hip level, knees slightly flexed, and the toes in the regular gripping position. The center of weight is over the balls of the feet. At the pistol shot, the toe muscles are relaxed, and the support is removed from the front of the feet and transferred to the heels. This shift of support to a point behind the center of weight causes the body to drop forward at a rapid rate.

As the body commences to drop, the knees are flexed, and the arms are then quickly swung forward so that their action coincides with that of the knees at the initial stage of the drive (Fig. 8-1, *D*).

Some power is lost during the drive since the arms have not gained sufficient speed. This deficit may be somewhat compensated for by the additional power gained from the swiftly falling body when the momentum is changed to a forward direction during the drive.

Motion picture studies show that nearly all sprint swimmers slightly relax the great toe and allow the weight to fall somewhat backward to the heels during the drop. This shift occurs naturally during all types of starts. The toe lift technique is merely an exaggeration of this natural tendency.

When the body reaches the beginning of the drive position, the toes again forcefully grip the edge of the pool. This prevents slipping and also provides a firm support for the drive from the edge of the starting station.

Flight. The swimmer leaves the take-off with his body in a nearly horizontal position. His body follows a parabolic curve as it is projected forward through the air.

The extension of the ankle during the final part of the drive tends to throw the legs upward. If this is allowed to occur, the body will be projected toward the water at too sharp an angle, and the swimmer will enter too soon and in a disadvantageous position. In order to avoid throwing the legs upward, the toes should remain in contact with the take-off until the ankles are fully extended (Fig. 8-1, *E*).

The angle of the take-off should be nearly horizontal. A take-off at an angle below the horizontal will result in an entry that is too near the starting mark, too deep, and lacking in momentum. On the other hand, if the take-off is nearly horizontal, the entry will be at a greater distance from the mark, the body will remain near the surface of the water, and the glide will be longer and faster due to the advantageous application of force (Fig. 8-1, *E*).

As the swimmer leaves the mark, his head is held up, and his eyes look forward. Care must be exercised that the head is not held so high that the body becomes arched. In an arched position in flight, the swimmer frequently enters the water with his legs dragging, which results in retarding his forward motion.

If the swimmer keeps his head up until near the end of the flight and then drops it between his arms, he has a tendency to raise his arms and lower his legs. This type of entry is thought by some to facilitate the first strokes because the shoulders are not submerged and thus the arms are free to start stroking. Repeated observations have shown, however, that the extended shallow glide is faster than the leg drag and early arm action.

The head should be lowered to a position between the arms in the early period of the flight, preferably as the feet leave the marks (Fig. 8-1, *E*). In this position the body is held steady on a horizontal level which facilitates a proper entry (Fig. 8-1, *F* and *G*).

Entry. If the take-off has been performed at a level approaching the horizontal and the body parts of the swimmer have been held in good alignment, the entry will be made at a maximum distance from the mark. The fingertips are first to enter, and the rest of the body follows at an angle of from 8 to 10 degrees beneath the surface (Fig. 8-1, *G*).

If the swimmer enters the water in a horizontal position, he will remain near the surface. If the entry is too angular, the swimmer will submerge too deeply, and his course will be curvilinear and time-consuming.

As the body enters the water, it is held rigid. The fingers and palms are held in line with the arms, the the feet and toes in line with the legs. The head is held low between the arms, and the back of the head in line with the upper surface of the arms. The arms are to be pressed against the sides of the head, and the thumbs and index fingers of the hands are held together. The whole body is in a streamlined position (Fig. 8-1, *G*).

Upon striking the water, the swimmer must press the arms downward in order to keep their alignment in the presence of the upward force of the water.

Observations have been made of the effectiveness of entering the water with the feet held in a narrow stride position so that the flutter kick can be commenced in the air or as soon as the legs are submerged. This early leg action was found to retard the forward motion instead of accelerating it.

Glide. As the body submerges, it is held stretched in the same streamlined position as during the flight (Fig. 8-1, *H*). The distance and speed of the glide depend upon the impetus given by the drive from the mark, the extent of the trajectory to the water, and the resistance of the water to the body in its forward motion.

The water resistance is greatest at the surface and is heightened by the whirling or eddying motion of choppy water. The glide, then, should be just far enough below the surface to allow all parts of the body to escape these swirls.

The fingers do not usually have to be planed upward in order to guide the body toward the surface. As momentum is lost, the body rises toward the surface due to the buoyancy of most individuals whose lungs are inflated.

Initial strokes. When the speed at the glide is reduced to a point where it is no greater than the maximum swimming speed, the initial strokes should be made. The swimmer can cultivate in practice the feel of the speed by noting the sensation caused by the friction of the water against the surface of the body at various rates.

At this point, the legs start their drive, and the arm opposite from the breathing side executes the first arm pull (Fig. 8-1, *I*). This prevents the temptation to turn the head for air during the first arm pull. Turning the head is detrimental to arm action and body balance at this point since the body is still low in the water and the head would have to be raised too high to get a breath. The swimmer should learn to hold his breath until he is well underway and his pace has been set. If adequate ventilation has occurred just before the start, this breathholding will not be uncomfortable.

The first arm pull is started while the body is still about 8 to 12 inches below the water's surface. The arm movement is started by depressing the hand and starting the pull backward. The elbow is then flexed, and the arm is drawn backward. The arm action does not start with a strong down stroke, as this would cause the body to be driven upward instead of forward, resulting in a loss of speed. The body is pushed forward and breaks to the surface with great speed (Fig. 8-1, *J*).

The head is held down during the first arm pull. It is then gradually raised to the swimming position with each succeeding arm stroke until the third arm stroke is reached. While the initial arm is pulling, slight supporting pressure is exerted on the other arm. This places it in readiness at the proper depth to start the arm pull as soon as the other arm has finished its stroke.

A forceful kick during the initial strokes lends stability to the arm action and aids in driving the body forward to the surface. The rhythm of the legs should coincide with the arm action from the beginning. A narrow, fast kick tends to cause a swimmer to speed up his arm action to a faster rate than that which he has been accustomed to using. If rapid leg action is started early, the arm action should not be started until the leg action has been reduced to the rate which is synchronous with the arm speed. The optimum speed of the initial leg and arm strokes is that which approaches the rate of the regular swimming rhythm.

Chapter 9

Coaching the sprint
crawl stroke

The modern crawl stroke is the fastest and the most efficient stroke used by competitive swimmers today. In all free style events from the short 50- or 60-yard dash to the long distance races, the crawl stroke is universally used.

There are two forms of swimming the modern crawl. The first, the sprint crawl stroke, is used for short dashes in which the conservation of energy is not a factor, and, the second, the distance crawl stroke, is used in races in which energy must be conserved and distributed over the course of the race. In the free style, races of 100 yards and less are generally considered as sprints. According to this definition, competitors who must conserve their energy by swimming at a speed slower than their maximum in order to complete a 100-yard swim must consider this race as a distance swim. Until they have improved their condition to such an extent that they can swim the 100 yards at maximum speed, the race, to them, is not a sprint.

The essential differences between the methods of swimming the sprint and the distance crawl strokes lie in the duration of the arm and leg cycles and the manner in which each arm performs the first act of the pull after it has entered the water. In order to lengthen the duration of the arm and leg cycles for distance swimming, a gliding movement is added to the arm stroke. The glide occurs just after the arm enters the water and before the pull is started. However, today there is a trend toward an opposition rhythm of the arm stroke for the sprint as well as for the distance swimmer. That is, the six-beat kick is diminished to less beats or merely a counterbalanced action of the legs in the longer distances, while the arms move in a windmill or opposite-action rhythm similar to the back crawl. This style entirely eliminates the glide of the arms after the entry but goes deeper for the catch.

This style was first seen in America in the Olympic Games in 1932 in Los Angeles. It was then called the European style simply because

Europeans used it. Teris of France almost defeated Buster Crabbe with it in the 400-meter race. The Holland women's team was most successful with this style at the games. At that time it was not well thought of by American coaches.

The duration of the glide depends upon the pace desired. In the sprint crawl stroke, the glide is reduced to a minimum, and the arm is pressed downward into the driving position as soon as it enters the water.

In order to obtain maximum speed, the modern crawl stroke is swum in the sprint style. This style is described in full in this chapter. Modifications of the sprint crawl which adapt it to middle distance and distance swimming are discussed later.

CHARACTERISTICS OF SPRINT SWIMMERS

A wide range of difference will be found among top-flight sprint swimmers. Competitors with only one leg have been among the place winners in county and state championships. In general, though, one will find that top-ranking swimmers possess robust, symmetrical bodies. A large number of these have developed from weaklings and poorly skilled individuals to powerful and smooth performers.

There are certain characteristics which will aid in sprint swimming performance. These can be divided into three classes, anatomic, physiologic, and psychologic.

The anatomic qualifications are probably the most important. These represent the equipment of the swimmer. The efficiency with which he uses this equipment depends upon his physiologic and psychologic functions. The frequently repeated rule that a good big man has the advantage over a good little man applies in top-flight sprinting.

A long hand will provide a good paddle, but it must be accompanied by powerful wrist and arm muscles if it is to be effective. Due to the wide range of movement of the shoulder girdle during sprint swimming, the muscles attached to this girdle must be flexible.

The muscles of the back and abdomen must be powerful since they are the muscles of fixation of the thorax and pelvis. The vigorous arm and shoulder movements and the driving leg action must originate and operate from and upon stable bases if these movements are to be effective. The body which sags in the middle and wobbles during the swimming action will not be streamlined, and greater resistance will be met in the water.

The hips should be thin, yet powerful. The sides of the buttocks should slope from the back to the thighs. A buttock which is undercut presents an abrupt surface which causes a drag in the water. Ideally, there should be no fold under the buttocks; they should be small and flat. In other words, the buttocks should be shaped more like a torpedo than like a rowboat.

The legs should be long and slender with flexible and strong muscles. An item of great importance is the ankle. This joint must be of the type which allows a large range of extension. Such an ankle is usually slender, and the joints in the ankle and foot are loose. A simple test of ankle flexibility is made by sitting on the floor with the legs extended forward and turning the feet inward and downward in a pigeon-toed fashion in an attempt to touch the floor with all the toes. Full efficiency in swimming the crawl cannot be realized until this degree of extension can be reached. This movement can be developed in most individuals through constant application of the few simple exercises which are presented in Chapter 16.

The question is often asked of the authors, by both coaches and swimmers, "Is it good or bad for swimmers to play football?" The only detriment observed by the authors is usually an enlargement of the ankles. This would cause them to be less flexible and efficient as the paddle end of the leg; especially is this true of the crawl, back, and butterfly swimmers. Then, too, the deltoid muscle, located on the upper and outward area of the shoulder joint, may become overdeveloped and hinder good flexible shoulder and arm action, especially in the crawl and butterfly strokes.

The feet should be long, slender, and flexible in order to achieve a free fishtail action. A foot that presents a long lever will be an efficient paddle since the leg muscles are capable of providing powerful action to it as the leg completes the upward and downward drive.

Individuals with short necks have difficulty in turning the head in breathing in the crawl stroke. In full-speed swimming the individual with a long neck can lift the head better in acquiring the desired planed position.

The foremost physiologic qualification is speed. A sprint swimmer must be a quick mover. He must have a fast response at the start and at the turn, and he must be capable of moving his legs at a high rate of speed in order to coordinate them with his driving arm action.

The muscles must be powerful in order to develop the tremendous horsepower needed to overcome the water resistance. As the speed is increased, the resistance of the water becomes greater, and consequently more power is required to keep the swimmer moving at a high rate of speed.

Endurance must be great since the entire body is at work during swimming. The heart muscle must be well conditioned so that it can pump blood continuously to all of the working muscles. The circulation of blood through the muscles must be adequate to supply large quantities of oxygen and foodstuffs and carry away the waste materials. This condition is gained only through frequently repeated vigorous exercise for several weeks. This means miles of daily swimming, including "wind sprints," for at least six weeks before a competitive season. The result is an increase in the quantity of blood capillaries within the work muscles. The improved circulatory condition in the muscles is felt by an increased ability to extend the distance of a swim at a fast pace.

The sprint swimmer who must move his arms and legs at a continuously rapid rate over a distance often becomes tied up. This occurs most frequently in those who are poorly coordinated. These individuals require more energy to overcome the waste movements. The sprint swimmer must train rigidly in order to derive a perfect stroke coordi-

Fig. 9-1. A-H, A series of ideal form for executing the modern sprint crawl stroke showing the six leg beats and one revolution of the arm stroke cycle. These figures also show the counterbalance of the arm and leg action, the turning of the head in taking air in the stroke, and the body position in relation to the surface of the water. **B** and **F** show the looseness of feet and ankles during the beat action.

nation. Some swimmers are faster learners than others and achieve this measure of skill in a relatively short time. Others must devote hours of conscientious practice in order to reach this stage of training.

TECHNIQUE OF THE SPRINT CRAWL STROKE

The components of the sprint crawl will be discussed in the following order: (1) body position, (2) leg action, (3) arm action, (4) coordination of the arms, (5) coordination of the legs and arms, (6) breathing, (7) coordination of breathing with the sprint crawl stroke, (8) sprint crawl turn, and (9) finish.

Body position. Nature has given streamlined bodies to fish, but the human body must be held in a position to follow the natural lines of streamlined flow in order to eliminate the turbulence which retards the motion of the swimmer.

Position of the head and neck. The head is carried well up, with the

Fig. 9-1, cont'd. For legend see opposite page.

face only in the water (Fig. 9-1, *A*). The water level varies from a position just below the eyes to one at the level of the hairline. This variation is in accordance with the height of the bow wave in front of the head and the buoyancy of the swimmer.

The wave in front of the head will be higher as the swimmer increases his speed and will lower as the speed diminishes. A difference in buoyancy will also affect the optimum height at which the head is carried. A great many sprinters are exceedingly muscular and have a heavy skeleton. This type of swimmer does not float as high in the water as do individuals with lighter skeletons, less musculature, and more fatty tissue. The less buoyant individuals will thus swim lower in the water with the water level near the hairline, even at maximum speed.

The eyes are directed forward in a natural position and are not peering upward from under the eyebrows or sideward from the corners of the eyes. The eyes are the main aids in the control of the body position. If they are directed in an upward or sideward position, the body will be easily thrown out of equilibrium, and the propelling motion of the arms and legs will be inhibited. The eyes are centered or "spotted" on the forward plane of progression. When the head is turned for an inhalation, the eyes are moved with it but are quickly returned to the centered position and remain fixed in this position until the next inhalation. Any sideward rolling motion of the body should not alter the stability of the vision.

The nose and chin are also held in a centered position, and, except for the turn of the head for breathing, they do not oscillate with any rolling movement of the body. After the inhalation they also recover to the center. The head cannot be held steady if the neck is too rigid. In this condition, any movement of the trunk is transmitted to the head.

It is commonly observed that if the head is returned too far past the center position during the exhalation phase of the crawl stroke, an unbalanced leg action will result. This reduces the driving power of the legs and thus should be avoided.

The chin is carried forward, away from the throat, except when turning for air. When the head is turned for air, the chin is tucked into a position in front of the shoulders and in line with the arm pit so that a relatively smooth surface is presented by the under side of the face, neck, and chest wall (Fig. 9-1, *C*) so that the water can flow under them with little resistance and the mouth will be in the trough formed by the bow wave flowing around the head.

The chin should not be held so far forward when centered that wrinkles appear in the back of the neck. This rigid posture is most likely to be found in individuals with short necks. A strained position of the neck will result in early fatigue since constant turning of the head in this position requires a greater effort. A rigid neck position usually is accompanied by a rigid body position also. In this condition muscles must work against each other as well as against the resistance of the water, and additional work must be done to overcome this additional load.

Although the head moves independently of the shoulder girdle and upper spine, the proper position of the head is aided by an accommodating posture of the shoulder girdle and upper spine. Likewise, a good body position is dependent upon the posture of the head and neck.

The speed developed by the powerful movements of the sprint crawl stroke will naturally elevate the head and shoulders. The swimmer, therefore, does not need to lift his head and shoulders. In fact, they are pressed somewhat forward and downward, giving the impression of swimming downhill.

A common fault of sprint swimmers attempting to get a good head position is to raise the head and neck too high. In this position too much energy must be dissipated by exerting the downward force of the arms which is necessary to hold the head high. Such a position also causes the lower trunk to compensate by sinking into the water. The stream of water flowing past the body in motion then offers additional resistance as it is broken into turbulence as large volumes of water close in over the back and are sent whirling off in eddies.

Position of the shoulder girdle and upper spine. The position of the shoulder girdle during the sprint crawl is designed to permit the maximum power and efficiency of the arm strokes. The shoulder blades should be held flat.

The shoulders are raised forward in the direction of the movement of the body. In this position the arms are able to execute a stronger pull, and the shoulder blades can move freely during the recovery.

The upper spine is also flexed slightly forward. In this position the sprint crawl swimmer presents the appearance of being somewhat hunchbacked (Fig. 9-1, *B*). This position affords a more powerful arm action due to the more mechanically advantageous position of the arm depressor muscles, mainly the pectoral muscles located in front of the chest and upper arm. It also places the trunk in a more streamlined position. The whole surface of the thorax and abdomen is flattened. As the swimmer propels himself through the water, his body level under the surface is parallel with the surface of the water, and the water can thus pass under this plane with the least amount of resistance due to turbulence.

Resistance is further eliminated by this plane position as the back and hips ride high in the water and a smooth, thin stream flows along the sides and past the hips in an unbroken sheath. The swimmer in this position experiences the sensation of swimming downhill. A common error in the position of the shoulder girdle and upper spine is to exaggerate their forward position. In this overly arched position, mechanical advantage of the arms is decreased, and power is therefore diminished. A high position of the upper spine also tends to result in a marked depression of the lower back and hips (Fig. 9-1, *B*), and large quantities of water are allowed to swirl over them and further energy is lost.

Position of the hips. During the sprint crawl stroke the hips remain level. They serve as a base for the articulations of the legs. The hips are carried slightly lower than the shoulders and move through the water just below the surface (Fig. 9-1, *B*).

The position of the hips varies among individuals, since the contour of the hips differs widely.

The water flows over narrow hips and small buttocks in an unbroken stream which causes very little resistance. Those with smaller, streamlined hips can carry them higher and out of the water, with the legs well down in the water, so that the body is held level and the legs are in the most favorable position for the propelling action of the flutter kick. Swimmers with large hips should submerge them more than those with small hips in order to permit the water to flow smoothly over them. The extra power from the larger muscles helps to compensate for the increased resistance.

Position of the legs. The legs are held in a loosely extended position. The ankles and knees pass close by each other in a supple movement. An efficient leg action appears as though the legs were made of rubber.

During the sprint crawl stroke the legs move well under the surface (Fig. 9-1) in order to gain maximum traction in the water. No propulsive force is gained by any part of the foot when it is out of the water; therefore, the feet should be beneath the surface at all times. If the hips are allowed to sink too low in the water, the feet are likely to be raised too high, and they break through to the surface and lose power.

Another common fault in the leg position is to allow the heels to drift apart in order to accommodate the toeing inward. In this spread position the legs lose some of their driving power, and the outward surfaces of the legs present a resistance to the forward motion of the swimmer.

In most individuals the proper alignment of the body position can be checked by drawing a straight line from the midpoint of the shoulder joint through the midpoint of the hip joint, the line being extended backward past the feet. If the body is in proper alignment, this line will pass exactly through a point which is midway between the ankle joints when the legs are fully spread in the stride position at the end of each beat (Fig. 9-1). In this position the legs are operating directly behind the body, providing the force in the most effective manner.

Leg action. The action of the legs in the sprint crawl stroke has been termed the "flutter kick." Because of its general usage and also because no really descriptive term has yet been assigned to it, the leg action will continue in this treatise to be called the flutter kick.

The legs neither "flutter" nor "kick" but oscillate forcibly and regularly, serving to push the water backward with each upward and downward beat. In order to derive maximum force from the leg action, the swimmer must have trained and strengthened his leg muscles to endure the continuous vigorous motion of the flutter kick. This may be accomplished by daily drills with the aid of the kicking board. While using the kicking board, the swimmer should ascertain that the body position simulates that of the regular sprint crawl position. Many bad swimming habits can result from careless use of the kicking board. The swimmer should strive not only to get his legs in top condition, but also to train his legs to perform in a manner which will allow him to derive the greatest amount of drive from each beat of the legs.

The most efficient sprint crawl leg action is one which resembles the action of a fish's tail. Although the swimmer's legs move in a vertical plane and the fish's tail in a horizontal plane, their propulsive action is derived from the same principle. The swimmer's leg propels him forward with both the upward and the downward swing just as the fish's tail propels him forward with each sideward swing.

The swimmer's leg, however, possesses a structural limitation which is not present in the tail of the fish. His knee joint restricts movement to a backward one only. If the knee joint allowed movement forward as well as backward, the swimmer could use his legs in the same range as that used by a fish during swimming. In order to compensate for this structural limitation, a slight variation from the fishtail action is made as the downward beat is completed. If the reader would sit on the edge of his chair and, leaning back slightly, go through the motions of pedaling a bicycle, he will get a good concept of what the compensated fishtail action ought to be. Note the action of each joint as well as the movements of the limbs. The pedal is pressed with the ball of the foot on the forward and downward stroke. The knee is straightened on the downward stroke, and then the foot is pressed more firmly against the pedal as it is pushed backward and then slightly upward. As the foot presses upward, the knee bends again, and the pushing power is diminished. This bicycle action can be observed in Fig. 9-1, *D* and *F*.

In the water the swimmer's leg action and range of motion are nearly identical to that of the bicycle rider. In riding a bicycle the pressure is always exerted on the balls of the feet, whereas in swimming the crawl stroke the pressure is exerted alternately on the soles of the feet in the upward tread and on the instep in the downward tread. Another example is to lie on a stool face down and pedal an imaginary bicycle.

The movement in the flutter kick leg action originates at the hip joint and is transmitted through the thigh to the knee joint. In whiplike motion the wave passes from the knee to the lower leg and next to the ankle and finally to the foot, which is lashed about like the free end of a rope which is being snapped. The initial movement is in the hips in both the upward and downward beat.

At the beginning of the upward leg movement, the thigh is slightly flexed upon the hip, and the knee and ankle are extended (Fig. 9-1, *D* and *F*). With the extension of the hip, the water is pressed backward by the back of the thigh, and the body is moved forward. This backward flow continues along the back of the leg and is finally whipped backward and upward by the sole of the foot. The flow of water is thus forced backward with ever-increasing speed, and, as it leaves the foot, the snap of the ankle sends the water backward with a tremendous driving force, thus propelling the body forward.

When the leg finishes its upward beat, the hips and knees are slightly flexed, and the ankles are extended (Fig. 9-1, *D* and *F*). The downward beat of the leg starts with the leg in this position. As in the upward leg beat, the action starts from the hips. A small flexion at the hips sends the water washing backward along the front of the thigh. The knee is then extended (Fig. 9-1). The water is thus driven backward along the anterior surface of the leg and down over the ankles as the body is driven forward.

The toes are turned inward in a pigeon-toed fashion during the down stroke (Fig. 9-1) in order to contact more water with the tops of the feet. Toeing in during the down stroke pushes the water backward at a more effective angle since the foot can be extended farther in this position.

In order to execute an efficient leg drive in this fashion, the leg muscles must be flexible, powerful, and able to relax to such an extent that they exert only a minimum of tension upon the joints which are being moved by their reciprocal muscles. Swimmers' muscles, when relaxed, give the appearance of being loose and elastic.

The advantage of possessing large feet and flexible ankles is apparent when the mechanics of the flutter kick are considered. The effectiveness of the kick will be limited by the degree of extension of the ankles. The lashing action of the foot provides the major propulsive action of the legs. If the ankle is stiff and movement limited, this lashing action is lost, and the legs do not provide their share of the propelling force.

The feet act as paddles, and swimmers with the largest feet naturally have the most effective paddles. The ideal foot for swimming is long, thin, broad at the instep, and flexible.

The ankles, however, can be made more flexible by stretching and limbering exercises such as those described in Chapter 16.

The upward leg action is as effective in propelling the crawl swimmer forward as the downward action. The slight knee flexion and powerful ankle extension as the leg completes its upward sweep contribute to the fishtail action which is capable of sending large amounts of water backward from the sole of the foot. This fishtail action is inhibited on the downward movement because of the anatomic limitation of the knee joint to flex both ways. The small amount of propelling surface presented by the instep as compared with that of the sole of the foot is also a restricting factor in the downward beat.

The width of the flutter kick stride should be from 18 to 26 inches, depending on the length of the swimmer's legs and the speed with which he moves. Due to the refraction of the water, the stride appears much narrower and appears to be from 12 to 18 inches wide. Since observation windows have been erected,* the swimming strokes can be analyzed with less refractive error.

Turbulent surface water that is swirling and eddying is an inhibiting factor to the driving force of the legs. The legs act best well below the surface of the water because surface water agitated by other swimmers or by waves striking against the side of the pool presents less traction than deeper water that is undisturbed.

Common faults in the sprint crawl leg action are as follows: (a) kicking with the legs too near the surface, (b) spreading the legs laterally so that the heels are beyond hip width, (c) kicking away from the vertical plane, especially during inhalation, (d) holding the ankles in a rigid extended position, (e) holding the feet toed inward during the upward stroke, and (f) holding the knees in a rigidly extended position.

Arm action. The arms provide about 85% of the total power of the sprint crawl stroke. Slight adjustments in body position and leg action made to accommodate the arm action are fully justified. In the sprint crawl stroke, the arms alternately drive forward into the water with reasonable force to pull the body forward over the surface. The arm which completes the stroke is then quickly recovered out of the water and placed in position in the water for the next arm stroke. For the purpose of analysis the sprint crawl arm stroke may be classified into the seven following components: (a) entry, (b) support, (c) catch, (d) pull, (e) push, (f) release, and (g) recovery.

Entry. The arm must enter the water in such a manner that it is

---

*Armbruster, David A.: Underwater observation windows, Intercollegiate and Interscholastic Swimming Guide, Spalding's Athletic Library, No. 491, pp. 71-73, 1940.

immediately placed in the most favorable position for a forceful stroke by taking hold of as much water as possible. In the sprint crawl stroke the hand begins its propulsive action as soon as it penetrates through the water's surface and the pressure is felt in the hand and fingers.

For the purpose of this discussion the arm entry will be defined as that period in the crawl arm cycle which starts when the hand passes in front of the shoulder following the recovery and ends when the arm is finally in the supporting position.

As the hand reaches forward and the arm is driven for the entry, the shoulder is held high and not allowed to reach forward to its fullest extent. Although the forward displacement of the swimmer's shoulder would increase the extent of the reach several inches, this displacement places the shoulder at a distinct mechanical disadvantage for the propulsive arm action. A shoulder displacement also tends to result in a sideward movement of the body which impedes forward progression.

With the shoulder in a fixed position, more of the body weight is held over the arm and represents potential energy for the arm drive. The shoulder and arm muscles are also in a better position to draw the arm downward and backward through the water.

The arm is dropped into the water directly in front of the shoulder. The shoulder remains high (Fig. 9-1, *E* and *F*), and, as the arm contacts the water, the hand and forearm are pressed downward. The tip of the elbow is pointing sideward and is held in this position to prevent hyperextension of the elbow and also to prevent the shoulder from dropping as the arm is pressed downward.

As the arm is pressed below the surface of the water, the swimmer's shoulder moves forward, not downward, so that as pressure is applied to the hand and forearm, the body weight moves over the arm as it goes into the catch. This action gives the sprinter the sensation of swimming downhill. Actually, however, the shoulder and the rest of the body are moving straight forward on a level with the surface of the water.

When the sprint crawl swimmer is at full speed, the bow wave in front of his head and shoulders causes the surface water in front of him to swell up into an inclined plane (Fig. 9-1, *E*). It is along the surface of this plane that the arm enters the water. The angle at which the arm drops into the water depends, therefore, upon the height of this wave, which, in turn, depends upon the velocity, size, and body position of the swimmer.

Common faults in the sprint crawl arm entry are (1) smashing the arm into the water with too much force, which splits the water and allows a great deal of slip, (2) pressing the hand into the water with the is made in front of the hip, much propulsive power is lost, and the recovery is opposed by a great deal of water resistance. Likewise, if the hand is carried upward past the hip joint too far before the release is made, the body will be pulled under the water, and the arm will be inhibited in its recovery.

Comment: Actually, the shoulder action and the shoulder arm muscles are the real motivating force of the crawl arm stroke. Too much stress cannot be placed upon the shoulder movement to compliment the arm action throughout the entire arm stroke cycle.

Recovery. The action of the arm from the release to the entry is termed the recovery. During the recovery the arm is carried forward out of the water from a position with the hand near the hip to a position with the hand ahead of its shoulder in preparation for the entry. The arm recovery is best accomplished when the shoulder has reached a position in its lift so that the water level is just below the armpit.

The action of the arms from release to recovery is continuous throughout. At no point are the arms arrested in their movement. A common fault is to pause the arms at the end of the release and at the beginning of the press. This practice causes momentum to be lost with a resulting loss of propulsion.

During the sprint crawl stroke, the recovery must be well controlled and executed in such a manner that the head and body position are not altered and that no lateral motion is affected. The driving action of the legs and opposite arm, likewise, must not be inhibited by the recovery.

At the completion of the propulsive action of the arm stroke, the water is released. The entire arm and shoulder are immediately lifted from the water by raising the elbow until the hand clears the surface. The forearm and hand are then elevated in an outward and forward circular motion with the shoulder acting as the axis. The forearm executes a quarter turn, and the hand is carried forward with the palm downward and the thumb forward (Fig. 9-1, *A*). As the elbow is carried forward, its elevation is maintained above the level of the hand for the remainder of the recovery and the entry. The forearm is nearly horizontal as the arm is carried forward past the shoulder. The hand remains in a line with the forearm. As the hand passes the head, the arm reaches forward. The upper arm is brought forward near, but not touching, the side of of the head. As the arm thus reaches for the entry, the shoulder girdle is maintained in an elevated position, the tip of the elbow above the shoulder level and pointing laterally, while the forearm points downward from the elbow as if to spear into the water at the point of the hand entry. The fingers are pointing forward into the water with the palm parallel with the water's surface and the wrist is slightly flexed downward (Fig. 9-1). The arm is now in a position preparatory to the entry.

There are many other styles of arm recovery during the sprint crawl stroke. Other styles include those in which the elbow is carried either high or low and the arm is recovered with the elbow either high above the shoulder or close to the surface of the water. These low, high, and medium recoveries with both the flexed and extended elbow have been used by different record-breaking sprint swimmers.

Timing of the arms. In the sprint crawl stroke, the opposition rhythm is recommended. That is, in the cycle of the entire stroke, the recovery of one arm is approximately opposite the propelling arm. This method almost entirely eliminates the slide between the arm entry and the catch (Fig. 9-1). This technique gives the sprinter the desired faster turnover of the entire armstroke cycle without actually going into a "dig-in-type" of stroke. The student should study the illustrated figures in Fig. 9-1 very carefully and note the position of one arm in relation to the other. This style of swimming the crawl, in order to obtain greater speed for both sprinting and distance competition, is being employed by most of the modern, top-flight swimmers.

Timing of the arms and legs. In the sprint crawl stroke the cadence of the legs is faster than that of the arms. This results in a motion which at first appears to be an unnatural one since it is unlike that used by man while walking and running. In walking and running the arms serve to counterbalance the driving action of the legs by swinging in an opposite direction to the legs. The legs and arms thus move in a 1-to-1 ratio during walking and running. In the crawl, however, the leg-to-arm ratio is 3 to 1. The legs perform three beats to each arm movement, or six beats to each complete cycle of both arms.

An analysis of the mechanics of the six-beat crawl stroke reveals that it is as truly balanced as is the counterbalancing action of the arms and legs in walking. That is, both arms and legs should be evenly balanced, one with the other. Not all top-flight swimmers have an evenly balanced leg action in relation to the arms. If they are unbalanced, compensation is made with the arms in order to obtain rhythm, counterbalanced, and a comfortable feel of coordination during competitive action. In order to facilitate a description of the timing of the arms with the legs in the sprint crawl, the stroke will be divided into six parts, and each part is discussed as a separate unit. The part of the stroke that is performed with the most regular rhythm is the leg action.

The legs move upward and downward in uniform periods, and each upward and downward beat of the legs marks a certain regular phase of the stroke. For the purpose of uniformity, the timing of the arms in relation to the legs is described in Fig. 9-1 in six parts. Each part commences with the instant the legs are completely spread in the stride position at the end of each beat.

It is impossible for the coach to detect errors in timing of the arms and legs of a swimmer sprinting at full speed by simply trotting by his side and watching his coordination. By the use of slow-motion and still movies, however, an analysis is made possible. Many of the newer pools are equipped with underwater observation windows through which such pictures may be taken.* Many coaches have made use of a diving bell for this purpose. If such equipment is not available, photographic records must be made above the water's surface. Above-water pictures are valuable even though the splashing and turbulence disrupt the actual movements and analysis is made difficult.

Once the record is obtained, a comparison may be made with the illustrations presented in Fig. 9-1, and the action of the swimmer compared with that described in the text. The coach and swimmer can study the timing and other mechanics of the stroke and determine objectively where the fault lies.

If the underwater movie method is not used, the coach must resort to an analysis of the arm action alone and then the leg action alone while the swimmer swims and attempts to detect an unbalance due to faulty mechanics. For example, the coach may watch the arm action during a certain phase of the crawl stroke when the right arm enters and the left arm should be completing its drive and vice versa, as the left arm enters, the right arm should be completing its drive (Fig. 9-1, *A*, *B*, *E*, and *F*).

Technique of breathing. Expiration through the nose and mouth under the surface and inspiration through the mouth above the surface is the traditional form of breathing in swimming the sprint crawl stroke. Although the nose is a natural inlet as well as outlet in the breathing mechanism, there are several objections to expiring under water through the nose alone. The nasal openings are very small to exhale all the air against water pressure. To exhale against the water, a forceful expiratory pressure would be required. This forceful expiration through the nose against the water resistance causes mucous discharge to pass toward the nasal and frontal sinuses and the middle ear and increases the liability to autoinfection.† When air is forced out through the mouth, the pressure against the ears and sinus regions is practically eliminated.

Experiments indicated that sprinters usually released air slowly through the lips or nose until just an instant before the head is turned

*Armbruster, David A.: Underwater observation windows, Intercollegiate and Interscholastic Swimming Guide, Spalding's Athletic Library, No. 491, pp. 71-73, 1940.
†Taylor, H. Marshall: Otitis and sinusitis in the swimmer, Journal of the American Medical Association 113:891 (Sept.), 1939.

out for the next inhalation and a forceful expulsion is made through the mouth. This is often called the "explosive" method.*

During inhalation, air should be taken rapidly through the mouth. As a general rule, inexperienced swimmers swimming the crawl stroke will fix the abdominal and back muscles, thus interfering with the function of the diaphragm. This rigidity occurs most frequently among swimmers who depress the hips too far, causing the fixation in the abdominal region and in the lumbar region. The tension in these groups of muscles is relieved by lifting the hips, which in turn permits deeper breathing.

Breathing may disturb the leg kick and arm rhythm. One can lie face down in the water, releasing the air with the head under the surface, and swim with the legs alone for some distance even after the air is expelled with no interference with the force of the leg kick. The same is found to be true when both arms and legs are used in the same manner. Thus the interference occurs not from diminishing the fixing action of the abdominal muscles, but from either faulty head turning mechanics or from depressing the hips.

One seldom has difficulty in inspiring if the mouth can be turned easily above the surface. In fact, usually too much air is breathed in too early in a race and not enough is expired. If the swimmer breathes regularly early in a race, he should not breathe so deeply but should increase the depth in proportion to the air requirement. The expiration should be adequate, or carbon dioxide will soon build up within the tissues and fatigue will set in early. Expert swimmers who have skillfully mastered breathing and relaxation of the abdominal muscles seldom have difficulty in breathing when under the exertion of swimming at great speed.

The question as to the number of breaths to take in a sprint race has always been a point of debate. It is a foregone conclusion that, if the head is turned less often, the fast rhythm of the arms and legs is least disturbed and, therefore, greater speed is developed.

The number of breaths to take during the sprint races depends upon individual differences such as breath-holding ability, relaxation, and the ability to accumulate an oxygen debt. One cannot lay down a "hard and fast" rule as to the number of breaths to take. However, in a 40- or 50-yard sprint, almost any good swimmer can cover the first length with one or two breaths and take only two or three breaths coming back. Some swimmers need to breathe with every other stroke after the first length. Others can breathe with every third arm stroke, which is a very good method if the swimmer can breathe properly on both

*Aycock, T., Graaff, L., and Tuttle, W. W.: An analysis of the respiratory habits of trained swimmers, Research Quarterly 3:199 (May), 1932.

sides. This method also tends to impart greater relaxation to the shoulder stabilizer muscles and maintain greater balance. A well-trained sprinter can swim the entire 50 yards without taking a second breath. The breath-holding interval should not be long enough to cause the swimmer to fight for air. This fault is recognized by a "wild eyed," taut, drawn expression upon the swimmer's face as his mouth is lifted high out of the water to get air.

Lifting the head out of the water for air at the turn slows the sprinter. At the start, and in coming out of the water after the glide, the head should not be turned for air on the first arm pull since the head is then too far below the surface. The swimmer should first get under way with at least four to six arm pulls. The head must rotate on its central axis and should not be raised backward or lifted sideward during breath-taking. The most important duty of the head other than the part which it plays in breathing is to keep the body on an even keel and maintain symmetrically balanced arm and leg strokes. The head must be turned for air and recovered as quickly as possible. For this reason the face is held below the surface most of the time to maintain equilibrium. At the proper moment in the stroke, the head is turned so that the least amount of interruption to the stroke balance will occur and the least amount of time will be consumed.

Between inhalations the face should be directly forward (Fig. 9-1, *B*). This plane should not be disturbed during the stroke other than during inhalation regardless of what the arms or shoulders are doing. The neck must be relaxed in order to isolate the movement of the head from that of the shoulder girdle. Many swimmers have the sensation of having the head aligned with the spine, when in reality it is turned toward the breathing side. This often causes swimmers to bear toward that direction across the racing lanes. Then, too, some swimmers will permit the chin to oscillate back and forth with the movements of the shoulder girdle while the arms are stroking and recovering. Relaxing the neck and holding the chin and nose on dead center will remedy this fault. Another fault commonly committed by the swimmer is to fail to recover the chin and nose fully to the center. Such a fault will inhibit the action of the opposite arm, especially in the push phase. The eyes should be on a horizontal plane so that the eyes can look ahead in almost normal forward vision. The tips of the shoulders should also be raised, and the upper spine should bend to conform to the planing position in sprinting. In the distance races, the bend in the neck and the spine is not quite as pronounced as in sprint racing. In the distance stroke, the eyes are just able to see straight forward by looking out from under the eyebrows.

As the body gains in speed and considerable friction occurs under the face, neck, and body, the swimmer should experience and actually feel that he is pressing down upon the water as he pulls and pushes his body forward over the water. The friction under the body created by the speed attained should not actually be permitted to force the body too high, but high enough to keep the water off the back as far down as the hips. When this position is assumed, breathing is then a simple matter. With the body in this position, a bow wave is created that curves around the head and sweeps in a downward curve on either side of the head at an outward angle. This in turn creates a deep trough inside the bow wave next to the body. The aim in turning the head to get air is to get the mouth into this trough and not into the bow wave. To accomplish this purpose, the head must turn on its longitudinal axis. The chin is turned to the side and pressed in close to the throat as the mouth is opened. The eyes play an important part in turning the head correctly to this point. They must sweep from the forward line of vision and focus on the surface of the water just in front of the chin and mouth. Many swimmers make the mistake of looking forward while turning the head. This causes the chin to move out into the bow wave, and for this reason it must be lifted farther to the side in order to get air. As the body rolls to the opposite side and the supporting arm slides from its balanced alignment, the pull and push phases of the arm stroke are shortened. While the head is being turned to the side for air, the water streams down under the chest. While turning the head, the face should be pressed against the resistance of the water to keep the water away from the front of the face (Fig. 9-1, *C*). If the head is permitted to lift away from the water, the planing effect of the face is lost, and the bow wave is broken, which causes difficulty in clearing the mouth to take air quickly.

The mouth should not open until the lips are clear of the water. Air is then taken in in the form of a gasp. In distance swimming, inhalation can be slightly slower because deeper breathing is necessary.

The mouth is closed immediately after air has been taken, and the head is quickly recovered in order to put the body again on an even balanced keel. During the entire movement of the head, the water level should always be maintained constant. There should neither be a sideward nor an upward or downward movement. To prevent a tendency toward lateral movement while turning the mouth out for air, press the head slightly toward the supporting arm, since the head is likely to be moved toward the side to which it is turning to get air. When the head recovers to the center, air is expelled immediately if a breath is to be taken at the next stroke. If more strokes are to be taken before air is again inhaled, the breath should be held and air bubbles should be permitted to escape until just an instant before the head is again turned out for air. Then the air which remains should be forced out in one larger bubble. This release of air should be skillfully timed so that the exhalation is finished as the lips and nose are breaking out to the surface. With the air being released in one large air bubble instead of emitting a series of small bubbles, the water is cleared away from the mouth by the air bubble as the lips break through to get a fresh supply of air.

All crawl stroke swimmers should learn to breathe on both sides. The reasons for this are obvious. A sprinter is not always able to come out even at every turn so that he can turn but one way. Thus, after he completes his turn he can take a breath as soon as the body is aligned at the surface. The habit of breathing on both sides tends to keep a more symmetrically balanced stroke. Finally, turning the head at certain intervals, especially during the fatiguing part of the race, releases shoulder girdle and neck tensions. After turning the head several times to the right and left, even though air is not always inspired, the competitor feels immediate relief if fatigue and muscular tension have already set in.

Relation between turning the head for breathing and the arm and leg cycle. The beginner usually breathes by turning the mouth to the side for air in the same rhythm with the breathing-side arm. This seems to be a natural method. The head thus turns for air just as slow or as fast as the cadence of the stroke. This method is inefficient, however, as it causes the head to remain at the side too long for the purpose of getting air. Whenever this unskilled method is used, one can almost always find that the body lies off keel, principally on the side opposite the breathing side. The body should be flat on the chest with the face forward on front dead center for a period at least twice as long as the time required to take a breath and return to the swimming position. It is the function of the head to maintain the body on an even keel, and this function is impaired if the head spends a large part of its time in getting air. This not only throws the body off balance, but the whole stroke equilibrium is disturbed and speed is reduced.

While turning the head to the side of inhalation, the body must remain stable so that neither the arms nor the legs are caused to deviate from their normal range of movement. In order to accomplish this maneuver, certain adjustments must be made. The neck must be relaxed in order that its movement can be isolated from that of the shoulder girdle so that the shoulder girdle will not be tilted to the opposite side to permit mouth inspiration. The opposite arm must have just entered the water for countersupport before the head is turned to the side for air. The head should start to recover as the breathing-side arm is lifted out of the water and should be fully recovered when the breathing-side arm is directly at the side of the head in the recovery. These accommodations permit the head to remain forward and on center four full beats of the legs. This permits the body to ride steadily and gives the arms and legs freedom to function without interference from the head. When improper breathing causes the body to roll, the arms and legs are less propulsive. Poorly timed head mechanics is a detrimental factor to speed. The well-trained swimmer should make every effort to turn his head for air and return it independently of the cadence of his arms. The head must move to and from air at a greater speed than the cadence in which the arms are moving. One can easily test the detriment of breathing by swimming the length of the pool at top speed without turning the head for air over the entire length and then swimming it at top speed, breathing with every stroke cycle. The former method will be very much faster. Note, too, how symmetrically balanced and smooth the arms and legs function when the head is maintained on dead center.

The breathing method referred to in the preceding may be designated as the two-count system. Note how skillfully the head is timed into the whole movement of the arms and legs. If the swimmer breathes on the right side, the head is turned at beat three (Fig. 9-1, *C*). The right arm is completing its push. The left leg is driving down for counterbalance in turning the mouth to the surface as well as for lifting the arm out of the water. The left arm is gliding forward and downward for the catch. At beat four, the right leg beats down while the head quickly recovers all the way to dead center (Fig. 9-1, *D* and *E*). At the beginning of beat four the recovery arm is just ready to enter the water. The inhalation has been accomplished in two counts or two beats of the legs. Therefore, the body remains balanced four out of six leg beats. The body on its keel and both legs and arms performing undisturbed for four beats in each stroke revolution is a tremendous factor toward greater speed and less energy expenditure.

If the swimmer breathes on the left side, the head is turned to get air during count six (Fig. 9-1, *F*). Another way to time this method other than by the count is to turn the head to the side the instant the opposite arm is beneath the surface. Care must be taken not to turn the head prematurely, that is, before the hand enters the water. The head is timed with the opposite breathing-side arm as it is entering the water. In either method the head should be fully recovered when the breathing arm has arrived in its recovery to a point directly at the side of the head. The sliding arm begins its pull as the head is completing its recovery.

A common error in this method is to drop the shoulder downward after the head has been recovered and after the breathing-side arm has entered the water. A shoulder drop in the crawl stroke violates sound mechanics in speed swimming. The shoulders must remain over the arms during the entry and propulsive phases. A shoulder drop is often caused by failure to maintain the head on dead center during exhalation. In turning the mouth for air, the head should not lift away from the pressure of the water, but both chest and the underside of the face should lie against the pillow of water while air is inhaled.

Common errors in breathing technique. Other common errors resulting from faulty head-turning mechanics are the following:

1. Lifting the chin forward and sideward to get air results in dropping the opposite elbow and shoulder, which causes the opposite arm to slide laterally. It also disturbs the leg balance, and propulsive force is dissipated.
2. Turning head in the same rhythm and cadence as the arms results in rolling the body.
3. Not fully recovering the head results in loss of body balance. The opposite shoulder drops, and the opposite arm pulls too wide, thus failing to complete the push drive phase. The pull is premature. The recovery-side arm has a tendency to freeze or lock at the entry.
4. Opening the mouth with the lips stretched back too far results in strangulation due to water entering the mouth. Facial muscles become tense. The lips should aid in guiding the water away from the mouth.
5. Moving the head out of its longitudinal axis results in a loss of symmetric arm and leg action and disturbs body balance, and thus propulsive force is lost.
6. Breathing on one side only results in the neck and shoulder muscles becoming cramped, loss of balance, and the inability of the swimmer to see the field on both sides during a race.

Turn. In order to execute a fast turn and one which will not become a mental hazard, the swimmer must be able to turn to either side equally well. When he is within 10 feet of the side of the pool, he must be able to judge accurately, with his eyes either above or below the surface, the number of arm strokes necessary to reach the turn. His decision as to which direction he will turn is made before he reaches the end. Some swimmers often become so engrossed in the race itself that they forget the wall until one arm hits it. Most modern pools have a warning mark 4 feet from the end, on the bottom. Often this is not seen because the swimmer's eyes are in turbulent surface water. Sometimes a pool wall has a peculiar color of tile on the end wall which is very difficult for the swimmer to distinguish from the water. This makes it hard for him to judge the approximate distance. Sometimes room lighting is very poorly arranged, resulting in shadows being cast on the inside wall so that a white wall looks dark. All lights over a swimming pool should be so arranged that the light directs its rays against all inside pool walls. In order to accomplish this the lights should be set inside the pool wall enclosure at least 5 feet. This eliminates all shadows, and, if the water is clear, it gives adequate illumination. Underwater lights should be shut off during competition since they tend to blind and confuse the swimmer at the turns.

Mechanics of the sprint turns. There are three types of turns which may be used by the sprint swimmer: (1) the lateral or closed turn, (2) the head-out or open turn, and (3) the somersault turn. In crawl events, a competitor is no longer required to touch the end of the pool wall with the hand in executing a turn. However, in the back, breast, and butterfly strokes, the hand or hands touch is definitely required with exacting and specific rules governing each style.

In the crawl events the turn, which is usually well timed by the competitor, can now be executed well out from the turning wall, as long as some part of the body does touch the wall, so that the feet touch in an ideal position for a fast drive-away.

The beginner, in learning to turn, is usually taught by the coach to use the hand touch at the turns. The next learning procedure is to have the swimmer do the closed as well as the flip turn in open water, that is, without the aid of the wall. The authors have used the hand touch in the illustrations for teaching purposes.

Lateral turn. This turn is sometimes called the closed turn because the head is held under. As the hand touches the wall, about 6 to 10 inches under the surface of the water, the elbow should bend slightly so that momentum can be utilized (Fig. 9-2, *B*). Simultaneously with the hand

Fig. 9-2. A-E, A series of ideal form showing the sprint crawl stroke lateral turn. **A,** The approach to the wall. **B,** The start of the turn.

touch, the legs are tucked tightly, with the knees together. Then the turn is made with the body remaining flat on the chest. The feet are tucked under to form a pivot upon which the body spins. After the tuck has been completed, the head and shoulders whip away from the arm which is against the wall, and the hips move around toward the wall (Fig. 9-2, *C*). The free arm assists the turn by whipping the hand in a sculling motion, starting from the side of the hips and sweeping outward and across to the chest in a short, quick, vigorous movement. The touching hand is quickly removed from the wall and tucked close to the body as it is brought to a position alongside the other hand under the head (Fig. 9-2, *D*). The feet are driven against the wall, the arms are extended with a thrust, and the head is lowered between the arms in the glide position.

In the glide, the body must be held straight, not arched (Fig. 9-2, *E*). It should glide slightly upward. The body should be stretched from toes to fingertips, with the legs held close together. The breakthrough to the surface should be executed as described in the start. The swimmer should extend his arms in a line with his spine and press down with his hands as he glides out. The legs should be held straight. Starting the kick prematurely is a waste of effort and slows down the swimmer if the push-off has been powerful. At the end of the glide, the swimmer should come out from under the surface, swimming hard. He should not turn his head for air on the first arm stroke. If the swimmer has a reflex of turning the head, even though he does not take air, he should

Fig. 9-2, cont'd. C, The position of the body at the quarter turn. **D,** Body set for push-out. **E,** The body in the glide position after leaving the wall.

be trained to pull through his opposite breathing-side arm first. His first movements should be concentrated in gathering speed or at least maintaining the speed gained from the turn. Many times a good swimmer can advance 1, 2, or even 3 feet beyond his opponent at each turn.

The body should be tucked before turning. When the body is elongated, it cannot be easily turned, but, when the radius is shortened, angular motion is accelerated and the body turns faster. The tuck phase is fast. The spine is flexed, placing the body in a ball-like position. Dropping the shoulders or ducking the head too low will cause the hips to lift; then the feet are placed too high on the wall, and the body is pushed toward the bottom. The head actually changes its position three times during the turn. When the hand reaches for the wall, it should dive under about 10 inches short of the wall; the head and shoulders should go down with the hand. Then as the body starts the turn, the head and shoulders should be lifted slightly. When it is nearly around to the front, it should duck down again as both hands come in to join each other under or just in front of the head. These movements keep the hips under control and do not allow them to lift too high.

Sprinters should not use the scum rail for the turn since this practice usually yields a slow turn. Also, not all pools have scum gutters at the ends.

The feet are set against the wall, with the ankles fully flexed. The balls of the feet rest against the wall with heels nearly touching. The balls of the feet are set on a level about midpoint between the knee and hip joints. This places the heels slightly below the spine line. The thighs are approximately parallel with the vertical wall against which the feet are pushing. The legs derive the greatest amount of power from a vigorous straightening of the hips and knees. The ankles are the last to straighten, just as in the start. However, it is the quick extension of the ankles toward the end of the turn that adds to the power and speed already gained by the extension of the knees and hips.

The elbow of the turning arm should be slightly bent. If the elbow is bent too much, the hips are brought too close to the wall, and the feet are placed too low. The body is pushed away from the wall by the legs, not with the turning hand.

When the turn is completed, the arms should be thrust out simultaneously with the leg drive. If the arms are set straight before the push-off, the body will go in the direction in which the arms are set. If the arms are pushed out simultaneously with the leg drive, the hands can guide the direction of the push-off more effectively.

Head-out turn. This turn is sometimes called the open turn because the head is lifted out for air. This type of turn is very fast and is used for middle distances and in the last turn of a sprint if air is needed to finish the race. This turn is executed exactly as the preceding sprint turn, except that, as the head turns away from the arm on the wall, the face is turned on its side facing the hand. It is turned as one would turn the face to the side to get air in the crawl stroke. As in the crawl stroke, the swimmer should avoid either turning the head too high or lifting it forward and upward. The head is held in line with the spine, and the entire body is slightly lifted, just enough for the mouth to reach the surface with the side of the face flat on the surface. The air should be taken as the turn is executed. When the body has completed the turn, the face is still on its side. The body is submerged with a vigorous downward plunge. As the arm is drawn away from the wall, it is tucked in close to the body and thrust forward beneath the water's surface. If the head and arms alone are thrust downward, the hips will rise above the surface, the feet will be placed against the wall too near the surface, and the swimmer will push off toward the bottom.

Many untrained swimmers use this method for the last turns of the 100-yard sprint. However, all turns in the sprint events should be underwater turns if breathing has been properly distributed over the distance.

*Somersault turn.** The somersault turn for the sprint crawl has been adapted from a similar turn used in the back stroke.

This turn is faster than the traditional turn by 0.4 to 0.6 of a second. One fact that makes this turn so fast is that the momentum is not lost. The somersault turn is performed by lowering the head and diving at the wall with the turning arm directly in front of the head. As the head is being tucked down, it is directed toward the armpit of the turning side of the body. This gives the somersault a diagonal plane rather than a vertical somersault. As the trunk reaches the point in its turn of standing on its head, the heels are then vigorously tucked tightly toward the hips, with the knees held together during the tuck. This hard tucking motion, executed at the right moment, will somersault the body and throw the legs against the wall under the surface and behind the hips with the additional aid of the free hand. (See Fig. 9-3.) When the somersault has progressed slightly farther than just past standing on the head, a quarter twist is made, but the somersault movement is continued until the trunk is in push-off position. As the push-off is made, the body completes the other quarter twist and leaves the wall, again righted and facing downward.

The success of the somersault turn depends upon tucking the heels up to the hips tightly as the swimmer goes over and then completing the twist when he is past standing on his head.

*This turn was devised by Armbruster in 1936 and used in competition for the first time in the 1938 N.C.A.A. championships at Rutgers University.

A variation of the somersault turn is one in which the legs are tucked and thrown over to the wall, but the body turns in more of a lateral motion. This lateral somersault turn may be used successfully by those swimmers whose equilibrium is impaired by a full somersault. This turn is performed in the following manner: the drive into the wall and the tuck and throw of the legs are the same as in the somersault. When the body is in the tuck position, however, the head and shoulders are turned laterally in the direction of the turn. The shoulders and the head lift in order to raise the forepart of the body to the surface. The turn is made with the chest downward at all times.

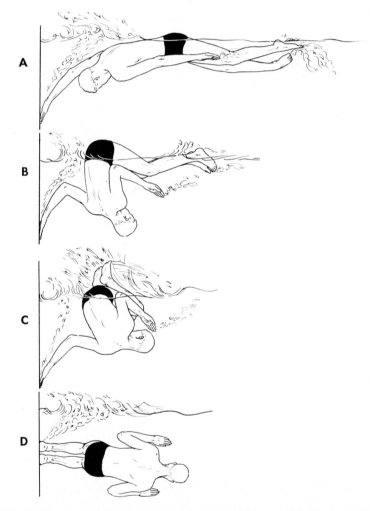

Fig. 9-3. A-G, The somersault turn. **A,** The head is turned, and the chin is tucked into the throat. **B,** The body is just beyond the point of standing on its head as the leg tuck is started. **C,** Note that the free hand assists in completing the turn. **D,** The body is set for the push-out, being partially on the face and side.

The no-hand-touch somersault turn. Since the competitive rules no longer require the hand to touch the wall in the crawl stroke turn, variations of the somersault turn are now being used to advantage. The no-touch turn is basically the same as described in Fig. 9-3 except for the action of the right arm. The right arm enters the water and compliments the diving action of the upper body. The amount of pull will be determined by the distance the swimmer is from the end of the pool. During the pull, the hand presses downward and across the body coming to rest below the left hip, in position to be extended when the feet push from the wall.

Finish. The finish consists of the approach to the finish wall and finish hand touch.

Approach to the finish wall. In the sprint events, especially in the 100-yard crawl stroke, in which the swimmer must rely upon endurance to finish with a burst of speed, too often the finish is made in poor form and the race is lost. A great many swimmers just lower the head and "barrel" in for the finish. This is a grave mistake. Even though the swimmer experiences a sensation of driving harder, in reality his speed is diminished. The reason his stroke feels more powerful is that his arms are going faster. The lowering of the head lets the water support the body, whereas, when swimming with the head and shoulder girdle elevated, the body is to some extent supported by the arms and legs.

Fig. 9-3, cont'd. E, The push-out. **F,** The body is turned face down with the aid of the feet as they leave the wall. **G,** The first arm stroke which propels the swimmer to the surface.

With the body held in sprinting position, the arms and legs are given additional purchase on the water at a more advantageous angle, and the arm speed provides the greatest traction.

In the approach to the finish some swimmers are coached to watch the field to see if they are gaining or losing. If the field is ahead, an occasional glance should suffice, but the swimmer should not look at the field every stroke, especially if he is tired or nearly "spent," because by looking forward he lifts the chin out and turns the head poorly and destroys stroke balance. Good sprinting form must be maintained at any cost in the approach to the finish.

Finish hand touch. In the touch at the finish, a swimmer should never reach out and slide in to the touch, but he should come in swimming hard and drive the hand in to the wall above the finish and stop short of it only an inch or two, with no more slide left. When one reaches, he stops swimming, and usually his head lifts up out of the water and the feet sink before the hand has touched. This situation is tragic for the swimmer in a close finish. He should swim until one hand hits and then stop swimming. If the hand touches under water, it is because he was sliding in too far. However, if one does slide in and touches underneath the surface, he then should not drive the other arm in just to make sure the judges will get his finish. If the hand touches in such a situation, the official is bound to judge him by the arm that comes in last, even though he did touch under water with the first. The judge is likely to be influenced by the action of the swimmer himself, by the fact that the swimmer knows whether or not he touched with the first hand. If the other hand is thrust forward, the judge will assume that he did not touch with the first. Even though a judge stands right over a lane and looks down, it is sometimes difficult to see if the touch has actually been made. If the judge is standing at the side, the angle of refraction of the arm under the water makes it difficult for him to judge as to where the touch is actually made. It is practically a guess. Should there be a question as to whether the underwater touch beat the opponent's touch above the surface in a close race, the touch above the surface is usually awarded the race.

RACING FUNDAMENTALS

The sprint race is one in which the maximum speed is maintained throughout the entire race. For practically everyone who swims in competition, a distance of 25 yards can be considered a sprint event. The swimmer simply plunges into the water and swims at his top speed over the whole distance.

As the racing distance is extended to 40, 50, or 60 yards, younger and inexperienced boys and girls will have to reduce their speed in order to finish the race. They cannot, therefore, consider these distances as being sprints.

At 100 yards, only seasoned, top-ranking competitors can cover the distance at top speed without regard for conservation of energy. A survey of split times of champions for the 100-yard crawl stroke shows that the time for each consecutive lap becomes greater from the start to the finish. This means that the swimmers had not made any attempt to reduce their speed at any point during the race but rather attempted to swim at top speed throughout. The cumulative factor of fatigue caused their speed to be reduced as the race progressed.

Swimming as fast as one can go does not mean making the arms and legs move as fast as possible. There is an optimum rate of movement which produces the greatest swimming speed for the individual. Fast, flailing movements of the arms only cut the water open and very little hold on the water is gained.

As soon as the sprint swimmer enters the water, he should attain the rate of movement which will produce the maximum speed and attempt to maintain this speed throughout the race. A common tendency among inexperienced swimmers is to break this optimum rhythm when they notice that they are being passed by a competitor or that they are behind the field. To break rhythm invariably results in an easily recognizable decrease in speed and, consequently, the loss of the race.

Thus, the answer to the swimmer's question, "How shall I swim this sprint race?" might well be, "Get off your mark as fast as you can, with a powerful dive. Come out of your glide swimming, not fighting the water, and build up into the rhythm of your greatest swimming speed. Hold your rhythm at this speed throughout the race to the best of your ability."

In order that a swimmer may compare his split times with those of champions, Table 9-1 is presented. By referring to this table, the swimmer can notice the part of the race which was swum too slowly. The next step to be considered is, then, the reason for this reduction in speed. The cause commonly is found to be improper breathing techniques, and these should be checked carefully. Improper breathing is usually associated with tying-up, and the swimmer often complains of being tired at this point.

The sprinter should not survey the field of competitors during a race. By lifting his eyes and head forward and sideward to look for his competitors, he drops his opposite shoulder and throws his body off balance, the rhythm of his arm and leg strokes is interrupted, and speed is lost.

Table 9-1. * Ideal split times for various racing times in the 100-yard crawl stroke (25-yard course)

ELAPSED DISTANCE (YD.)	ELAPSED TIME (SEC.)	SPLIT TIME (SEC.)	ELAPSED DISTANCE (YD.)	ELAPSED TIME (SEC.)	SPLIT TIME (SEC.)
25	9.1	9.1	25	11.0	11.0
50	20.1	11.0	50	24.0	13.0
75	32.1	12.0	75	37.9	13.9
100	44.0	11.9	100	52.0	14.1
25	9.5	9.5	25	11.5	11.5
50	21.2	11.7	50	25.0	13.5
75	33.6	12.4	75	39.4	14.4
100	46.0	12.4	100	54.0	14.6
25	10.0	10.0	25	12.0	12.0
50	22.1	12.1	50	26.2	14.2
75	35.0	12.9	75	41.0	14.8
100	48.0	13.0	100	56.0	15.0
25	10.5	10.5	25	12.6	12.6
50	23.1	12.6	50	27.2	14.6
75	36.5	13.4	75	42.5	15.3
100	50.0	13.5	100	58.0	15.5

*****How to use Table 9-1:** (1) Select your best total time that you now swim for the 100-yard free style race. (2) Record your own split times from this race, and compare them with the split time divisions made by swimming champions. (3) To improve your best time for 100 yards, use the split times shown for the next faster total race time.

Sprint swimmers have a tendency to race the arms at a faster rate of speed than is possible to attain with the legs. This causes a loss of rhythm between the arms and legs and can only result in a loss of speed. If a faster rhythm is desired to close a margin or provide a burst of speed at the finish, the speed of the leg action should be just as great as that of the arm action. The speed ratio between legs and arms is then balanced and will result in greater propulsive speed.

TEACHING AND LEARNING
PROCEDURES OF THE CRAWL STROKE

The instructor explains the entire stroke to the class gathered before him. He then explains and demonstrates each part of the stroke.

Kick. Land explanation and demonstration by the instructor (see the discussion of leg action earlier in this chapter). Land drill for this kick is not recommended because of the limitation of the thigh action on the down movement.

Water drill. The water drill is practiced using the side of the pool for support or, if out-of-doors, arm depth shallow water with the hands supported on bottom. The class faces the wall of the pool, with left hands grasping the hand rail with the elbow bent down against the wall directly beneath the hand, giving support to its shoulder which is maintained at a submerged level. The right hand reaches down against the wall, arm extended and directly under the right shoulder, but far enough down until both shoulders are level and horizontal with the surface of the water. The chin is submerged with the water level just below the lips. The body is extended out to the rear by the aid of the hand supports, until the entire body is just under the surface. With the shoulders and chin at this level and the back relaxed, a deep arched sway back is eliminated. This position of the body affords the proper freedom of action for the legs to perform this kick.

Half of the class will perform and execute the kick, while the other half will observe his designated partner and offer constructive criticism. The partners then change, the student teacher becoming a pupil and the performing pupil now acting as a teacher. The instructor moves among the class correcting outstanding errors.

These kicking drills can be given for a duration of from two to five minutes at a time, or may be repeated with rest intervals. As the class begins to relax into the movements, a full respiration can now be added with each series of six beats of the kick. At first, breathing can be done with the face out of the water; then in and out of the water with each respiration within the six beats. At first, the instructor may count off, in a loud voice, the desired cadence and tempo, then let the class pick it up individually, and each student performs at random. (See discussion of breath control, Chapter 2.)

Kick board drill. The student is instructed to hold the kick board with both hands and the arms fully extended along its sides, just far enough ahead so that the near end of the board is just beyond the face. This position of the board will permit the head to move in and out of the water for breathing practice along with the kicking exercise across the pool. If the class is large, flights can be staggered moving all the way across the pool, with proper rest intervals.

During these exercises the instructor will stress hip lift to a constant maintained point near the surface. This is controlled by emphasizing the down beat of the kick so that the foot action is just under the surface. If the kick is properly performed, a boiling effect of the water rather than a splashing effect results. The instructor will also urge the class to mentally concentrate on using a six-beat rhythm or cadence, which action will later in the learning progression fit itself naturally to the arm stroke coordination.

These drills are continued until all members of the class can make progress across the pool. The instructor devotes most of his attention to the slower students. Any practical floating device may be substituted for the kick board.

Water drill without kick board. The student lies on the surface of the water, face down, the body and arms extended. In this position the class is again staggered in flights and instructed to kick as far as possible without a breath, then stop, catch air, and again push-off from bottom and in this way continue across the pool. This drill may be performed with half the class interchanging with partner as teacher and pupil. At this point the kick board can again be reverted to, and the class is now urged to cover a greater distance with continuous kicking and breathing—even as far as 100 or 200 yards.

Arm stroke and breath control. The class is again staggered in flights, this time walking across the pool, with the body bent forward to the water level and using a windmill action of the arms. This arm action is sometimes referred to as an alternating opposition rhythm. The primary purpose of this phase of learning is to recover the shoulder above the water. Maintaining a good shoulder lift throughout the entire arm recovery is of great importance in the success of learning the crawl stroke. Continue these drill repetitions with the added skill of breathing, the head turning techniques, and timing with the arms.

At this point the class is urged to walk slowly across the pool while concentrating on learning these timing techniques. Continue many repetitions of this drill while the instructor points out glaring errors. (See discussion of technique of breathing earlier in this chapter.) During this drill the student can practice turning the head to either side, or both sides, while these learning habits are being formed. The instructor constantly stresses shoulder lift during the arm recovery, and also that the shoulder lift must be maintained until the hand and arm have entered the water. He should also stress pulling the arm down under the body during the propulsive phase. When these skills have been sufficiently learned, the instructor demonstrates in the water a lower and bent elbow recovery, as well as a bent arm pull under the body (see discussion of arm action earlier in this chapter).

Whole stroke. When the class has sufficiently learned the skills of the head action in breathing, the arm recovery, and pull, the whole stroke is now attempted by coordinating the six-beat kick with the arm and breathing action. Some instructors get best results during this learning phase by using supports as an aid.*

Again the instructor will urge the student to successfully complete as many individual stroke repetitions as possible, with breathing. When he is successful in completing more than four strokes with supports,

*See Brockway, David L.: The effectiveness of flotation aids in the teaching of beginning swimming, Masters thesis, 1961.

the supports can be removed. The student is urged to strive for an ever-increasing number of strokes consecutively. It is then a question of increasing the distance during each class session until the student can swim easily and comfortably, breathing with relaxation.

Chapter 10

Coaching the middle distance crawl stroke

Middle distance races include any swimming event between 150 and 300 yards.

MIDDLE DISTANCE CRAWL STROKE

The 200-yard freestyle crawl had been classified in our previous revisions of this book as requiring a distinct speed somewhere between the 100-yard top sprint distance, and the 400-yard or 1-mile distance.

In modern, competitive swimming of today, the 200-yard freestyle crawl is no longer considered a middle distance race but a sprint race. This distance in top-flight swimming requires allout swimming speed with a short, fast tempo and an evenly measured six-beat kick.

To compete in this 200-yard sprint event requires and calls for tremendous endurance, stamina, and skill, and the swimmer must therefore condition himself mentally and physically to participate in a very rugged and vigorous period of training in order to become a successful competitor and winner.

However, the authors have in mind that not all swimmers competing at the middle distance level are top-flight competitors. Instead of competing at a maximum energy output, at the beginning of his competition experience he should at first be trained to compete at a more evenly distributed energy output.

CHARACTERISTICS OF THE MIDDLE DISTANCE SWIMMER

There are some individuals who possess the speed of a sprinter plus the stamina and endurance of a long distance swimmer. These are the ideal qualifications for the middle distance swimmers. Many long distance swimmers have developed into excellent middle distance swimmers.

The wide range of difference in physical characteristics of middle distance swimmers prohibits a description of an "ideal" build. The buoyant individual, however, has an advantage over a heavy-muscled

one and one half body length. This is commonly called the danger line in racing tactics. Very frequently in such a close race, one relies upon the other to be carried along at an optimum stroke cadence and keeps the leading rival near enough to sense quickly any change in tactics. Frequently a leading rival will go out at a terrific rate of speed with the idea in mind of causing his rival to press his stroke, throw him off his stroke rhythm, and in this way outmaneuver him to the finish.

An experienced swimmer knows his own best pace and will not allow a competitor either to entice him into early exhaustion by a great effort early in the race or cause him to swim so slowly at first that even an all-out accelerative effort will not enable him to finish well. Swimmers are in lanes by themselves and can be attentive to their own pace.

Passing an opponent. A middle distance swimmer who relinquishes an early lead to his rival may wish to challenge in the later stages of the race. He may attempt faster turns after the first half of the race and gradually build up the margin relinquished. Some swimmers like to sneak up and pass a less alert rival on a blind lap. These tactics may cause a less experienced swimmer no end of worry. Passing a swimmer is costly, and the passer must be prepared to pay the price to stay ahead and meet a counterchallenge.

In the final stages of a race, if a margin must be closed, it should be closed gradually. The swimmer should close the margin early enough in the final stages of the race so that it is within the limits of accomplishment. If the opponent is tiring rapidly near the finish, then a final effort is made to overtake him. The swimmer must always be on the alert in going for the finish and use good judgment by swimming in good form and not making a "dog-fight" out of the finish. It is well for him to keep in mind that his rival may be tiring more rapidly than he is. In other words, while in the water be alert and smart at all stages of the race.

Meeting a challenge. The start may be considered as the first challenge in a middle distance race. When the field gets underway, the swimmer must decide if the speed of his opponents is approximating that of his own plan or whether it is too fast or too slow. He has the option of either electing or rejecting the challenge. He may desire to conserve his energy early in the race and then in the closing seconds of the race elect to challenge for the lead.

A challenge may occur at any stage of the race. One may be swimming at his own best pace and may ignore passing tactics of an opponent. On the other hand, he may accept the challenge with the idea of breaking down excessive amounts of energy being spent by the challenger and later reducing his stroke cadence. Quite frequently in a race a swimmer must decide quickly which is the wiser plan to follow, even

though it does not fit into his predetermined race plan. In the last 50 yards of the race he should be ready to meet any challenge if he has hopes of winning the race. Middle distance swimmers may well follow the rule of swimming the first part of the race with the head and the last part with the heart.

Disastrous effects may be the direct result of accepting a challenge at a most inopportune time of a race if the challenge interferes seriously with the effort distribution of the accepting swimmer.

Pace. A swimmer should be thoroughly disciplined and schooled in the technique of pacing. Perhaps the ideal way to swim a middle

Table 10-1. Ideal split times for various racing times in the 200-yard crawl stroke (25-yard pool)

ELAPSED DISTANCE (YD.)	ELAPSED TIME (SEC.)	SPLIT TIME (SEC.)	ELAPSED DISTANCE (YD.)	ELAPSED TIME (SEC.)	SPLIT TIME (SEC.)
25	9.8	9.8	25	12.0	12.0
50	21.8	12.0	50	26.1	14.1
75	34.0	12.2	75	40.6	14.5
100	46.25	12.25	100	55.2	14.6
125	58.50	12.25	125	1:10.2	15.0
150	1.10.80	12.30	150	1:25.3	15.1
175	1:23.15	12.35	175	1:40.5	15.2
200	1:35.00	11.85	200	1:55.0	14.5
25	10.4	10.4	25	12.6	12.6
50	23.0	12.6	50	27.3	14.7
75	35.8	12.8	75	42.4	15.1
100	48.7	12.9	100	57.6	15.2
125	1:01.6	12.9	125	1:13.2	15.6
150	1:14.6	13.0	150	1:29.0	15.8
175	1:27.6	13.0	175	1:44.8	15.8
200	1:40.0	12.4	200	2:00.0	15.2
25	11.0	11.0	25	13.2	13.2
50	24.1	13.1	50	28.5	15.3
75	37.5	13.4	75	44.2	15.7
100	51.0	13.5	100	1:00.0	15.8
125	1:04.6	13.6	125	1:16.2	16.2
150	1:18.2	13.6	150	1:32.6	16.4
175	1:31.9	13.7	175	1:49.1	16.5
200	1:45.0	13.1	200	2:05.0	15.9
25	11.6	11.6	25	13.8	13.8
50	25.3	13.7	50	29.7	15.9
75	39.3	14.0	75	46.0	16.3
100	54.4	14.1	100	1:02.5	16.5
125	1:07.6	14.2	125	1:19.3	16.8
150	1:21.9	14.3	150	1:36.3	17.0
175	1:36.3	14.4	175	1:53.4	17.1
200	1:50.0	13.7	200	2:10.0	16.6

distance race is to be able to distribute the rate of speed and effort evenly in proportion to the distance covered. The swimmers who are breaking the records are swimming the first part of the race at only fractions of a second slightly faster rate than the latter part of the race.

A general plan is presented and recommended showing the beginner how energy may be distributed effectively for the middle distance swimming races (Table 10-1).

Maintaining the stroke rhythm. To maintain and preserve a smooth, relaxed, and economical stroking cadence from the starting stages through the challenges and to the final stages of a race is a most commendable achievement in competition. If one is too easily excited under racing conditions so that the mind is diverted from the stroke rhythm, he can hardly expect to maintain any stroke balance. Sometimes swimming near the path of another swimmer's feet causes one to lose hold of the disturbed water.

In the middle distances one should turn the head occasionally to both sides for three reasons: first, to relax the neck and shoulder girdle muscles; second, to facilitate respiration; and third, to observe the position of his opponents. Care should be taken so that the body does not roll with this head movement.

TEACHING AND LEARNING PROCEDURES

For teaching and learning procedures for the crawl stroke, see Chapter 9.

Chapter 11

Coaching the distance
crawl stroke

A distance swimming stroke is built around the idea of getting a swimmer rapidly through the water with the least possible expenditure of energy. The distance crawl stroke resembles the sprint crawl stroke, except that the distance swimmer strokes with a minimum output of energy yet maintains effective speed. Relaxation is stressed, and the stroke action is smooth. The distance crawl stroke further differs from the sprint crawl stroke in that the trunk angle is slightly flatter and takes on a stretched appearance; the arm action is less strenuous, and the strokes are longer and more deliberate; the height of the recovery arm is lower than in the sprints; the six-beat kick may or may not be broken and breathing is deeper.

A distance for this category of swimming is considered anywhere from 400 yards upward to 1 mile. Training for the distance events is performed quite differently by the top-flight swimmers than for the sprint events. The authors will not attempt to recommend an ideal style for swimming the distance events because of the number of variations being used in the kick. There is a steady trend by modern distance competitors to employ the use of an interrupted or broken kick tempo. There are, however, quite a number of the good swimmers who will adhere to the six-beat kick throughout the entire distance. Swimmers using the broken kick tempo or drag style kick are usually extremely buoyant. They depend on the arms to provide the main propulsive force, using the minor beats of the kick for counterbalance and one or two major beats to compliment the propulsive force of the arm action.

Practically every top-flight distance swimmer has developed a characteristic broken style kick of his own, one that is designed to conserve energy and effort output.

Those swimmers who do use an interrupted or broken tempo kick as a general rule will revert to a regular six-beat sprint crawl kick in the closing moments of a distance race.

CHARACTERISTICS OF DISTANCE SWIMMERS

The type more often advancing into the top-flight performance is tall and rangy, with well-developed endurance. Their muscles are usually long, rather than short and thick. They range in height from 5 feet 8 inches to 6 feet 4 inches. The weight range is from 150 pounds to 195 pounds.

QUALIFICATIONS

The first prerequisite for any type of competition in which endurance is a factor is a good, sound body. The estimate of prerequisite physical condition is best obtained by a medical examination which includes observations of body functions during strenuous physical exercise. If the health conditions are satisfactory, the next question the candidate should consider is whether or not he is willing to "pay the price" exacted of him in the way of training for such strenuous exertion as that demanded by the distance swimming events.

To withstand systematic, rigorous training the candidate should have a strong heart. There have been studies made as to the actual size of the heart of swimmers. In nearly every case, the better type swimmer had a large heart. Since the heart is a muscle, it will naturally increase in size due to exercise in the same manner as any muscle. Individual hearts differ in size just as one's nose or ear differs in shape and size. Whenever one is endowed at the outset with a large, strong heart, he seems to be at an advantage. If a distance swimmer desires to go far in competition, it is essential that he must either possess a strong heart or acquire one through training. The heart then becomes a powerful pump which continuously not only carries oxygen from the lungs and feeds it to the oxygen-hungry working muscles, but also carries away toxins thrown off by the working muscles. When this healthy situation exists, through a rugged and well-directed program of good conditioning and training, fatigue is delayed.

The distance swimmer must be of at least medium height, strong and durable, yet flexible and supple. He must be streamlined at the hips and legs. An individual with a pair of long, supple, or "rubbery" legs usually makes a better distance or middle distance swimmer than a sprinter. This is an essential adaptation to distance swimming. The kick must be delivered with an even, smooth, and powerful continuous flow of propulsive force if a six-beat kick is used. Long feet and big hands are an aid. He must possess a good sense of rhythm in order to be able to make adjustments to either an increased or decreased cadence. He must be buoyant so that he can rely on the water to hold him up.

A winning complex is essential, and a determination to extend and spend one's self is necessary. Courage to drive a tired body in the closing moments of a race to the finish wall with a burst of speed is an essential quality to cultivate.

TECHNIQUE OF THE DISTANCE CRAWL

Position of the body. The body should ride high in the distance stroke, but not as high as in the sprint crawl stroke. It should be stretched so that water does not flow over the back. The speed and distance to be covered are the criteria which regulate the riding angle of the swimmer; the greater the speed, the greater will be the angle.

Position of the head and neck. The head position is slightly below or above the hairline. The neck should be somewhat relaxed with the shoulder girdle kept loose.

Position of the hips. The hips ride near the surface and are maintained there by pressing down constantly on the hands and legs. If the broken kick tempo is being used, the hip and shoulder girdles will tend to roll considerably to compliment the leg and arm action.

Position of the legs. There is no departure in leg position from that already described in the sprint crawl stroke. Long rubbery legs are an asset to a distance swimmer. The six-beat kick should be kept just under the surface for traction. Enough depth should be maintained to permit the water to wash down over the legs so that the legs are beating in solid water, not in a mixture of air and water.

Leg action. The technique of the distance flutter kick is, in principle, exactly the same as that discussed in the sprint kick. There is, however, a general difference in the width of stroke of the legs. This is due to the fact that the slower the speed, the wider becomes the leg stroke. The reason for this is that the legs must obtain traction in the water, and, when they kick less rapidly, less propulsive action is obtained. Therefore, wider action of the legs increases their pressure against the water and provides the traction. It is for this reason that rubbery legs are desirable for distance swimming. However, some six-beat crawl distance swimmers will use a shortened, major and minor, six-beat kick that gives the legs an appearance of dragging, or trailing along.

Common errors in leg action technique. Common errors in the distance crawl stroke are most likely to occur in the leg action. Such errors are often not due to the leg action itself but to some other phase of the stroke which is affecting efficient kick performance. One of the most common of these is badly performed head-turning mechanics in breathing.

A distance swimmer requires deep breathing in his race, and, instead of using an independent head-turning action in relation to his arm action, he usually falls into a slower rhythm coincident with the arm action. This action turns the head to the air and returns the head to the water too slowly. This causes the body to tilt and roll over to its opposite side, rolling the hips with it and, in turn, causing a lateral spread of the legs and an unbalanced kick. It is impossible to manipulate the legs in a vertical plane if the hip level is tilted at an angle. It is this fault or deviation from the true six-beat crawl kick that has brought about the broken or interrupted kick rhythm tempo that has considerable following by top distance swimmers. However, most of these distance swimmers will revert back to the six-beat kick in the closing moments of the race.

The feet should not be fully extended or fully pigeon-toed continuously throughout the kick. This will keep the calf of the leg muscles and the plantar region of the foot muscles under a constant state of contraction, and the leg will soon fatigue.

Transition from slow (early season) to faster (later season) tempo. During the early season conditioning of squads, distance swimmers as well as sprinters usually take longer distances at very moderate speeds. It is through these longer swims that the sprinter must adjust his stroke rhythm and somewhat alter the arm slide and length of stride in the kick in order to cover the distance without having to stroke too fast. He does this by gradually drifting into a delayed arm slide on the arm which has entered the water. He loafs on the anchored arm. Over a period of swimming in this cadence the leg stride has gradually widened without the swimmer being conscious of the gradual change.

There comes a time when the swimmer begins to work on starts and short sprints. He experiences difficulty with the rhythm and finds it hard to obtain purchase or hold of the water with either hands or legs. What is now commonly taking place is that he is reducing the slide of the arms and digging them in, while the legs are still kicking in the slow and deep stride. Naturally, the first few times sprinting rhythm cadence is used, the legs cannot readjust themselves to the rapidity of the arms, and the legs thus miss a beat or two and the kick becomes generally irregular in an attempt to keep up with the racing arms. This is a natural result of distance swimming and is not difficult to adjust. Many coaches will avoid this phase of conditioning procedure by not permitting sprinters to swim distances continually. A week or ten days of orientation in special work on the kicking board, working for a reduced stride and a more rapid cadence of the legs, will soon have the legs in a higher gear ratio to mesh with the faster arm action.

Drag kick. There are some distance swimmers who have a very ineffective leg action but a fast and powerful arm action. These swimmers will then rely upon a reduced leg stride, called the "drag" or broken tempo flutter kick. There is in this type of kick just enough hip and knee action to feather the legs with the legs held almost straight and merely giving counterbalance to the arms. There will be just enough effort expended in the kick to maintain the body near the surface and every effort should be made to offer as little surface friction along the legs as possible. The water must slip smoothly under, over, and past the legs.

Arm action in the distance crawl stroke. In order to slow the arm action and allow greater relaxation, the arm in the distance crawl stroke is allowed to glide forward during the catch. However, to obtain the longer catch, the arm reaches out to enter at a very shallow angle and then slides into the catch. Then the elbow is bent more in order to shorten the arm lever so as to obtain greater driving power by driving the arm almost straight backward with some downward pressure. During the distance crawl stroke, while the swimmer is using the gliding arm stroke, he relies upon a flattened arc to propel his body forward. This gives the body efficient forward action from the drive as the elbow and wrist extend in a follow-through delivery. After the completion of this arm delivery, the elbow is then bent again and lifted above the surface, and the forearm is flung around laterally to the reach and entry. Unless one has an efficient driving leg action kick to support a sliding arm stroke, the swimmer should reduce the slide and rely upon the arm action for nearly all of the power.

Reach. The reach may be made from either a high bent elbow or from a low bent elbow recovery. Both types are commonly followed.

In the high recovery, care should be taken not to let the forearm hang down vertically from the elbow because then the hand is too close to the armpit during recovery. When the elbow extends for the reach from this position, the hand usually overreaches in nearly every case, and the shoulder is dropped before the hand entry. The reach is made slightly slower than in the sprint type. However, if it is too slow the shoulder will roll down. Again in this type of stroke the shoulder must remain above the arm during the propulsive arc. The arm should not reach to its full extension above the surface. From the high elbow recovery, the arm comes down from above for the entry. In the low bent elbow recovery, the reach is very close to the surface and goes into the entry slightly sooner, usually with a press type of entry similar to the one described in the sprint stroke.

Entry. The arm should be pressed into the water, and it should continue under the surface to the catch and pull. It should be constantly pressed at the wrist and hand, not the elbow and shoulder, to allow the shoulder to move over the arm. The press allows contact to be held with the water while waiting for the completion of the leg cycle. The entry should not be prolonged because the loss of arm propulsion will be far in excess of the very slight advantage given to the legs by the delay.

Glide or support. During the glide the pressure should be felt in the fingers. This causes the arm to glide downward slightly below the level of the shoulder, which causes the body to rest on that arm, but the shoulders and head are not permitted to lower. The water level at the head should remain constant throughout the entire slide. Throughout this slide the elbow should never be stretched or overextended. There should be a natural full reach and elbow extension. The tip of the elbow should be pointing to the side, not downward, during the slide. If the tip of the elbow is pointing downward, the elbow has been extended too far and will cause the shoulder to drop below it. The action of the arm from entry to catch must be rapid and forceful yet be skillful in preparing itself for an effective catch. The phase from entry to completion of the release must be executed fast and skillfully in order to assure a fast turnover of the propulsive arm stroke, so that the opposition rhythm balance is maintained with the recovery arm. (See Fig. 9, *A*.)

It is during the glide phase of this stroke that the shoulder joint should be extended forward after the elbow joint has completed its extension. The shoulder is submerged in the water. This increases the length of the arm leverage as it commences the propulsive phase. The body glides on the arm from the drive of the other arm and from the constant flow of power delivered from the flutter kick.

If the arm is permitted to glide on or just barely under the surface, it is too shallow, and the entry has lost some of its propulsive effectiveness. The entry to the catch should be a propulsive phase of the stroke, even though minor in force to the major propulsive arc. The arm, while sliding, should move downward. From the study of underwater movies, the actual depth of proficient swimmers, riding below the surface, is approximately 6 to 10 inches at the completion of the glide. From above the surface it appears very much shallower and has the appearance of 2 to 4 inches in depth.

Catch. The catch is effected at the completion of the glide the same as described in the sprint type of stroke. The pull or catch is initiated in the hand; then the forearm and upper arm follow in rapid succession. The elbow should never lead during the pull phase. The mechanics of the adjustment from pull or draw to push and drive takes place exactly the same way as it is performed in the sprint crawl stroke. Some swimmers use a decided elbow bend, almost a boomerang position, whereas others use a slight bend in adjustment. Whenever a decided bend is used, in order to maintain good leverage in the movements, care should be taken not to let the hand move too far outside the line of the opposite shoulder. Otherwise, the mechanical advantage of the pull and drive is lost.

Pull, drive, and release. The pull, drive, and release are identical in mechanics to that of the sprint type of stroke. The essential difference in the release from that of the sprint type is that it occurs farther back. As a general rule it takes place slightly beyond the hip joint. It is also essential in the release to notice if each hand has the same length of drive to the point of the release so that balance is maintained.

Recovery. The recovery of the arms may be accomplished as described in the sprint crawl arm recovery. Some swimmers employ a quick recovery, sometimes called a "flip" recovery, whereas others usually use a slightly slower recovery. Most distance swimmers recover the arm in a low, outward sweep of the entire arm, maintaining the hand well out from the elbow, with the arm rotator muscles adjusting the hand and elbow for the proper entry.

Timing of one arm with the other arm. A very simple and accurate timing method can be used. The recovery arm is used as a guiding basis. As the recovery arm is entering the water, the driving arm must be well beyond the shoulders in its concluding drive. In executing this significant and dominant phase of the timing technique, one should experience the same feeling as in ice skating. For example, in skating as one drives with the hindmost leg, the foremost leg swings forward to contact the ice to receive the force of the driving leg. This same principle is true in the crawl stroke, that is, the driving arm under the body transfers force and momentum onto the entering arm. (See Fig. 8-2, *A-D.*) Note how this timing has established the opposition rhythm of the arms as well as the legs. The legs will naturally "dovetail" into the arm and shoulder movement for counterbalancing action of the entire stroke. Once this timing pattern has been established, it is very easy to maintain it throughout the distance to be covered. The weight of the body must not be shifted onto the recovering arm as the catch and pull begins but must be shifted when the recovery arm is in the water and is in a position to furnish support. It is this timing point that many swimmers miss. The speed derived from this type of stroke is in a large part due to this timing. One derives a feeling of continuously sliding downhill if the entire stroke is performed well.

Timing ratio of the arms and legs in relation to each other. The same timing is used as described in the sprint crawl stroke, except that, when an arm slide is used, a slightly longer kicking stride is necessary to coordinate with the arms.

Relation of the head turning for breathing to arm and leg action. There is little difference in the timing of the head other than has been discussed in the sprint crawl stroke. Even though more time is allowed for the taking of air because deeper breathing is essential in distance swimming, actually no less time is or should be consumed in going to the air and in coming away from it. However, many inexperienced swimmers will, because they are stroking slower, move the head slower to and away from the air. This will disturb the whole stroke rhythm as well as body balance.

The distance swimmer must learn to turn the face equally well to either side for air. Occasionally, by alternating the breathing side, the shoulder muscles gain rest and relaxation.

Common errors in head action technique. A common error is either not turning the head fast enough to the point of inhaling or recovering it back to dead center after air is obtained. This is usually due to a rigid neck. If fatigue sets in too early in a race, breathing should be checked to see if it is adequate and properly executed.

One should not retard the recovery arm as it approaches the point of entry. This fault permits the shoulder to lower and submerge before the hand enters. The hand must drop immediately into the water as it nears the point of entry.

Lateral-spin turn for distance crawl stroke (with head out for breathing). This turn is similar to the sprint turn except that the mouth is out of water to obtain air. (See Fig. 9-2.) The tumble or somersault turn is not recommended for beginning distance swimmers because of the need for air at the turn. However, somersault turns are being used extensively by highly conditioned distance swimmers. (See Fig. 9-3.)

As the body coasts in to the wall, it is turned slightly to the side as the under hand touches the wall. The fingertips are turned upward, and the elbow is bent to permit the head to come in close to the wall. The tuck is started at this point, and the body turns partly on its side and face. The head lifts out and away from the water and wall to get air. The head is turned for air in such a manner that the cheek is flat on the surface and the mouth is facing to the rear. The free hand sweeps down from the hips in front of the body and across the chest. The body is tilted nearly in a sitting position. The turn is actually end-over-end in a tucked position. As the body is thrown away from the wall to a point just beyond a vertical sitting position, the hand is driven away from the wall above the surface, elbow bent, and speared into the water with tremendous speed. The hand enters slightly in front of the head and face. The arm is pushed down and forward to join the other hand in front of the head. The shoulders and head plunge down with the arm, and as the arms extend forward the legs drive into the wall for the push-out. The body is actually tilted on its side slightly at the time of the push-off. Extending the turning arm out hard under the water tends to flatten the body. The speed of execution of this turn depends largely upon the speed with which the turning arm is literally jerked away from the wall and plunged into the water. The turning arm continues to push forward to help right the body again to the push-out position. Some swimmers will remain on the side after the turn

Table 11-1. Ideal split times for various racing times in the 500-yard crawl stroke (25-yard pool)

ELAPSED DISTANCE (YD.)	ELAPSED TIME (SEC.)	SPLIT TIME (SEC.)	ELAPSED DISTANCE (YD.)	ELAPSED TIME (SEC.)	SPLIT TIME (SEC.)
25	11.0	11.0	25	12.0	12.0
50	24.4	13.4	50	26.4	14.4
75	37.8	13.4	75	40.8	14.4
100	51.2	13.4	100	55.2	14.4
125	1:04.7	13.5	125	1:09.7	14.5
150	1:18.2	13.5	150	1:24.2	14.5
175	1:31.8	13.6	175	1:38.8	14.6
200	1:45.4	13.6	200	1:53.4	14.6
225	1:59.1	13.7	225	2:08.1	14.7
250	2:12.8	13.7	250	2:22.8	14.7
275	2:26.5	13.7	275	2:37.5	14.7
300	2:40.2	13.7	300	2:52.2	14.7
325	2:54.0	13.8	325	3:07.0	14.8
350	3:07.8	13.8	350	3:21.8	14.8
375	3:21.6	13.8	375	3:36.6	14.8
400	3:35.4	13.8	400	3:51.4	14.8
425	3:49.2	13.8	425	4:06.2	14.8
450	4:03.0	13.8	450	4:21.0	14.8
475	4:16.6	13.6	475	4:35.6	14.6
500	4:30.0	13.4	500	4:50	14.4
25	11.5	11.5	25	12.5	12.5
50	25.4	13.9	50	27.4	14.9
75	39.3	13.9	75	42.3	14.9
100	53.2	13.9	100	57.2	14.9
125	1:07.2	14.0	125	1:12.2	15.0
150	1:21.2	14.0	150	1:27.2	15.0
175	1:35.3	14.0	175	1:42.3	15.1
200	1:49.4	14.1	200	1:57.4	15.1
225	2:03.6	14.2	225	2:12.6	15.2
250	2:17.8	14.2	250	2:27.8	15.2
275	2:32.0	14.2	275	2:43.0	15.2
300	2:46.2	14.2	300	2:58.2	15.2
325	3:00.5	14.3	325	3:13.5	15.3
350	3:14.8	14.3	350	3:28.8	15.3
375	3:29.1	14.3	375	3:44.1	15.3
400	3:43.2	14.3	400	3:59.4	15.3
425	3:57.7	14.3	425	4:14.7	15.3
450	4:12.0	14.3	450	4:30.0	15.3
475	4:26.1	14.1	475	4:45.1	15.1
500	4:40.0	13.9	500	5:00.0	14.9

Table 11-1. Ideal split times for various racing times in the 500-yard crawl stroke (25-yard pool)—cont'd

ELAPSED DISTANCE (YD.)	ELAPSED TIME (SEC.)	SPLIT TIME (SEC.)	ELAPSED DISTANCE (YD.)	ELAPSED TIME (SEC.)	SPLIT TIME (SEC.)
25	13.0	13.0	25	14.0	14.0
50	28.4	15.4	50	30.4	16.4
75	43.8	15.4	75	46.8	16.4
100	59.2	15.4	100	1:03.2	16.4
125	1:14.7	15.5	125	1:19.7	16.5
150	1:30.2	15.5	150	1:36.2	16.5
175	1:45.8	15.6	175	1:52.8	16.6
200	2:01.4	15.6	200	2:09.4	16.6
225	2:17.1	15.7	225	2:26.1	16.7
250	2:32.8	15.7	250	2:42.8	16.7
275	2:48.5	15.7	275	2:59.5	16.7
300	3:04.2	15.7	300	3:16.2	16.7
325	3:20.0	15.8	325	3:33.0	16.8
350	3:35.8	15.8	350	3:49.8	16.8
375	3:51.6	15.8	375	4:06.6	16.8
400	4:07.4	15.8	400	4:23.4	16.8
425	4:23.2	15.8	425	4:40.2	16.8
450	4 39.0	15.8	450	4:57.0	16.8
475	4:54.6	15.6	475	5:13.6	16.6
500	5:10.0	15.4	500	5:30.0	16.4
25	13.5	13.5	25	14.5	14.5
50	29.4	15.9	50	31.4	16.9
75	45.3	15.9	75	48.3	16.9
100	1:01.2	15.9	100	1:05.2	16.9
125	1:17.2	16.0	125	1:22.2	17.0
150	1:33.2	16.0	150	1:39.2	17.0
175	1:49.3	16.1	175	1:56.3	17.1
200	2:05.4	16.1	200	2:13.4	17.1
225	2:21.6	16.2	225	2:30.6	17.2
250	2:37.8	16.2	250	2:47.8	17.2
275	2:54.0	16.2	275	3:05.0	17.2
300	3:10.2	16.2	300	3:22.2	17.2
325	3:26.5	16.3	325	3:39.5	17.3
350	3:42.8	16.3	350	3:56.8	17.3
375	3:59.1	16.3	375	4:14.1	17.3
400	4:15.4	16.3	400	4:31.4	17.3
425	4:31.7	16.3	425	4:48.7	17.3
450	4:48.0	16.3	450	5:06.0	17.3
475	5:04.1	16.1	475	5:23.1	17.1
500	5:20.0	15.9	500	5:40.0	16.9

is made, push out on the side, then right themselves with the first pull. This is a retarding movement and should not be practiced. The righting of the body face down should be performed at the wall. It should be fully completed with the feet as they leave the wall. The push-out in this turn and the break into the surface are the same as in the sprint crawl stroke.

A common error in the execution of a distance turn is that it is usually performed too slowly. This fault is usually due to the habit adopted in early season swimming of making all turns in the same tempo as the stroke rhythm. Turns in practice distance training should always be executed faster than the stroke cadence. Inexperienced swimmers rely upon the turn for rest, and the experienced swimmer relies upon it to gain in speed and distance on a napping opponent. The slow turning swimmer must then swim faster to regain what he loses at the turn.

Some swimmers lift the head and body too high above the surface in getting air. The turn should be done quickly, and the inspiration should be executed rapidly.

In any turn the legs should be tucked simultaneously as the turning hand touches the wall. Some swimmers will execute a quarter-turn before tucking the legs. This is decidedly slow and should not be practiced.

Finish. Racing fundamentals for the finish of a distance event are the same as those described for the finish of the sprint crawl stroke. A swimmer should swim through the last 20% of a race with all the speed and effort that he possesses.

RACE

All racing fundamentals discussed for the middle distance swimmer also apply to the distance swimmer. The longer the race, the more carefully the swimmer must plan the distribution of his efforts.

For the benefit of the inexperienced swimmer an individual race plan table is presented (Table 11-1). By observing this composite pace of championship swimming, one can observe that as the length of the race increases there is a tendency to cover the entire distance at an even distribution of effort and stroke cadence. There is no abrupt acceleration or deceleration at any portion of the race. Deceleration gradually takes place after the first 150 yards are covered. This is because speed decreases as the distance increases due to fatigue.

It has been recommended that by using a special pacing device a swimmer should be able to swim each length of the pool in proportional time from start to finish (excluding the first and last laps) and in this way preserve energy and perform the entire distance vastly more economically. Experience has shown this method of swimming to be difficult. The swimmers claim that they cannot swim slow enough at the start. Then, too, they find difficulty in maintaining a uniform stroke cadence as the race progresses and fatigue sets in.

TEACHING AND LEARNING PROCEDURES

For teaching and learning procedures for the crawl stroke, see Chapter 9.

Chapter 12

Coaching the back crawl stroke

The back crawl stroke is of more recent origin than that of its sire, the crawl. Since its origin in approximately 1912, its speed has been improved more than either the crawl or the breast stroke. A comparison of the fastest times recorded for the four strokes from 1912 with those of the present time is given in Table 12-1.

When the back crawl stroke first became known as the fastest means of swimming on the back, the preferred technique of stroke mechanics varied widely among coaches and swimmers.

Some of the questions considered were: Should the arms be recovered straight or bent? Should they be placed in the water behind the head, straight back from the shoulder, or outside a line with the shoulder? Should the arms be pulled deep or shallow? Should they be pulled straight or in a bent position? Should the head be carried in line with the body or held up facing the legs? Should the body roll more than in the crawl stroke? Through a long process of trial and error, a general agreement had been reached as to the best style so that we had but one style universally accepted. This style will be called the Kiefer style since it was introduced by him. Practically every world's back stroke record has been established by Adolph Kiefer. However, the modern trend of the top-flight swimmers is now away from this style and favors a more vertical recovery of the arms. It is believed that a faster turnover of the stroke is obtained through the latter.

One must bear in mind that in swimming the back crawl style the man is on his back, and structural limitations at the shoulder joint prevent him from pulling the arms through the propulsive phases under the body as in the crawl stroke. However, to partially offset this limitation, he is able to maintain his breathing apparatus above the surface, which is a great advantage. The fact that the swimmer does not need to turn or lift his head out to the side or to the front for breathing air, as is the case with the crawl, breast, and dolphin butterfly strokes, makes

Table 12-1. A comparison of speed for the four competitive strokes (1912 to 1967)

STROKE	1912 100 YD. (SEC.)	1967 100 YD. (SEC.)
Crawl	0:58.0	0:45.6
Butterfly*		0:50.2
Back crawl	1:12.0	0:52.5
Breast	1:10.0	0:58.5

*Note: The dolphin butterfly stroke was not originated until April, 1935, by Armbruster and Sieg. Sieg's best time for 100 yards at that time was 1:00.2.

this stroke one of the most mechanically balanced of all the competitive strokes. Because no head-turning mechanics are required for breathing, resistance to water is minimized, and, as a result, this is the smoothest of any of the swimming strokes.

PHYSICAL QUALIFICATIONS FOR THE BACK CRAWL SWIMMER

Almost anyone endowed with ability in water and better than average strength can swim the back crawl stroke reasonably well. However, those who have ambitions of reaching the top should possess reasonably good height of at least 5 feet 11 inches, with large hands and feet and a snakelike type of build. Along with this, they must be endowed with strength and endurance. The 200-yard back crawl is probably one of the most difficult races on the college swimming program. A fast flutter kick is essential for speed. There are many boys who have long rubbery legs but who do not possess either the power or speed to drive them fast enough for either 100 yards or 200 yards to be top-flight swimmers. Many shorter-built swimmers are endowed with extremely fast driving legs and powerful arms and make up for their lack of long legs and arms by their speed and endurance.

The back crawl swimmer moves his arms and legs at about the same cadence as the sprint swimmer, and yet he must cover a distance which is beyond that of the 100-yard sprint. His physiologic characteristics are, therefore, a combination of the sprint crawl and the middle distance swimmer.

He must be able to move his legs rapidly, he must have powerful arms and flexible shoulders, and he must also have a considerable amount of endurance. His sense of rhythm must be well developed.

TECHNIQUE OF THE BACK CRAWL START

The back crawl stroke start requires an entirely different technique than the crawl, breast, and butterfly strokes. In most instances the back crawler is put to a disadvantage in competition because of the lack of a secure foot support. This is a disadvantage which should be

Fig. 12-1. A-F, A series of ideal form showing the start positions for the back crawl stroke start. **A,** The preliminary stance. **B,** The "set" position. **C,** Leaving the mark.

corrected. Some type of starting blocks* should be made with a hand bar for the competitor to grasp (Fig. 12-1, *A*). With the use of adjustable starting blocks, it has been proved that the starting time for back strokers is significantly faster. The bar can be constructed so that it is in line with the starting wall. A more advantageous start could be made with hand rests approximately 18 inches above the surface. Adjustable footrests upon which to place the feet should be constructed to prevent slipping and to give substantial support to the foot to any depth beneath the surface. With this equipment a more powerful start is made, which would enhance the flight through the air and give an advantage to the start similar to that of the other events.

Starting position. If no starting rail is available, the hands grasp the scum rail about shoulder width or spread slightly wider than shoulders. The feet take a position beneath the hands parallel to each other and spread hip width. The toes are from 0 to 4 inches under the surface and are never spread farther than the width of the hips. The feet are placed firmly against the wall (Fig. 12-1, *A*).

Another position of the feet is a walking stride stance, with the toe of one foot placed about level with the heel of the other foot. Either of these two methods of foot placing and spacing is used.

The body must assume a closely bunched tuck with the hips placed close to the heels. The body is out of the water. The arms may be held either straight or slightly bent at the elbows.

*Valett, Herbert B.: An experimental study of the back stroke start in swimming with the use of starting stirrups, University of Iowa Thesis, 1948.

Fig. 12-1, cont'd. D, Body entering the water. **E,** The start of the stroke at the end of the glide under the surface. **F,** The position of the body as it comes to the surface.

If a handrail is used, it should be grasped with the first two joints of the fingers, and the heel of the hand should take a position below the hand grasp on the hand starting rail. At the signal to start, the hand throw can be executed faster with the quick extension of the wrist against the hand rail.

The above stance is assumed (Fig. 12-1, *B*) when the starter gives the command, "Take your marks." At the report of the gun, the body is catapulted backward as if it were crouched upon a powerful compressed spring which was suddenly released (Fig. 12-1, *C*).

Leaving the mark. The aim of the throw-away action in the back stroke start is to make a backward racing dive by projecting the body out over the surface, entering the water, and utilizing the momentum derived from the start in the glide under water.

At the gun, the starting movement consists in releasing the hands with a wrist snap, and driving the arms vigorously backward laterally, not upwards, to a full arm extension beyond the head and in line with the spine. (See Fig. 12-1, *B* and *C*.) This arm movement is executed with tremendous speed. The head is driven backward simultaneously with the arms. The legs then begin extending at the knees and hips with explosive speed. When these joints are fully extended, then the ankles are extended. The final snap of the ankles gives added speed to the body. This should throw the body into a stretched position with the back slightly arched and the hips well above the surface of the water (Fig.

12-1, *C*). If no handrail is provided and the body is sitting in the water at the start, the hips must be lifted at the throw-away; otherwise they will drag through the water, causing resistance.

The swimmer should grasp the handrail in the starting stance, with the toes at the surface line. In this position the body can be driven far out above the surface with a very much faster start and a greater penetrating power into the water.

Entry. The position of the body is somewhat arched so as to gain a clean-cut entry at the proper angle. As the hands enter the water, the head is held well back between the extended arms (Fig. 12-1, *D*). The arms are fully stretched beyond the head, in line with the spine. The wrists should be held straight in line with the forearm. A common error is to hyperextend the wrists, which causes the body to glide too deep into the water. The hands and arms should be separated the width of the head and the neck and face. The moment the head and shoulders have entered the water, the head should be raised in order to prevent the body from going too deep.

Glide. The glide under water should be continued to a point at which the speed derived from momentum slows to a rate equaling that of the swimming speed. Overanxious sprinters have a tendency to start stroke action prematurely and thus do not take full advantage of the momentum gained from the start.

As the momentum is retarded to the swimming speed in the glide, the flutter kick begins just before the arm stroke action begins.

During the glide, air may either be expelled gradually or held until just prior to breaking through to the surface.

Breath control in the back stroke start. When the arms are thrown back laterally beyond the head, away from the starting wall, the chest region is lifted and expanded, causing air to rush into the lungs easily through a wide-open mouth (Fig. 12-1, *C*). The breath is held during entry and during most of the glide.

When one is lying on the back under water, the opening from the nose into the throat is directly down. In this position water can enter very easily, causing considerable respiratory distress to the inexperienced back stroke swimmers, especially during the glide phase of the start and also at the push-out at the turn.

There are several ways to prevent this distress of water entering the throat by way of the nasal passage. One method is to curl the upper lip and press it up against the external nasal openings. This closes them entirely and prevents water from entering the outer nasal and sinus regions. At the instant before swimming into the surface of the water and at the moment the nose has cleared the surface and the outer nostrils are free of water, the exhalation is started and the upper lip is removed.

The mouth is then opened for an inspiration. A more conventional method is to expire air slowly through the nose continuously throughout the glide from the start and also throughout the push-out from the turn. This method is most difficult to control by a beginner because, while lying on the back, the swimmer finds the pressure of water difficult to overcome by a sustained expiration. This pressure causes the air held in the lungs to be forced out through the nose unchecked early in the glide. When the air has escaped in this manner, the inexperienced swimmer then finds himself just as helpless to prevent water entering the lungs through the nose before he comes to the surface.

Start of the stroke action. The arm stroke action begins while the body is still under the surface (Fig. 12-1, *E*). The swimmer then comes up forward to the surface swimming.

While the first arm begins its pull under water, the other arm should remain firmly anchored under the surface and straight ahead in line with the body. Downward pressure on this arm is necessary to keep it under the water and prevent it from shooting out of the water. Maintaining the arm under the water streamlines the body and eliminates considerable resistance. The arm that is pulling should pull fast and hard. This first pulling arm should bend at the elbow to effect quick forward propulsion to the body, which is already moving fast from the start.

If the initial pulling arm is pulled in a straight-arm position, it will lead to two errors: first, it will push the body out of the water instead of driving it straight ahead; second, the straight arm cannot pull through the water fast enough to maintain the speed. The body must come out of the glide swimming fast. The head should be raised as the first arm is pulled (Fig. 12-1, *F*).

In the alternating type of initial arm action, the body slides through the surface under continuous application of power. The body rides on a supporting arm which is preparing itself to catch the water the moment the other arm releases the water. As the body is swimming out into the surface, the stroke continues with regular rhythm. The head has been raised to the proper position in the next two or three arm strokes.

TECHNIQUE OF THE BACK CRAWL STROKE

The arms perform in reverse order to the crawl stroke. The back stroke is more easily mastered than the crawl, breast, or butterfly strokes because it does not have the complex breathing skills to be mastered. The arms move in a regular cycle in opposition to each other. The kick is similar in action to the six-beat crawl kick.

Once the stroke is mechanically mastered, it seldom gets out of line.

Sometimes a strong swimmer who is not highly endowed with motor skills makes a very fine back crawler.

Position of the body in swimming the back crawl stroke. The body is held nearly in a horizontal position and is maintained as near the surface as possible, with the hips just low enough to keep the legs under the surface (Fig. 12-2, *A*). The hips should not sag downward. The body should constantly be maintained in a stretched position. The chest and abdomen are flattened so that the water slipping around from the side of the head and neck can wash smoothly over the shoulders and chest

Fig. 12-2. A-H, A series of ideal form for executing the back crawl stroke showing the six leg beats and one revolution of the arm stroke. These figures also show the counterbalance of the arm and leg action and the position of the body in relation to the surface. All of these figures show the stroke, body from both sides, and head-on positions. **A,** The right arm has completed the drive as the left arm enters and catches the water. **B,** As the right arm recovers, the left arm starts the drive. **C,** Note the opposition rhythm of the right and left arms, also the bent arm drive. **D,** Opposition rhythm of the arm stroke.

with as little resistance as possible. The back of the spine presents a slightly convex position to the water. The back is curved just enough to cause the small of the back to conform to a continuous curved line from the hips to the shoulders. Stretching the body and relaxing the spine will place the body in this position.

Position of the head. The head is carried in line with the body (Fig. 12-2, *B*). The position of the head aids materially in forming the proper spinal curve. It also aids in balancing the body. The chin should be lowered, reasonably close to the throat so that the eyes can easily see toward the feet. The back portion of the head below the ears should ride under the surface. The head in this position serves as a rudder.

Fig. 12-2, cont'd. E, The left arm is slightly bent for relaxation as it lifts out of the water for the recovery. The shoulder lift is also shown. **F,** The arm is again straight in the recovery. The height of the arm above the surface is also shown. **G,** Note the position of the legs, hips, and shoulder. **H,** Note the head and right arm as the left arm prepares to enter the water.

The position of the head in the water will vary somewhat with characteristics of the individual and the amount of speed generated. Usually the lower tips of the ears are at the water level.

The eyes, nose, and chin should be centered on the line of progression. Under no circumstances, except when glancing for the turn, should the chin move out of this alignment regardless of the movements of the shoulder girdle while stroking. In spite of a slight rolling of the body caused by the shoulder action of the arm stroke, the chin must remain centered and pressed down toward the throat. The body requires this stability of the head in order to maintain body alignment and balance during the stroke action.

Position of the neck. A long, flexible neck is a definite aid to a back stroke swimmer because it offers a lesser amount of resistance to water than a short neck. In both the short- and the long-necked individuals, relaxation is essential. Unless the neck is relaxed, the chin will not be able to remain fixed while the shoulder girdle is oscillating. However, if an individual has a long neck, then instead of having to hold the body in an angular position in order to elevate the head, he can hold the body in an almost horizontal line, with the shoulders completely submerged (Fig. 12-2, *C*). The neck is projected upward, with the chin tucked toward the throat, and the back of the head presses into the water. In this position the water washes down smoothly over the entire length of the body.

Position of the shoulder girdle and upper spine. Ordinarily a swimmer who has a normal spine while walking will have the proper contour of his shoulder girdle and upper spine if he tucks his chin in, stretches the body, and relaxes the spine and neck (Fig. 12-2, *A*). In this position the cervical spines, from the shoulder to the base of the skull, will form a convex curve in line with the thoracic spines. A hunchbacked position would diminish power because the back muscles would be stretched and the pectorals would be shortened. The shoulder girdle muscles should be stretched daily to keep them supple and strong throughout the season. It must be remembered that the arms in the back crawl stroke work in reverse gear. Therefore, if the pectorals are allowed to become shortened when the arms reach back for the entry, they will prohibit the arm from stretching backward comfortably, and the body will have to roll over too much to accomplish a proper entry. The pectoral muscles should be stretched thoroughly so that there will be no resistance to the freedom of the arm action, especially in the recovery and the entry where efficient muscular performance is absolutely essential to great swimming speed performance in back stroke swimming.

The major characteristic of swimming the Kiefer style of back crawl is in the method of recovery. The arms sweep back from release to entry in a low, lateral swing. The authors recommend that in learning the back crawl stroke the beginner should first be taught the Kiefer style, or lateral arm recovery. This style has several advantages for the beginner over the style that employs a high vertical arm recovery for the following reasons: First, one is not apt to sink one's face or splash water over one's breathing equipment, the nose and mouth, causing unpleasant choking and strangling. Second, due to the structural limitation of the shoulder socket, if the arm is recovered vertically, the shoulder socket tends to lock itself just as the arm is extended overhead and about to enter the water. In this position the forearm and hand cannot be placed into the water unless the body is rolled over or the arm rotated, palm facing outward and downward. However, if the arm is swung back low over the surface and placed into the water just outside the shoulder joint, with the palm down, the joint does not bind and lock itself; neither does the body need to roll over to accommodate the movement.

The third advantage to this style is that the arm will not go into the water as deep as it usually does following a vertical recovery. By going deep, both the latissimus dorsi and the pectoralis major muscles are placed at a mechanical disadvantage. In the shallow pull both of these muscles pull with a very good mechanical advantage.

The modern trend in back stroke competition is definitely going to the high or vertical arm recovery. The advantages of the high arm recovery are as follows: First, it affords a faster turnover. Second, the recovery at the completion of the arm drive, a more natural continuous movement, is obtained, rather than a change of direction by swinging the arm laterally away from the body to initiate the recovery phase as is the case in the Kiefer style. Third, if the arm completes the drive and starts into the recovery, the thumb breaks through the surface first, then the hand and entire arm need only execute a quarter-turn inward in order to unlock the shoulder socket for an easy entry (Fig. 12-2, *D* and *E*.)

Position of the hips and lower (lumbar) spine. A common tendency for back strokers is to permit the hips to sag downward. This is brought about by carrying the head too high and rounding the neck and shoulders too much. This is true in the crawl stroke as well as the back crawl stroke. This sag is eliminated by stretching the body while swimming. Not only should the body be stretched in order to lift the hips, but downward pressure must be exerted on the two points of support— the arms as they enter and press and the down beat of the kick. The upper brim of the pelvis is tilted backward to straighten a deep curvature of the lower back (Fig. 12-2, *C*).

The hips do not have as much oscillation as in the crawl stroke. There is, however, just enough undulating movement in the hips for counterbalance between the beats of the legs and the pelvis.

Lateral sway of the hips should be eliminated. This is usually caused by overreaching in the arm entry.

Action of the legs. As in the crawl stroke, the six-beat kick is the most efficient and practical because of its natural counterbalance rhythm in stroke cadence with the arms.

There is little difference between the back crawl flutter kick and the crawl kick, as far as mechanics are concerned. The hip, knee, and ankle joints undulate the same way in either kick. There are, however, two essential differences (Fig. 12-2).

First, the feet do not kick into or break through the surface. However, the legs lie just under the surface, and at the completion of the up kick the leg has straightened at the knee, but the knee and foot have not kicked through the surface. Underwater study of champions, including Kiefer, reveals the absence of air bubbles in the back crawl. This does not support the theory that air bubbles give added friction for the feet to get traction in the water. By the use of the underwater camera method, it is seen that the air bubbles pass backward at an angle and do not again come in contact with the other leg in either the down or up beat in either the back or the crawl flutter kick.

The second significant difference between the two flutter kicks is that, on completion of the up beat, in the back crawl kick the upper surface of the leg is on a straight line with the upper surface of the hips, abdomen, and chest.

In general, in the back flutter kick, the foot and toes bend inward in the up kick more so than in the down beat of the crawl kick. They do not remain in pigeon-toed position on the down beat. On the down beat the foot may or may not be fully extended.

In the up beat the knee bends and then quickly straightens to create a whiplike action in the ankle. During the bend of the knee, the inexperienced swimmer will very often bend or lift the knees too far and break the surface. This should be avoided. The water should be permitted to slip or wash down over the legs from the hips downward and not be retarded or resisted by poking the knee through the surface. To streamline the legs and avoid this knee lift, the legs should be stretched from the hips toward the feet. If the knee is lifting, the foot is not pressing against the water and is naturally ineffective. On the up stroke, the knee bends and does rise to the upper level of the body but does not break water. When the knee straightens, the foot whips up so that at the completion of the knee extension the leg is in a straight line with the upper surface of the body.

The axis of action for this kick is in the hip joint as in the crawl

stroke. At the completion of this up kick, considerable water is thrown above the surface. The initiating movement is in the thigh, driven by the power of the pelvis and thigh flexors and hip extensor muscles. Initiating the movement in the thigh creates an action in the foreleg and foot, giving them an appearance when in motion of waving fishtails. Power is transmitted downward through the legs by means of pressure at effective angles against the resistance of the water, giving this back flutter kick its propulsive force in water.

The most frequent errors are those of holding the head either too high or too far back. Holding the head high will round the back too much. Holding it too far back will flatten it. Lifting the hips and thighs above the surface of the water will cause too much surface friction and therefore slow the speed. Each individual should experiment with head level to find the best level for creating least resistance to forward speed. Anatomic characteristics make some differences among different individuals. Sometimes the legs are held too stiffly and not relaxed to give free play to the joints. This is especially true in the action of the ankle.

Arm technique and mechanics of the back crawl stroke. The movements of the arms in the back crawl stroke differ from those of the crawl stroke in mechanics. However, arm-and-leg cycle ratio is 1 to 6, the same as in the crawl stroke.

Recovery of the arms. When the hand has completed its drive at the side of the thigh and below the hip (Fig. 12-2, *E* and *F*), the initiating movement in the recovery is started with the hips rolling slightly to the opposite side to give counterbalance to the opposite arm recovery. The shoulder lifts slightly as the body weight is shifted over onto the opposite arm as it enters. The elbow of the recovering arm bends slightly as the arm is lifted out of the water (Fig. 12-2, *F*). The wrist is turned so that the palm faces toward the surface. It droops slightly to permit it to relax and drain the water from the arm as the arm lifts out of the water. Bending the elbow slightly as the arm is lifted out of the water serves the three following essential purposes: First, it releases the tension of the arm flexor muscles and permits them to rest. Second, it permits the water to wash down the arm and drain off the fingertips as the arm is lifted out of the water, thus reducing the added weight of a curtain of water which is a retarding factor to speed. Third, the palm is turned toward the body, so that the thumb side of the hand will break through the surface.

The moment the fingertips have cleared the surface, the arm moves overhead vertically in line with the outside of the body to the entry. The wrist can be slightly drooped during the recovery.

A slight error is to maintain a bent elbow throughout the entire recovery, thereby causing the shoulder and elbow to enter the water before the hand and wrist enter.

Entry. The entry should follow the recovery without any retardation. The movement of the arm is slightly accelerated just prior to the entry. As the fingertips enter the water, the arm should be pressed into the water and should disappear immediately below the surface. This is the most important timing point in the arm action of the back crawl stroke. There are far too many back crawlers who believe that their entire wrist, hand, and forearm are in the water at the entry when actually only the shoulder is submerged and half the forearm is projecting above the surface.

The correct hand entry is with the palm facing the surface (Fig. 12-2, *E*). The wrist is slightly flexed at an angle of nearly 60 degrees. The fingers are parallel with the line of the arm. The wrist should be straight, not abducted. The palm is now in a position to slide forward and into the water ahead of the shoulder, the same as in the crawl stroke. The outer extremity of the arm, that is, the outer edge of the wrist, hand, and fingers, presses into the water and gives support to the whole body and prevents the shoulder from dropping below the hand. The hand should be pressed in quickly. When the hand approaches the entry position, it must enter before the shoulder. It should not be smashed but forced and pressed, so that the arm will slide down to the catch and pull effectively.

The hand should enter the water not more than 6 inches outside the shoulder line. The left hand should enter about 1 o'clock and the right hand at 11 o'clock, if one is swimming toward the face of the clock. The entry should be a quickened movement in order to keep the shoulder above the hand. If the movement is slow, the shoulder will ease down below the hand.

Press-slide. In the back crawl stroke, as in the crawl stroke, there is a definite momentary press-slide phase (Fig. 12-2, *A*). Even though brief, it is present in top sprinters, and it is there for a very definite purpose.

The hand and forearm press downward and slide forward to a very shallow depth in preparation for the catch. This is not deep, as in the crawl stroke, but just inches under the surface level. In this position the muscles which depress the arm have a good mechanical advantage. The shoulder is behind as well as above the arm in its drive. The palm is faced downward at an angle so that during the pressing phase, pressure is felt on the fingers.

During the entry, the body should not roll into the arm. After the arm has entered, the head and body are moved toward the extended arm. The trailing hand pushes as the recovering arm is extended. This slight inclination toward the sliding arm also helps to lift the opposite arm out of the water. A sensation of driving forward is achieved.

There is but little roll of the body in this type of back crawl stroke.

The fundamental movement occurs in a loose, flexible shoulder socket which gives the arm the freedom of action it requires. Tight-shouldered individuals cannot swim this stroke until they loosen their shoulder girdle by using daily stretching exercises for the shoulder girdle muscles.

There are some authorities who believe that the arm should enter and "dig" or go immediately into the drive. There are some very good back crawlers who use such a type of stroke. This is a more or less "windmill" type of stroke sought by those who use purely an opposition type of stroke, thereby gaining a faster "turnover" stroke which results in greater speed. However, it reverts back to the smash entry, and with a smash entry it is doubtful if a full cycle of six full-measured kicks can be executed on one stroke revolution. Again, there are some coaches who advocate anchoring the arm into the water and watching the body go by. This is the sensation one has when the stroke is properly executed, but actually the arms are not anchored. They definitely drive through the water, even though it seems that the body goes by stationary arms.

Catch, pull, and push drive. The catch, pull, and push or drive phase of the back crawl stroke will be considered as a whole, rather than broken down into its separate parts. In this stroke it is possible to pull the arm through to the release in either of two ways, straight or bent.

STRAIGHT ARM PULL. There are really few back crawlers who keep the arm straight after they have been swimming for several years. In learning, a swimmer will find that it is best to start with a straight arm pull. Later, the skill of bending the elbow for the push drive phase can be learned. There are, however, many top swimmers using the straight arm pull. Any strong, rugged boy can successfully use the straight arm pull all the way from the catch to the completion of the drive. If the arm is long, it requires powerful muscles to drive the arm through very fast. The straight arm back strokers usually develop a slow, lazy looking pull. In sprinting, the swimmer must move the arms more rapidly through the water, and the hand must fasten onto the water and not be permitted to slip. The longer-armed boys who are less rugged would find a more productive speed stroke with the arm bent at the elbow. In this way the lever arm is shortened, which gives greater advantage to the muscles.

The catch in the straight arm pull is no different than for the bent arm pull. The fingers, hand, and wrist must not be fixed. They resist when pressure is applied against them. The first movement of the catch is in the fingers and the hand, which curve and press downward and backward with a quickened movement. The palm is faced outward and toward the feet as the pressure is increased in the pull. The arm pulls very shallow in this movement, approximately 2 to 6 inches under the surface, until the hand and arm reach a point directly out

from the shoulder, where the depth is increased to 8 to 16 inches. From this point to the release the whole arm presses downward to the finish on a plane in line with the body and against the leg. The palm is faced rearward and completes its drive tight alongside the thigh, executing a quick push at the finish.

BENT ARM PULL. The bent arm pull and drive is now almost universally used by all competitors. The catch is started with the hand and fingers the same as in the straight arm action. The pull is at a greater depth and is slightly faster. Instead of being stretched out to its full length as in the straight arm pull, the arm reach is gradually shortened as the pull progresses. A firm grip upon the water is maintained with the hand by bending the elbow down. When the arm and hand have reached a point just slightly ahead of the line with the shoulder, a mechanical adjustment takes place. The shoulder girdle is prepared for the transition from a pulling or drawing action to a pushing or driving action. During this transition the propulsive force is not weakened, and no dead spot appears in the pull. On the contrary, during this phase the forearm muscles spring into action and begin a powerful forearm drive, followed by a continued contraction of the depressor muscles of the arm. As the forearm executes this drive, the elbow is bent downward and slightly forward and moves in advance of the wrist and hand. The action is similar to that of a baseball pitcher who is in the act of throwing with the arm poised over and behind the head. The elbow is brought forward slightly ahead of the ball, but, as the powerful forearm flexors come into play, the forearm and the hand give a final flip to the ball as it leaves the hand in the followthrough stages. The back stroke swimmer uses the same arm action as the baseball pitcher in order to throw the water to the rear, enabling him to get great speed for the drive. The swimmer's hand describes a letter "S." If swirls appear on the surface during any part of the arm drive, the hand and arm are pulling too shallow. Although the hand does come very close to the surface in this stroke during the forearm whip, the hand in this movement should not break into the surface or pass through the surface water, for it will lose its hold against the water.

At the completion of this drive, the arm and hand finish at the side of the thigh as in the straight arm action. This type of propulsive arm drive should prove to be ideal for the long- and weak-armed individuals. It is a movement that can advance the arm with speed and force through the water in the propulsive phase. Sometimes swimmers are unable to pull a straight arm through the water fast enough during the latter portion of the race when they are fatigued. The bent arm type of drive is then used to advantage.

Release. The hand and fingers complete a whip or push from the wrist

in the final stages of the drive of the arm in both the straight and the bent arm styles. The hands press the water directly backward and downward toward the rear. At the same time that the upper arm and elbow are actually squeezing the water out from between the arm and body, the hand and wrist snap in an attempt to give a final push just before the arm has released its hold on the water. This final whip finish of the hand, arm, and shoulder gives a lifting impetus out of the water quickly and smoothly with the thumb uppermost as the hand breaks through the surface, and moves rapidly into the recovery phase (Fig. 12-2, *B* and *F*).

There are a great many coaches who advocate a feathering motion in the final stages of the drive. This is simply sculling with the hand. The idea is to give the arm a greater propulsive finish to its drive. Some back crawlers employ this sculling motion very skillfully. Whatever is gained in propulsive power is likely to be lost in the additional time it takes to complete the movement. The opposite arm must make up somewhere else the time lost in the stroke revolution. This delay usually takes place in the recovery or the glide.

There is another claim that this sculling of the hand is a supporting movement to the hips and that it holds them at the proper level. A hip sag can be eliminated by maintaining a constant stretch to the body with pressure placed on the arms during the entry and pull phase of the arms and slight emphasis placed on each down beat of the legs. This method gives sufficient support to maintain the hip elevation.

Timing of one arm in relation to the other. In the back crawl stroke there is no independent movement of one arm from the other. It is just like an elementary windmill action. One arm is always directly opposite the other throughout the entire revolution of the arm stroke cycle (Fig. 12-2). Both arms should be even with the shoulder as one is recovering and the other pulling as they pass each other at the shoulder line. As the driving arm arrives at the side of the thigh, the recovery arm enters the water.

If the recovery arm is too slow, the drive of one arm is completed while the recovery hand of the other arm is still in the air. This is a very common error in timing the back crawl stroke, and, when it is violated, the swimmer permits his shoulder to drop and the body to roll toward it.

Another serious error is to permit the arm to pause too long at the side of the body at the completion of the drive. This causes the body to lose momentum as the catch is made, and the body moves along in a jerky manner. As one arm is completing the drive, the recovering arm must be entering the water (Fig. 12-2, *A* and *E*) so that the body drives forward onto the arm entering. One must experience two sensations in swimming the back crawl stroke. As the arm enters the water, one must have the sensation of moving forward on it. Again, when it pulls, one has the sensation of going past the hands.

Pulling the arms too deeply below the surface lessens muscular advantage as well as secures an ineffective purchase on the water with the arm and hand.

Timing the arms and legs. Some back stroke swimmers rely upon the feel of smooth rhythm to judge their timing. Sometimes this method does not give accurate mechanical timing since there may be some part of the stroke deliberately delayed for which some other part must either mark time momentarily or gain time to offset the unbalanced movement.

When this stroke is perfectly timed, the back crawl stroke is performed even smoother than the crawl stroke because there is really nothing to disturb its working parts from a symmetrical balance. This stroke also falls into the category of a fast, executed, turnover type of stroke, the same as do all of the other competitive styles of strokes.

Breathing while swimming the back crawl stroke. While swimming the back crawl stroke, the swimmer will find that breathing is just about as elementary and simple as when walking. However, the traditional method of expiring through the nose and inhaling through the mouth is strictly adhered to. If one should inspire through the nose, he is almost certain of sniffing droplets of water into the throat and causing strangulation. The chance of breathing in through the nose in the back crawl stroke is a chance a swimmer cannot afford to take. One splash of water into the nose may cause the loss of a race as well as some most distressing moments.

In former styles of back stroke recovery techniques, a curtain of water from the arm as it passed over the face caused considerable difficulty. With the present lateral and vertical arm recovery, this water hazard has been eliminated, and breathing can now take place under almost normal conditions except when the swimmer is under water at the turn or start. The tension of the abdominal muscles in the back crawl stroke during the up kick inhibits freedom of action of the diaphragm in breathing for the untrained swimmer. A swimmer who trains daily and increases the daily load of work in proportion to conditioning these abdominal muscles eventually becomes very efficient and permits almost normal breathing, even during strenuous racing.

The number of breaths per length depends upon the individual. For distances of 100 yards or more, breathing every stroke throughout the race is almost essential.

Technique and mechanics of head action in the back crawl stroke. The most stabilizing factor of the entire back crawl stroke is the head position. The head is fixed, with the chin and nose remaining constantly on a central plane, while the body rotates about it on its longitudinal axis, even though the body oscillates slightly from side to side with each arm pull. In order for the head to be maintained in a steady position while the body oscillates during the stroke action, the head action must be isolated from that of the trunk. This is effected by maintaining a relaxed neck. By maintaining the head in a centered position, the body rides on an even keel and is prevented from rolling (Fig. 12-2). It also prevents lateral sway which would move the body out of alignment. The head should lean in the same direction as the line of progression. The swimmer should not look around more than necessary because each change of head position is likely to alter the body position and the timing of the stroke. The inspiration and expiration phases are carried on in a normal way. Inspiration takes place through a wide-open mouth, with the lips curled out away from the teeth. Expiration should be through the nose to prevent strangulation and to maintain the nasal canals clear of water droplets.

Back stroke tumble turn. The reach to the wall is made with a drive under water just as the reaching inverted hand is about 12 to 16 inches from the wall. The head is lowered back with the arm. The hand dives to a depth of about 6 to 10 inches under the surface. The elbow bends so that the head comes close to the wall (Fig. 12-3, *A*). Air is taken just before the head is submerged. The free-arm shoulder is slightly dropped. The body is brought into a very close tuck position, throwing the knees at an angle over the shoulder of the contact arm (Fig. 12-3, *B*). As the knees come over, the body has already half turned around and is nearly flat on its back (Fig. 12-3, *C*). By use of the contact arm on the wall and a sculling motion of the free hand, palm inverted, the remaining half turn of the body is made while at the same time the feet plant themselves against the wall (Fig. 12-3, *D*). The head should incline toward the angle of the knees which is a partially oblique plane. This turn is not a somersault. The head in this turn is a guide and controls the entire turn, especially the placing of the feet on the wall. The body spins directly on its back while tucked. In the tuck, the knees should not spread apart. The body is now in push-off position. The arms are poised ready for the thrust, and the elbows are flexed, palms up, one on either side of the head close to the ears, just over the shoulders. The chin is tucked down toward the throat (Fig. 12-3, *E*). A vigorous drive of the legs is made, while at the same time the arms are thrust out to full extension beyond the head for the coast to the surface (Fig. 12-3, *F*).

This turn is often confused with the somersault turn. The body does not somersault but merely permits the trunk and head to submerge,

Fig. 12-3. A-F, A series of ideal form showing the back stroke tumble turn. **A,** The touch at the wall. **B,** The tuck. **C,** The turn. **D,** The completed turn. **E,** The driving position. **F,** The glide after push-out.

with the trunk remaining in a horizontal plane throughout the entire turn. This turn is called the tumble turn. It is similar in general principles to the touch, tuck, spin, and push with head out as explained in the sprint crawl turn. This turn is the fastest of all the back stroke turns. In approaching the wall for the turn, speed is of utmost importance to flip the turn fast. Coasting to the wall slowly will result in a poorly executed turn.

Finish. A great many sprinting back crawlers make a serious mistake of turning the head to the side when pressed for a close finish. Instead of turning, they should press the head back into the water deeper in the last two or three firm strokes so that the approaching end can be seen over the forehead. This also gives a longer stretch to the body as well as permits the touching arm to drive low over the shoulder to the finish wall or finish curtain. In this manner the swimmer can accurately judge the distance to the finish wall, and the fully extended arm reach can be thrust at the wall with tremendous speed. In this way the swimmer can gain at least a foot advantage in reach over an opponent who remains in swimming position. However, the head should not be lowered earlier than the last two or three arm strokes.

The touch on the finish wall should be made with the fingers reaching downward and the palm of the hand flattened against the wall. This prevents injury to the fingertips.

The back stroker, while in the natural swimming position, is tempted to watch the other competitors in a race. This is wrong because it keeps his mind from concentrating on the number of strokes to the approaching finish. Not only that, but he is not centering the head on its longitudinal axis and will cause his body to flounder from side to side, which loses speed for him when speed is most needed.

Another error often made in approaching the finish is to look for the finish wall over one shoulder. In doing so, the opposite arm will never take the full reach, the stroke is shortened, and rhythm is lost right at the finish where driving speed is absolutely essential. Furthermore, fixing the eyes on the finish wall over one shoulder as he approaches causes him to veer to the opposite side, and the touching hand will reach the wall at an angle to the side of the wall. The head should be centered and lowered, and the hand should reach directly back in line with the spine.

Many swimmers, rely upon markings on the ceiling when swimming in indoor pools. Roped markers should be stretched above the center of each lane for the back stroke races, for both indoor and outdoor races, to aid in guiding back stroke competitors. Surface lane markers should also be of a contrasting color about 10 feet from the end wall as a warning to the back stroker. End walls above the surface should also be of a contrasting color from the surface so that they can be easily distinguished through the water-blurred eyes of a back stroker. A wall that is not easily distinguishable to water-blurred eyes often causes an optical illusion of the wall appearing either farther away or nearer than is actually the case. This causes the swimmer to reach for the finish or turn either too soon or too late, which may mean the loss of a close and hard-fought race.

Back strokers should be constantly trained to keep driving their legs as they are reaching for the finish. They often cease all stroke movements when reaching for the finish. This should never be tolerated in practice. While reaching for the wall and just inches short, the swimmer should hold the finishing arm straight and on the surface as the legs drive him in.

As a general rule, if the reaching arm for the finish is less than 14 inches short of the finish, the arm should lie on the surface, and the swimmer should rely upon the legs to drive him home to the finish. If the fully extended arm is farther than approximately 14 inches away from the finish line, the arm should be pulled through and the other arm driven into the finish wall.

RACING FUNDAMENTALS

Pace. The 100-yard back stroke can be grouped in the sprint event, and, for all purposes of training, the sprint type of training should be followed as discussed in the sprint crawl stroke.

In the 200-yard event, a large amount of endurance combined with speed is essential in competition. The stroke cadence is just slightly slower than that used for the 100 yards. Usually the 100 yards elapsed time on the way to 200 yards varies just from about one to two seconds. It is practically full sprinting effort. A great deal of sprinting, as well as distance endurance swimming, is necessary in training for this race. The standard table (see Table 12-2) for the 200-yard back stroke should be carefully studied in planning for competition. Both the sprint and middle distance techniques of racing fundamentals should also be studied.

A common error of racing in this style is to look over to the side or over the shoulder to watch an opponent. This should be avoided, and, if done at all, the head should again be centered after each glance. When one does glance to the side, the body rides off keel, and the opposite arm does not take its full reach. A back stroker should cultivate a sense of knowing where a rival is with only occasional glances in his direction.

TEACHING AND LEARNING PROCEDURE

The back crawl stroke is demonstrated before the class. The instructor explains the advantages of the stroke and the major characteristics. The instructor then breaks down the stroke into its component parts and teaches them to the class.

Back crawl kick. Land explanation and demonstration are again given by the instructor.

Land drill. The class is seated on the side of the pool with the legs extended over the water. The hands are placed just behind the hips

Table 12-2. Ideal split times for various racing times in the 200-yard back crawl stroke (25-yard pool)

ELAPSED DISTANCE (YD.)	ELAPSED TIME (SEC.)	SPLIT TIME (SEC.)	ELAPSED DISTANCE (YD.)	ELAPSED TIME (SEC.)	SPLIT TIME (SEC.)
25	11.6	11.6	25	13.0	13.0
50	25.2	13.6	50	28.2	15.2
75	39.2	14.0	75	43.6	15.4
100	53.4	14.2	100	59.4	15.8
125	1:07.8	14.4	125	1:15.4	16.0
150	1:22.6	14.8	150	1:31.6	16.2
175	1:37.4	14.8	175	1:47.9	16.3
200	1:52.0	14.6	200	2:04.0	16.1
25	11.8	11.8	25	13.4	13.4
50	25.8	14.0	50	28.9	15.5
75	40.2	14.4	75	44.8	15.9
100	54.8	14.6	100	1:00.8	16.0
125	1:09.6	14.8	125	1:17.2	16.4
150	1:24.8	16.2	150	1:33.8	16.6
175	1:40.0	15.2	175	1:50.5	16.7
200	1:55.0	15.0	200	2:07.0	16.5
25	12.4	12.4	25	13.8	13.8
50	26.6	14.2	50	29.6	15.8
75	41.4	14.8	75	45.8	16.2
100	56.4	15.0	100	1:02.3	16.5
125	1:11.6	15.2	125	1:19.2	16.9
150	1:27.2	15.6	150	1:36.2	17.0
175	1:42.8	15.6	175	1:53.2	17.0
200	1:58.0	15.2	200	2:10.0	16.8
25	12.6	12.6	25	14.2	14.2
50	27.4	14.8	50	30.4	16.2
75	42.5	15.1	75	47.0	16.6
100	57.8	15.3	100	1:03.8	16.8
125	1:13.6	15.8	125	1:21.0	17.2
150	1:29.4	15.8	150	1:38.4	17.4
175	1:45.3	15.9	175	1:55.8	17.4
200	2:01.0	15.7	200	2:13.0	17.2

for support. The legs move up and down from the hips in an alternating action. Emphasis is placed upon keeping the feet and toes pointed in an extended position. The knees bend to facilitate the desired whip action in the legs. The instructor corrects the individual's faulty technique and stresses the positive desired action to the group.

Water drill. The water drill is practiced, using the side of the pool for support. The pupil stands facing away from the side of the pool and leans backward in order to rest the neck on the scum gutter. The hands reach up and grasp the gutter above the shoulders. Elevate the hips to a supine position. Where the side of the pool cannot be utilized, a partner may be used to give the needed support. Half the class executes the kick action while the other half observes a designated partner and offers constructive criticism. The partners change, the teacher becoming the pupil and the pupil acting as a teacher. The instructor moves among the class correcting outstanding faults.

Kick board drill in the water. The pupil is instructed to lie on his back, in the water, holding the kick board on his chest by wrapping both arms over and across the board. The pupil is instructed to bend his knees to assume the above position, lean backward slowly, and place the back of the head and ears into the water. The feet and knees then extend, resulting in a supine floating position with the body supported by the kick board. The drill is continued until all members can make progress across the pool. The instructor devotes most of his attention to the slower students. Any practical floating device may be substituted for the kick board.

Water drill using kick without floating device. The instructor reviews the hand sculling action. The class reviews the use of sculling with a back float, hand sculling just outside the hips and well below the surface. Half of the class attempts to kick approximately 40 yards; using the sculling action of the hands to help maintain a high hip position, just beneath the water surface, is encouraged at this point. Partners observe and offer constructive criticism. The remainder of the class attempts the skill.

Kick 200 yards. At this point the pupil is encouraged to depend only upon the kick for support and forward progress. The hands are held at the sides of the body, arms relaxed. The goal of each student is to complete 200 yards without stopping. If he is forced to stop, he rests momentarily and again continues.

Kick test. The arms are extended and stretched beyond the head, beneath the surface. The hands are held together. The head is lowered so that the chin is on the chest. The pupil attempts to kick 20 or 25 yards in this position.

Back crawl arm action. When the pupil is skilled with the kick to the point at which he can make suitable progress through the water without depending upon the arms for support, he is ready for instruction in the arm action. The straight arm low recovery action is taught to the beginner, because water is less apt to be thrown over his face, and progress is rapid. (See discussion of low arm recovery earlier in this chapter.)

Hand action explanation and demonstration is given by the instructor. Major points such as arm position, recovery, entry, and propulsive force are discussed.

The class, now standing erect, imitates the instructor, slowly going through the arm action. Faulty technique is noted and corrected.

Water instruction by the instructor. The class is assembled about the corner of the pool deck where all can see and hear the instructor. The instructor is supported by a member of the class while demonstrating the arm action.

Water drill. Pupils stand in shoulder depth water, holding the arms out straight to the sides of the shoulders and moving the arms forward and backward in opposition to each other. The pupil is instructed to imagine that a broomstick is held behind the neck and to extend the arms to the sides on the imaginary stick. This gives the student the feeling of moving the arms in opposition to each other, which action is significant in learning the action of the back crawl arm stroke.

Walking backward across the pool. Pupils bend their knees to maintain a neck depth level of the surface. Emphasis is placed upon lifting the shoulders first in the recovery. The elbows are kept straight throughout the entire action. During the entire recovery the palm is held facing the surface, and the head is held still with the chin on dead center.

The student is instructed to breathe regularly, inhaling through the mouth and exhaling through the nose. This skill is repeated until the pupil achieves desired relaxation, coordination, and rhythm.

Whole back crawl stroke. The instructor demonstrates the whole stroke. The body position and timing between arms and legs are stressed.

The student now practices the whole stroke and is encouraged to make as many stroke repetitions in succession as possible before stopping. The student is cautioned not to race the arms ahead of the six-beat kick but to work easy and relaxed.

At this point the instructor gives a great deal of his attention to encourage regular and natural breathing. During most of the learning progression previously discussed, the student has employed very irregular breathing habits. Swimming easy and relaxed will aid the student to breathe normally. He should be taught to inhale through the mouth and exhale through the nose. Nose clips are not recommended.

Chapter 13

Teaching and coaching the breast stroke

The breast stroke was the first of the competitive swimming strokes. Its original form has been altered more than the other strokes. The breast stroke, with all of its newest additions, can now be classified into the following two competitive divisions:

1. The conventional or orthodox breast stroke
2. The dolphin butterfly stroke

CHARACTERISTICS OF BREAST STROKE SWIMMERS

It is difficult to say which type of body build is best suited for the breast stroke. One is able to find all sorts of body builds among championship competitors. This may be due to the fact that the stroke can be readily adapted to any type of build. The technique can be modified for either the tall, medium, or short contestant. In recent years, any one of these types has been able to go to the top in breast stroke swimming.

Physical condition is a prime factor in success in breast stroke competition. A candidate for breast stroke swimming must possess strength, endurance, and a stout heart. The dolphin stroke especially requires a tremendous amount of energy, even for the 100-yard race. The 200-yard event is a race long enough (with the use of the flying stroke) to demand special emphasis on endurance since the problem in the race immediately becomes one of energy distribution. The dolphin butterfly stroke employs muscles of the back which are not commonly brought into play. Thus months of training are necessary to develop the heavy back musculature needed in the dolphin butterfly stroke.

TECHNIQUES OF THE BREAST STROKE START

The various stances and techniques of the take-off described for the crawl stroke start also apply to the breast stroke start. *Deep breathing* while the swimmer stands ready to take his mark is especially important in the breast stroke since the first stroke of the race is swum under water. Three or four deep breaths will enable the swimmer to hold his breath much longer without discomfort.

Line of flight. There are some authorities who recommend a slightly higher line of flight than that used in the crawl stroke start. They recommend that the head be lower and the arms dipped for a deeper entry than that used for crawl stroke starts. Caution should be used in deviating too far from the traditional line of flight used for the crawl stroke start; otherwise, penetrating power is lost.

Another method of attaining a deeper glide is to adopt a slightly sharper downward angle of flight than is used in the crawl stroke start. The slightly sharper downward angle of flight is the most generally adopted method for the breast stroke start.

Entry. The entry, in all respects except that of the angle, is exactly as described for the crawl stroke as far as position concerning the arms, head, body, and legs. The angle of entry is slightly deeper than in the crawl stroke start because of the fact that a full stroke is permitted under water. Where the dolphin stroke is to be used, all "flyers" will immediately come swimming to the surface on the first arm stroke after the entry. In this case the angle of entry as well as the line of flight through the air should be like that of the sprinting start used in the crawl stroke.

Glide under water. The body, whether the glide is shallow or deep, should be maintained in a straight position from the fingertips to the toes. Preserving this body alignment at the point of entry and throughout the glide depends largely upon the action and position of the head. The head should be held between the arms and low, with the chin tucked in. This position will do a great deal to streamline the swimmer's body and will offer the least resistance while keeping the body at proper depth.

Since the breast stroke is the slowest of all the competitive strokes, it is essential to get all the speed advantage possible from the start. The body will glide with less resistance beneath the surface than on the surface. Therefore, the swimmer can make greater speed by remaining under water on his first stroke. The breast stroke swimmer is now limited in the two styles of breast stroke competition to one complete stroke under water at either the start or after the push-off of the turns. The purpose of this rule is to keep the swimmer on the surface.

Swimmers differ as to physical contour and have different resistances to water. Some swimmers have low water resistance and slip through the water without any apparent slowing down during the glide after the start, after the push-out from the turn, and during the glide following a stroke. Others with higher resistance may drive just as powerfully but seem to drag down to a stop as if brakes were applied. A swimmer who has slow speed in the glide under water should be carefully checked with the watch to study accurately just where the starting momentum has subsided to a swimming speed and where he should begin to swim. As the swimmer progresses under water, he should gradually bear upward so the angle is not too abrupt as he strokes to the surface. He should never lie much deeper than 2 feet before the break to the surface is made.

Technique, mechanics, and timing of the underwater stroke. The underwater breast stroke is discussed here for purposes of class instruction. (See N.C.A.A. and A.A.U. rules.) The underwater breast stroke differs in technique and mechanics from that generally used on the surface. The essential difference between the underwater and the surface stroke is in the length of the arm pull. On the surface, the hands and arms are not pulled very far beyond the line of the shoulders in the traditional breast stroke. If they are pulled fully beyond the shoulders, the hands no longer can hold the body and head well up out of the water. This will cause the head to drop below the swimming level of the surface, and the swimmer will bob excessively. While the swimmer is under water, this is not true. The arms can be pulled all the way back to the hips and still not alter body balance.

The full arm pull may be executed in two ways:

1. The arms may be pulled by sweeping them laterally and holding the arms almost entirely straight. The arms should not be pulled downward because the downward press would push the body up toward the surface. During the lateral sweep of the arms, they should actually pull slightly below the line of the body so that at the finish of the pull the hands are actually pressing upward, which aids in pressing the shoulders and head downward and helps to maintain the body in its straight course. The body, while submerged, usually tends to float upward due to buoyancy. The swimmer must acquire skill with the hands in order to maintain the proper plane of the palms throughout the arm drive and to cause the body to remain under the water in a straight line of progress.

2. The second method, which is more generally used, is to pull the arms with the elbows bent in a boomerang position. The upper arm is carried almost in a horizontal line with the shoulder, and the forearm is directed vertically downward and inward. In this movement, the hands start the action with a quick digging hold of the water, and from there the arm drive is continued. The forearms press outward slightly, and, when they arrive almost in line with the shoulders, a transition takes place from a pull action to a swift push or driving inward action to the hips. The arms finish alongside the hips, fully extended, with palms upward. Here the arms drift momentarily during a brief glide

on the momentum gained from the powerful arm stroke. The arms should be permitted to drift in this position, but not too tightly to the body, so that the water can wash and flow down the arms and sides of the body freely. If the arms are held too close to the body, the water is pocketed between the arm and body and thus increases resistance. The arms should drag in line with the back. During this arm pull, the legs are held straight but relaxed and slightly spread so that the water freely washes down the legs without interference from turbulence between the legs.

The legs remain straight while the arms start the recovery movement. In the recovery of the arms, the elbows are bent, and the arms slide closely along the under side of the body to a point under the chest or chin where both hands join palms down. This movement continues uninterrupted, and the arms thrust forward to the fully extended gliding position.

The recovery of the legs begins just as the hands are about to join under the chest. The legs should recover in a fairly rapid movement with not too much of a drag, or the timing point with that of the arm thrust is likely to be missed. The leg drive should be executed when the arms are not quite, but almost, fully extended in the forward thrust. The arm pull starts as the legs begin their drive so that both arms and legs act together. The legs thrust and whip in their propulsive drive. At the completion of the leg drive the body again glides momentarily from the momentum gained from the leg drive. The leg drive, as well as the arm drive, is an individual unit of power in the underwater stroke. Some swimmers prefer the arm pull to begin almost immediately upon the completion of the leg drive, or as soon as the legs have closed from the kick.

Surfacing. There are two essentials to bear in mind in breaking to the surface:

1. The body should be at the proper depth below the surface of the water just before the breakthrough. If the body is too deep, the angle which the body must make to reach the surface in one stroke is too sharp, and the forward speed will be decreased. Additional loss of speed from rising at too abrupt an angle comes from expending forward motion when the body shoots above the swimming level. This deviation from good form will also force the legs too deep for good propulsion on the first kick.

2. The break to the surface should be initiated by the kick, not the arm pull. This is accomplished in the following way: When the arms are thrust forward from under the chin, they should be directed at a slight angle toward the surface. At the same time the head is raised, and the legs drive the body upward. However, when the body arrives

at the surface, it should be sliding forward, not upward. When the legs drive the body to the surface, the arms are already placed in pulling position. This method prevents any break in forward motion which would cause the legs to lose traction. According to all present competitive rules, the start of the second arm pull must not occur until the head has surfaced.

TECHNIQUES OF THE ORTHODOX BREAST STROKE

General position of the body. The position of the body in the orthodox breast stroke in the water does not differ essentially from that described in the crawl stroke. The body must be maintained in a streamlined stretch, but at the same time in a comfortably relaxed position. This is controlled principally by the position of the head. During the glide phase of the stroke the head should be held comfortably well up and maintained there (Fig. 13-1, *A*). This is especially difficult for individuals who have short necks. The head in this position is in front of the center of weight of the body and in this position will tend to balance the legs over the center of weight.

Classification of leg kicks. Many attempts to improve the orthodox breast stroke kick have been made in order to keep it abreast with the arms. Rather than relying upon the traditional kick which consists of

Fig. 13-1. A-F, A series of ideal form for executing the orthodox breast stroke. **A,** The legs are closing, and the arm pull is started. **B,** The head is lifting to clear mouth for air. **C,** Both arms and legs begin the recovery at the completion of taking air.

a wide knee spread and wide whiplash of the legs, new methods have been devised. The knee spread has been narrowed, the heels have been lifted, and the downward thrust has been executed in a circular motion. Many variations are used.

The variations of the kicks were naturally developed because of anatomic limitations of breast stroke swimmers. Some swimmers are naturally crotch bound, which prevents a wide knee or leg spread. Others are very flexible and supple and possess a wide lateral range of leg movement. It was formerly believed that the wider the spread of the legs, the greater was the propulsive force which could be obtained because more water could be squeezed out from between the legs while completing the leg drive. However, this theory was discredited when crotch-bound swimmers with a narrow knee and leg spread seemed to get as much, and in some cases more, propulsive drive from this narrow thrusting drive than did others using the wide whipping drive.

Coaches now generally select the type of kicks to be used according to the physical attributes of the individual; that is, the height, strength, and build determine the general type of kick to be used.

The short-legged, rugged individual may rely upon the wide whiplash and squeeze type of kick. This lateral sweeping leg drive is a very

Fig. 13-1, cont'd. D, The hands are preparing for the forward thrust, and the legs are preparing for the leg drive. The feet should be well spread. **E,** The ideal timing position to start the leg drive in relation to the arm thrust forward. **F,** The arms are in the downhill coasting position, and the legs are completing the drive.

mechanically weak position because one can only rely upon a weak group of muscles to sweep the legs together. Some coaches have advocated rotating the legs outward by turning the feet outward during the kick phase so that the swimmer could bring stronger muscles into play. A long, broad foot on a short-legged individual gives him a decided advantage. However, a long foot is seldom seen on a short leg. The modern trend is away from the wide knee spread and toward the narrow knee spread because of a lessened resistance in spreading the knees.

The tall swimmers with long legs and long, broad feet should not adopt the squeeze kick. If this type of individual spreads his legs wide, the lever is too long and thus too weak. The legs should be drawn up toward the pelvis instead of spreading them, and then a thrust, or screw type of kick, is made with the forelegs followed by the extension of the long feet. This narrow knee spread and heel lift permit the long-legged swimmer to take advantage of a shorter mechanical lever; he is then able to execute the drive faster, more powerfully, and more efficiently.

The third classification is for the individual of medium height and build. This kick is a combination of the two types described and has as a basis a modified and limited spread of the knees, so that a powerful thrust can be executed, combined with a snap or squeeze to complete the drive of the legs. This type of kick is powerful and is most generally used by the average swimmer. All of the preceding kicks should be executed quickly and powerfully.

Orthodox kick. This kick may be used most efficiently by swimmers with short, powerful legs. The kick is started from a moderate spread of the knees. Both legs are rotated outward so that the feet turn out and remain extended so that the soles of the feet almost face each other (Fig. 13-1, *C*). The knees are spread wide, and, as the heels are drawn outward to a spread, they are drawn as closely as possible toward the hips (Fig. 13-1, *E*). There should be a continuous rapid-action recovery and leg drive. From this position, the feet may either be drawn out as far as possible or partially turned out, and the toes flexed toward the knees so that, as the thrust is being made, the soles of the feet immediately engage the water (Fig. 13-1, *F*). Just prior to the knees becoming fully extended, the thighs are driven and squeezed together. The feet extend fully during this whip phase. This movement, if accurately timed, gives a tremendous propulsive whiplash to the legs. The squeeze or snap of the legs should continue from the whiplash, so that the feet do not lose hold of the water. Too often in this kick, swimmers do not follow through in this squeeze movement but instead permit the legs to drift together, and therefore the kick loses some of its effectiveness. As speed is reduced, force is lost. The kick is performed with a thrust, whip, and squeeze. As the legs close, they should relax and drift slightly apart. There is a counteraction from the end of the down kick which gives the swimmer a feeling of lift of the legs to the surface.

Narrow kick. This kick corrects for weak mechanical advantage in swimmers with long legs. Its action is to recover the knees using a narrow spread. The thighs are pressed down while the legs and heels are drawn, just under the surface, toward the hips. The heels are drawn up to the outside of the hips. Here the toes and feet are turned outward and immediately go into a quick outward and inward circular thrust, with the thighs snapping together just prior to the knees being fully extended. This entire kick is executed from a narrow knee spread. This type of kick not only corrects for the wide knee spread with a poor mechanical advantage but also permits the legs to force the water back along the longitudinal axis of propulsion.

A variation in this kick in the propulsive phase or drive phase may be made. Instead of driving the legs and feet outward and inward in a circular motion, they are driven and directed downward, and the thighs are driven backward and together just prior to the full extension of the knees. This gives the knees a rotation inward and an upward movement, giving the foot a screw-drive effect. The down drive, theoretically, gives greater resisting force against the foot, whereas in the backward inward snap of the thighs and knees the powerful hamstring extensors spring into action to assist the thigh adductor group of muscles. Caution must be exercised in manipulating the feet on the downward thrust so that the toes are turned down and drawn toward the knees when the legs are "cocked," so that the soles of the feet engage the water on the downward action of the feet. This type of kick gives the leg action a vertical range of movement as well as a lateral range. This kick is very effective in propulsion, especially if the swimmer is endowed with a long, broad pair of feet and powerful legs.

Modified narrow kick. Swimmers with medium long legs will do best to maintain a moderately narrow kick. The recovery of the legs is similar to the recovery in the short-legged individual, except that the feet and the knees are not turned out nearly as wide. The heels are drawn up very close toward the hips and well spread. From this point the feet are turned out, and the outward circular thrust is made. The motion is a circumduction with the hip joint as the axis. The water is engaged at the start of the thrust with the inside of the foot as the knee begins to extend. Before the knees are fully extended, they execute an inward and backward snap, giving a simultaneous whip to each leg, which gives tremendous propulsive power.

In all types of kicks, a common error is to draw the knees too far forward. The most effective results from the breast stroke kick are obtained by not flexing the thighs upon the pelvis farther than approximately a 45-degree angle with the spine. This limitation streamlines the thighs and causes the water to slide under the legs as they are drawn up.

The heels and feet should be drawn up as closely to the line of the hips as is anatomically possible. The feet there are able to engage the water nearer to the line of the hips. In this way, the feet are able to hold and push the water over a longer range, giving the legs a greater area for propulsive pressure against the water during the leg drive. Too many swimmers are likely to kick the feet diagonally back, rather than pressing the feet directly out from the hips, before the backward thrust is delivered.

The legs are drawn up quite rapidly and immediately start the thrust.

Orthodox arm stroke action. The arms pull simultaneously in a lateral, downward, and backward movement. From an extended position in front of the face the arms are pulled to a point under the upper chest. Here the hands join each other and are thrust forward to the starting position. The entire movement is continuous and uninterrupted. In the traditional arm stroke, the hands should never pull more than a few inches beyond the shoulder line. Most top-flight breast stroke swimmers, for the shorter sprint events, use a very short arm pull, to a point just ahead of the chin, and a very narrow, fast, leg kick, in order to obtain a faster stroke turnover for greater speed. If the hands are pulled too far beyond the shoulder line, the support is taken from under the shoulders and head, and the body sinks, causing body balance to be destroyed. When the hands release pressure upon the water, they should relax.

Press-catch with arms and hands. The catch begins from the glide position (Fig. 13-1, *A*). The arms are extended in front of the face at a depth of 4 to 6 inches below the surface. The catch is initiated with the arms stretched forward and the fingertips and hands turned downward. The wrists flex slightly in a quickened movement. At the same time, the shoulders lift in an attempt to get the shoulders over the forearms and behind the press and pull so that the water level at the face is not changed.

Pull and push. The pull is very similar to the crawl stroke pull except the movement in the breast stroke is made laterally as well as downward in a semicircular movement. The path of both hands may best be described as drawing the upper half of an elongated letter O. The fingers should direct the path of the arms. The catch begins by a quick press and pull outward and downward of both hands and forearms. At the same time the shoulder blades rotate forward, giving the arm tremendous mechanical advantage in the shoulder arm-push position while the arms are still well in front, but at 8 to 15 inches in depth. Both arms give lateral balance and support to each shoulder, and the center of body weight is not altered. While both arms are pressing and pulling, the shoulders tend to be lifted out of the water (Fig. 13-1, *B*). The lift should be minimized and converted into forward motion along the surface.

The pull phase of the breast stroke is of short duration and really is a continuation of the press-and-catch movement. It is during the press-and-catch movement that the shoulders adjust themselves for the push phase. The press-and-catch draws and lifts the body. The movement must be a quick and forceful action of the hands and forearms. In order to perform this with skill, an active, flexible, strong wrist joint is absolutely essential.

The hand must have freedom of movement while in the water. During the press-and-pull phase the hand should be slightly flexed at the wrist in order to hold the water against the arms. Some water is allowed to wash down the arm to give greater planing resistance against the arms. If the arms pull with the wrist set at a slight angle, a greater resistance is obtained by deflecting the water from the heel of the hand toward the fingertips. With the wrist cocked at an angle of 20 degrees, the wrist flexor muscles have a good mechanical advantage during the catch-and-pull phase. The wrist straightens as the shoulders move forward to get in front of the hands and arms. Although the swimmer does not actually anchor the arms in the water and then draw the body over them, he appears to do so. The swimmer should not be misled by this appearance and strive merely to set the arms in the water. He must actually pull and drive them through the water so that water will slip off the arm and form suction swirls behind the hands and arms which give traction with the water. With a quick movement of the hands at the catch, swirls form which give greater propulsive efficiency earlier in the stroke. The water pressure should be felt in the palm. The fingers should not be flattened to full extension but to a very slight saucer shape. This gives greater strength to the fingers and is less fatiguing. During the catch-and-pull phase of the stroke, the arms should be spread downward, until the hands have reached a depth of 14 to 16 inches. At this depth the arms are still ahead of the shoulder line, and maximum propulsive force has been attained.

There is a great deal of difference of opinion as to how the arms should complete the push phase and the recovery. There are two generally recognized methods. In one, the elbows spread wide, and the hands pull in under the elbow and toward the chest wall, followed by an elbow squeeze toward the body. The other method is to pull the elbows back and toward the body with the hands and forearms following the elbows. Those favoring the first method rely chiefly upon the rotator muscles of the upper arm and the forearm flexors to assist the rotators in driving the forearm downward and inward. When the arms are on a line with shoulders, the upper arm and elbow are then squeezed in to the under side of the chest wall. The hands follow, planing at an angle and pressing against the water.

Those favoring the latter method advocate a flexed elbow leading the arm in a movement backward and inward to the underside of the upper chest wall. Here the pulling force is not from the weaker upper arm rotators but from the powerful arm depressors. In both movements, the elbows begin to flex early in the catch-pull phase of the stroke and increase in flexion as the drive continues through its maximum depth and to the completion of the arm stroke under the chest. The theory is advanced that in the wide-spread elbow technique there is more arm surface area presented against the water. To offset the weakness of the muscles brought into action in the movement, the swimmer should train to strengthen these muscles.

Swimming speed can be increased by shifting from a wide lateral arm movement to a more downward movement to get the arms under the body. Speed is also the chief objective in breast stroke competitive swimming. To obtain greater speed in this, the slowest of all the competitive strokes, the range of hand and arm movement is shortened, and the hands take on an appearance of sculling in a horizontal plane to obtain faster turnover speed of the entire stroke cycle.

Release and recovery. The pull phase in the breast stroke is actually completed when the hands have released backward pressure, which occurs when the hands arrive at the upper chest wall. This release is accomplished with a wrist whip, and the hand rotates upon the wrist joint, forcing the water to the rear. The hands are then relaxed and recovered to a point under the chest. This is a common method of release and recovery. A more skilled method is to continue the press of the hands at the end of the push toward a point near the chest, still pressing the water down and back and then releasing the pressure and cocking the wrists so that the fingers point forward from under the chin, palms down. Although the movement is one of recovery, the hands actually do not release the pressure of the water while they complete the elongated letter O.

Arm thrust. The thrust is a continuation of the release and the recovery. There must be no separate motion of release, recovery, and thrust. It must be continuous. At the beginning of the thrust, the hands are aligned together under the chin, palms down and the elbows close to the sides of the chest (Fig. 13-1, *D*). The thrust should be as streamlined as possible, with the least amount of resistance offered by the elbows and the shoulders. In some swimmers less resistance is obtained if the hands are separated from 3 to 6 inches during the thrust and glide.

This depends upon the physical characteristics of the individual swimmer.

When the arms are being thrust forward, they should be moved rather quickly at an upward angle, but not thrust out of the surface or even close to it (Fig. 13-1, *E*). When the arms are nearly fully extended, downward pressure should be made upon the hands and forearms. They glide deeper and cause the body to slide downhill. The whole technique is as if an obstruction such as a partially submerged log is lying across the path of the swimmer, and he guides his hands up and over the submerged log and coasts down on the other side.

Arms in glide position. The glide position of the arms may be made with the hands aligned together or with the hands apart (Fig. 13-1, *A*). Under no condition should the arms become so relaxed that the elbows assume a slight bend and the hands and forearms fail to press slightly to afford a planing surface to the upper part of the body. If the arms are permitted to spread, water will be carried along between the arms and against the head and cause considerable resistance to the forward gliding motion. The arms should remain comfortably straight, so that water washes down the arms in a straight path and passes on underneath the chest wall to the rear. At the end of the glide and just prior to the catch for the next stroke, the hands should be submerged 3 to 6 inches in depth.

Timing the arm action to synchronize with the leg kick action in the orthodox breast stroke. There are two types of timing to be used, depending upon whether a wide or narrow knee spread is being used.

Timing of the wide knee-spread kick. The arms pull lateral to the shoulders; then the legs recover (Fig. 13-1, *B*). The arms then recover to a point under the chin and go immediately into the thrust (Fig. 13-1, *D*). While the arms are recovering, the legs are spreading and turning the feet out, poised for the leg drive. When the arms are almost fully extended in the thrust, the leg drive is made (Fig. 13-1, *E*). The start of the leg recovery in the stroke must be fast. There must be no hesitation or slowing down between the leg spread and the leg drive.

Timing in the narrow knee-spread kick. The difference in timing in the narrow knee spread and the wide knee spread is that it does not take so long to recover the legs in the narrow spread as it does in the wide knee spread. Therefore, in order to coordinate with the arm stroke, the knees should not be recovered until the hands are recovered to the front and lateral side of the head or the chest wall. The drive of the legs is made at the same time in the arm thrust as in the wide knee spread. The legs lift up into the recovery very quickly, and this movement can be executed while the arms move from the chest wall to the proper point in the arm thrust.

When a swimmer with a wide kick attempts to learn a kick with a narrow knee spread, he must readjust the timing of the recovery of the legs in relation to the arm recovery. Otherwise, difficulty will be experienced in the timing of the stroke.

In both types of kicks, the arms should remain in the glide position until the legs have closed from the kick. Then the catch in the next stroke may be started immediately after the legs close for a sprinting type of stroke. For longer distances, more time may be consumed in the glide position after the legs have closed, depending upon the individual's strength and condition.

In short races the swimmer uses a quick, narrow kick with a quick pull following the kick, almost entirely eliminating the traditional glide following the stroke. Top-flight breast strokers no longer depend upon a resting glide but train and condition themselves to eliminate as much of the glide as possible in order to acquire great speed. He, therefore, naturally speeds up his stroke, not only by shortening the glide, but also by speeding up the execution of both arm and leg action. The quick spread of the knees is narrow so that the legs may execute the kick movement as fast as the arms execute the arm movement of the stroke. This quickened kick movement has geared up the orthodox stroke to a higher speed level. This geared-up ratio tends to give the orthodox breast stroke an almost continuous propulsive action, rather than single units of power delivered at intervals in series. The entire stroke must have a rapid turnover. Usually one who uses a long glide will start the arm pull slowly as a means of gathering himself to deliver a powerful leg stroke. This slower gathering-up phase has been discarded, and instead more strokes per length of pool are used.

Timing of the head action in breathing for the orthodox breast stroke. Generally there are two types of timing of the head action used to synchronize and balance the arm and leg action.

1. The better method is to elevate the chin for air as the arms go into a stretch-and-press action, and, by the time the mouth has cleared the surface, the arms go into the catch-and-pull. The head must be maintained high after air has been taken and must remain on the surface throughout the race except at the start and turns. This tends to ride the body high on the surface and prevents it from bobbing up and down, thus reducing resistance.

2. The second method is delaying the head lift in the arm pull. The chin is lifted for air after the arms have passed well back beyond the catch to about the point where the pull ends and the push begins. Unless one is skillful, this delayed head action causes the body to lift out of the water too high and to unbalance the arm and leg action. Considerable motion will be wasted. In the action of lifting the chin for

breathing, the level of the body should be kept as nearly constant as possible. The body should remain in alignment with the level of the water and the forward plane of progress.

The head is not lifted backward, but the mouth is drawn forward to the air above the surface (Fig. 13-1, *B*). When the eyes appear above the surface, they should focus on the surface in front of the mouth and be on guard for any choppy movement. The mouth is opened, and, simultaneously with the opening, air should be gasped quickly. The mouth may be opened with the lower lip extended forward beyond the upper lip, curled out to ward off wavelets around the mouth on the surface. Another method of opening the mouth is to catch the tip of the tongue behind the lower front teeth and then "belly" the tongue forward into the mouth opening, leaving a narrow opening above the bulge of the tongue and the upper lip.

A most frequent and common error in lifting the head for air is to lift it backward out of the water, as if trying to press the ball of the head back between the shoulder blades. This faulty head movement is very detrimental to both forward progression and body balance. The head should be moved toward the line of progress, not against it.

Very often a swimmer will pull the arms too slowly during the press-catch-and-pull to accommodate the head lift in getting air. This slow arm action at the inception of the arm stroke retards accurate mechanical timing in stroke performance. In practice, a quick and independent head action should be stressed, especially in the longer distance workouts. The longer the distance of workout, the more a fault is liable to be practiced.

Another common error is usually developed in slow long distance workouts. This is a "frozen" wrist joint. A wrist joint should be flexible and sensitive at all times to the pressure of the water.

Coaching methods and techniques used for daily practices. The following land and water drills, used in daily practices, aid in the development of arm and leg action.

For the development of the leg action. Four methods of leg development are suggested to be used. One is Danish gymnastics for stretching the ankle ligaments and stretching the crotch muscles. Abdominal muscles should be strengthened as well as the back extensors by using body-bending and leg-lifting exercises and wall weights. Second, the heavy kicking board should be used early in the season and continued throughout the season with the load increased or decreased as the leg strength and skill develop. Some swimmers can perform the kick without the kicking board by holding the arms extended beyond the head. For other swimmers this position arches the back too much and therefore should not be practiced without the board. Breast strokers should also use a type of fast kicking movement by whipping the legs continuously without a pause at any point. This improves the leg flexibility. The third method is to use an elastic check rope and belt. This can be made from several bicycle inner tubes, with one end fixed to a rope attached to a belt at the swimmer's waist and the other end fastened to a wall. The swimmer then kicks against this resistance. The fourth method is to practice the dolphin breast stroke kick which will aid in maintaining a limber, supple back and rubbery legs.

For the development of the arm action. Here again land drills may be used as a way of stretching shoulder joints and strengthening arm and shoulder muscles by use of weights and wall weights. The use of the elastic check rope and belt is perhaps the best method for conditioning the arms. The breast stroker should develop himself until he is sturdy and rugged. The hands should not flatten to a hyperextension of the fingers during the press and propulsive phase, nor should the fingers be over-cupped. The fingers and the wrist joints should be slightly bent in flexion to give the finger, hand, and wrist flexor muscles a greater mechanical advantage, especially during the press-catch-and-pull phase of the stroke. This position of the hand and arms also gives proper tonus to the arm muscles and thus delays fatigue as late as possible in the race. Special attention should be given to keeping the neck relaxed. Tension on the neck muscles will cause early fatigue which will spread quickly to the other muscles of the shoulder girdle group.

Breast stroke turn. The breast stroke turn consists of the approach to the wall, tuck, turn, push-off, glide, and stroke.

Approach to the wall. A swimmer must drive into a turn, not coast in slowly. Momentum gathered must be utilized to carry the body well up to the wall and for the tuck and turn. The swimmer should come into the wall with his hands about 4 to 8 inches apart. The head is lowered just before the hands contact the wall. The hands are placed flat on the wall, with the fingers turned up and slightly projecting above the surface. The elbows bend until the head almost touches the wall.

Tuck. The tuck of the legs is made simultaneously with the bending of the elbows. With a slight sideward pressure of the hands the hips are turned laterally.

Turn. The head may either snap up for air or remain entirely under water as the turn is made. For sprinting events of 50 to 100 yards, the head should remain under. For greater distances, the head should lift out, and the mouth should be turned to the side to get air. The upper back should rise during the first half of the turn. If the turn is to the left, the left arm is jerked away from the wall and assists in the spin by a scooping motion across the chest. It then meets the other hand which has been on the wall and is now on its way forward. The body

turns at a point slightly less than an arm's length away from the wall. When all these movements are timed perfectly, the body first rises slightly then sinks in rhythm for the push-off.

Push-off. The feet are set against the wall just as in the crawl push-off. The feet and knees are set at a hip-width position against the wall. The knees are then extended, and the body is stiffened. Simultaneously with the drive of the legs against the wall, the hands, which have joined under the chin after assisting in the turn, are now thrust forward simultaneously with the push-off. The body is directed forward

Table 13-1. Ideal split times for various racing times in the 200-yard breast stroke (25-yard pool)

ELAPSED DISTANCE (YD.)	ELAPSED TIME (SEC.)	SPLIT TIME (SEC.)	ELAPSED DISTANCE (YD.)	ELAPSED TIME (SEC.)	SPLIT TIME (SEC.)
25	12.4	12.4	25	14.8	14.8
50	28.0	15.6	50	33.0	18.2
75	43.8	15.8	75	51.4	18.4
100	1:00.0	16.2	100	1:10.0	18.6
125	1:16.2	16.2	125	1:28.6	18.6
150	1:32.6	16.4	150	1:47.5	18.9
175	1:49.0	16.4	175	2:06.6	19.1
200	2:05.0	16.0	200	2:25.0	18.4
25	13.0	13.0	25	15.6	15.6
50	29.0	16.0	50	34.2	18.6
75	45.6	16.6	75	53.2	19.0
100	1:02.4	16.8	100	1:12.4	19.2
125	1:19.2	16.8	125	1:31.8	19.4
150	1:36.3	17.1	150	1:51.2	19.4
175	1:53.4	17.1	175	2:10.8	19.6
200	2:10.0	16.6	200	2:30.0	19.2
25	13.6	13.6	25	16.4	16.4
50	30.4	16.8	50	35.4	19.0
75	47.6	17.2	75	55.1	19.7
100	1:05.0	17.4	100	1:15.0	19.9
125	1:22.4	17.4	125	1:35.0	20.0
150	1:40.0	17.6	150	1:55.0	20.0
175	1:57.8	17.8	175	2:15.2	20.2
200	2:15.0	17.2	200	2:35.0	19.8
25	14.2	14.2	25	17.2	17.2
50	31.6	17.4	50	37.2	20.0
75	49.4	17.8	75	57.4	20.2
100	1:07.4	18.0	100	1:17.8	20.4
125	1:25.4	18.0	125	1:38.2	20.4
150	1:43.8	18.4	150	1:58.8	20.6
175	2:02.0	19.0	175	2:19.6	20.8
200	2:20.0	18.0	200	2:40.0	20.4

and slightly upward, so that the head will break the surface before starting the second arm pull.

Glide and stroke. In the glide the body should remain absolutely straight from fingertips to extended toes. The back should not be arched. The head should be held low between the arms. The arms may be held together at the thumbs or separated, depending upon the individual. Legs also may be slightly separated or held together. Anything which causes resistance to forward progression should be minimized.

Finish. In general, the finish is no different from the approach to the wall in the turn. However, in a close finish when the swimmers' heads are even and it looks like a tie or dead heat, one swimmer may be going into the pull of another stroke while the other swimmer is thrusting the arms forward in the recovery. The latter will appear to finish first. The one who is approximately an arm's length away from the finish at the end of the glide has the disadvantage because he cannot afford to coast in, even with the head low, since most of this momentum is already spent. He must, therefore, outwit his competitor and effect a quick catch of the hands and thrust for the finish without the kick. A full stroke would use up too much time and pull his head too close to the finish mark, and he would arrive at the finish with the hand touch too late to win the race. In this situation, the swimmer should accurately measure the remaining distance to the finish in terms of strokes with the head held high and the eyes having clear vision to the wall, so that, when his body has arrived close enough to the wall, with the last arm thrust he hits the finish at full arm extension. The head should be held up even though air is not taken during the last two or three strokes. The swimmer should not turn the head to the side and watch his competitor as the finish is approaching. He should look straight ahead at the finish.

TEACHING AND LEARNING PROCEDURES

The stroke is explained and demonstrated before the class. The instructor then breaks down the stroke into its component parts. He explains, demonstrates, and teaches each part to the class.

Breast stroke kick. Land explanation and demonstration are given by the instructor. (See discussion of kick earlier in this chapter.)

Land drill. It is difficult to give land drill for this kick unless canvas backless stools are available.

Demonstration in the water. The instructor demonstrates the kick after he has demonstrated the whole stroke before the class. In his explanation and demonstration he emphasizes the following:

1. The amount of knee spread in the recovery of the kick; that is, if narrow or wide spread is to be used

2. How far to flex the thigh upon the hip joint in relation to the body during the recovery phase

3. When and where to cock the ankles; that is, flexing the feet toward the knee joint just prior to the leg drive

4. During the kick phase, how to drive the thighs together before knee joints are fully extended (This technique, if executed properly, with fairly relaxed legs, results in the desired whiplash of the leg drive.)

5. That the kick is the major propulsive function of the entire stroke, not the arms

Water drill. The water drill is first practiced using the side of the pool for support. This phase of the drill gives best results if the partner system is used. The partner stands just in back of the performer's legs in order to best give aid with hands to correct faulty movements.

Another good teaching method is for the instructor to place himself on a deck stool, in view of the entire class, supported at the sides of the pool, following and imitating the kick movements of the instructor. He may use the count system if desired. For example, on count 1, he drags the legs slowly during the recovery phase so that the class is able to follow. On count 2, the heels are separated, and the ankles cocked. On count 3, the drive is executed. On count 4, the legs are held together straight for a definite pause.

Kick board drill. When the kick is sufficiently learned at the side of the pool, the kick board is employed for best results because the swimmer is able to breathe above the surface and continue practice of the kicks over a longer period of time. One after another, flight waves can be sent across the pool in rapid sequence. This drill is performed with the face out of water.

As the class progresses, the breathing skill can now be added as the flights move across the pool. The instructor demonstrates when and how breathing is executed in the stroke. (See discussion of breathing earlier in this chapter.) The face is lowered and raised in and out of the water, between extended arms supported on the kick board and just behind the board. Air is inhaled during leg recovery and expired during leg drive and glide during the pause of the kick after completion.

Another skill can be added to the kick and breathing, that of using the arms with the aid of the kick board. This is performed by drawing the kick board down under the chin while the legs are executing the recovery phase. During this movement the face is lifted out of the water, and air is inhaled. As the drive of the legs is now executed, the arms thrust the board forward to the starting position, while the face is again lowered and air is expired during the glide phase. At the completion of this entire exercise, the pause and glide received from the impetus

of the kick are stressed by the instructor. This exercise is given to prepare the student for the whole stroke coordination. This exercise is very helpful to the student, since the whole stroke coordination of the breast stroke is very difficult for most students to grasp. It is therefore very essential that the student is well schooled in the kick and performing the preceding preliminary coordinating exercise. Too much emphasis cannot be placed on overlearning the kick.

Arm stroke water drill. The arm stroke is again explained and demonstrated by the instructor as the class is gathered about him in a large circle in waist-deep water. In this formation the class will bend down to the water level and imitate the instructor going slowly through the movements of the hands and arms. After sufficient practice by the class, flights are formed to walk slowly across the pool, taking one step forward as the arms are executing the forward movement from under the chin. After a pause the arms then pull sideward and downward to shoulder level in the propulsive phase. As the recovery and arm thrust are again executed, the second step forward is taken. This exercise of both arm and leg movements gives the student the sensation of a glide which is so greatly desired in the learning of the whole stroke.

The breathing skill can be added to this drill as the class progresses. (See discussion of breathing technique.)

Whole stroke drill. If no supports are being used, the class can lie on the surface, face down in the water, and attempt to execute three or four strokes without a breath.

Some instructors favor a partner system, with the partner in front, catching the hands of the performing partner at the end of each stroke. He holds the hands momentarily to emphasize the glide at the end of the stroke.

Other instructors favor supports placed under the body as an aid, without partners. This method is advantageous, because then the student can move all the way across the pool without a stop. Regardless of which system is used, the student is constantly urged to take as many unhurried stroke repetitions as possible without a stop. To obtain best results in this phase of learning the coordination of the stroke, supports as an aid are highly recommended.

Once the stroke has been quite well mastered by the class, the instructor then stresses the finer timing movements and skill techniques of the stroke.

DISTANCE ORIENTATION

The student is now urged to swim farther each class session without stopping to rest. The instructor should at this point commend distance achievement accomplished by the students.

Teaching and coaching the dolphin butterfly stroke

The dolphin butterfly stroke was developed at the University of Iowa in 1935.* This stroke is a further development of, and a step forward in, speed in the different types of breast stroke swimming. If changes could be made in the arm stroke of the orthodox breast stroke and still stay within the scope of the competitive breast stroke rules, then it would seem logical that the leg stroke could also be altered so long as the legs performed in unison, as to the arms. The flying arms were powerful and created greater speed, but the two movements, flying arms and orthodox breast stroke kick, were not a good basic mechanical combination of movements. The kick was a retarding type of action compared to the faster, more powerful action of the flying arms. Retarding factors in the kick action had to be eliminated. A kick had to be developed which eliminated a recovery phase as well as the tail suction it created behind the legs. This was the dominating factor which led the author to create this stroke.

The discovery of this stroke was merely an assembling into a perfectly timed combination of skills of arm and leg actions which had already been known for years. The kick was a simultaneous undulating action similar to a double flutter kick.

The dolphin butterfly stroke kick is fundamentally like that of the crawl stroke, the only difference being that both arms and legs move together in unison, while in the crawl stroke the same performance of both arms and legs is executed in alternating movements. One may further say that the flying arms in the breast stroke should not be classified as a breast stroke but as a crawl breast stroke, because it is a combination of two styles of competitive swimming.

The dolphin butterfly stroke is amazing in speed performance.†

*Armbruster, D. A., and Sieg, Jack: The dolphin breast stroke, Journal of Health and Physical Education 6:23 (April), 1935.
†Armbruster, D. A.: The new dolphin breast stroke on trial, Swimming Guide, New York, 1937, American Sports Publishing Co., p. 52.

It has left the butterfly breast stroke far behind. The kick itself produces greater speed than the alternating crawl flutter. However, on basic physical principles, it is doubtful that this stroke will ever develop the speed of the crawl stroke, even though the kick is faster. However, this stroke ranks second in competitive speed to that of the crawl stroke, and it is getting dangerously close. The dual arm action never will be as fast as the alternating arm action because there is a non-propelling phase during the recovery. In the crawl movement one or both arms are always in the water propelling. An alternating arm action with the dolphin fishtail kick does not synchronize naturally.

TECHNIQUE OF THE DOLPHIN BUTTERFLY STROKE

The dolphin butterfly stroke is definitely dominated by the kick, which resembles the tail movement of a flat-tailed dolphin.

Kick. The leg action is exactly like that of the flutter kick in the crawl stroke. The feet have the same slant on the up beat as the crawl kick. The knees bend as the legs pass the central axis of body progression. At the end of the up stroke, the feet relax (Fig. 14-1, *A-D*). At the beginning of the down stroke the toes are turned inward, and the foot is hyperextended. On the downward stroke of both legs, the knees are somewhat bent until almost the end of the down beat. The knees straighten quickly, giving a tremendous downward whip to the feet. While this whip is completing its downward stroke, the thighs are already in the upward motion, causing the loose knee to straighten as the whole leg continues upward. The up stroke is started with the legs straight until the legs reach the central axis of progression where the knees again bend in order to effect the propulsive action of a fishtail. As the legs wave up and down, they press backward against the water at an angle as the water washes down the legs. This action supplies the propulsive power of the kick.

The kick has several better and more efficient principles for delivering speed than does either the alternating crawl flutter kick or the orthodox breast stroke kick. First, there is less resistance at the thighs than in the crawl flutter or the traditional breast stroke kick. Second, there is less retarding resistance to forward motion than an alternating motion of the legs. Third, there is no waste return motion such as in the orthodox breast kick recovery. Fourth, there is no counterpropulsive reaction due to motion opposite to the direction of progress. For example, the orthodox breast stroke kick has a reciprocating jerk so that, when the legs kick backward, the kick ends with a jerk due to the backward momentum of the feet.

In the dolphin kick, both the legs and trunk weave up and down in the water, placing the axis of motion somewhere in the spine, well up in the shoulder region. In the crawl flutter kick, the axis of motion is in the hip joints. In the dolphin kick, the whole body weaves as if made of rubber.

Arm action. The arm action includes the entry, support, catch, pull, push, release, and recovery.

Entry. The entry of the arms should be at a point in front and in line with the shoulders. The arms are naturally extended and relaxed, with the hand slightly bent down at the wrist (Fig. 14-1, *A*). The hands and arms should be dropped into the water rather than carelessly smashed into the water. The hands enter the water about 10 to 12 inches apart. The resistance of the water should be felt on the palms during the entry.

Support. The arms and hands serve to propel the swimmer forward as soon as they enter the water and continue this propulsive action until they are removed for the recovery. The main propulsive action does not begin until the arms are in a favorable driving position below the surface of the water. The interval between the entry and the position at which the arms start their major propulsive action is the support phase of the dolphin butterfly arm stroke. The support phase aids in maintaining a desirable body position in the water. It is not a glide but rather a downward and slightly outward press of the hand and forearm which is timed with the down beat of the legs. As the hands move downward the shoulders follow in a dropping movement that helps to facilitate an elevation of the hips, resulting from an action–reaction of the legs in their downward drive. During the dropping movement of the shoulders, care should be taken not to allow the shoulders to become lower than the level of the hands. If the shoulders drop below the hands, the result is a decided mechanical disadvantage in the arm pull. In the shorter sprint events, the drop of the head and shoulders are decidedly reduced, and retained at a higher level.

Catch. The path of the arm action with its changing directional line of drive can best be described by the hand forming an elongated and reversed letter S if one were to look down upon the stroke. The hands first press outward, then inward, and, as the arms finish the stroke, they again press outward. The initial outward movement takes place during the support phase. The catch starts at the completion of the down kick of the legs. The catch takes place as the arms finish their outward movement and begin their inward action. This transition consists of a quickened skillful movement involving the supination of the hand and forearm. The pressure of the water must be maintained in the hand and forearm during the catch action.

Pull. The pull immediately follows the catch and continues until the hands are in a position immediately below the shoulder level. During the catch and pull the elbows move slightly outward, and, just before the shoulders are over the hands, the arm and shoulder action shifts from a quick press to a push action. There is an element of lift during the support, catch, and pull, but this lift should be kept to a minimum. Forward, not upward, motion of the body should be the objective. This is based upon mechanically sound principles, giving advantageous leverage as well as efficient muscular action. The principle is exactly the same as that applied in the crawl arm action.

Push. The push phase of the arm action begins at a point at which

Fig. 14-1. A-H, A series of ideal form for executing the dolphin butterfly stroke. These figures also show the ideal position in relation from both side and head-on of the body in relation to the surface. **A,** The legs have completed the up drive and are beginning to drive downward. The arms are in the glide-and-catch position. **B,** The legs complete the first down beat, and the hips get an action-reaction upward. The arms press and spread into the downward catch. Note position of the entire body. **C,** The legs are beating upward to complete the first beat of the kick. The arms have completed the catch-and-pull and are beginning the push phase of the stroke. The head is kept in line with the body. **D,** The legs begin the second down beat while the arms are well in the push phase of the stroke.

the hands reach a position slightly ahead of the shoulders at the end of the pull. As the transition from pull to push takes place, the elbows turn toward the chest wall, and the hands almost meet under the body as the arms drive back, toward, and on a line with either hip in a direct push (Fig. 14-1, *C-E*). The push of the arms coupled with the second downward drive of the legs results in a powerful forward thrust of the body. As the arms approach the front of the hips in completion of the push, the hands whip backward to give a last additional drive to the arm stroke.

Fig. 14-1, cont'd. D and **E,** The legs are driving down through the axis of progression while the arms have released the water and begin the recovery. Note at this point air is being taken. **E,** During the push drive, air is taken as the legs complete the down beat. **E** and **F,** The arms are midway in the recovery, and the legs begin the final upward beat in the stroke revolution. Again note action-reaction of arms and legs. **F,** Shows the arms clearing the surface and the legs beginning the up beat. **F** and **G,** The arms are about to complete the arm stroke revolution. The legs continue the up beat to complete the arm stroke revolution. The legs continue the up beat to complete the two-beat leg kick revolution. (See **G** and **H.**) **G** and **H,** Show the low straight arm recovery and entry. The legs have completed the up beat and are in position for the next stroke cycle.

Release and recovery. After the hands push and drive backward from shoulder to hip, each hand releases the water just beyond the hip joint (Fig. 14-1, *E* and *F*), knifes outward to the surface, and moves rapidly into the recovery.

The arms should recover in a low, lateral, sweeping movement above the surface, with rotation of the arms to accommodate the movement (Fig. 14-1, *G*). A rapid initial forward movement carries the arms forward to a position opposite the shoulders, with the elbows and the little fingers of each hand slightly facing upward. The arms are held as relaxed as possible in this position. As the arms pass the shoulders, there is a rotation at the shoulder joint which accommodates the forward movement. The rotation continues until the palms are facing downward. In this position the arms are in readiness for the entry. While the hands are in the air during the recovery, the body has a tendency to sink. This sinking of the body can be reduced by a rapid recovery. Those swimmers who are less buoyant especially should stress the point of recovering the arms as quickly as possible without smashing them into the water.

The body should progress over the surface at as nearly a constant level as possible; undue climbing and dropping results in increased resistance and slower speed.

Timing of the arms and legs. The best rhythm found for this stroke was two beats of the legs to one cycle of the arms. Since the kick dominates the stroke, the timing elements should be analyzed from its action. There are some top-flight swimmers now using only one beat of the legs to one cycle of the arms. This action needs further experimenting. The first timing movement is begun (Fig. 14-1, *A*) with the arms in the support phase, just after entering the water. The legs at this point are driving downward in their first beat.

The arms catch and press into the pull while the hips elevate at the end of the down beat of the legs (Fig. 14-1, *B*). In Fig. 14-1, *C*, the arms are pulling while the legs are driving upward. Note the counteraction of both arms and legs in relation to the hip in Fig. 14-1, *B* and *C*. In Fig. 14-1, *D*, the legs begin the second down beat, and the arms are making the transition from the pull to the push phase. Note the pigeon-toed feet and the narrow spread knees on the down beat. In Fig. 14-1, *E*, the legs have completed the second downward beat, and the arms have released the water and are beginning to recover. Note how both the arms and legs are in line, since the arms have completed the push. The body at this point is in its highest position and is in readiness for the inhalation of air in the breathing cycle.

Fig. 14-1, *F*, shows the arms already rotated in the recovery, while the legs are moving upward in the second kick. Fig. 14-1, *G*, illustrates the legs completing the upward drive as the arms are about to enter the water.

The most troublesome difficulty many swimmers fall into, after having learned the stroke, is in obtaining the best timing movements of the arms and legs. The basis of the fault lies in the fact that the swimmer does not pull the arms through the water fast enough nor recover the arms fast enough. He should also check the kick and shorten the range to adjust to the faster arm action.

Timing of breathing with the arms. At the end of the push phase of the arm action, the legs have finished the down beat of the second beat of the kick. The body at this point is at its highest position, and it is the ideal time to inhale the air in the breathing and stroke cycle. Buoyant swimmers may start the exhalation of air immediately following the inhalation. Those less buoyant should retain the air until just prior to the end of the push phase of the arms and then exhale in a strong blast, through the mouth. It is very common to breathe once every two strokes. However, the swimmer must consider the possibility of building an oxygen debt in a race over 100 yards. The question remains, does the ease and mechanical advantage gained by breathing every other stroke give the individual performer an advantage in this method over the possibility of paying for an oxygen debt later in the closing moments of a race?

Start. The techniques and mechanics of the moving parts of the dolphin butterfly start are no different from those presented for the crawl stroke start. (See Chapter 8, Figs. 8-1 and 8-2.)

The entry and glide technique also are the same as that described for the crawl start.

The swimmer comes out of the water, from the glide, flying on the very first arm pull, since more swimmers can fly faster on top of the water than swim under it.

The distance to be traveled under the water in the glide to the beginning of the first stroke depends also upon the penetrating power derived from the start and the velocity maintained, which, in turn, depends upon individual characteristics. Some men are more streamlined in physical contour and present less frictional resistance to the water. However, most any swimmer should be out at least 18 to 20 feet before beginning the first stroke. Starting too early in the glide will slow down the speed of the stroke.

When the hands and arms spring into action, the arms should press and pull downward, slightly wider than the shoulder width, and pull toward each hip. The pull should be executed in such a way that, as the body pops through the surface, it is in a forward movement, not upward.

Dolphin butterfly turn. There are very few differences between the techniques in the dolphin butterfly stroke turn and those used in the conventional type. In the approach one should time the strokes so that as the arms recover they lunge into the wall above the surface. The head remains lowered. In case the throw of the arms is short, the momentum will drive the body forward into the wall. The turning mechanics are the same as in the conventional breast stroke turn. After the turn is made with both hands, one hand is removed to execute an outward finning action which aids in turning the hips around during

Table 14-1. Ideal split times for various racing times in the 200-yard dolphin butterfly stroke (25-yard pool)

ELAPSED DISTANCE (YD.)	ELAPSED TIME (SEC.)	SPLIT TIME (SEC.)	ELAPSED DISTANCE (YD.)	ELAPSED TIME (SEC.)	SPLIT TIME (SEC.)
25	10.2	10.2	25	12.6	12.6
50	23.0	12.8	50	28.1	15.5
75	36.1	13.1	75	43.8	15.7
100	49.5	13.4	100	59.6	15.8
125	1:02.9	13.4	125	1:15.6	16.0
150	1:16.6	13.7	150	1:31.9	16.3
175	1:30.7	14.1	175	1:48.4	16.5
200	1:45.0	14.3	200	2:05.0	16.6
25	10.8	10.8	25	13.4	13.4
50	24.3	13.5	50	29.4	16.0
75	38.0	13.7	75	45.6	16.2
100	51.9	13.9	100	1:02.0	16.4
125	1:06.0	14.1	125	1:18.6	16.6
150	1:20.5	14.5	150	1:35.6	17.0
175	1:35.2	14.7	175	1:52.8	17.2
200	1:50.0	14.8	200	2:10.0	17.2
25	11.4	11.4	25	14.2	14.2
50	25.5	14.1	50	30.8	16.6
75	39.9	14.4	75	47.6	16.8
100	54.5	14.6	100	1:04.6	17.0
125	1:09.3	14.8	125	1:21.9	17.3
150	1:24.3	15.0	150	1:39.5	17.6
175	1:39.6	15.3	175	1:57.2	17.7
200	1:55.0	15.4	200	2:15.0	17.8
25	12.0	12.0	25	14.6	14.6
50	26.8	14.8	50	32.0	17.4
75	41.8	15.0	75	49.5	17.5
100	56.9	15.1	100	1:07.1	17.6
125	1:12.4	15.5	125	1:24.9	17.8
150	1:28.2	15.8	150	1:43.1	18.2
175	1:44.2	15.9	175	2:01.5	18.4
200	2:00.0	15.9	200	2:20.0	18.5

the tumble movement. When the turn is completed and if the swimmer is sprinting, the push-off should be shallow so that the body can immediately be driven to the surface on the initial arm stroke.

Finish of the dolphin butterfly stroke. For the finish, the same principles apply as recommended in the finish of the traditional breast stroke.

Coaches should train swimmers to practice the finish approach just as much as they practice starts and turns. There seems to be no advantage to practicing starts and turns consistently if the swimmer is destined to lose in the last 10 yards of the finish what he gains by a good fast penetrating start and fast turns earlier in the race.

By referring to Table 14-1, the dolphin butterfly stroke swimmer can plan his race in accordance with the ideal split times throughout his race.

TEACHING AND LEARNING PROCEDURES

Land drill. The class is seated on deck on the side of the pool. Legs are extended out above the pool water. Arms are extended backward with the hands placed on the deck supporting the body. The instructor reviews and demonstrates a single one leg action of the back crawl kick. The class practices the movement with one leg. The instructor then demonstrates the action of the dolphin kick—both legs moving up and down as a single unit—following the same pattern as previously executed with one leg. The class continues to practice the action.

Water bracket drill using the side of the pool for support. The instructor reviews the key points of the crawl stroke kick. The class then executes the crawl stroke kick, concentrating on the mechanics of its action. The instructor now demonstrates the dolphin kick, waving both legs up and down similar to the crawl but as a single unit. Action–reaction will necessitate movement of the hips and upper body, which is encouraged at this point. The drill is continued until all members can keep the legs together in the execution of the kick.

Underwater drill. The student is instructed to push from the side of the pool so that the body is in a submerged prone position. The hands and arms are held loosely at the sides of the body. In this position the kick is practiced, keeping the eyes open to avoid submerging too deep. Repeat several times until all pupils get the feel of the propulsive movement of the fishtaillike action.

Side drill. The students push off on their right side and execute the kick several times. The breath is held, and the eyes are focused backward toward the legs to observe their action and technique. Repeat on the left side. Alternate right and left.

Back drill. The kick is practiced in a supine position.

Kick board drill. Using the board as a floating support, the student attempts to kick 200 yards while on the face. If he is forced to stop, he rests momentarily and continues until he has covered the full distance. During this exercise the student should attempt to hold the up and down action of the hips to a minimum. When the class becomes proficient to the extent that all can cover the distance, they are ready for instruction in the arm action technique.

Arm action of the dolphin butterfly stroke. The instructor should review the coaching techniques of this stroke in this chapter and then discuss and demonstrate the arm stroke action, stressing important points.

Land drill. The land drill is preceded with flexibility exercises of the shoulders. Pupils face the instructor and imitate his arm action. The instructor emphasizes a speedy and relaxed arm recovery. He also cautions class not to drop the shoulders at the arm entry.

Shallow water drill. Pupils take position and stand in waist-deep water. The legs are spread with the knees bent. The body is inclined forward at the hips so that the shoulders are in the water. The class simulates the arm action as taught in the land drill.

Leg support drill. A kick board or other floating device is used to support the legs in a floating position. The swimmer uses his arms to propel him through the water, with the face in the water. As he improves this skill, he is encouraged to elevate his head toward the end of the arm push and inhale. (See Fig. 14-1.)

Combined arm and leg action. It has been observed by the authors that, if the swimmer will utilize the arm action and merely trail the legs, the legs will move up and down slightly, twice during a complete arm cycle, due to body action reaction. The swimmer then attempts to lengthen the size and range of this natural movement of the legs, until he feels the balance and power from the kick. If he has difficulty in recovering the arms above the surface, a common problem in learning and coordinating the whole stroke, the beginner should pull and recover the arms at a greater speed. This faster arm action not only aids coordination but also helps to prevent the shoulders and head from sinking during the arm recovery and entry.

The beginner has a tendency to lengthen the range of movement in the kick. As he becomes skilled, he should strive to shorten and minimize the size and range of the kick.

The up and down action of the hips caused by action–reaction from the kick should also be held to a minimum.

The instructor should stress the point at this time of too much up and down movement of the head and shoulders during the breathing action. This is commonly known as "climbing" to get air, instead of moving the head and shoulders forward to inhale (see the discussion of breathing in this chapter).

Chapter 15

Relay racing

Relay racing is that form of competition in which two or more men swim the same specified distance, one relieving the other at the end of the distance.

Relay racing is fun for most swimmers as well as spectators because of its spirited competition. Each portion of the relay race is designated as a "leg." Points in relay racing run very much higher than in an individual race. For this reason relays become the highlights of the meet.

TYPES OF RELAY RACES

There are usually two types of relays in swimming: medley (including the four competitive styles of swimming) and the free style relays, which may be classified as sprint and middle distance races, that is, for each individual portion of the race. The length of each leg is quite definitely standardized for high school, college, and Olympic competition. Other types or varying distances come under the heading of noteworthy relay performances. The standard types are as follows:

High school:
(1) 200-yard medley (75-foot pools) (4 x 50)
    160-yard medley (60-foot pools) (4 x 40)
    (Four swimmers on each team, each to swim one fourth the distance; first, back stroke; second, breast stroke; third, butterfly; fourth, free style)
(2) 400-yard sprint free style relay (75-foot pools) (4 x 100)
    400-yard sprint free style relay (60-foot pools) (4 x 100)
    (Four swimmers, each to swim one fourth the distance)
College and A.A.U.:
(1) 400-yard medley relay (4 x 100)
    (Four swimmers on each team, each to swim one fourth the distance; first, back stroke; second, breast stroke; third, butterfly stroke; fourth, free style)

(2)   400-yard sprint free style relay (4 x 100)

(Four men on each team, each to swim one fourth the distance)

(3)   800-yard free style relay (4 x 200) (college championship meets)

Olympic and A.A.U.:

(1)   800-meter free style relay (4 x 200)

(Four men on each team, each to swim one fourth the distance)

(2)   400-meter medley relay (4 x 100)

(Four swimmers on each team, each to swim one fourth the distance; first, back stroke; second, breast stroke; third, butterfly; fourth, free style)

ARRANGEMENT OF A RELAY TEAM

When selecting members of a relay team and the order in which they swim, a coach must first consider a number of factors as to the qualifications of the candidates before making a decision. A number of these factors are as follows:

1.   Who is a fast starter and calm under fire of competition?
2.   Which one will swim best when behind?
3.   Who swims best when in the lead?
4.   Who is the weaker competitor?
5.   Which lead-off man will give the most stability to the team?
6.   Which anchor man will give most confidence to the team?

Another question which must be answered is whether all men should be selected on a tryout basis; that is, for the particular meet for which a tryout is held, should those who win be on your team because they were fastest on the day of the tryout?

Some coaches will rely entirely upon tryouts. Others will wait until well along in the meet to see how certain individuals performed in earlier races and then nominate the men for the relay team. If a meet is close and depends upon the last relay event, some coaches will often select, at the last minute, a slightly slower man but one who has been tried and true. This is selecting on a percentage basis and is considered an advisable procedure. One cannot take chances and experiment when the meet is close. A faster man may be an "in and outer," or an inexperienced man may fold up when the going gets tough. After the men have been selected, the next question to be decided is: In what order should they be placed in competition? We must now go back to the preceding questions as to personal characteristics and qualifications.

For the sake of simplicity, let us list the men in the order of their speed as 1, 2, 3, and 4, respectively. The most commonly used order is 2, 3, 4, and 1. This arrangement places the weaker man in the number 3 position, with two good men in front of him and the fastest man behind him. This should give the weaker man confidence.

Another commonly used plan is 2, 4, 3, and 1. This places the fastest man at anchor and the second fastest in the lead-off position, with the weaker man in the number 2 position. This arrangement is made with the hope that the second fastest man will hold his own or hand over a lead to the weaker man. Should those two men lose the lead, there are still two good men left to make up lost yardage.

Another order of swimming the sprint relay, and one which is often used to confuse opponents, is to arrange the competition in the order 1, 2, 3, and 4. The idea is to put the faster man out in front to get the lead and the number 2 man to further gain or at least hold the advantage, so that by the time the weaker "anchor" man comes up, he has been given a substantial advantage. In case things do not go well for him, he still has quite a margin. In each race, the team standing in the meet and the opponents' possible lineup should be the determining factors in arranging the team. If a lineup has been decided upon before meet time, a last minute change is likely to disturb the composure and confidence of the team.

TECHNIQUE OF THE TAKE-OFF

The swimming take-off in relay racing differs from that in track relay racing. In track, the competitor receives a baton from his predecessor within a limited zone. He then must carry this on and pass it to his succeeding teammate. Such passing cannot be accomplished in swimming relay racing.

In the swimming relay the preceding swimmer finishes his "leg" by touching the finish wall. Poised above this finish lane and wall is the succeeding teammate who takes off as soon as his teammate touches the wall. There is some latitude given the swimmer at the touch-off comparable to the zone advantage given a runner. The starting swimmer may be in motion, such as arm swing or body lean, but his feet must not leave the take-off wall until his teammate has touched it. In competition this is checked in two ways: (1) A take-off judge stations himself in such a position that he can place his finger on the foot of each swimmer (after the first one) and at the same time see the end of the pool, and he judges whether the swimmer leaves his position before the preceding swimmer touches the end. (2) The more common method is the honor system. The judge stations himself at the side of the finishing end of the pool and merely observes that the rule is not violated.

There are several methods by which a swimmer may judge when to start his wind-up for the take-off. The swimmer must use his own judgment about when to begin preparation for his take-off. A safe method is for the swimmer to begin preparation for his take-off when the head of his teammate is approximately 3½ feet from the finish wall. When the teammate's head reaches this point, the starting swimmer can drive with tremendous force and still have his feet on his mark when the "leg" is finished. The finishing swimmer must practice driving in with the finishing hand in order to time it perfectly. The starting swimmer must observe and practice judging a distance of 3½ feet. He looks down at the swimmer below him but must hold his head well up. If the head is held low, he is likely to lose balance, or, when he does dive, he is likely to dive short.

In a shorter sprint where speed is greater, a 4-foot margin can be allowed.

In breast stroke swimming in the medley relay, the following free style swimmer may allow not more than 2½ feet from the head to the finish wall since the speed of the incoming swimmer is slower

Chapter 16

Conditioning

Conditioning may be defined for our purpose as preparing the body for activity. It includes the building of health, strength, endurance, and speed. Training is defined here as the process of adjustment to the competitive situation and improvement in the skill in which the athlete is to perform.

A common occurrence in athletic literature is the use of the words "conditioning" and "training" synonymously. They are usually considered as being so closely allied in preparing an athlete for competition that no distinction is made between the terms. For example, as an athlete undergoes certain forms of physical movements in acquiring a skill, he is also by this exercise improving the quality of his muscles. Thus, while he is training, he is also improving his condition.

From the coach's viewpoint in considering the preparation of an athlete for competition, the problem of conditioning and training presents a logical sequence. The body as a machine must be strong and be able to overcome the processes of fatigue to such an extent that the performance of the skill may not be hampered by the lack of these faculties.

Theoretically, a man can be in excellent condition and still not be trained in any skill. Also, on the other hand, he may be well trained to perform a specific skill, but he may lack the physical capacity necessary to complete the performance or continue the performance for any length of time.

As an example, a boy may report to the coach at the swimming pool each day and there may receive the best education in swimming technique which the coach is able to give. As a result of this training, the boy is able to demonstrate a very highly skilled performance. His stroke mechanics are refined to the utmost degree. His timing of the stroke is perfect. However, if on leaving the pool he continues to violate good hygienic habits, he is thereby reducing his condition. After a period his performance in the pool becomes characteristic of a man who is well trained in technique but in poor condition. His stroke mechanics are still excellent, and over a short distance and at a slow speed he gives all the outward appearances of a champion. But if he is asked to increase the speed, even for a short distance, he finds it difficult to do so. We can now say that the man is in poor condition and still is well trained. Conditioning the athlete for competition requires months to achieve, but it can be destroyed within a very few days.

Although the processes of conditioning and training are carried on at the same time during a season, still each of the procedures may be considered separately. This chapter is devoted to measures which will improve the athlete's physical condition. The emphasis here will be on strength, endurance, and flexibility.

Before reporting for a program of conditioning for swimming competition, the swimmer should report for a thorough medical examination. This examination will bring to light any functional organic disorders.

Strength, endurance, and flexibility can be improved by a carefully regulated program of conditioning procedures. These procedures include diet control, frequent and graded exercises, adequate rest, and observance of certain hygienic principles.

The coach usually imparts information concerning these procedures by the distribution of printed material, by posting a list of rules, and often by classroom sessions during the preseason meetings of the squad. The material pertaining to conditioning which appears in this chapter has been prepared in such a form that the coach can easily lift it from these pages and transfer it to his own rules for his swimmers.

SWIMMER'S DAILY SCHEDULE OF LIVING

The cardinal principle for conditioning one's self for strenuous activity is to have a regulated schedule for daily routine events. The student has a schedule of academic hours for every day in the week. He should also budget his study hours for every day in the week. Meals should be eaten at regular hours every day. He should set his bedtime and rising hour at a regular time. His training period is also arranged at a regular time each day of the week. Such a regulated schedule will keep the swimmer mentally and physically alert and healthy.

Regular diet. The first consideration will be that of the diet. As most swimming squads do not have the advantages of a training table, the most effective presentation of diet control will be in the form of a discussion of foods which are recommended and other foods which should be avoided. Food, the right kind and enough of it, is a significant factor involved in acquiring strength, endurance, and alertness.

There are six essentials of nutrition: proteins, carbohydrates, fats, vitamins, minerals, and water. These are easily attainable by the individual through a properly chosen diet.

During the swimming season the swimmer's daily energy consumption is increased over his everyday average. Large amounts of body heat are lost during submersion and exertion in the water, body substances are broken down faster, and a strain is thrown on the body processes. The food substances taken into the body must be increased to supply the necessary elements for yielding energy for muscular work and heat, for building and restoring tissues, and for regulating body processes.

Foods may be classified according to function as follows:

1. Fuel foods or sources of energy
   (a) Carbohydrates
       (1) Sugars
       (2) Starches
   (b) Lipids
       (1) Fats
       (2) Lipoids
   (c) Proteins
       (1) Animal proteins
       (2) Vegetable proteins
2. Body builders or tissue formers
   (a) Proteins
   (b) Lipids
   (c) Mineral salts
   (d) Water
3. Regulators of body processes
   (a) Mineral salts
   (b) Water
   (c) Accessory food substances—vitamins

Carbohydrates. Of the six essential foodstuffs, the carbohydrates are the most abundant and also the most economical source of energy. Most of the body energy is derived from the carbohydrates. Other foods are used, but these foods are ultimately in the carbohydrate form when used for body energy.

Carbohydrates are derived almost entirely from the vegetable kingdom. They form the chief constituents of roots, tubers, and seeds. The most available sources of carbohydrates for human use are the cereal grains, potatoes, rice, tapioca, sugar (cane, beet, and maple), honey, and sweet fruits. The only direct animal sources of the carbohydrates are liver (glycogen), milk (lactose), and blood (glucose).

The carbohydrates yield energy when burned in the body. That in excess of the body needs may be stored as glycogen, chiefly in the liver but also in the muscles and other organs. If greater quantity than can be burned and stored as glycogen is ingested, it may be converted and stored as fat.

Sugars are soluble carbohydrates with a more or less sweet taste. We are most concerned with glucose (grape sugar), lactose (milk sugar), and sucrose (cane sugar).

Glucose occurs in nature as a syrup; it is less sweet than cane sugar. Other sugars have to be changed to this form by digestion before the body can use them. Glucose is found throughout the vegetable kingdom, chiefly in fruit and plant juices. It is especially abundant in grapes; it may constitute 20% of the weight in grapes. Glucose is a fuel food in a very readily absorbable form. It is an economical form of energy.

Sucrose is chemically the same as cane sugar. Maple sugar has the same composition except for its impurities. Sucrose is derived from the sap or juices of a large variety of plants; from sugar cane, sugar beet, and maple tree. The common fruits and vegetables contain considerable amounts of this sugar. The solid product is obtained by evaporation and purification of the saps. The sucroses are valuable sources of energy. They must be used with discretion, however, for two reasons:

1. Large amounts of too highly concentrated solutions are irritating to the lining of the stomach.
2. Because of the quickness of their absorption, they may either satisfy the appetite before the needs of food have been met or they may blunt the appetite so that other foods necessary to ensure adequacy in the diet may become distasteful.

Lactose occurs in the milk of all mammals. It is less sweet and less soluble than cane sugar. Because of its mild flavor and because it is less irritating to the gastric mucosa, it is widely used in infant and invalid feeding. Warm milk before retiring is soothing to the nervous athlete. It forms a valuable source of fuel. Cow's milk contains about 4.8% of lactose.

Starch occurs widely in the vegetable kingdom. It is found in large amounts in seeds, roots, tubers, bulbs, and sometimes in the stems and seeds of plants. It constitutes one half to three fourths of the matter of the ordinary cereal grains and three fourths of the solids of mature potatoes. Commercially, starches are obtained from wheat, corn, rice, potato, and tapioca.

Fats. Fats are almost as widely distributed in nature as are carbohydrates and constitute a more concentrated form of fuel for the supply of energy in nutrition. They form part of animal tissue and are contained in many plants.

The chief sources of fats in the diet are milk (cream and butter), olive oil, and other vegetable oils, meat fats, lard, bacon, salt pork, beef suet, and nuts. Less expensive forms of fat are found in the margarines which are made from fats such as cocoanut, cottonseed, and corn oils. Oleomargarine is made from beef fat churned with milk. These fats have the same fuel value as butter but differ in their vitamin content unless artificially fortified.

The fats tend to check secretion of gastric juice and retard motility of the stomach, thereby retarding the rate of digestion. The softer fats (butter) are digested more easily than the solid ones (suet). Heating fats to too high a temperature may decompose them and give products which are irritating to the lining membrane of the stomach. Foods fried in fat are coated with or permeated by it and are, therefore, less quickly digested.

Lipoids are fatlike substances closely related both chemically and biologically to the fats. Lipoids occur widely in nature and are essential constituents of every living cell. The two most important of these lipoids are lecithin and cholesterol.

Lecithin occurs in considerable quantities in brain substance, blood corpuscles, and other nitrogenous tissues; it is present also in egg yolk. Lecithin is also found in plants, especially seeds.

Cholesterol is present in animal cells and in blood. There are considerable quantities in the brain and skin. It acquires antirachitic properties on irradiation. It is believed that light forms antirachitic vitamin D from cholesterol or ergosterol, another sterol, in the skin. It is present in cod liver oil, egg yolk, and green vegetables.

Proteins. The proteins supply both energy and body-building foods; i.e., certain parts of these substances are taken and built, with other substances obtained from other sources, into body tissues. The proteins form the only source of organic nitrogen, which is an indispensable constituent in animal and plant cells.

The proteins are found in nearly all solids of animal and vegetable organisms. Animal foods are richer in proteins than plant foods. Meat, fish, eggs, and milk furnish large amounts of proteins. They are found both in the whites and yolks of eggs. Legumes are the only plant foods which compare with the animal foods in their content of protein. Some of these are peas, beans, and peanuts. Certain nuts, such as almonds and pine nuts, contain considerable protein.

Nitrogenous extractives are nitrogen-bearing substances found in muscle juices having little if any food value and are useful as stimulants to the flow of gastric juice. They give meats their flavor. These extracts of meat, such as beef tea and bouillon, are used widely in the diets of invalids or in healthy persons as a first course. As a part of the menu of the precompetition meal, they improve the appetite and, secondarily, the digestion.

Cooking proteins at high temperatures tends to toughen them. Better results are obtained by cooking them for longer periods of time at lower temperatures because this renders them more tender.

Minerals. Mineral substances enter into body functions and structure. They are important elements in the diet. Mineral salts function in the following ways:

1. As bone constituents, giving rigidity and relative permanence to skeletal structures
2. As essential elements of the organic compounds which are chief solid constituents of soft tissues (muscles, blood cells, etc.)
3. As soluble salts held in solution in body fluids

The soluble salts give these fluids their influence upon the elasticity and irritability of muscle and nerve by supplying the material for the acidity or the alkalinity of the digestive juices and other secretions and yet maintaining the neutrality or alkalescence of the internal fluids as well as their osmotic pressure and solvent power.

Calcium and phosphorus are essential for hard bones and teeth. Iron is essential for building the red blood corpuscles. Calcium and phosphorus are the minerals most often inadequately supplied. Calcium occurs in milk, cheese, egg yolk, vegetables, and molasses. The calcium of milk is easily assimilated. Phosphorus is present in milk, cheese, egg yolk, whole grain cereals, vegetables, lean meat, and fish. Iron is present in liver, kidney, egg yolk, spinach and other green vegetables, potatoes, whole grains, fruits, and lean meats.

Sodium and chlorine are received as table salt. These are lost in great quantities in early season by swimmers, especially if the water is warm. Replacement should be made by adding more table salt to food items at mealtime. Salt tablets may be used if more than 3 pounds of body weight are lost during a workout. One tablet may be taken for each 2 pounds of weight lost. At least one glass of water should be taken with each salt tablet.

Sulfur is present in almost all protein foods and is adequately supplied in the diet, provided a variety of proteins are fed. Magnesium is adequately supplied in the ordinary foods since little is needed.

Iodine is necessary for normal functioning of the thyroid gland. It is found almost solely in the ocean and, therefore, found largely in sea food, in table salt not too highly refined, in water from regions near the sea coast, and in plants and animals raised on a sea coast land which contains iodine. Little is known of the exact quantity of iodine in the foods.

Vitamins. The lack of any of the vitamins in the diet may give rise to a decline of physical efficiency long before outstanding or readily recognizable disease appears. Vitamin deficiency constitutes the principle "hidden hungers."

The people in some communities frequently have a diet which is deficient in nicotinic acid. The workers are easily fatigued and are often discontented and sunk in apathy and despair. In other communities, thiamine is more commonly lacking in diets than is nicotinic acid. Many of these thiamine-deficients are nervous and apprehensive or irritable, tired, and listless. Deficiency of vitamins of the B complex, including thiamine, nicotinic acid, and riboflavin, is due, in part, to the milling processes which remove the vitamin-containing portions of sugar and flour. Many people do not like brown bread. The new "enriched flour" and "enriched bread" have an increased content of thiamine, riboflavin, nicotinic acid, and iron.

Vitamin C is present in suboptimal amounts in many diets. Scurvy always has been a problem in Northern regions. The lack of vitamin C increases susceptibility to tuberculosis and other infections. Vitamin C is abundant in fresh fruits, especially citrus fruits, and vegetables. It occurs also in animal products.

Uncertainty still surrounds the fat-soluble vitamins, vitamin A and vitamin D. Many diets are too low in vitamin A, and lack of this vitamin provokes night blindness and lowers the integrity of epithelial structures, notably the cornea. The fish liver oils and butter fats are rich in vitamin A.

Vitamin D is obtained by the effect of sunlight on the sterols in the skin or by the ingestion of substances such as fish liver oils or foods which have been suitably fortified. Vitamin D functions in the proper utilization of calcium and phosphorus, which is accelerated in exercise.

Fluids. Whether the constant use of caffeine beverages is harmful or harmless is a debated question. There is fairly unanimous agreement that excessive amounts are definitely injurious. It is likewise agreed that athletes should drink milk. Because only limited amounts of liquids will be taken in a day, it is important that coffee, tea, and other beverages do not entirely replace milk.

Approximately 60% of the body is water. Water is constantly being eliminated by the skin, lungs, and kidneys. The loss is replaced conveniently by drinking water. Since thirst is a poor guide to water needs, some forced drinking of water is indicated when weight losses during workouts exceed 3 pounds.

On trips away from home where only water of a questionable purity may be available, the use of good bottled waters is recommended. They serve as refreshing drinking water with a maximum assurance of safety.

All foods except the simple mineral foods and water contain chemical energy available for use by the healthy body to support the many activities and life processes and incidentally to maintain temperature. This use of the term "energy" in defining the caloric or energy value of foods should not be confused with the popular usage signifying activity, vitality, strength, vigor, or endurance. These conditions depend on many factors, including freedom from disease, natural constitution, physical environment, habits, and others. Good nutritive condition, a necessity for health, requires far more than food energy only; all the nutritional essentials of a complete well-balanced diet in adequate amounts are demanded.

Precontest diet. The precontest diet on the day of competition should be carefully planned. Some of the factors to be considered are the following:

1. A high carbohydrate diet will improve endurance. During the period prior to participation, the major portion of the increased food intake should be carbohydrate. The meals immediately before the contest should be low in fat and very high in carbohydrate. For example:

Breakfast (7:30 A.M.)
   One half grapefruit with one tablespoonful of sugar
   Cereal with milk and one tablespoonful of sugar
   Two poached eggs and lean baked ham
   Two slices of toast with honey or jelly
   Glass of milk

Luncheon (3 hours before afternoon competition)
   Consommé or bouillon soup
   Baked potato with one small patty of butter
   Broiled lean beef steak or two lamp chops
   Two slices of toast with jelly or honey
   Choice of clear Jello
   Weak tea (green) with sugar

2. In a diet leading up to a contest, it is well to increase the alkali reserve by eating fruits and vegetables which will increase the potential alkalinity of the blood stream. This alkaline reserve will help to neutralize the acids which are produced by muscular activity and cause fatigue. (These fatigue acids have no relation to gastric acidity.)

3. Avoid heavy pastries and greasy and highly spiced foods.
   Bread: Avoid hot bread, biscuits, waffles, and pancakes.
   Condiments: Avoid chili sauce, meat spices, catsup, and any form of relishes such as olives and pickles.
   Gas-forming foods: Avoid cooked cabbage, beans, raw onions, sauerkraut, bell peppers, melons, apples, and cauliflower.

Postcontest diet. Materials which have been used and excreted from the body during competition should be replaced between events and following the competition. Those replacements include the aforementioned glycogen and alkaline substances. Salts are also diminished by exercise and should be replaced.

Foods rich in protein are needed for tissue building and repair requirements.

Elimination. The human body rids itself of waste materials through defecation, urination, perspiration, and respiration. The swimmer need concern himself principally with the elimination of the fecal matter. This elimination should occur at regulated period of the day such as immediately following breakfast. Irregularity is the forerunner of constipation.

Cathartics should not be taken unless prescribed by a physician to relieve a severe case of constipation. Usually constipation can be avoided by regular habits of defecation and by the careful selection of certain foods. If too much roughage is consumed to correct this condition, it may lead to other gastrointestinal disturbances.

Rest. The youth who is attending high school or college and participating in athletics is usually a creature of extremes. He eats his meals hastily. He worries about his classwork and his standing on the team. He may have to work to pay his expenses at school. To these he may add inordinate social obligations.

The intensity of such activity taxes the resources of the nervous system to the extent that sleep offers the only sure means of recuperation.

The amount of sleep required by the athlete depends entirely on the individual, the determining factors being his age, daily activity, physical and mental development, and personal peculiarities. It is possible for an individual to obtain too much sleep. Temperance in sleeping is just as essential as temperance in eating and other habits of life.

A period of eight hours of sound sleep is far more restful than a twelve-hour span of semiconsciousness and tossing in bed. Absolute rest presupposes dreamless slumber. The result obtained is the desire to arise and be up and doing—a feeling that the capacity for work has never been greater. Except in cold weather, people sleeping out of doors or in amply ventilated rooms as a rule sleep deeply; hence, because of the quality, they require less sleep. If a large number of blankets are required to keep warm, the weight of these will be a retarding factor in sleep. Normal and refreshing sleep is favored by moderate fatigue and reduction of sensory stimuli.

Swimmers should be taught a healthy sleep habit founded on the following principles:

1. Arise at a regular hour, regardless of early morning fatigue.
2. Stay awake all day.
3. Determine the number of hours of sleep usually required to pro-

duce a feeling of absolute rest upon awakening. Calculate the hour of retirement accordingly. Establish the habit of retiring regularly at this hour.

4. As you undress for bed, shed your worries with your clothes. Go to bed to relax, rest, and sleep.

5. Have the sleeping room dark, well ventilated, and as quiet as possible. If you cannot escape noise, make up your mind to become adjusted to it.

6. If nervous excitation is marked or physical fatigue unusual, take a hot bath before retiring.

Exercise. Recent analyses of the factors which make for success in athletic performance have shown that strength is extremely important.

This is not surprising when the structure of the body is considered. The bones of the body are attached in such a way as to form levers which are moved by the muscles. The levers which are employed in sports, such as those of the arms and legs, are practically all of the type in which the muscle is attached quite near the end of the bone. The weight to be lifted is at the free end of the lever and far from the muscle which is to move the weight.

While this arrangement may be very convenient for movements of speed in which little resistance is encountered, it puts the muscle at a great disadvantage where moving against resistance, as in swimming, is concerned. To move against resistance, an extraordinarily large force is required in the form of muscular contraction.

For peak performance in swimming, the muscles, which are the sources of power, must be strong. As a rule the practice of the sport itself is not sufficient to develop the muscles to their greatest strength. The addition of strength-building exercises can be used to supplement this muscular development.

In many instances, swimmers reach a peak in their event that represents only the skill side of the activity. Further improvement is impeded by their limitations in strength. If they will increase their strength, they may extend their peaks considerably.*

The exercises used for conditioning and for the warm-up will vary with each individual.

The conditioning exercises should be easy to perform, should require no special apparatus, and should utilize the large muscles since it is through the activity of these muscles that general physical condition is most improved. A program of this type increases the following:

1. The size of the general musculature
2. Strength

*Morehouse, Laurence E.: The physiology of athletics (strength), Scholastic Coach 10:25 (Sept.), 1940.

3. Endurance

4. Efficiency of performance

The warm-up exercises used before practice and actual competition have these immediate effects: (1) increase body temperature to that most favorable for muscular activity, (2) improve muscle tonus, (3) shorten the length of the relaxation period, (4) remove the effects of possible early contraction, and (5) decrease the chances of injury.*

One need only give a general strength test to a squad to determine that some of them lack strength in many important muscles. Some of these weak areas may be found in the forearms, wrists, hands, pectoral region, shoulder girdle, pelvis, spine erectors, lumbar region, abdomen, legs, and feet. The shoulder girdle and pelvis regions especially require rugged support and stability, giving sturdy anchorage against powerful arm and leg action. The soles of the feet require strength for starts and push-offs in turns. These should be strengthened by special exercises.

Some swimmers have muscles that are overdeveloped and shortened which require stretching to give them suppleness and amplitude of motion. A stretched muscle is more efficient and responsive than an unstretched muscle. That is one reason why one should warm up before taking part in violent exercise. Muscles shorten under constant use. If the crawler or the flying breast stroker hopes to recover the arms above the water easily and not pull against tightly stretched muscles retarding these movements, he must give some attention to keeping the muscles stretched throughout the entire season. The hamstrings also shorten easily, hindering freedom of action of the legs. To have supple feet, muscles which control the ankles and those over the tarsal and metatarsal bones must be stretched regularly.

The diving squad most certainly should include stretching exercises in its daily program of training. Divers must present a symmetrical and well-built body. Divers must emphasize flexibility in the following areas: shoulder joints, spine, hamstrings, ankles, and toes. All joints of the body must have freedom of movement. The trunk should flex upon the thighs deeply and easily. The back should be as if made of rubber, yet it should have strength.

Breast strokers should stretch the crotch muscles so there is no tension in the spread of the legs.

Back strokers should develop an especially loose shoulder joint so that arms can press into the water easily on the entry phase of the stroke without a roll of the body to accommodate tight shoulder-arm muscles.

*Morehouse, L. E., and Baumgartner, A.: Conditioning and warm-up exercises, Scholastic Coach **10**:28 (April), 1941.

SPECIAL FLEXIBILITY EXERCISES FOR SWIMMERS AND DIVERS

A few exercises for the purpose of limbering, stretching, and strengthening the major muscles used in swimming and diving are outlined below.

Exercise 1—light exercise. Start the work with light exercises such as running in place, gradually increasing the cadence of the run. While running, emphasize ankle rock. The foot or ankle should be fully extended before the big toe leaves the floor—in other words, depress the toes as the foot is lifted while running. In making contact with the floor again the toe should touch first with the ankle fully extended.

This is good strengthening work for the feet in starting, push-offs, turns, and springboard work. At the same time it serves to warm up the body. As running continues, have the squad increase the height of raising the knee in an upward movement until the knee is on a line with the hips.

When perspiration is starting to come to the surface, ease down the running to a jog—a walk—and stop. The muscles are now prepared for stretching.

Exercise 2—stretching of shoulder and chest muscles. This is accomplished by swinging the arms sideward vigorously over the head. Start this movement from a cross-arm position in front of the hips. On the up swing, the palms are turned in. Press the arms back as far as possible during the upward swing without forward movement of the hips and stomach.

Exercise 3—rotating trunk on longitudinal axis. Position: Stride stand. Arms extended at sides, shoulder level; palms down. While doing exercise, keep feet fixed flat on floor. Relax muscles and turn body briskly as far as possible from side to side so that there is a strong resistance met at the end of the range of movement.

Exercise 4—stretching hamstring or leg flexor group in back of legs. Bend down quickly in an attempt to touch the toes. On the first attempt do not go all the way down, but on each succeeding dip bend lower and lower until fingertips touch toes—then gradually try to touch whole palm to the floor. The diver should stand on an elevated object from 6 to 10 inches above floor and should easily bend over and touch floor with knees straight. Recover quickly and pause for relaxation between each succeeding dip.

Exercise 5—ankle stretching. Sit on the floor; cross right leg over left. With the left hand, grasp toes of right foot with palm along sole of foot. With right hand, grasp leg above ankle to steady the foot. Left hand now manipulates foot in a rotary motion. Pull on fingertips over top of toes when foot is in extended position so that foot is extended to its fullest position. Repeat with left foot.

Exercise 6.

The crab (for divers only).* Arch backward until hands touch floor. This exercise stretches the abdominal and spinal ligaments to permit the spine to bend as freely as rubber. Try walking forward and backward on all fours.

Handstand against wall. Arch back and stretch body to its fullest extent.

Exercise 7—shoulder girdle loosening and stretching (performed in pairs). Subject sits on floor, legs together, knees straight, toes pointed, trunk vertical and straight. Operator stands behind sitting subject and places one knee between shoulder blades and grasps subject's arms below elbows and slowly elevates them forward-upward, pulls them slowly back, and lets them move sideward-outward and down again. During the movement, firm resistance is offered with knee against back. This is repeated slowly several times. The last two or three times, cross arms slowly behind the head.

Exercise 8—stretching spine in thoracic region (extreme stretching for pectorals). The use of the stall-bars is necessary. Subject grasps round high above head, back to wall. Operator steps between subject and bars facing bars. Stand on lower round, hands on rounds shoulder height. Place shoulders against subject's shoulders. Slowly push subject out and up until feet lift off floor. Use caution on this exercise. Work slowly and do not lift too high.

Exercise 9—crotch stretch. Breast strokers who are crotch-bound should stretch the adductor muscle groups. This can be done by doing leg-spreading exercises, lying on the back with legs lifted upward.

SPECIAL BODY BUILDING EXERCISES FOR SWIMMERS

Exercise 1 (performed in pairs). Subject lies on floor on back, arms at sides of body. Operator places his hands on subject's feet to give support. Subject now slowly lifts his shoulders from floor about 12 inches, holds this position momentarily, and recovers to floor to relax. Repeat four to six times.

If abdominals quiver, the muscles are weak. Increase number of exercises and hold longer before lowering to the floor in third and fourth weeks.

Exercise 2—development of back extensors. Subject lies on the edge of the pool, face down, so that hip joint comes directly over the edge of the pool. Helper places hands over heels of subject and supports him. Subject now raises trunk slowly up into deep arch, then lowers body as far as possible. Repeat several times. Then circle trunk several times to left and then to right. This exercise is especially good for the develop-

*See special exercises for divers, Chapter 18.

ment of all the back extensors. Crawl swimmers should have strong extensors along spine and especially in lumbar region to afford stability between pelvic girdle and the shoulder girdle.

Exercise 3—stationary running. Repeat sequence used for stretching warm-up. Strengthens ankle ligaments and plantar region of foot.

Exercise 4—handstand balancing and walking. All swimmers should develop strong wrists. This exercise can be done in several ways. Novice should lean legs against a wall from a handstand (use caution on hard floors while learning). Helper can steady legs of subject. Stretch body, keep knees straight, toes pointed. Walk on hands. With helper supporting legs, do a wheelbarrow exercise, walking using arms.

Barbell exercises.

Most college coaches recommend training with the barbell weight during the fall conditioning months. However, care should be taken to select only those exercises that will develop the forearm and upper-arm, both the biceps and triceps muscles. For arm flexors and biceps, a two-hand snatch, as well as curling, is the best exercise. The bar weight should be heavy enough so that not more than five or six repetitions can be performed. The supine press is performed by lying on the back and pressing the bar from the chest upward to full arm extension.

Excellent exercises for swimmers' forearm, upperarm, and pectoral muscles are performed by lying prone on the back on a shoulder-width bench and using straight-arm lifts with either iron dumbbells or a horizontal barbell. These lifts can be performed with arms extended over the head as well as from the sides of the body, and the weights are moved vertically above the shoulders, then lowered, and the exercise repeated.

In exercises for the legs and feet, the horizontal bar is placed on the back of the shoulders, and deep knee bends are performed. With the bar in this position, the balls of the feet are placed on a two-inch thick board and lifted up and down to toe stand and returned.

The legs can be further strengthened by doing the flutter kick, wearing iron boots from the prone position on both the front and back sides. It should be performed from a table, and the legs should be extended out over the end of the table.

Wall weights can also be utilized for both the arms and shoulders. However, they should be heavily loaded so that only a few repetitions can be performed.

It is now well known that this overload principle is better in developing strength than using many repetitions with lighter weights. For abdominal and back muscles, the inclined sit-up board is recommended.

OTHER CONSIDERATIONS

Trip away from home. When a trip is made, regardless of the mode of transportation, competitors should make every effort to get themselves there in good condition. Athletes must be good travelers. If travel is by auto, a stop should be made every seventy-five miles, and all men should get out and shake the legs loose. Positions in the car should be changed when again ready to travel. At the end of the journey, limbering-up exercises should be undertaken as soon on arrival as possible. Sitting in auto seats, as well as train seats, tends to tire the buttocks and the thigh muscles. These muscles should be exercised by kicking in the water until they gain function normally. This may require several workout periods in the water. Swimming easily in the water several times is no more fatiguing to well-trained swimmers than walking several blocks for exercise. The swimming workouts restore those car- or train-fatigued muscles to normal condition.

Travel by air in flights longer than four hours presents special problems. The trip should preferably be made at least one day before competition so that the swimmers can recover from motion sickness and constipation and have an opportunity to work out sluggish muscles before the meet. The team physician may wish to prescribe Dramamine or some other drug to prevent motion sickness in those who are known to be susceptible. These drugs should not be offered indiscriminately, especially on the day of a contest, for they might lower maximum performance.

Weight chart. At the beginning of school the swimmer should weigh and record his weight. From the preliminary through the entire competition season, accurate recordings on a weight chart should be made at least two or three times a week. If a gradual loss in weight is noted, the coach should be informed. This may be a danger signal of overwork or an indication of the presence of an infection. The weight chart, therefore, serves as a guide for the coach in prescribing the amount of work for each individual swimmer. Some swimmers will gain steadily and thrive on the work, at least so far as weight fluctuations may indicate. Fluctuations which are only normal do occur and should not necessarily be a disturbing factor to swimmer or coach.

During the competition season, as various swimmers on the squad begin to reach the peak of condition, a careful check on the weight chart should be maintained. Accurate scales and a weight chart and pencil should be placed near the showers in the dressing room. Swimmers should keep a daily record of nude weight before practice. Moderate reduction in body weight can be expected in those swimmers who are overweight or out of condition at the beginning of the season. Any loss in weight should receive immediate attention. It may be due to overwork, worry, sleeplessness, illness, excessive fatigue, or loss of appetite. The athlete may become irritable and quarrelsome, and his whole attitude toward the event is changed. Sometimes a few days' rest away from the pool, prescribing outdoor hikes, is an excellent antidote. In moderate cases, merely decreasing the load of work will be sufficient. His diet should be checked by having him bring in a three-day dietary history. This can be studied for a possible deficiency, and corrections and suggestions can be given by the coach or school dietitian.

Ultraviolet rays. Swimmers should seek out-of-door work or activities during summer vacations as much as possible, especially in those climatic areas where winter indoor swimming is necessary. However, this does not mean that one should overexpose to the sun's rays. The skin of the swimmer should be nicely tanned. He should attempt to maintain this healthy tan color throughout the year by means of the ultraviolet ray lamp.

Ultraviolet rays should be used late in the fall and be continued daily. The best time for exposure is before the bath or workout in the daily routine schedule. The ultraviolet rays react upon the oil in the skin. If these oils are washed off the body in the shower or in the pool, the rays lose their beneficial effect.

Massage. In this discussion, massage will be referred to only as a means of bettering the performance. Massaging as an aid to the repair of injured tissue will not be considered. That should be left to the physician or trainer.

Massage consists in kneading, rubbing, and thumping various parts of the body. In swimming its principal use is to loosen tightened muscles. There is a difference of opinion among coaches as to the benefits of massage. Some coaches prefer it as an aid to the warm-up before the competition. Others believe that the only way to loosen tightened muscles is to swim easily until the tight muscles feel loose to the swimmer.

A rubbing massage is restful and relaxing and gives a swimmer a feeling of well-being. For this reason, many coaches use it as an aid for its soothing and quieting effects upon a swimmer between events.

An oil ingredient is usually used to prevent irritation and friction to the skin areas. Oil is also used in massaging a swimmer with the purpose of lessening body surface friction to water in competition. Some swimmers normally have a very dry skin. Swimmers lose some of the natural oil in the skin during the winter months, and the skin often becomes dry and chapped. An oil massage two or three times a week is very beneficial to a swimmer with a dry skin.

Common cold and its prevention. Any sinusitis or any throat infection should be reported for proper treatment to the physician at the very earliest possible moment. A swimmer is more susceptible to the common cold than perhaps any other athlete. His body is continually subjected to constantly changing temperatures during the course of an afternoon's training period. He comes from outdoors, undresses in the locker room, goes to the swimming pool, exercises, takes a shower, and then goes into the pool. He comes out of the water and goes in again, and finally comes out to shower, dry off, and dress for the street. Each of the aforementioned changes produces stresses upon the swimmer's temperature-regulating mechanism. The swimmer should not increase this stress by sitting in draughts or sitting on cold tiled floors. After the workout he should thoroughly dry his body, hair, and ears before going out into the cold air. He should dress for the street adequately to meet changing weather conditions. In the Northern states generally, an epidemic of colds is brought on by the arrival of a cold wave.

If a swimmer has his health and condition seriously at heart, he will report a cold with the very first symptom of a sniffling nose. A cold then can usually be checked or cured. If it is permitted to go on without proper treatment for several days, little can be done for it except to let it run its course.

Young men who contract a common cold often treat it altogether too lightly at the beginning, which may give serious complications and later prove to be very disheartening to a boy who had been anticipating keen competition for that season. If it develops into influenza, it is very doubtful if that swimmer will again reach his peak of performance in less than six weeks, if at all for the entire season.

If proper preventive measures are adhered to throughout the season, colds can be held to a minimum. Some of these measures are (1) personal health habits of proper sleep, rest, and diet; (2) wiping and rubbing one's self thoroughly dry before dressing; and (3) dressing adequately for any weather condition, such as dressing warm, keeping feet dry, wearing hat, and keeping shirt collar buttoned.

Chapter 17

Training

An athlete who is not trained for swimming may have followed all the rules of diet, rest, and exercise and give evidence of being in top physical condition by being able to play a full game of football without undue fatigue, yet, when he attempts to swim any distance, he may tire within a few seconds. The reason for this lies not in the factor of condition, but rather in that of training. The muscles of the football player and those of a swimmer may be equally strong, and their blood equally capable of carrying away wastes and supplying oxygen. Still, athletes in such nearly identical states of physical condition will experience an earlier onset of fatigue in sports in which they are untrained and a delayed onset of fatigue in sports in which they are trained.

The onset of fatigue during exercise depends upon the rate and intensity of the work and the frequency and duration of rest periods during the work. The athlete trained for a certain sport prolongs the onset of fatigue by maintaining a certain degree of relaxation during participation. However, when he performs in another sport for which he has not trained, he endeavors to compensate for his lack of skill by tightening up in an effort to play harder. He thus reduces his rest periods to such an extent that fatigue toxins accumulate faster than they can be removed and local fuel supplies are exhausted.

A common characteristic among champions is the extraordinary amount of relaxation which they maintain, even under stress of competition. The "natural" or "all-around" athlete possesses the same quality. He is able, through a proper balance of relaxation during work, to establish a steady state of activity in which the recovery mechanisms are able to maintain a muscular environment which is relatively free from toxins and is rich in food.

The athlete trained for swimming executes his movements in a most economical manner. He has reached a high degree of neuromuscular coordination. His working muscles can contract powerfully while the muscles which oppose them are nearly completely relaxed.

During swimming, the movements are so executed that the muscles work alternately. The muscles which contract during a flexion thus become the antagonistic muscles during extension. Likewise, the extensors are the working muscles during extension and become the antagonistic muscles during flexion.

If the swimmer remains tense during performance and does not allow his antagonistic muscles to relax while his working muscles are contracting, he deprives his muscles of the rest periods they need for recovery and thus hastens the onset of fatigue. In addition, tense antagonistic muscles act as brakes, adding to the load of the working muscles.

Training furnishes two refinements to performance. First, the movements become so timed that rest periods are allowed, and second, antagonist brakes are released.* As a matter of fact, the training procedures for the teacher and pupil in the various levels of swimming and the training procedures for the coach and competitor are in all respects very similar. Only the intensity of the training and the objectives differ. The ultimate objective of the class swimmer is utilitarian, that is, to be able to swim quite a long distance comfortably for pleasure and safety. It also serves as a preparation for lifesaving techniques as well as being a "feeder" for varsity competition. The competitor's objective is to be able to swim as fast as it is humanly possible—in short, to win races.

TRAINING PROGRAM

Records in swimming continue to fall every year. The competitive swimmer who hopes to attain record performance finds that in order to meet the challenge he must extend his training to a year-round program. The training plan is designed to improve the swimmer's level of skill in starting, in stroke mechanics, in the turns, and in finishing and to educate him as to pace and race efficiency. All of these factors are combined in one objective, namely, to win swimming races. Each item in training should contribute to this objective.

In general, the training program can be divided into six phases:
1. The winter precompetition period (3 months)
2. The winter dual-meet period (3 months)
3. The championship period (1 month)
4. The postcompetition period (2 months)
5. The summer period (3 months)
6. The special summer age group period (3 months)
   (a) Summer precompetition period
   (b) Summer swim meet period
   (c) Summer championship period

*Morehouse, L. E., and Cooper, J. M.: Kinesiology, St. Louis, 1950, The C. V. Mosby Company.

Precompetition period

This period starts at the first practice session and continues until about two weeks before the first scheduled meet. In most schools, the coach calls his squad together for the first formal meeting about the latter part of September or the first of October. Prior to the first squad meeting the swimmers may work individually or in small groups, conditioning away from the pool area. A weight-training program designed to strengthen the swimming muscles is in order at this time in the season. The method of running outdoors is fun and will develop wind endurance. The swimmer should discuss his plan with the coach who can prescribe the proper weight exercises and guide his program progressively and intelligently at the first squad meeting.

At the first squad meeting certain phases of training and conditioning are discussed, and the plans for the season are outlined. The overall plan of training is explained by the coach.

The following handout material may be given to each member of the squad:

1. The swimmer's log, a personal notebook including mimeographed pages designed to keep a record of workouts, times, split times, individual comments, goals, pulse counts, etc.
2. Heavy and light weight training exercises for specific strokes
3. Diet and the Swimmer (see Chapter 16)*
4. A short, well-prepared article designed psychologically to stimulate and motivate the swimmer's mental attitude, e.g., the desire to improve, to excel, to take pride in self and the team, work, and self-sacrifice
5. Several copies of the season's swimming schedule including dates and times

Many successful coaches have their squads play water polo during the precompetitive period. This plan works out very well for several reasons. It is a fine swimming conditioner, and it breaks the monotony of a steady, year-round swimming program. It develops teamwork and, above all, it is fun to play. Weight training, water polo, swimming drills, and condition swims complement the program.

Most squads practice in the latter part of the afternoon after academic appointments are completed so that the swimmer can devote his entire concentration to his sport. The swimmer should try to leave his worries in his locker and enter the pool with a buoyant spirit ready to enjoy himself in healthy recreation and pleasurable exertion. He meets his teammates in common bondage and feels he belongs to a group which is interested in him and he, in turn, is seeking his interest in them.

*See also Morehouse, Laurence E.: The physiology of athletics (strength), Scholastic Coach **10:**25 (Sept.), 1940.

The squad member should prepare to devote at least an hour and a half to his daily practice so that he does not have to rush through his work and thereby eliminate the rest periods between the workout events. The swimmers should practice in the water every day and during the precompetition period should continue performing the strengthening and flexibility exercises along with the regular daily schedule of practice.

In general, the swimming workout for all men, including sprinters, during this period consists of distance swimming and repetition swimming during which the coach attempts to iron out the faulty swimming mechanics and difficulties of breathing, body position, relaxation, timing, and balance. The effectiveness of this training is checked by noting the ease which the swimmers acquire, the increased distance they can achieve, and the sustained good form of stroke they can achieve without undue fatigue. During this season the coach should accomplish the spade work for the entire season.

First through third week of precompetition period

The weekly plan of work for the first three weeks of training is designed to build up endurance, speed endurance, and speed in the water as follows: to develop muscular strength through heavy weight exercises twice a week; to develop strength endurance by using light resistance exercises in sets of increasing numbers twice a week; and to develop cardiovascular improvement by running distance one day and repetition of shorter distances the next. In addition, a short series of stretching exercises selected to increase flexibility precede the daily water work.

A water warm-up, such as a 400-yard individual medley, is advisable in early precompetition period. Through practice of the dolphin, back, breast, and crawl strokes, the swimmer's arms, legs, and body acquire certain adjustments to the water that later aid and condition him in swimming any one stroke with greater ease and efficiency.

Major corrections of stroke technique should be made in the early seasons rather than in the competition season. When making corrections, the coach should remain with the swimmer until the desired movement is accomplished. The swimmer should then attempt to duplicate, time and time again, the desired movement pattern until it is thoroughly mastered.

Following is a suggested practice schedule for the first three weeks of precompetition period:

FIRST WEEK

Monday, 2 hours
1. Run 1 mile, relaxed (under 8 minutes)
2. Heavy weight-resistance exercises; number of repetitions, amount of weight, and exercise set by coach

3. Stretching exercises (deck of pool)
4. Warm-up swim 400-yard individual medley
5. Group A (distance men and flyers) crawl stroke 1,000 yards
6. Group B (back, breast, individual medley, and sprinters), 400 yards (3 times)
7. Group A, pull 500 yards (2 times)
8. Group B, pull 300 yards (3 times)
9. Group A, kick 500 yards (2 times)
10. Group B, kick 300 yards (3 times)
11. Whole team, sprint 50 yards (5 times) on the minute

Tuesday, 2 hours

1. Run ⅛ mile slow (warm-up), ⅛ mile fast, 30 seconds; continue running, alternating every ⅛ mile slow and fast, total distance 1 mile
2. Light weight-resistance exercises, pulley-weight or surgical tubing; exercise and number of repetitions determined by the coach
3. Stretching exercises
4. Warm-up swim 400-yard individual medley
5. Group A, crawl stroke 200 yards (5 times), 1-minute rest between swims
6. Group B, 2 sets of 200 yards (3 times), 2-minute rest between swims, 5-minute rest between sets
7. Group A, pull 200 yards (2 times), 100 yards (4 times), 50 yards (4 times)
8. Group B, pull 100 yards (5 times), 50 yards (10 times)
9. Group A, kick 200 yards (2 times), 100 yards (4 times), 50 yards (4 times)
10. Group B, kick 100 yards (5 times), 50 yards (10 times)
11. Whole squad, butterfly, arms only, 50 yards (5 times)

Wednesday

1. Run mile under 7 minutes
2. Increase amount of weight slightly or increase number of repetitions over that of Monday; heavy weight-resistance exercises
3. Stretching exercises
4. Warm-up swim-400 yard individual medley
5. Group A, swim 1,000 yards
6. Group B, swim 500 yards (2 times)
7. Group A, swim 1,000 yards
8. Group B, pull (breast strokers kick) 500 yards (2 times)
9. Group A, swim 1,000 yards
10. Group B, swim 500 yards (2 times)
11. Whole squad, kick 50 yards (5 times), butterfly pull 50 yards (5 times)

Thursday, 2 hours

1. Run ⅛ mile slow, ¼ mile fast, ⅛ mile slow, ¼ mile fast, ⅛ mile slow, ¼ mile fast, ⅛ mile slow, and ¼ mile fast
2. Light weight repetitions increased
3. Stretching exercises varied
4. Warm-up swim 400-yard individual medley

5. Group A, crawl stroke, 100 yards (10 times) starting on the 1 minute and 30 seconds
6. Group B, 2 sets 100 yards (5 times), favored stroke, starting on the 1 minute and 30 seconds, 3-minute rest between
7. Group A, repeat step 5
8. Group B, repeat step 6
9. Group A, pull 100 yards (5 times)
10. Group B, pull 100 yards (5 times)
11. Group A, kick 100 yards (5 times)
12. Group B, kick 100 yards (5 times)
13. Whole squad, butterfly, 50 yards (5 times); 10 push-ups after each 50

Friday

1. 15-minute run (fun running)
2. Stretching exercises; back and abdominal groups stressed
3. Time 400-yard individual medley
4. Time 100-yard kick, favored stroke
5. Time 100-yard pull, favored stroke
6. Continuous relays or water polo

Saturday

If the team can work out on Saturday, it is suggested that the Friday workout be similar to Monday and Wednesday and the Saturday workout be that suggested for Friday.

It cannot be too strongly stressed that the suggested workouts will not fit all situations. The coach must be guided by the time available for workout, the need for strength building, the caliber of his swimmers, and, above all, the individual's capacity for work. The coach who is familiar with the physiology of exercise can utilize the heartbeat count to aid him in determining rest intervals and individual work capacity.

SECOND AND THIRD WEEK

The same general pattern is followed. The swimming work load is gradually increased at the coach's discretion. The procedure should be well organized so as to allow the coach time to study individual stroke technique and make corrections.

Fourth through sixth week of precompetition period

The daily plan of work for these three weeks varies in accordance with the needs of individuals. In general, hard and easy workouts are alternated each day. The load of work should consist of a 1,000-yard warm-up swim, a 500- to 1,000-yard kick board drill, arm pulling for the next 500 to 1,000 yards, swimming for 500 to 1,000 yards, and a series of short sprints at the finish. Speed should be fast enough so that swimmers do not break the good stroking mechanics and accurate timing of the movements.

The daily program can be varied in any number of distances, just so total yardage for the day is beyond the range of 1½ miles. Individual

swimmers differ as to capacity to perform this type of work, and some can easily swim 2 miles or more. The work load must be gradually increased for conditioning.

The style of stroke can also be varied. The kicking and arm pulling should be increased for strengthening legs and arms in the water. The check rope can be used to good advantage in developing power in the arms and legs.

There are many variations that can be used to keep the daily program interesting. If the load of work has been exceptionally hard for some individuals on a certain day, the work for the following day should be modified. Distance need not be shortened if speed is lessened. Sometimes the speed need not be modified, but the arrangement of the sequence of work can be altered, or slightly more rest can be given between each item of work on that day's program.

On at least one or possibly two days, permit the swimmers to go through to the full mile without rest, either with one style of stroke or with all three, with the kicking and arm pulling alternating between the swimming strokes.

At this stage of early season swimming an objective should be an appreciation of the distribution of effort over a longer distance. This is essential for learning pace later in the seventh and eighth weeks.

At the end of the precompetition period the swimmer should have acquired better breathing habits through relaxation, water strength should have been gained, hands and feet should be more sensitive and effective, and the entire body should be better adjusted to the water.

The squad members are now ready for pacing patterns to be drilled daily. They have an appreciation of distance but not of time over a given distance. Up to this point little timing with the watch has been given. However, some authorities believe in timing the swimming at once during distance work, so that time as well as distance may be judged more accurately at an early period in the training.

The inexperienced swimmer should be encouraged constantly to extend and improve in his distance swimming and to sustain a steady stroke cadence. This type of swimming tends to relax him and facilitate breathing habits.

Seventh week of precompetition period

In swimming a distance at which a maximum speed cannot be maintained, the swimmer must attempt to distribute his effort in such a manner that he can cover the distance in his shortest possible time. When this proper energy distribution is accomplished, we may say that he has reached the highest degree of race efficiency.

The untrained swimmer invariably becomes excited during compe-

tition and swims the first portion of his race faster than he should. As a result, he tires quickly and is forced to reduce his velocity to such an extent that his swimming time for the event is very poor. Following proper and sufficiently long training, he develops a greater ability to estimate his speed and his reserve strength, and his efficiency is improved.

Training also produces a greater immunity to the exciting effect of competition.* The longer the race, the more attention the swimmer must give to the distribution of his energy. An observation of the summary of the finals of the Seventeenth Annual National Collegiate Swimming Championship† revealed that the variations in speed were less as the distances became longer. In other words, as the length of the race increases, there is a tendency for trained swimmers to cover the entire distance at a more even rate.

The strong desire of the inexperienced swimmer to take the lead at the start may be due to a transfer of training in track-racing fundamentals. In the track races, which are usually run without lanes around a curve, it is an advantage for a runner to obtain the lead and pole position by sprinting at the beginning of the race. He can then appreciably reduce the pace and force his opponents either to do likewise or to run around him. This track-race strategy does not apply to swimming since swimming races are always swum in lanes and the man in the lead does not block those behind him.

Swimming a certain distance at a given time at a steady rate requires a little less work than swimming the same distance in the same time at an uneven rate. According to Karpovich,‡ the work done in swimming may be expressed as Work = Force $\times$ Distance. It was found that the approximate force developed in swimming the crawl stroke may be calculated by the formula: Force = $0.65V.^2$ Thus, Work = $0.65V^2$ $\times$

Distance, or $W = \dfrac{0.65d\ (d)^2}{t^2}$ where d = distance reckoned in feet trav-

eled in a given t = time reckoned in seconds. To show the effect of a very slight variation in speed upon the work done in swimming 220 yards in 2:13.0, a comparison of two plans of distribution of effort is shown in Table 17-1.

The first 50 yards are covered in a shorter time in both plans because of a time advantage of about 3.4 seconds due to the starts. The figure representing the time advantage due to the start was calculated

---

*Karpovich, Peter V.: Physiological and psychological dynamogenic factors in exercise, Arbeitsphysiologie 9:626-629 (August), 1937.

†National Collegiate Athletic Association, Official rules for swimming, fancy diving and water polo, New York, 1963.

‡Karpovich, Peter V.: Analysis of the propelling force in the craw' stroke, Research Quarterly (Suppl. 6:49-58 (May), 1935.

Table 17-1. Comparison of two race plans of distribution of effort

	DISTANCE (FEET)	TIME FOR EACH 150 FT. (SECONDS)	WORK DONE (FOOT POUNDS)
Race Plan A (steady rate)			
	150	27.6	2,878.5
	150	31.0	2,281.7
	150	31.0	2,281.7
	150	31.0	2,281.7
	60	12.4	913.9
Totals	660	133.0	10,637.5
Race Plan B (unsteady rate)			
	150	26.5	3,169.0
	150	30.5	2,361.4
	150	31.7	2,183.1
	150	32.1	2,129.0
	60	12.2	943.3
Totals	660	133.0	10,885.8

by comparing the time for the first 50 yards with that of the second 50 yards in the summary of the finals of the 100-yard free style race in the 1940 National Collegiate Swimming Championships. If it may be assumed that the entire 100 yards were swum at a maximum rate, then the shorter time required to swim the first 50 yards may be attributed to the advantage gained at the start. The advantage ranged from 2.8 seconds to 4.0 seconds and averaged 3.4 seconds.

In Plan A, the swimmer assumed a steady rate of 50 yards in 31 seconds and maintained that rate throughout the race. The last 20 yards, swum in 12.4 seconds, are swum at the same rate as that in the preceding laps.

In Plan B, the swimmer sprinted for the first 100 yards, then reduced his velocity for the next 100 yards, and sprinted the last 20 yards to the finish.

The difference in the work required to swim Plan A (steady rate) and Plan B (unsteady rate) is 248.3 foot pounds. By utilizing the extra work done in swimming Plan B more efficiently, the swimmer could have considerably reduced his time for the 220-yard race.

In order to improve the untrained swimmer's ability to estimate his speed and reserve strength, a system of training in race efficiency was devised. This system involved the use of a pacing machine.

Since the University of Iowa swimming pool is 150 by 60 feet and practice and competition are held over the long (50-yard) course, the pacing machine was set so that the marker traveled along the length of the pool. The marker was a small black flag attached to a continuous cord 288 feet in length. The cord was stretched over two 3-inch pulleys, one at each end of the pool. The pulleys were held in place by steel rods which were fastened to the ends of the pool and were of such a length that the pulleys were 3 feet from each end of the pool. This extension allowed for the gain in velocity which the swimmer achieves at each turn. One pulley was operated by an electric motor and a device by which the speed of the driving wheel could be adjusted so that the marker could travel 144 feet at any desired interval, from 20 to 60 seconds' duration. The motor was $\frac{1}{4}$ horsepower and ran on a 110 volt, 60 cycle, 5 ampere, alternating current. The motor developed 1,750 revolutions per minute. The speed adjustment mechanism was a 12-inch cast aluminum disk which was held against the motor's driving wheel by a coiled spring. The motor's driving wheel was covered by a rubber tire and measured 2 inches in diameter. The motor was set on an adjustable platform which could be moved 6 inches backward or forward by means of a crank attached to a threaded rod screwed into two grooved pieces of metal, one attached to the motor's platform and the other to the fixed base. The velocity of the marker could thus be increased by moving the motor closer to the center of the aluminum disk and also could be slowed by moving the motor toward the outer edge of the disk.

During the early season of training the pacer was set so that the swimmer would swim one length in 50 seconds (see Table 17-2). Emphasis was made on swimming form, and condition was developed by long-distance swims (800 to 1,000 yards) at this rate.

As the swimmer improved his form, the speed was increased gradually from day to day until it was noticed that he had difficulty in maintaining that rate for 500 yards. This difficulty usually occurred when the speed was lowered to 42 seconds for 50 yards, or 7 minutes for 500 yards. The pacer was then left at this rate until the swimmer improved his ability to swim 500 yards at this rate. Faults were being corrected, and good form was still being stressed at this period.

After continued swimming with the pacer, the swimmer learned to judge his rate and needed to glance at the marker only once each 50 yards in order to check his velocity. A further check was made at this period by having him swim 500 yards without using the pacer and estimating his ability to swim 500 yards in 7 minutes.

When the swimmer was able to gauge his speed so that he was able to swim 500 yards in 7 minutes with an error of no greater than 10 seconds, then the speed of the pacer was again gradually increased, and the fastest rate at which the swimmer could swim 400 yards was de-

Table 17-2. Pace training (time per 50 yards necessary to swim the crawl stroke)

TIME PER 50 YARDS (SEC.)	100 YARDS TOTAL TIME	150 YARDS TOTAL TIME	200 YARDS TOTAL TIME	300 YARDS TOTAL TIME	400 YARDS TOTAL TIME	500 YARDS TOTAL TIME
50	1:40	2:30	3:20	5:00	6:40	8:20
49	1:38	2:27	3:16	4:54	6:32	8:10
48	1:36	2:24	3:12	4:48	6:24	8:00
47	1:34	2:21	3:08	4:42	6:16	7:50
46	1:32	2:18	3:04	4:36	6:08	7:40
45	1:30	2:15	3:00	4:30	6:00	7:30
44	1:28	2:12	2:56	4:24	5:52	7:20
43	1:26	2:09	2:52	4:18	5:44	7:10
42	1:24	2:06	2:48	4:12	5:36	7:00
41	1:22	2:03	2:44	4:06	5:28	6:50
40	1:20	2:00	2:40	4:00	5:20	6:40
39	1:18	1:57	2:36	3:54	5:12	6:30
38	1:16	1:54	2:32	3:48	5:04	6:20
37	1:14	1:51	2:28	3:42	4:56	6:10
36	1:12	1:48	2:24	3:36	4:48	6:00
35	1:10	1:45	2:20	3:30	4:40	5:50
34	1:08	1:42	2:16	3:24	4:32	5:40
33	1:06	1:39	2:12	3:18	4:24	5:30
32	1:04	1:36	2:08	3:12	4:16	5:20
31	1:02	1:33	2:04	3:06	4:08	5:10
30	1:00	1:30	2:00	3:00	4:00	5:00
29	:58	1:27	1:56	2:54	3:52	4:50
28	:56	1:24	1:52	2:48	3:44	4:40
27	:54	1:21	1:48	2:42	3:36	4:30
26	:52	1:18	1:44	2:36	3:28	4:20
25	:50	1:15	1:40	2:30	3:20	4:10
24	:48	1:12	1:36	2:24	3:12	4:00
23	:46	1:09	1:32	2:18	3:04	3:50

termined. In a like manner, each swimmer's best time for the 500-yard, 400-yard, 200-yard, 100-yard, and 50-yard free style, as well as for the 200-yard and 100-yard breast stroke and the 200-yard and 100-yard back stroke, was determined. The coach could now advise each swimmer as to his best events, and the swimmer could concentrate his efforts on these events.

The pacing machine was employed throughout the early season and the midseason to establish paces at lower levels than were first recorded during the preseason period. In many cases, swimmers achieve their fastest times while "racing" with the pacer. If a pacing machine is unavailable, the coach or manager with a stop watch as a guide can walk off the pace. Another method is to have a large clock with a sweep second hand located at each end of the pool. It should be large enough and so placed that it will be clearly visible to the swimmer as he turns.

Eighth week of precompetition period

By this time the swimmer has learned some concept of pace and can estimate to some degree his speed in the water. By increasing his swimming speed and maintaining a steady pace over shorter distances, he has some idea of the manner in which to cover a distance in the shortest possible time.

The rate at which champions swim successive laps of a middle distance or distance event slows very gradually as each lap is undertaken. This gradual slowing is due not to forgetfulness of pace but to the accumulating effects of fatigue which tend to make the swimming strokes less effective as the distance is prolonged. This factor must be taken into account when planning a race.

The eighth week of the precompetition period is devoted wholly to schooling in swimming the first 100 yards of a middle distance or distance race in either the crawl, back crawl, or breast stroke in a certain set time. For example, a swimmer who can repeatedly swim the 100 yards in less than 1:05 minutes is asked to swim 100 yards in 1:10 minutes. At his first trial he will usually be surprised that he has swum the 100 yards in about 1:06 or 1:07 minutes. He is then told to swim the same distance in 1:12 minutes. This time he comes closer. The third trial at which he tries again for 1:10 minutes is usually within a second of that mark. He practices this distance at this time until he can remain within a 0.5-second error consistently. He is then asked to hit this 1:10 mark on the way to a 200-yard distance. After he has accomplished this, the time for 100 yards is lowered to 1:07 minutes and the swimmer repeats the procedure described previously.

In all events over the 100-yard distance, the way the swimmer swims the first 100 yards is of great importance. The nature of the race after this point depends largely upon the energy he has expended during the first 100 yards. If he has allowed the excitement of the race to cause him to increase his swimming time for the first 100 yards beyond that which is a safe limit in his distribution of effort, only a partial amount of his finishing energy remains, and he is left floundering hopelessly during the challenging moments of a race.

Dual-meet period
First week

This phase of training introduces the factor of speed to the swimming workout. Until this period, the swimmers have been covering long distances in order to refine stroke mechanics, establish a perception of pace, and increase swimming efficiency.

The coach introduces the starting gun and increases the use of the stop watch for checking swimming time.

At each practice, after limbering exercises and swims, the technique of starting is taught, and a series of practice starts is given. After each start, the swimmers should continue across the pool, make a fast turn and push-off, and return to the starting edge. The time of the first width is noted, and each swimmer is encouraged to lower the time.

The turns are made as fast as possible, and, after the first three days of this drill, the time for the two widths is noted. The importance of constant drill in the technique of making rapid and powerful starts and turns cannot be overemphasized.

Relay starting technique can be started at this time by practicing the touch-offs. All swimmers can participate in this practice in preparation for the medley and free style relay events.

Drills in pacing are continued throughout this week, and each swimmer begins to concentrate upon the event in which he shows the most promise in relation to the rest of the squad. The squad is notified that time trials will be made on Saturday.

A careful record, complete with the split times of each man in each event, should be made during the time trials on Saturday. These are studied by the coach, and each swimmer is advised as to his achievement and as to ways of improving his times.

Second week

Drills in starts, relay take-offs, turns, and pacing are continued, as are frequent attempts to lower the swimming time for the events in which the swimmer plans to specialize.

Either a freshman-varsity or an intersquad meet is scheduled for the Saturday of this week. On each succeeding day of practice an increasing effort is made to simulate actual meet conditions. On Saturday, officials are present, and the meet schedule and organization are exactly like those of a regular dual meet. Spectators are invited, and each event and its results are announced. By a careful observation of the behavior of each competitor, the coach will gain a fairly accurate estimate of the racing ability of each squad member during competitive conditions.

The divers perform the dives they intend to use during the first dual meet. The dives are scored as in regular competition, and the coach makes notes on each dive and discusses the weakness of each diver after the meet.

The swimming time and the split times of each competitor are recorded for comparison with the previous performance.

Week of the first dual meet

On Monday the data and notes collected from each individual during last Saturday's competition are discussed with each member of the squad. Comparisons are drawn with the results recorded during the first time trials. Improvement or decline in performance is noted.

From these records the coach sets up a reasonable time which the swimmer should attain in his event for the dual meet this week-end. The remainder of the week is devoted to achieving consistency in attaining the set time.

Fourth through twelfth week of dual-meet competition (interval and repetition training)

During this period, interval and repetition swimming are stressed. This type of training as applied to swimming is an outgrowth of methods used by famous track coaches and runners. It reached its height of recognition with the lowering of the mile record below 4 minutes. Runners using the interval method of training would alternate a fast run with a slow run—fast, slow, fast, slow, etc.—over a set distance, with each run timed. Every effort was made to run the fast runs in a predetermined time. The interval or slow run was timed to allow for sufficient recovery between fast runs. As the athlete's stamina and condition increase, the interval of rest is gradually decreased, and the speed of the fast runs is increased.* Repetition running consists in repeating a series of fast runs, say a group of 440-yard runs for example, at a pace slower than an all-out effort, with adequate rest for recovery between runs. This method is designed to increase the appreciation of pace over a set distance and to develop stamina and endurance.

In swimming, this method of training can apply to all strokes for any given distance. The arms and legs may be trained independently and together as a whole stroke.

The technique involved is based upon the overload principle to develop speed and cardiorespiratory endurance. The overload principle, stated simply, means that cardiorespiratory endurance develops according to the demands placed on the lungs and circulatory system; to improve endurance, increased demands must be systematically made on muscles, lungs, and the circulatory system.

In planning the workout program the coach must give careful consideration to the individual swimmer, his present physical condition, and his capacity for work.

*Franz Stampfl on Running, London, Herbert Jenkins (reprint, 1956).

Interval and repetition training is unique in that it offers so much variety, makes workouts more interesting, and can also be patterned to the needs of the individual swimmer.

A series of repetition swims is designed for each swimmer. The rest interval between each swim is established and the time limit for each swim determined. A hypothetical illustration is as follows:

Swimmer A:

1. Swim 200 yards (3 times), 2-minute rest between; time goal under 2:10 seconds for each 200 yards
2. Swim 100 yards (5 times), 1-minute rest between; time goal: 62 seconds for each 100 yards
3. Swim 2 sets of 50 yards (10 times), 45-second rest between; time goal :30 seconds for each 50 yards

If the swimmer misses the time goal on one swim of a set, he may be given an additional swim in that set or be required to repeat the whole set after the complete workout. Should he stay under the time goals for the whole set, the coach may increase the number of repetitions, reduce the rest periods, or lower the time goals for the next session.

The coach has a wide range of selection for the repetition swims, such as repeats of longer swims for distance men and inclusion of kicking and pulling for breast, back flyers, and sprinters. Predetermined time goals selected by the coach should be easily attainable by the swimmer at first and gradually lowered to motivate the swimmer.

Another method of utilizing the repetition and interval method in swimming is illustrated in the following schedule. Again the authors stress the point that the distances and number of repetitions are arbitrary and should be patterned to the ability of the swimming squad.

Monday

1. Land flexibility exercises
2. 15- to 20-minute warm-up swim
3. Kick 200 yards for time; coach lists in individual's performance data card for future use
4. Rest 3 to 5 minutes
5. Pull 200 yards for time; coach posts data for future use
6. Rest 3 to 5 minutes
7. Swim 200 yards for time; coach posts data for future use
8. Rest 5 minutes
9. Swim ¼ mile
10. Sprint 50 yards (3 times); 30 seconds rest between each 50 yards

Tuesday

1. Land flexibility exercises
2. Warm-up swim 5 minutes each stroke (back, breast, and crawl strokes)

3. Kick 100 yards (3 times), 2 minutes rest between each 100 yards; effort should be made to keep time below ½ the time posted for the 200-yard kick on Monday
4. Pull 100 yards (3 times), 2 minutes rest between each 100 yards; effort made to keep time below ½ the time posted for the 200-yard arm pull on Monday
5. Rest 5 minutes
6. Swim 100 yards (3 times), same procedure as steps 3 and 4 above
7. Rest 10 minutes
8. Swim 300 yards
9. Sprint 75 yards or more; 50 yards or more (2 times)

Wednesday

1. Land flexibility exercises
2. Warm-up swim 880 yards
3. 300 yards interval kicking (100 yards all out effort; 1 length slow easy kicking; 100 yards all out effort; 1 length slow easy kicking; 100 yards all out effort)
4. Rest 5 minutes
5. Pull 600 yards, ¾ effort
6. 300 yards interval swimming—100 yards fast (3 times), 1 length slow, etc.
7. Rest 5 to 7 minutes
8. Swim 300 yards
9. Sprint 50 yards or more (4 times)

Thursday

1. Flexibility exercises
2. Warm-up 15 minutes; count the number of lengths covered
3. Kick 1,000 yards, ¾ effort
4. Pull 300 yards interval style
5. Rest 5 minutes
6. 300 yards interval swimming
7. Rest 10 minutes
8. Continuous relay 50 yards sprints (6 times)

Friday

1. Flexibility exercises
2. Warm-up, swim 15 minutes, attempt to increase number of lengths covered on Thursday
3. Repetition kicking: *Time* 50 yards (5 times), 1-minute rest between each 50 yards; attempt to keep time below ½ the speed posted for 100 yards on Tuesday
4. Repetition pulling: *Time* 100 yards (5 times), same procedure as step 3 above
5. Swim 1,000 yards
6. Repeat step 3
7. Repeat step 4
8. Practice starts and turns

Saturday

    1. Repeat Monday's workout; compare times

Sunday

    1. Rest

Following is a suggested workout plan for the week of a dual swimming meet for all styles of swimming which are competed in at a distance up to 200 yards:

Monday (Rest periods and predetermined times to be established by the coach)

    1. Warm-up flexibility drill on deck
    2. 15-minute warm-up swim
    3. Swim 100 yards (3 times) interval swimming (100 yards fast, 1 length slow, etc.)
    4. Kick 100 yards (3 times) interval method
    5. Pull 100 yards (3 times) interval method
    6. Swim 100 yards (3 times) interval swim
    7. Swim ¼ mile
    8. Sprint 50 yards (3 times) repetition method

Tuesday

    1. Warm-up flexibility exercises
    2. 1,000 yards warm-up swim; vary pace and change strokes
    3. Swim 150 yards (4 times) favored stroke repetition method
    4. Kick 800 yards
    5. Pull 500 yards
    6. Swim 50 yards (5 times) repetition method
    7. Swim easy 200 yards to tone down

Wednesday

    1. Warm-up flexibility exercises
    2. 15- to 20-minute warm-up swim
    3. Work on pace plan for coming race; repeat ½ of race distance 3 times
    4. Swim 75 yards (5 times) repetition method
    5. Kick 75 yards (5 times) repetition method
    6. Pull 75 yards (5 times) repetition method
    7. Swim 50 yards (5 times) repetition method
    8. Swim easy 200 yards

Thursday

    1. Warm-up flexibility exercises
    2. 15-minute medley warm-up swim, 5 minutes each stroke (back, breast, and crawl strokes)
    3. Pace work, swim ¾ of race distance, repeat 3 times
    4. Kick 800 yards
    5. Pull 500 yards

6. Swim 50 yards (5 times) repetition style
7. Swim 25 yards (10 times), using gun start

Friday

1. Squad meeting; discuss meet plan
2. Warm-up flexibility exercises
3. 15-minute warm-up swim
4. Continuous relays; vary strokes, vary distances
5. Gun starts, 25 yards (10 times) with turn
6. Practice turns, 20 with each arm, breast stroke 30 turns

Saturday (day of competition)

Warm-up on day of meet; best results can be obtained if warm-up is performed about 20 to 30 minutes before meet time. Some coaches favor an early morning light workout on day of meet.

1. Warm-up flexibility exercises
2. Warm-up swim followed by short sprints 20 to 30 minutes prior to competition
3. Keep warm till event

Distance swimmers can add variety and interest to their workout plan by using interval and repetition training. The distances will naturally be longer, ranging from sets of 800-yard repetitions for speed endurance down to 50-yard repetitions for speed.

Championship period
Two weeks before the league championship meet

During this period finer adjustments are made in racing fundamentals, and the swimmer's condition is watched closely. Special attention is given to the diet, rest, exercise, and hygienic habits of the swimmers. All swimmers who are eligible to compete in the championships should be nearing the peaks of their condition and performance.

In order to approximate the work which will have to be done at the championships if the swimmer is fortunate enough to proceed to the finals, time trials of the swimmer's events are repeated the number of times that are scheduled in the championships. This trial is given about 10 days before the championships so that the swimmer is given ample time to improve his condition after he recognizes what may be demanded of him.

The sprinters should swim three fast 100 yards with 20 minutes between each trial. The middle distance swimmers should swim 200 yards 2 times with 30 minutes of rest between. The distance swimmers and back and breast strokers should also attempt this schedule with a 45-minute rest between trials.

Through weeks of continued training throughout the entire season, relaxation is increased; efficiency, pace, and timing have also improved. The swimmer should experience sensations of power, speed, and relative freedom from fatigue. In other words, he has the sensation of power throbbing "under the hood." Breathing becomes effortless. All of the preceding swimming fundamentals coincide, and the result is water-efficiency.

During this period the emphasis is placed on quality repetitions rather than quantity. The rest period is increased between swims and the distance of the repetitions shortened.

When the swimmer arrives at this stage of his training, he is now in readiness for specialized training for his race. Starts become a daily event in his training for the purpose of improving faster reaction time. Timing and speed in performance of turns are emphasized. In the midseason of training, swimmers should not be permitted to make turns slowly. The turn rhythm should be independent from the stroke rhythm.

Postcompetition period

The first week of this period should be devoted to loosening up. All swimmers should swim every day.

At the end of the first week after the last meet, a time trial should be given to each man in his best event. It is frequently observed that the swimmer will turn in his best time of the entire season at this trial. Here is a good opportunity for the coach to demonstrate the effect of worry and overstrain of competition.

The remainder of the two months is usually devoted to lifesaving, water safety, and water sports such as water polo or all-round inter-squad competition. Much of this time should be given over to experimentation and photographic and other forms of study of swimming technique. Radical changes in technique can be made during this period. Ample time is now available for refinement. The swimmer should now ease down his training gradually, just as he gradually trained up.

Summer period

To become a champion today a swimmer finds that he must spend more and more time in the water. The workout of twenty years ago is hardly more than a warm-up for the modern champion. The summer period offers an opportunity for two, or in some cases three, workouts a day.

Special summer age group period

The summer program has become the backbone of competitive swimming in this country. The success of its program has contributed in no small degree to the success of the 1960 and 1964 American Olympic Teams. The growth of the summer competitive program during the past ten years has flourished to such a tremendous degree that the authors feel it necessary to discuss some of the aspects of the program, which will be of assistance to the summer period coach.

The season extends over a period of three months, June, July, and August. Most of the state and National championships are generally scheduled in August. However, due to the short season, age group, open A.A.U., invitational, and dual swimming meets are held about every week during the summer. The coach is faced with the problems of training a large group of swimmers with a wide range of talent in a short period of time. He must also teach mechanically sound strokes and strive for perfection in technique.

If practice time available to the team is limited, each period must be well planned. The first meetings should include instruction in the competitive strokes. Individuals at this stage are encouraged to swim all of the strokes. When the group is unusually large, older skilled swimmers assigned to small groups have helped to speed up the teaching process. In a situation where the team is limited to the use of the swim pool for a period of only an hour and a half a day, the coach might well consider the possibility of holding additional meetings elsewhere. At these meetings he could show swimming films of champions, lead the group in flexibility exercises, discuss diet, rest, and the physiologic aspects of swimming, or discuss the workout plan for the day. A discussion prior to the first out-of-town meet pertaining to conduct, eating, transportation, etc., is well worth the time spent.

The coach that has a pool available to his team throughout the day is indeed fortunate. His problem then becomes one of grouping his swimmers by ability, sex, or age, so that the group will be best motivated and benefit by his instruction. He can easily accommodate two, and in some cases three, workouts a day.

A typical plan would be to have the best swimmers, regardless of sex and age, representing about 25% of the total group, report for practice at 8:30 to 10:00 A.M. The remainder of the experienced swimmers would report at 10 A.M. and work to 11:00 A.M. The younger and less experienced group would meet from 11:00 to 12:00 A.M. This type of arrangement would stimulate competition within groups, allow adequate pool space for advanced swimmers, and permit the coach to bring each group along at its own pace.

A similar arrangement could be scheduled for the afternoon, or the coach could have the whole group report for sprint type workout from 3:00 to 5:00 P.M. The hours from 1:00 to 3:00 P.M. may be utilized by the divers.

A small swimming area can accommodate a large group of swimmers if the following patterns are utilized for a six lane pool.

Two lane weave. Swimmers line up on deck behind lanes one, four, and five. The swimmers behind lane one will swim down one and return in lane two. Swimmers behind lane four will swim down four and back in lane three. Swimmers behind lane five will swim down five and back in lane six. The coach may line up the swimmers according to their speed and set them off at a set interval. Each swimmer attempts to touch the swimmer in front of him; if he is successful, he will change positions with him in the next swim.

Whole pool weave. All swimmers line up behind lane one. The first swimmer swims down lane one, back lane two, down lane three, back lane four, down lane five, and back lane six. He then climbs out of the pool and joins the end of the line. The second and succeeding swimmers follow the same pattern, allowing a 2- to 3-second interval between swimmers.

One length wave. All swimmers are lined up behind the six lanes. The first six swimmers start and swim one length of the pool. As soon as they are 10 feet away from the start, the second flight of six start, and so on. After swimming one length of the pool, each swimmer climbs from the pool, walks to the starting end, and takes his position at the end of the line in his lane.

Swimming across the pool. The purpose of this is to utilize the practice of starts and turns. The whole team lines up and swims across the pool and back, responding to gun starts while concentrating on turn technique.

Summer precompetition period

This period starts with the first meeting of the summer swim team and continues for three weeks. During this period emphasis is placed upon stroke technique, flexibility and weight training or muscle development programs (see Chapter 16), and a gradual development of distance swimming designed to create a sound foundation of condition for the coming weeks of competition.

The length and extent of flexibility exercises and muscle development will be determined by the time available and the needs of the individual. Group exercises led by the coach should be demonstrated to the team. The benefits to be derived from the particular exercise should be explained. At least thirty minutes will be required the first few meetings until the team is familiar with the exercise routine. The flexibility portion of the workout can then be done individually as soon as the swimmer arrives at practice. The swimmer should select those exercises most suited to his strokes.

PRACTICE SCHEDULES FIRST WEEK OF SUMMER PERIOD

Monday

1. Coach conducts organization meeting. Plans for the summer, schedule, conduct of squad, etc.
2. Crawl techniques are explained and demonstrated by the coach, including breathing, arm action, leg action, body position, the turn, etc.
3. Team executes crawl kick, supported by side of pool. The coach checks each swimmer. When the swimmer is able to demonstrate sufficient skill in the execution of the kick, he is instructed to kick 400 yards with a kick board for support. Inexperienced swimmers are told to stop and rest when fatigue sets in but to make every effort to minimize the number of stops. Skilled swimmers kick the full distance without stopping and work for relaxation and efficiency. (As the better kickers finish, they may assist the poorer kickers.)
4. Group is assembled in chest depth water, facing the coach. Group simulates the arm and proper breathing action. Coach checks each member's technique. When satisfactory skill is attained, each swimmer pulls 400 yards with a floating device supporting the legs. The lesser skilled swimmers follow the suggestions mentioned in step 3.
5. Divide the team into three groups. Groups 2 and 3 are instructed to practice the whole stroke under supervision of older team members or lifeguards. Group 1 is assembled at one end of the pool with the coach. One swimmer at a time will swim before the coach and group. Coach will comment on faults and how to correct them. Group 1 is then instructed to swim 400 yards, concentrating on coach's comment relative to his technique. Coach then works with group 2 and finally group 3, following the same procedure as with group 1.
6. Four short sprints complete the workout.

Note: The length of time available for the use of the pool by the swimming team may require the coach to adjust the preceding into two sessions rather than one.

Tuesday

1. Meeting; training and conditioning
2. Back crawl techniques explained and demonstrated by the coach
3. Follow same procedure listed in steps 3, 4, and 5 of Monday's workout, substituting back crawl stroke for crawl stroke
4. Crawl 100 yards; back crawl sprints, 50 yards (2 times)

Wednesday

1. Meeting; health habits, care of ears, athlete's foot, etc.
2. Breast stroke techniques explained and demonstrated by coach
3. Follow same procedure listed in steps 3, 4, and 5 of Monday's workout, substituting breast stroke for crawl stroke
4. Crawl stroke, 100 yards; back stroke, 100 yards; and breast stroke, 50 yards (2 times)

Thursday

1. Meeting; mental attitude toward practice and competition
2. Dolphin butterfly stroke explained and demonstrated by coach
3. Follow same procedure listed in steps 3, 4, and 5 of Monday's workout, substituting dolphin butterfly stroke for crawl stroke
4. Crawl stroke, 100 yards; back stroke, 100 yards; breast stroke, 100 yards; and dolphin butterfly stroke, 50 yards (2 times)

Friday

1. Meeting; sportsmanship, team loyalty, and pride
2. 200 yards individual medley (50 yards dolphin stroke, 50 yards back stroke, 50 yards breast stroke, and 50 yards crawl stroke)
3. Pull 100 yards dolphin, kick 100 yards dolphin, swim 100 yards dolphin
4. Pull 100 yards back stroke, kick 100 yards back stroke, swim 100 yards back stroke
5. Kick 100 yards breast stroke, swim 100 yards breast stroke
6. Pull 100 yards crawl stroke, kick 100 yards crawl stroke, swim 100 yards crawl stroke
7. Continuous medley relay races; each man swims 50 yards

Saturday

1. Meeting; explanation of day's workout. Each swimmer to be timed for 100 yards in all strokes, less skilled and younger swimmers for 50 yards. This will help the coach and swimmer to determine the stroke or strokes in which to specialize.
2. 100 yards or 50 yards dolphin butterfly stroke for time trial. The number of stop watches available will determine the number of swimmers to swim at one time. Alternate method: the coach can call out the time as each swimmer finishes, and the manager can record the time.
3. Allow each swimmer a minimum of 12 minutes rest between races
4. Breast stroke, 100 yards or 50 yards
5. Rest 12 minutes
6. Back stroke, 100 yards or 50 yards
7. Rest 12 minutes
8. Crawl stroke, 100 yards or 50 yards

Note: When time permits, it is suggested that water games, relays, and water fun be incorporated into the workout.

PRACTICE SCHEDULE SECOND WEEK PRECOMPETITION

Monday

1. Muscle development and flexibility exercises
2. Swim 200 yards individual medley
3. Kick favored stroke; 1 length fast, 1 slow, 2 fast, 2 slow, 3 fast, 3 slow, 4 fast
4. Pull favored stroke; 1 length fast, 1 slow, 2 fast, 2 slow, 3 fast, 3 slow, 4 fast

5. Swim favored stroke; 1 length fast, 1 slow, 2 fast, 2 slow, 3 fast, 3 slow, 4 fast
6. Sprint 50 yards dolphin butterfly stroke, 50 yards breast stroke, 50 yards back stroke, and 50 yards crawl stroke

Tuesday

1. Muscle development and flexibility exercises
2. Swim 100 yards dolphin butterfly stroke, rest, 100 yards back stroke, rest, 100 yards breast stroke, rest, 100 yards crawl stroke
3. Kick 300 yards time favored stroke
4. Pull 300 yards time favored stroke
5. Swim 300 yards favored stroke
6. Continuous relays, each swimmer to sprint 25 yards (10 times)

Wednesday

1. Muscle development and flexibility exercises
2. Swim 200 yards individual medley
3. Kick 100 yards fast, 25 yards slow, 100 yards fast, 25 yards slow, 100 yards fast, 25 yards slow, 100 yards fast
4. Pull 100 yards fast, 25 yards slow, 100 yards fast, 25 yards slow, 100 yards fast, 25 yards slow, 100 yards fast
5. Swim 100 yards fast, 25 yards slow, 100 yards fast, 25 yards slow, 100 yards fast, 25 yards slow, 100 yards fast
6. Sprint 50 yards (5 times)

Thursday

1. Muscle development and flexibility exercises
2. Kick 500 yards
3. Pull 500 yards
4. Swim 500 yards
5. Sprint 100 yards (2 times), 50 yards (2 times), 25 yards (2 times)

Friday

1. Flexibility exercises
2. Warm-up, 200 yards individual medley
3. Group works on start and turns
4. Swim 300 yards, rest 5 minutes, 200 yards, rest 5 minutes, 100 yards, rest 5 minutes, 50 yards, rest 3 minutes, 25 yards
5. Relay races, 25 yards; repetitions

Saturday

1. Flexibility exercises
2. Warm-up, 200 yards individual medley
3. Time 100 yards favored stroke
4. Time 50 yards favored stroke
5. Games

THIRD WEEK PRECOMPETITION

Monday

1. Flexibility and muscle development
2. Warm-up, swim ¼ mile

3. Pull 500 yards
4. Kick 500 yards
5. Swim 500 yards
6. Sprint 50 yards (4 times)

Monday P.M.

1. Flexibility exercises
2. Swim 100 yards (5 times), with 5-minute rest to establish average
3. Rest 15 minutes
4. Pull 50 yards (5 times), time to establish average
5. Kick 50 yards (5 times), time to establish average
6. Relax swim

Tuesday A.M.

1. Warm-up, 100 yards butterfly stroke, 100 yards back stroke, 100 yards breast stroke, 100 yards crawl stroke
2. Kick 200 yards (3 times)
3. Pull 200 yards (3 times)
4. Swim 200 yards (3 times)
5. Sprint 50 yards (4 times)

Tuesday P.M.

1. Flexibility exercises
2. Warm-up swim
3. Swim 100 yards (5 times), time, 5-minute rest interval
4. 15-minute rest
5. Kick 50 yards (5 times), time, 5-minute rest interval
6. Relays of 25 yards

Wednesday A.M.

1. Flexibility exercises
2. Warm-up, 200 yards individual medley
3. Swim 800 yards

Wednesday P.M.

1. Isometric and muscle building routine
2. Repeat swim of 100 yards (5 times), 5-minute rest unless goal was reached; if so, 100 yards swim (5 times) with 4-minute rest
3. Pull 50 yards (5 times), 5-minute rest, attempt to beat established average
4. Pull 75 yards (5 times), no time
5. Sprint 50 yards (4 times)

Thursday A.M.

1. Warm-up, swim 200 yards individual medley
2. Swim 1 length fast, 1 slow, 2 fast, 1 slow, 3 fast, 1 slow, 4 fast, 1 slow, 3 fast, 1 slow, 2 fast, 1 slow, 1 fast, 1 slow
3. Kick 100 yards (3 times)
4. Pull 100 yards (3 times)
5. Sprint 25 yards (5 times)

Thursday P.M.

1. Flexibility exercises
2. Warm-up, swim individual's discretion
3. Attempt to attain goal, swim 50 yards (5 times)
4. Attempt to attain goal, kick 50 yards (5 times)
5. Attempt to attain goal, pull 50 yards (5 times)
6. Games, water fun

Friday, one workout; meet on Saturday

1. Flexibility exercises
2. Warm-up, 200 yards medley
3. Time one half distance of Saturday's race, coach establishes time to hit for pace, repeat 4 times
4. Starts, turns, relay exchanges
5. Sprint 25 yards (5 times)

Summer championship period

This period starts 3 weeks prior to the final championship meet of the season and ends the special summer period.

This is a period for fine adjustment. The swimmer is working harder at shorter distances, with more rest between swims. The objective is to have the swimmer reach his peak at the championship meets. Special attention is given to the diet, rest, exercise, and mental attitude of the swimmer. The coach should be closer to the swimmer than at any other period. It is a period of mutual understanding of the effort and sacrifice necessary to achieve the desired goal. The coach must instill confidence that the swimmer can achieve the final goal he has set for himself. Unless the swimmer honestly believes he can do well in the race, he will fall short of the goal. Rhythm, timing, pace, and mental conditioning are stressed during this period.

If the squad has been working out once a day prior to this time, two workouts a day would be in order. This is the time when some coaches work out three times a day.

A few days prior to the championships, the coach will ease up the swimmer's work load and allow him to rest and store up energy. The length of the rest period varies with various coaches.

Chapter 18

Teaching and coaching
springboard diving

D **INTRODUCTION**

iving was developed in Europe as an outgrowth of outdoor aerial acrobatics and tumbling. It became a competitive sport in England in 1905. Fundamentally, diving consists in leaping from either a platform take-off or a springboard take-off and descending vertically into the water, either head or feet first.

Competitive springboard diving is really a form of aerial acrobatics. The water serves merely to ease the shock of alighting, just as a net catches the trapeze acrobat. Needless to say, springboard diving is as spectacular as it is intrinsically difficult and is related more closely to acrobatics than to swimming. It offers a thrill to the spectator as well as the performer.

Diving consists in projecting the human body high into the air and there performing a series of breathless, swift, and gracefully controlled maneuvers, such as bending, twisting, and somersaulting. Then the body is suddenly righted and poised for a straight entry into the water. Springboard diving attracts and challenges the most stouthearted youth. It provides an opportunity to cultivate a supple and graceful body through skilled movements.

Some dives, when performed efficiently, cause the diver to move with the rhythm and tempo of "poetry in motion," especially such dives as the layout dives. Any dive performed in the layout, pike, or tuck position, whether slow or rapid in motion, must always have force, yet have the appearance of being performed with ease, comfort, and simplicity. When power and ease of performance are achieved, the dive is well balanced. When expertly timed and controlled, the springboard dive is a thrilling acrobatic feat. It leads to confidence and poise in body control.

An ambitious beginner who has hopes and aspirations of becoming a top-flight diver should first master the fundamental dives before attempting the more intricate dives. Then, advancement will be easier, and the difficult dives will be more easily mastered. Many inexperienced divers, as soon as they are able merely to perform a dive, without any regard for good form, seem to be satisfied with their efforts. One should not stop here but should make every effort to "dress up" the dive by improving the style and mechanics, even to the smallest detail, in order to give the dive personality.

If the movements, such as the lift from the board, are not well timed, the dive will appear unbalanced, and will also seem to require great effort. Any dive, no matter how intricate, if well timed from the take-off to the entry, will have the appearance of being performed effortlessly.

A diver must possess an awareness of muscular movement. In the performance of intricate dives, he must be able to make one group of muscles perform one movement while another group performs independent of the other group or groups. If a diver wishes to become a champion, he must possess perseverance, courage, and patience. He must be willing to spend several seasons developing fundamental skills in the elementary dives in order to go far in competition.

PHYSICAL QUALIFICATIONS

The build of a diver should be reasonably well proportioned. It is particularly advantageous to have a flexible shoulder girdle so that when the arms are extended overhead they can easily squeeze tight next to the head. When the legs are extended straight for the entry in the water, the aesthetic appearance presented by a graceful curve of the ankles and toes does much to improve the beauty of the dive. If the diver's ankle joint is not flexible, it will then be a definite detriment to his diving. Ankle exercises do improve the flexibility of the ankles. A diver could weigh 190 pounds and be over 6 feet tall and be just as great a diver as a man 5 feet tall, weighing 120 pounds, so long as each has a well-proportioned body and similar muscular coordination.

EQUIPMENT

Divers should be equipped with snugly fitting trunks of some type of elastic which conforms to the contour of the hips when the body is either bent or straight. The suit should be high-waisted, giving the diver a more pleasing appearance. The diver should have at least two suits, one for practice and another for competition.

TRAINING AND CONDITIONING EXERCISES

To attain a pleasing physique and maintain good poise and posture, a diver must practice some preseason and daily conditioning. A good diver must develop firmness in the muscles of his body, especially in the stomach and legs. There is considerable impact when the body strikes the water, and the diver must be strong and firm in order to hold his body in straight alignment for a perfect entry. All the muscles of the body must be held tense to keep the body from collapsing on the entry. Control of the stomach muscles is particularly important in many dives, especially in the back and reverse dives done in pike position. In these pike dives the muscles of the stomach contract to draw the legs close to the body, and then they extend to straighten the body and again are held taut at the entry.

To strengthen the stomach muscles, the diver should do sit-ups from the floor or from an inclined board. If the diver uses an inclined board, the feet should be attached to the high part of the board, and the head should lay on the lower end. After the diver is able to do this many times in succession, he should try holding an extra weight behind the head.

The legs and toes must extend firmly on the diving board on all take-offs and must be held firmly throughout the execution and entry into the water. To strengthen the legs and toes, the diver lays on his back in a supine position and does repeated leg lifts. He should hang from a horizontal bar by the arms and do repeated leg lifts up to the bar. He should try to increase the number of times he does this exercise each day.

To exercise the flexibility of the ankles, kneel on a towel, with the toes pointing backward. Then, sit back on the ankles, and rock up and back, slightly supporting the body weight with the hands placed on the floor beside the legs. The knees will lift off the floor as the body rocks back on the ankles. This exercise is used to strengthen the ankles and increase the flexibility and should be practiced daily before and during the season. A towel should be kept beside the diving board, and before every dive the diver should turn his toes downward and exert a little pressure in extending the ankle. This will help to increase his thought and awareness of the toe point in the actual dive.

A number of stretching exercises are important at the beginning of a workout in order to loosen the muscles in the back, shoulders, trunk, and legs. Some of these exercises are as follows:

1. Run in place, lifting the knees high toward the chest.
2. Bend down, keeping the legs straight, and touch the ankles. Then straighten up, and arch the back with the arms over the head.
3. Rock back and forth in the kneeling position while sitting on the ankles.
4. Jump up and down on the balls of the feet like skipping rope.

5. Stand erect, with the arms stretched laterally, and twist at the trunk from side to side. Bend over at the waist with the legs straight, and repeat the exercise.
6. Press into a handstand and balance without an arch in the back.
7. Stand with the back against a flat wall with the heels, calves, hips, shoulders, and head touching for a sense of posture alignment and correction. Tilt the pelvis back to straighten the spine, allowing just the thickness of the hand to be inserted between the spine and the wall.

DAILY WORKOUTS

A competitive diver with the aspiration of becoming a champion must enjoy a lot of hard work. A competitive diver should work out at least once a day and, if time permits, twice a day. When practicing once a day, the diver should first loosen up with some stretching exercises along with some practice approaches on the board. The diver should then execute about three each of the required dives and the optional dives. The diver may find it helpful to practice the first four compulsory dives in the pike and layout positions during the beginning of the season to aid in muscle tonus and orientation to body position in the air. Once the diver has completed his full list of dives, he should make repeated attempts at those which cause him the most trouble. The diver should experiment with new dives he wishes to learn at this time.

When practicing twice a day, the diver should not execute the compulsory and optional dives more than three times in each workout. The two practices should be separated by at least two hours of rest. In practicing from both the 1-meter and 3-meter boards, the diver should devote one practice session to the 1-meter and the other practice session to the 3-meter board. The practices from the different heights may be switched from day to day. The diver should occasionally start the second practice by executing the optional dives then the required dives to add variety to the practice. He should then finish the practice with any particular dives that he wishes to give extra attention. At least twice each week, the second workout should be as though the diver were in actual competition—that is, he should do each dive on his list of competitive dives without repeating any dive. Also, it is important to have someone judge his diving at this time.

The diver should be taught to create a visual picture in his mind before attempting a dive. When learning a particular technique, the diver should draw an imaginary picture in his mind and strive to achieve this very thing as he does the dive. Perhaps in a jackknife he will imagine that he is lifting his hips over an imaginary pole, wire, wall, or whatever he wishes in striving for the hip action involved. In a somersault, he may think that he has heavy weights on his feet and that he must throw them over his head.

The diver should visualize whatever image best describes the action to him and then perform it. The action and the coordination of the dive should be thoroughly thought through by the diver before trying it. Once he has decided to try a dive and has launched his body into the air, he should go through with it as he has pictured it in his mind, and he will usually be successful. If the diver changes his mind in midair, he will generally make a bad landing and "take a beating." Therefore, it is suggested that once a dive is started, make every effort to finish it.

Water temperature is something the diver may have no control over, but, if he does, he should practice diving when or where the air temperature and water temperature are warm. Goose bumps and muscular coordination just do not go together.

Eating habits do not have to be restricted or controlled for diving. However, the diver should not eat anything for at least two hours before a workout or competition.

A diver should never practice alone. First, it is not safe because the diver could possibly have an accident. Secondly, the diver must have someone observe and correct his technique if he is ever going to learn. A coach must observe the component parts of a dive. He does not simply note whether or not the body causes a splash forward or backward, but what action takes place from the time the diver takes off from the board until he enters the water. It is better to look at one single thing at a time. For example, if in a front jackknife the diver continually lands on his stomach and is short of the vertical entry, the coach should observe the action of the legs ONLY to see if they lift upward and backward to cause enough rotation. If the action seems right, then on the next few attempts he observes ONLY the action of the arms. Perhaps the diver touches his hands to his toes too far in front of him. Or possibly after the proper touch, he may be straightening his body and reaching too far forward with the arms instead of directly for the bottom of the pool. If there is no coach around, the diver can tell another diver or observer what to watch in his dive.

It takes attentive concentration to spot the errors in the take-off as the diver leaves the board. The most common error is simply "rushing" into the execution of the dive as soon as the diver lands on the board after the hurdle. This, however, is not easy to correct, and gives reason for mastering the required dives before spending much time on the optional dives. Thus, it is also valuable to spend a lot of time on board work, using the sand pit or, if none is available, just practicing the approach with jumps. When a diver learns to land on the end of the board in perfect balance, his dives will be more consistent, and he will be certain to gain more success.

Since skill in diving depends much on the building of one skill upon another, the diver, whether a beginner, a novice, or a skilled performer, should pay strict attention to each detail underlying diving performance. The basic skills are not learned simply by the process of smoothing out a complete performance but are learned more easily by starting from scratch and practicing each step until it is learned thoroughly. Through this process, the first skills become a part of the diver's reflex behavior as the succeeding, more difficult skills are added to the performance.

If faulty skills are learned first, the unlearning and relearning of new reflexes are time-consuming, very difficult, and often discouraging to the learner.

TEACHING AIDS

Watching a champion diver at first hand is certainly a great inspiration and an asset in learning to dive. Not everyone has a chance, however, to see champion divers. Therefore, the next best thing is to study movies or slides. Motion pictures of diving champions in action provide excellent devices for helping the student learn the parts of each dive.

With the modern advances in motion picture projection, it is possible to stop the action precisely where you wish in order to study every detail of a dive at a precise moment. Slides, too, offer an excellent opportunity to study the mechanics of the dive at a given moment.

It is quite impossible for a person to know how he himself looks in a dive. It is very important to have motion pictures made of himself in order to observe his own technique. Watching one's self in an actual dive is a vivid way of observing mistakes. This is a much more impressive lesson for the diver than an explanation by a coach. Sometimes, viewing films is the only way a diver can actually "get the feeling" of the action involved in a dive.

Use of the trampoline. Basically, divers use the trampoline to aid in the quick development of muscular coordination, balance, and kinesthetic sense. The trampoline provides the diver with the opportunity to learn and attempt fundamental dives and advanced dives with the use of spotting and safety apparatus which reduces to a bare minimum the chance of injury. Divers also find the trampoline useful in physical conditioning and in the development of endurance. They can learn certain diving techniques and body mechanics on the trampoline much faster than on the diving board. Many new dives have been perfected in recent years that were first tried on the trampoline.

Use of the dry land pit. In recent years the sand pit has been replaced by the port-o-pit, which is a large sack filled with foam rubber. This provides the diver with a much softer landing than sand and also allows him to land on his back, stomach, etc., which is not possible when sand is used. Whatever type of dry land equipment is used, the diver can practice nearly twice as fast as in the pool, for he does not have to keep climbing out of the water. The pit permits the diver to practice diving techniques on dry land when a cold or minor injury may have prevented him from going into the water. The use of the dry land pit is usually emphasized just before and after the swimming season, but it may be very helpful during the season in correcting fundamentals. The approximate size of the pit is 8 x 14 feet.

It is imperative that the diver spend much time perfecting an approach with a good take-off as this is vitally necessary in the execution of a good dive. The diver will find the pit a great aid in obtaining this objective. In addition to the approach, take-off, and practice jumps from the board in the pit, the diver can practice somersault dives, with feet first landings, when using the sand pit, and various other landings when using the port-o-pit, from all five of the diving groups. Single somersault dives can be practiced with reasonable safety, but a safety belt should be considered when multiple somersaults or somersaults with twists are attempted. The important thing is to perfect the take-off and the start of the somersaults since the beginning actions are basically the same for the more complicated spins. When practicing with sand, it should be piled to within two feet of the board, for a long drop to the sand is very hard on the legs and ankles.

FUNDAMENTAL TECHNIQUES OF THE FRONT APPROACH, HURDLE, AND TAKE-OFF

It is at this point that the various finer aspects of the finished performance should be instituted so that, as the diver repeats these polished movements, they become natural to him.

The approach to the hurdle consists of (1) mental and physical poise in the starting position, (2) the walk, (3) the hurdle, and (4) the take-off from the board.

In the starting position, the diver should assume an erect, active position. The head is held erect, with chin in and chest well up, but not extremely exaggerated. The abdomen is drawn in. The center of body weight is over the balls of the feet, not over the heels. The back is erect, the arms are at the sides, and the palms rest at the sides of the thighs. The fingers and thumbs should be held straight and slightly squeezed together, with the palms flat from the moment the diver steps onto the board. The legs and heels are held together. The eyes are focused on the far end of the board, without lowering the head to do so.

While in the starting position, the diver is concentrating upon the particular dive that he is going to perform. He should visualize his body going through the entire dive. Then he should concentrate on the approach and hurdle as he moves to take the first step. The eyes sight the end of the board throughout the approach until the feet are ready to alight on the board following the hurdle. The eyes then shift to an approximate point in the water where the entry will be made. As the feet make contact with the board following the hurdle, the diver again concentrates on the dive to be executed. When performing dives requiring the diver to stand on the end of the board with his back to the water, he concentrates on the dive to be executed as soon as the arms are set in the backward stance. Before a large audience a diver in the starting position is a human magnet for hundreds of pairs of eyes which are attracted toward him. As he becomes quietly and deeply engrossed in concentration on his announced dive, so, too, will the audience come to attention. This moment gives him inspiration. All outside stimuli about him are blocked out, and everything is centered on the performance of the dive. Throughout the stance the diver should express confidence, strength, personality, and poise.

Walk. The walk must be smooth and forceful. A diver should not give the appearance of any awkwardness. If he is too tense, he will usually shorten his normal steps, and his hurdle will be too long.

The walk should consist of at least three steps before the hurdle. A natural walk is better for accuracy in dropping to the end of the board from the hurdle than one that is hurried or forced.

The first step is slightly shorter than the others, and each succeeding stride is slightly longer than the one previous. The take-off foot in the hurdle should reach a point approximately 2 to $3\frac{1}{2}$ feet from the end of the board. Some divers try to put too much power into the step just prior to the hurdle, causing the step to overreach and giving the body a crouched appearance or unbalanced position.

In the three-step approach, start the first step with the foot opposite the one used when kicking a football. Assuming the starting foot to be the right foot, it is then the left foot that is lifted in the hurdle.

In the four-step approach, start the first step with the foot used in kicking a football so that you will come out right at the hurdle step.

During the run the arms should coordinate in rhythm with the legs (Fig. 18-1, *C*). The arm swing should be natural and not exaggerated. The rhythmic run is best accomplished by swinging the arms slightly forward and backward from a hang at the sides of the hips. It is important that the arm swing be timed so that at the hurdle step both arms are ready to come forward from slightly behind the hips with the hurdle

A

B

Fig. 18-1. A series of ideal form showing the various types of springboard diving take-offs. **A,** Standing take-off with the body facing the water. **B,** Standing take-off with the body facing the springboard. **C,** Three-step run, hurdle, and take-off.

C

take-off (Fig. 18-1, *C*). In the three-step run, the arm swing is very simple. The arms swing moderately from a shoulder hang, and the diver merely attempts to coordinate the movement with the run, as in walking. Then, at the hurdle step, the arms move simultaneously behind the hips and swing forward then upward and slightly lateral with the leap. The arms should be extended. In the four-step approach, the only variance from the three-step approach is that the diver starts the approach with the opposite foot. To obtain a smooth walk, it is important that the diver makes sure to alight on the heel of the foot in each step.

Hurdle and take-off. In order to derive optimum lift from the springboard, the diver must drop onto the end of the board in such a manner that he is in the proper position to depress the board. The elongated jump or spring to the end of the board is known as the hurdle (Fig. 18-1, *C*).

The hurdle is basic for all front running dives. There are numerous basic techniques to be learned in an accurate hurdle to give a true and powerful lift from the board.

When placing the foot on the board on the last step (assume it to be the right) before the hurdle, the body continues to move forward until the center of body weight is over the ball of the right foot. The right leg is slightly bent at the knee. A powerful upward spring is given by extending the knee and powerfully extending the ankle (Fig. 18-1, *C*). Simultaneously with this movement the left leg, bent at the knee to form a ninety degree angle, is lifted, and the ankle and toes extend toward the board. The arms move forward and upward from slightly behind the hips. As the arms are lifted upward, the shoulder girdle is pulled up erectly from a slightly forward lean; the hips are pressed forward until the body is straight. The head is forward just enough that the eyes may maintain focus on the end of the board. The left leg is then quickly stretched downward as the right leg moves forward alongside. All of these movements should take place by the time the body reaches the highest point in the hurdle. Both legs and body are now stretched straight down toward the tip of the board (Fig. 18-1, *C*).

The hurdle leap must be accurately directed so that the body is at its highest point just behind the very end of the board. Here the body is prepared for the descent to the board. Too much power sometimes is attempted, causing the diver to crouch too deep during the approaching steps to the hurdle, which causes loss of springing power as well as rhythm and timing. The result is an unbalanced take-off. The hurdle is an important skill and requires weeks and weeks of practice. In the descent, the toes, ankles, legs, and the entire body must be stretched and directed toward the end of the board. Check any overforward lean with the shoulders in the drop or descent. There should be approximately a degree or two of lean, just enough to place the center of weight of the body behind the tip end of the board.

In the descent from the hurdle, the arms are delayed in their descent until the weight of the body is about to drop onto the board (Fig. 18-1, *C*). Then the arms are driven downward slightly behind the hips, swept forward at the side of the hips, and then lifted upward. This delayed descent of the arms gives perfect timing with the board and with the take-off. Most divers get the arms down too soon, which results in ineffective timing of the take-off movement. The arm descent should be delayed because the board must be pressed down by the body weight; then the arms are brought forward, transferring their downward momentum to the body at the end of their swing to assist in giving greater downward bend to the board. The descent should not be forced. One can only drop as fast as gravity permits. Some beginning divers will flatten the feet several inches above the board, with a slight bend of the knees, and then stomp the board for the take-off. Most boards today are slow and flexible. They should not be stiff and quick. A stiff board causes the diver to stomp, which develops the dreaded shin splints. The diver should drop onto the end of the board with his feet settling as lightly as a feather.

An important movement takes place as the balls of the feet land on the board. About one inch from the board during the descent, the toes lift upward. The ankles remain extended so that the balls of the feet can contact the board first. As the feet come in contact with the board, the fall is broken, and the weight is distributed over the entire foot by letting the ankle flex gradually as the toes and balls of the feet, then the heels, alight on the board.

The knees and hips also act as shock absorbers and prepare for the lift. They flex slightly as the body drops onto the board. These mechanics prevent the diver from stomping the board and allow for a quiet descent.

With the weight of the body depressing the board, the knees and hips flex slightly as they take up the landing shock. While the board is being depressed further, the knees and hips cease to give, and the full weight of the body settles onto the board. As the board approaches its fullest depression, the knees and hips begin to extend and drive against the board, pressing the board farther toward the water.

As the board recoils, the knees and hips continue to extend and propel the body upward. When the board has completed the recoil, the knees and hips reach full extension, and it is then that the ankles execute the final lift which sends the body soaring into the air. The extension of the ankle and foot is vigorous, and even the toes contribute to the snap upward as the feet finally leave the board.

The action of the arms must be turned into this whole springing movement. The arms serve to control body balance and also to supply a further force in the depression of the board and upward lift of the body.

As the body is above the board ready to drop into it, the arms slowly move into a position in preparation for the downward swing as the body descends. The arms are outstretched, with the hands slightly more than shoulder width and just above head height. The palms are face downward and somewhat forward, and there is a comfortable flexion in the elbow joints.

The arms describe a slow outward motion, and, as the body nears the board, the slow outward motion is converted into a rapid downward and backward swing, with the hands reaching the hips just as the board is being depressed.

The arms move downward to a position just alongside and slightly behind the hips and then swing forward and upward with the palms of the hands facing the hips. This sudden change in direction from downward and backward to forward and upward transfers the downward momentum from the arms to the body. As the hands pass the hips, the downward extension of the legs against the board is made. The arms lift upward as the board is depressed to its fullest extent so that, as the board starts upward, the arms are nearly at shoulder level.

At this position the arms must be carefully controlled so that body balance will be maintained. The hands now aim upward to the required position necessary to guide the dive.

While practicing the hurdle, the diver should enter the water head first at the completion of the take-off. This practice will drill the diver in the proper drop onto the board and in the proper angle of take-off. Bouncing up and down repeatedly on the end of the board is dangerous. An approach with a SINGLE bounce is reasonably safe and often very helpful in getting the feel of the board. Once the approach to a dive is started, the diver should go through with it and not balk.

Take-off. As the lift from the board is executed, the arms extend forward and reach upward (Fig. 18-1, C). Just at what angle or how far the arms should reach depends upon the dive to be performed. This will be discussed further with each dive. However, when the board is depressed to its maximum bend, the diver times the arms to reach beyond the head and in the intended line of flight of the body as it leaves the board. Too often the inexperienced diver swings the arms upward too abruptly or ahead of the recoil of the board and presents an awkward, unbalanced position. Note in each dive the position of the hands and arms as the feet leave the board. The eyes should be steadily fixed upon the tip of the board until the feet drop onto it. The eyes then sight down at the water until the arms begin their upward reach. What the eyes see after the arms are lifted depends on the dive to be executed.

The amount of lean in the body as it drops to the board in the hurdle also differs with each dive. In every forward dive there must be just enough lean to permit the center of the body weight to pass just beyond the base of support when the feet are on the end of the board. One must distinguish between proper lean and the common fault of falling forward. This moving-lean will give a faulty take-off and reduce height and balance. A plain front header and the backward dive are half somersaults, and any somersault dive passes through a line of flight which is angular in motion. This angular motion can be obtained by merely having the body approximately one or two degrees off center. It might be said that there should be no forward movement at all once the desired degree of lean is obtained from the hurdle. Usually, angular forward motion continues once the diver has landed on the end of the board. The forward motion should be so slow, and the lean so slight that it can hardly be perceived. To illustrate, place one end of a stick 5 feet long on the floor and perfectly balance it. Then move it just off its center of support. Notice that the early falling movement is so slow that it appears to be balanced. As gravity begins to take effect, the falling speed is accelerated.

With a diver, this falling fault usually starts in the descent of the hurdle if it has not been sufficiently counterchecked in the ascent of the hurdle. Through constant trials and practice, the diver acquires a sense of lean and just the exact amount of lean required during the ascent and descent of the hurdle necessary for the type of dive to be performed. He must, therefore, train to acquire different angles of lean at the take-off for dives requiring a greater or lesser amount of lean to obtain a desired line of flight. These body leans may possibly vary only from one to ten degrees. One may readily note that to achieve such slight angles consistently requires accuracy in performance. Unless this fundamental is thoroughly learned, a diver can never hope to perform consistently in competition. It is the amount of lean that determines the distance a diver goes out from the board. A diver must then not "groove" himself to learn one angle of take-off for all dives, but he must be able to take-off at several different angles of varying degrees, depending upon the type of dive to be performed.

The flight will vary as the angle of take-off varies. Some dives require a flatter line of flight than others. The center of motion of the body describes the line of flight. In layout dives the center is just slightly above the hip joint. In pike dives the center of motion is not in the body but just outside and in front of the hips. In the tuck position the center of motion lies just outside of the body, in front of the hips between the abdomen and the thighs. An attempt is made to group these dives as to the amount of distance of entry from the end of the board. They are as follows:

1. Those dives entering farthest from the end of the board with a more or less flattened line of flight; the plain headers, all of the forward somersault dives whether tuck, pike, or straight; the front dive with one-half twist and front dive with one twist in the layout position; and the forward somersault twisting dives

2. Those dives entering nearest the end of the board with a more vertical line of flight; the forward dive, pike; the inward group of dives; the jackknife dives with twists; all of the reverse dives including those with twists; and all of the backward dives.

A common error most divers make is that, as the dives become more difficult to perform, the more hurried the hurdle and take-off become. Then, too, there is a tendency to become more tense in the approach and hurdle, causing an inefficient take-off. Divers must remember to be properly relaxed in the approach of a difficult dive and perform the preliminary arm movement of the standing take-off slowly.

In the take-off, the hands, arms, head, and shoulder girdle should conform to the intended angle and line of flight of the body at the exact moment the body stretches off the board. The eyes then assist the body in the air by constantly spotting or focusing upon some object to inform the diver as to his bearings and balance. The head of the diver should not move awkwardly out of body flight alignment for the purpose of focusing.

Height and line of flight. Height in diving is the vertical distance of the highest peak reached by the body's center of motion in the line of flight. The line of flight is the path described by the center of body weight from the take-off to the entry. To obtain optimum height in a dive, all essential movements must be rhythmically timed and balanced from take-off to the entry. If this is attained, the body lifts effortlessly into the air. Whenever one observes a diver making tremendous effort to obtain height in a dive, the body usually appears jerky in its motions and unsymmetrical or unbalanced. Muscular power must be skillfully controlled. Height, then, is a natural result when the run and hurdle are well controlled and timed.

Some divers have a natural gift of good springing muscles in the legs, so it is not practical for all divers to attain the same height. However, each diver should utilize all of the potential lift from the board. When this jumping force is properly transmitted through the central longitudinal axis of the body, the body will derive maximum height.

Entry. The point of entry of a dive should be at a point directly under the center of weight of the body, on a line with the descending flight of the body. From the surface, the line of flight should be projected directly down to the bottom of the pool. The diver's body should follow this projected line of flight to the bottom so that every part of his body will pass through the same opening in the surface of the water. In the feet-first entry dive, the pointed feet and legs must guide the body down this line so as to draw the shoulders and head into the hole without side, forward, or backward casts. Nearly every dive requires a different position of the body, legs, head, and arms to effect a good entry. A technique used by high platform divers to reduce the splash after a feet-first entry is to pull the toes up as soon as the feet are under water. This blunt entry cuts down the splash and leaves nothing but a mound of bubbling water.

In all feet-first dives, such as the inward somersault or the reverse somersault, the diver's body should be held straight with only a natural standing arch in the back. This will prevent splash or side casts. To prevent a large curvature in the back, the arms should be closed along the sides of the body with the palms of the hands curving along and slightly in front of the thighs just below the hips. This arm and hand position will prevent the elbows from protruding behind the line of the spine. The legs must be straight with the ankles extended, toes pointed, and the head held erect in all feet-first entries. If the mechanics of the dive are correct and well timed and the dive is not short, the arch is straightened to a minimum. If short, or over, then the amount of arch varies from a deepened arch to a straight line. Too much arch will never drive the diver to the bottom on a projected line with his line of flight but will cause him to veer just under the surface and cause his feet to splash on the surface if his legs remain straight.

In header dives the hands should be held extended. As a general rule in most types of dives, a smoother and less noisy entry is made when the hands are clasped one over the other with the thumbs locked and the arms held tightly against the head. It also presents a more streamlined effect to the head and shoulders when entering the water.

In the head-first dives, the head should be lowered slightly just as the hands clasp together for the entry. The back of the head should be well above the back line of the arms at the entry. The head in this position preserves the unbroken and continuous arch from the head down the curved line of the spine to the feet. In all head-first dives the arms, when extended above the head, should be pressing against the ears and in a straight line with the upper spine. If the arms are extended too far, the arch will be too great.

MECHANICS AND TECHNIQUE FOR THE
TAKE-OFF FOR BACKWARD DIVES (BODY FACING BOARD)

This take-off is executed without a run. The back faces the water at the end of the board where the stance is assumed (Fig. 18-1, *B*).

Approach. The diver steps on the board and assumes a momentary stance before executing the approach. In this position the diver must have confidence in his poise as well as be mentally alert for the dive he is about to perform.

The diver then walks briskly, yet poised, head and chest held high, and arms swinging naturally and alive as he takes natural, moderately spaced strides to the end of the board. Some inexperienced divers make the error of walking out too slowly and showing a nonchalant attitude. The eyes may spot the end of the board as he walks out to it, and the head should not be lowered. The head does an about face as the diver pivots with his feet and focuses the eyes on the rear of the board.

Pivot step. The pivot action of turning the back to the water may be performed in the following manner: The walk to the end of the board is identical to that used when making a forward approach except the hurdle is not executed. The diver starts toward the end of the board on the same foot as when performing the forward approach. When the foot of the last step in the approach is planted on the board, the body should be approximately two feet from the end of the board. The weight of the body is then placed on the ball of this foot, and the diver pivots a half turn. The pivot is controlled and stopped by stepping back with the other foot, after the pivot is made, and placing the ball of this foot near the end of the board. Part of the body weight is then transferred to the back foot to maintain balance. When balance is accomplished, the back foot is placed in position over the end of the board, and the forward pivot foot is moved back along the other foot ready for the stance.

Stance. With the back to the water, the arms are placed at shoulder height and shoulder width as the feet are placed in proper position. The body must be straight and not arched. The curvature at the small of the back must be straightened by tilting the pelvis back. The center of body weight rests on the balls of the feet and the toes. The heels are level with the board.

If a stance is assumed for any of the inward dives, the body should assume more of an incline toward the board, with the center of body weight over the big toes. This slight incline accommodates a more efficient hip lift at the take-off. In a backward dive or backward somersault, the center of body weight should be well back in the heels, even though the heels do not rest on the board.

Take-off mechanics of arms and legs in action. The arms are lowered slowly to the sides of the body so as not to off balance the diver. Throughout the entire preliminary arm action of the take-off, the center of weight must be maintained over the base of support.

With the arms extended, they lift laterally and slightly forward from the sides of the body. The arms lift upward to either shoulder height or slightly above shoulder level. No matter to what height the arms lift, they must always move in front of the spine during the up phase of the arm swing. If the arms are moved behind the spine on the up swing, the shoulders pull back, the chest bulges forward, and the lower spine arches, which causes the body to lose its balance over its base of support.

As the arms lift, the body is raised well upon its toes (Fig. 18-1, *B*). The arms move up strongly enough to just ease the weight of the body off the end of the board. This sets the board in motion and in rhythm with the arms and legs for the remainder of the take-off. A deep breath is taken through the mouth during this motion, and then the mouth is closed.

The initial arm lift is the most important phase of the mechanics of the backward take-off, and the success of the dive depends upon the accuracy of its performance. Usually a diver drives the arms up too hard and fast, which lifts the shoulder girdle high, causing the body to lift off the board (crowhop), which results in the body leaning backward prematurely at the take-off.

The final down swing of the arms is now executed as the knees are bent in preparation for the final push on the board (Fig. 18-1, *B*). In this action, the arms drive down with force as far as the hips, where they suddenly change direction, further transmitting downward force, while the arms begin the final upswing. Together, with a sudden extension of the knees and ankles, the arms lift and reach up into the line of flight (Fig. 18-1, *B*). The diver should attempt to keep the arms straight throughout this entire action. While the arms swing down, the heels remain above the board and the knees bend, the hips move back and down very slightly with the knee bent forward, extending beyond the toes as if to sit down on the heels. However, the body or trunk remains in a vertical line above the hips and does not bend forward. (See Fig. 18-1, *A*.) This movement does not give the body a falling appearance. At the same time, it gives it true balance, and the diver is able to keep the body under control on the take-off, as well as throughout the dive.

The movements for the standing take-off, body facing the water, are very similar to those described for the take-off with the back of the body facing the water (Fig. 18-1, *A*).

FUNDAMENTAL JUMP DIVES

The jump dives are devised mostly for the beginner so he may learn the proper approach and take-off. The beginner should not attempt the advanced dives until he has learned these rudimentary skills of diving. The diver's proficiency should then improve rapidly because his technique is sound.

In all of the jump dives it is a question of balance in the air. This the beginner should control right from the take-off. When in the air, he should rely upon the head and arms to accurately control the body. When consistency in balance is developed, the arms are relied upon less, and the head takes over in slight adjustments in midair.

The jump dives should first be attempted from a standing take-off (Fig. 18-1, *A*). The technique used in executing the standing take-off with the body facing the water is the same as that described for the take-off with the back facing the water (Fig. 18-1, *B*). The only difference is that the diver can curl the toes over the board when facing toward the water.

When he has adjusted himself to the feel of the movement of the arms and legs with the board, he can proceed with the approaching run and hurdle as described in Fig. 18-1, *C*.

Front jump—straight. As the body leaves the board, the arms reach forward and upward at shoulder width to a position above the head. As the body reaches the peak of the jump, the arms stretch upward, fingers squeeze together, and the head and shoulders press backward to keep the body well aligned. After the peak of the dive has been reached, the arms move downward so that the hands are placed at the sides of the thighs at the entry. The head is held erect with the eyes sighting the water near the other end of the pool. At the entry, the toes stretch toward the water (Fig. 18-2, *A*).

Front jump—pike. The arms reach for the ceiling as in the front jump, straight. After the body has left the board, the legs should lift to a position nearly parallel with the water. The flexion is in the hips as the thighs are lifted. The legs are kept extended, the ankles stretched, and the trunk and head held erect throughout the dive. The arms are lowered toward the legs as the legs reach hip level in a horizontal plane. The ankles are brought up to touch the hands as the peak of the dive is reached. The body should straighten immediately after the peak of the dive has been reached. The hands simply slide along the front of the legs to the entry position in the front of the thighs. This dive requires a considerable amount of body control in order to effect a vertical entry. (Fig. 18-2, *B*.)

Front jump—tuck. This dive is harder to perform than the pike. The body is stretched momentarily as in the front jump, straight. After the body leaves the board, the knees are brought up to the chest, and the knees and ankles are held together. At the same time the hands are lowered and grasp the legs at the shins and pull them in so that the heels are brought toward the buttocks in a tight tuck. The hips and knee joints must be relaxed.

As the diver reaches the peak of the dive, he should hold his trunk firm and his head erect with the eyes directed forward. The tuck is held for a moment after he has passed the peak when the legs are released and shot downward. The hands slide down the legs and are held against the sides of the thighs at the entry. (Fig. 18-2, *C*.)

Backward jump—straight. As the body leaves the board, the arms lift forward to a position above the head. The arms are stretched upward. As the body jumps upward and backward from the board, the head and body must be held erect. A falling take-off should be avoided. As the diver descends from the peak, the hands are lowered to the thighs, and a vertical entry is made.

If the feet tend to come out from under the diver, then the head should be tilted according to the direction in which the feet move. For example, if the feet move back on the jump, then the head should be dropped. (Fig. 18-2, *D*.)

Backward jump—pike. At the lift from the board in the take-off, the body leans slightly backward. The center of weight is in the heels, which project beyond the board, as in Fig. 18-1, *B*. As in the front jump, pike, the hands lift forward and upward above and slightly in front of the head before the pike is made. The arms do not jerk to a stop, and they are not lifted to a full reach above the head, since either of these actions would cause a transfer of momentum from the arms to the body, and the body would be thrown out of alignment. The legs should be held extended, and the toes pointed. The hips should flex easily as the legs are lifted to the pike. The legs are slightly short of horizontal when the pike is effected. The diver should unpike immediately after the peak is reached.

The entry should be made in the vertical position at a point from 4 to 5 feet from the tip of the board (Fig. 18-2, *E*).

Backward jump—tuck. The diver executes a straight back jump lay-out before the tuck is started (Fig. 18-2, *F*).

At the peak of the dive the head is erect, and the eyes are directed forward. The body is leaning slightly forward. As the knees are drawn up forward, the arms are lowered until the hands grasp the shins. The heels are held close to the buttocks, and the knees and ankles are closed tightly together. The toes are in full depression, and the ankles are extended.

The diver should untuck soon after the peak is reached and attempt to gain a vertical entry with the body in good alignment, not arched.

A

B

C

Fig. 18-2. A series of ideal form for executing the elementary jump dives. **A,** The standing or running front jump dive, layout. **B,** The standing or running front jump dive, pike. **C,** The standing or running front jump dive, tuck. **D,** The standing or running front jump dive, layout. **E,** The standing back jump dive, pike. **F,** The standing back jump dive, tuck.

COMPETITIVE DIVING

All dives are combinations of the forward or backward dive with either a somersault or a twist in one of the straight, pike, or tuck positions. The first dive of each group is the fundamental movement, and and succeeding dives contain added movements which increase the complexity of the dive.

In learning the dives the diver should accomplish the most elementary of the dives in each of the groups first. As these are mastered, the successively more difficult dives are attempted.

The following order may be used in learning all of the required and a few of the more elementary of the optional dives:

Order*	Group	Dive
1	I	Forward dive—layout
2	I	Forward dive—pike
3	II	Backward dive—layout
4	V	Forward dive half twist—layout
5	IV	Inward dive—pike
6	I	Forward somersault—tuck
7	II	Backward somersault—tuck
8	III	Reverse dive—pike
9	I	Forward one and one half somersault
10	III	Reverse dive—layout
11	IV	Reverse somersault—tuck
12	IV	Inward dive—layout
13	IV	Inward somersault—tuck
14	I	Forward somersault—pike
15	IV	Inward one and one half somersault—tuck
16	II	Back one and one half somersault—tuck

SPRINGBOARD DIVING FROM THE ONE- OR THREE-METER HEIGHT

Forward dive—tuck. This dive is, in reality, a one half somersault. The one half somersault tuck dives require a great amount of body control in order to maintain the body in good balance and alignment throughout the flight in the air. It is helpful to perform these dives to improve the diver's control and alertness for a perfectly aligned entry into the water.

The dive begins the same as the plain front header. As the feet come in contact with the board at the end of the hurdle, the eyes are lifted from the board and look at the front wall. The arms reach overhead and slightly forward as the diver rises from the board. The face is held directly forward. As soon as the legs have made the final extension onto the board, the hips are lifted slightly, and the knees are brought for-

*See Rules for springboard diving, Intercollegiate Swimming Guide and A.A.U. Swimming Handbook.

ward under the chest. The hands lower to grasp the shins just as the knees are about to reach the chest. This contact in the tuck position is made at the peak of the dive. The head tilts downward slightly, keeping the eyes focused on the water. This causes enough rotation to put the diver's body almost in a complete head-foremost position. The legs are immediately snapped straight just short of the vertical alignment. The hands slide from the shins to the sides of the hips as the body straightens. Then the hands reach laterally outward and are stretched downward toward the water. The arms are pressed firmly against the head for the entry. (Fig. 18-3, *A*.)

A common fault in executing this dive is to bring the arms together too slowly and too near the surface of the water. The arms should be brought together quickly since the body has fallen to within a few feet of the water.

Forward dive—jackknife, pike. The take-off is made with the hands held shoulder width apart in a modified reach above and in front of the head. The hips lift almost immediately on the take-off from the board. The feet point straight down, the arms depress, and the hips lift above the head as the body rises to the peak of the dive. The eyes sight the water at the approximate point of entry. As the peak of the dive is reached, the hands are brought in contact with the feet. The legs at this point are in a vertical position, with toes pointing downward.

As the body drops from the peak of the dive, the arms reach toward the water. The legs then lift slowly as the body starts to open up, and

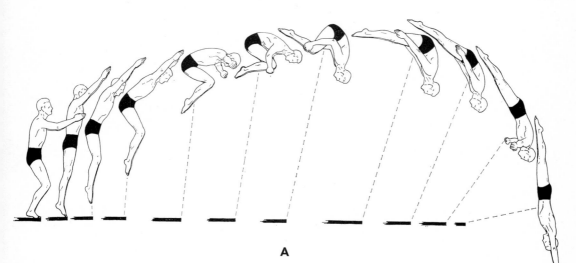

A

Fig. 18-3. A-L, A series of ideal form for executing the various forward somersault dives from either the 1- or 3-meter springboard selected from the standard table of springboard dives as listed in the N.C.A.A. and A.A.U. Rule Books. **A,** Forward dive, tuck.

B

Fig. 18-3, cont'd. B, Forward dive, pike.

the continued rotation of the body places it in a vertical position for the entry. As the legs lift upward, the arms reach downward to a position along the sides of the head, and the hands clasp together at the entry.

Common errors in executing this dive are as follows:

1. The head lifts on the take-off, and the arms fail to reach overhead.
2. The hands touch the feet before or after the peak of the dive is reached.
3. In unpiking, the hands follow the legs back too far, giving the body too much rotation forward with the loss of entry control. (Fig. 18-3, *B*.)

Forward dive—layout. This dive is commonly known as the swan or plain front dive. It is, in reality, a one half somersault. The difficulty of this dive lies in the large amount of body control required to maintain the body in alignment throughout the flight through the air. As the feet

Fig. 18-3, cont'd. C, Forward dive, layout.

come in contact with the board at the end of the hurdle, the eyes lift from the board and focus on a point at the other end of the pool that is usually lower than the height of the board. The face is held directly forward until after the peak of the dive has been reached. When the diver leaves the board, the body should stretch, with the feet pressing downward and backward. The arms raise overhead at a position wider than the shoulders and then spread out to a position straight from the shoulders with a slight angle forward. A line across the upper back should follow along the top of the arms when the body is in the layout position.

The whole body should be straight, and the legs held close together, with the toes pointed backward.

As the peak of the dive is reached, the body rotates forward around its center of weight which is just above the hip joint. This rotation lifts the legs upward and levels the trunk so that the heels are just above the head level when the body is at its peak.

The rotation continues as the body falls from the peak, and the head remains in line with the body as the eyes shift to the point of entry. The hands clasp as the vertical entry is made.

Fig. 18-3, cont'd. G, Forward one and one half somersault, pike.

The pike should be initiated by lifting the hips up and over the head. With the upper part of the body curled under, the radius of rotation becomes shorter, which increases speed of angular rotation. (Fig. 18-3, *D*.)

Forward somersault—tuck. As the diver leaves the board the arms reach overhead and the eyes sight the water at the approximate point of entry. The legs then extend, and the hips push upward. At the same time the arms and head start a downward movement, and the body starts to rotate. When the hips start their upward movement behind the body, the knees draw toward the chest with the heels making an upward and backward movement toward the buttocks. The spinning motion is induced by the downward motion of the arms and head toward the knees. Caution should be taken not to bring the knees up to the hands.

The knees draw tightly to the chest by grasping the shins with the

H

Fig. 18-3, cont'd. H, Forward one and one half somersault, tuck.

hands and holding the elbows close to the body. On passing the peak of the dive, the body approaches a "sitting" position at which time the tuck is released by letting the legs slide from the hands. When approximately three quarters of the somersault is completed, the legs extend with a slight bend in the hips. The legs then move down toward the water while the head and chest lift to bring the body to an upright position. The arms press against the sides, and the hands are placed on the thighs for the entry into the water. (Fig. 18-3, *E.*)

Flying forward one and one half somersault—tuck. This dive is more easily performed from the high board but is also a good dive from the low board if the diver obtains a sufficient amount of height from the spring.

The legs lift upward and backward as the feet leave the board and continuously press upward past the peak of the dive. The arms stretch sideward, and the body arches with the head up.

When the body has reached the peak of the dive and the legs are nearly vertical, a fast tuck is made and released when one and one quarter somersaults are completed. The radius of the body is shortened in the tuck which greatly increases the speed of rotation. When the legs are released, the body begins to straighten with the arms reaching for the

Fig. 18-3, cont'd. I, Forward double somersault, tuck.

water, and the eyes sighting the water. The body completely straightens with the arms stretched overhead and the hands clasped for a near vertical entry into the water. (Fig. 18-3, *F.*)

Forward one and one half somersault—pike. In this dive the diver should concentrate on his center of rotation, which is in front of his hips when the body is piked. This dive is very similar to the forward somersault, pike, but the rotation is exaggerated by the continual pressure of the hips backward and the head and shoulders forward. The hips must be relaxed so that the pike can be deep. The dive may be performed in the open or closed pike and, in this case, the open pike is demonstrated. The open pike requires the arms to be placed laterally at shoulder level during most of the dive.

While the body is descending from the peak, the diver completes one somersault and the water can be sighted.

The legs are driven backward and upward, and the trunk remains firm as the body straightens for the head-first vertical entry. The arms move laterally as they reach downward toward the water, and the head is brought between the arms as the entry is made. (Fig. 18-3, *G.*)

Forward one and one half somersault—tuck. The diver reaches overhead with the arms and he sights the water directly in front of the board as the body lifts from the board.

The tuck is begun directly in the reach from the board, and the hips lift as the head and shoulders are depressed. The heels are brought

Fig. 18-3, cont'd. J, Forward two and one half somersault, pike.

sharply to the buttocks. The chin is tucked in as the head is brought toward the knees and the back is rounded. The tuck starts to open when the body passes, in horizontal position, the one and one fourth turn. The legs extend and press backward as the body is straightened. This elongation of the longitudinal axis decreases the speed of rotation.

The arms reach for the point of entry, and the body slides down the parabolic line of trajectory and into the water.

A common error in executing this dive is that the arms do not reach high enough on the take-off then move sidewards for the tuck, instead of straight down in front of the body (Fig. 18-3, *H*).

Forward double somersault—tuck. With the increased complexity of the dive, the diver is likely to stomp the board with the idea that this will give him an additional lift from it. The diver should not stomp the board but should drop onto it with the toes pressing into the board and make use of the rocking action of the ankles and the full spring of the board in order to get ample height. To obtain greater height, a higher hurdle should be effected so that gravity acting upon the body from this

K

Fig. 18-3, cont'd. K, Forward two and one half somersault, tuck.

height will increase the force exerted upon the board when the body lights onto it, thus bending it deeper. Naturally it follows that the deeper the board is being depressed, the greater will be the recoil, as well as the greater the lifting force imparted to the diver.

The forward double somersault, tuck, should only be done from the low board. It is probably the most difficult step in achieving the more intricate dives. The execution of the dive requires the diver to depend entirely upon feeling in opening from the tuck spin for the entry. There is only a split second of visual perception for adjusting the angle of entry. Success with this dive is dependent upon determination and trial and error since there will be many times when the diver will misjudge the snap opening. It is much safer and easier first to learn this dive on the trampoline or the port-o-pit before attempting it from the board.

The emphasis is on the swiftness of the arm swing from the reach

L

Fig. 18-3, cont'd. L, Forward three and one half somersault, tuck.

of the arms on the take-off to the tuck position. As the body weight depresses the board, rock forward slightly and tilt the head down a little to sight the water as the arms reach upward in front of the head. Extend the legs and follow immediately with a snap up of the hips and feet in the direction of the forward spin. Almost simultaneously, the arms thrust downward toward the bending legs as the hands grasp the shins and the head is pulled down hard. There is a feeling of "chasing the knees with the head and arms" and a continual tightening of the tuck. The diver holds the tuck tightly until he feels the body turn into a sitting-down position. As he senses this feeling, he straightens his body, keeping the eyes open and the mind alert for a last split-second correction of body alignment. As the legs thrust downward, the toes point so that, as the feet strike the water, they pierce the surface with a minimum of splash and sound. The hands slide from the shins to the front of the thighs as the body straightens, and the shoulders press backward. The head is held erect with the eyes focusing far down the pool. (Fig. 18-3, *I*.)

Forward two and one half somersault—pike. The pike and the somersaults are made in the same manner as that of the forward one and one half somersault, pike, except that more power is applied in the spin and the dive is executed in the closed pike position. The eyes lift toward the anticipated point of entry as the diver depresses the board, and, immediately as the board recoils, the diver rocks forward, lifting the hips and vigorously extending the ankles onto the board. The ankles and toes extend swiftly as to almost scrape the toenails on the board as the arms swing down in front of the body in chase of the legs. The legs move backward and upward over the body into the forward spin. The hands catch up to the legs and are clasped just behind and above the knees. It is important to clasp behind the legs, above the knees, rather than below the knees to ensure a faster spin.

As the diver increases the number of spins, he may have a tendency to close the eyes. The eyes should be kept open at all times, and he should learn to orient himself to his surroundings throughout the dive. As the two and one half turns near completion, the head is tilted slightly down, and the eyes focus slightly forward where the water can be sighted. The hands reach slightly forward for the water as the legs press back, straightening the body for the entry which should be made at an angle slightly short of vertical. (Fig. 18-3, *J*.)

Forward two and one half somersault—tuck. The diver should be able to do the forward double somersault, tuck, from the low board before he attempts the forward two and one half somersault, tuck, from the low or high board.

The take-off should not be hurried, and the tuck must not be started too soon.

The opening is made as the trunk is beyond the horizontal after two and one fourth turns have been made. The body snaps open as the arms release the legs which quickly extend. The arms shoot downward and continually stretch toward the water as the legs straighten upward. This stretching movement gives support to the straightening of the legs as they spring open.

The diver should be alert for the instant the opening should take place. (Fig. 18-3, *K*.)

Forward three and one half somersault—tuck. In the initiation of a successful three and one half somersault, the emphasis is on getting into the tuck position as soon as possible without rushing the take-off and thus reducing the lift of the dive. As the body weight depresses the board, rock forward slightly, and bring the head up erect with the eyes sighting the water where the entry is to be made. The arms simultaneously reach upward in front of the head. Extend the legs straight and follow immediately by an upward snap of the hips and feet in the direction of the forward spin. Almost simultaneously the arms are quickly forced downward toward the legs with the hands clasping the shins and the head pulling down hard. As the arms first reach downward for the shins, the arms should extend straight, making a reaction movement which aids the lifting of the hips to accelerate the rotation.

The emphasis is on "chasing your knees with your head and arms" and a continual tightening of the tuck. The diver holds the tuck tightly until he feels the head turning downward into the completion of the three and one half turns. The diver must sense instinctively when to straighten his legs and thrust his arms down toward the water. Straighten the body keeping the eyes open and the mind alert for a last split-second correction of body alignment. (Fig. 18-3, *L*.)

Back dive—tuck. The diver springs from the board as in a back jump. As the body rises upward and slightly backward from the board, the head and body must be held erect. In the lift the arms reach directly overhead and hold stationary while the knees lift up toward the chest. The hands are lowered to grasp the shins just at the instant the knees reach the chest. The hands clasp about the upper shins at the peak of the dive; then the legs snap upward, the body straightens downward,

A

Fig. 18-4. A-J, A series of ideal form for executing the various dives selected from the backward group of dives, performed from either the 1- or 3-meter springboard. **A,** Back dive, tuck.

Fig. 18-4, cont'd. B, Back dive, pike.

and the hands slide from the knees to the sides of the body. The shin remains tucked toward the chest as the body is straightened for a momentary look at the legs. This instant peak orients the diver to the position of his legs, thus giving him better judgement for the entry into the water. Next, the diver swiftly extends his arms out laterally and downward toward the water for the entry. while the head tilts back to sight the water. (Fig. 18-4, *A*.)

Back dive—pike. After the arms press the board downward and the knees and hips flex, the diver sits slightly backward and jumps straight up. The arms aim directly overhead. The hips must not push forward. The emphasis is on stiffening the legs on the final thrust into the board and immediately lifting them up toward the hands. The stomach and thigh muscles contract very tightly. At the peak of the dive, the arms press slightly forward in the touch to "check" the legs overhead slightly short of vertical. The eyes peer where the hands will touch the instep. The head does not tilt back until a firm touch is made. To open out of the pike position, the diver must hold the leg muscles firmly as the

C

Fig. 18-4, cont'd. C, Back dive, layout.

stomach muscles relax for the body to arch back head-first. The head and arms press back simultaneously for the entry. The arms reach out laterally before closing together over the head for the entry. (Fig. 18-4, *B*.)

Back dive—layout. As the body lifts from the board, the eyes focus high on the rear wall. The arms reach upward slightly above shoulder level and spread laterally to a position at right angles to the body. At the peak of the dive the head tilts backward, and the eyes commence to look for the water.

During this head action, the back should be arched, and the knees and ankles must be stretched. The arms are brought together when the body has dropped to a point near the water, and the entry is made with the hands together and the head between the arms. (Fig. 18-4, *C*.)

Back somersault—layout. This dive is similar to the back dive except that the arms are lifted vigorously overhead, then extended laterally. The head and back continue arching backward until the body is well past the horizontal. The emphasis is on the initial arm thrust upward from the board.

The hands drop forward from the arm-spread position to the thighs

D

Fig. 18-4, cont'd. D, Back somersault, layout.

as the horizontal is passed. The shoulders lift upright, and the eyes focus on the edge of the pool under the board as the entry is made. (Fig. 18-4, *D.*)

Back somersault—pike. The diver reaches overhead with the arms, shoulder width apart, the eyes sight the hands as the legs are drawn up to the hands, which remain stationary. The hands grasp behind the legs slightly above the knees. The legs are released as the diver completes about three quarters of a somersault. The eyes sight the water as the body begins to straighten. The arms slide up the legs to the sides as the body straightens for the near vertical entry. (Fig. 18-4, *E.*)

Back somersault—tuck. The tuck is made soon after the upward reach so that the body is tucked at the peak of the dive. The tuck is made by lifting the knees to the chest and the hands grasping the legs just below the knees.

When the chest is horizontal to the surface and well above the board, the legs are thrust to full extension, and the toes are kept pointed. The head and shoulders are lifted erect so that the body is perfectly aligned at the entry.

As the body is opened, the eyes can focus on the board until the entry

E

Fig. 18-4, cont'd. E, Back somersault, pike.

is made. The hands simply slide from the shins to the front of the thighs. (Fig. 18-4, *F*.)

Back one and one half somersault—layout. As the body leaves the board, the initial pull backward is made with the arms and head. The diver should not attempt to gain as much height in this dive as in the backward header but should use this energy to accelerate his backward rotation. This is obtained by vigorously swinging the arms and head back on the take-off. Then as the legs lift from the board, the arms are forcefully moved forward to the waist of the diver. This reverse action of the arms gives added lift and rotating motion to the legs. The back of the diver must be made supple in order to decrease the radius of the body movement and obtain the desired speed to the rotation at the peak of the dive. The knees must be stiffened very forcefully as the legs are thrust upward. The board can be sighted between the first half to three quarters of the first somersault, which helps in adjusting the speed and position of the dive.

F

Fig. 18-4, cont'd. F, Back somersault, tuck.

As the horizontal position is reached when one and one fourth turns have been made, the arms are thrust straight toward the water. The body should arch in the entry.

As the water is sighted, the head is adjusted so that a vertical entry is made with arms stretched, legs extended, and toes pointed (Fig. 18-4, *G*).

Back one and one half somersault—pike. After the vertical reach of the arms, at shoulder width, the legs lift upward between the hands and backward over the head in the pike position. When the body is piked, the head is stretched slightly backward. The hands grasp the backs of the knees and hold the legs in a pike.

The pike position is held for a full somersault. When the body has made one and one quarter turns on the three-meter board, the opening of the pike is made, and the body straightens for the entry. The diver must keep his eyes open, and he should see the board at the completion of the one and a quarter somersaults when the legs are in line with the board.

When the legs are aimed directly at the board, the opening is made.

Fig. 18-4, cont'd. G, Back one and one half somersault, layout.

The legs are held as if anchored in position as the body drops away from the pike for the straightening before the entry.

The eyes do not spot the water until the body is nearly straight. The arms open laterally from the knees and reach for the water below the head. (Fig. 18-4, *H.*)

Back one and one half somersault—tuck. A full extension of the body is made as the diver leaves the board. The chest lifts as the arms swing up above the head in front of the face. The head also lifts up with the eyes directly sighting the hands. The knees then drive upward toward the hands. When the knees drive into the chest, the hands grasp the tucked legs just below the knees and pull them tight against the chest.

H

Fig. 18-4, cont'd. H, Back one and one half somersault, pike.

As the body completes one and one quarter somersaults, the hands release the legs just as the legs pass above the horizontal level. The legs extend with a snap as the arms quickly extend laterally over the head and the body straightens for the entry. In reaching for the entry, the back arches slightly, and the head tilts backward until the water is seen. (Fig. 18-4, *I*.)

A common error in executing this dive is reaching down for the legs on the take-off, rather than lifting the legs to the arms that are overhead. The opening should be initiated by snapping the knees straight with great speed and holding them in place, and then the arms and head reach backward for the entry.

Back two and one half somersault—tuck. The dive is started with the

Fig. 18-4, cont'd. I, Back one and one half somersault, tuck.

arms held straight at the elbows and at shoulder width as they reach directly upward and slightly backward. The toes, ankles, and knees extend forcefully to push the body upward. As soon as the legs have straightened in the downward push on the board, the knees are lifted directly upward. The hips must not push forward. As the knees lift upward, the arms swing slightly forward to catch the shins. Immediately upon contact of the hands on the shins, and pulls firmly as the diver tightens the tuck position into a close ball. As the diver senses the completion of the two and one fourth turns, he should feel the legs pulling up toward the board when the body is snapped straight. The legs straighten upward, aiming directly at the tip end of the diving board as the arms stretch directly at the water. (Fig. 18-4, *J*.)

Reverse dive (half gainer)—tuck. The diver jumps forward and upward from the board, lifting his arms directly overhead and pointing his hands a bit forward as he rises from the board. Immediately as the diver jumps from the board, he begins to lift the knees up forward in front of the chest. The head is held erect, and the eyes directed forward.

Fig. 18-4, cont'd. J, Back two and one half somersault, tuck.

The emphasis is on holding the trunk and arms steady as the knees lift up toward the chest. The arms lower just at the instant the knees reach the chest. The hands clasp about the shins momentarily at the peak of the dive; then suddenly the legs snap upward, the body straightens downward, and the hands slide from the shins to the sides of the body. The chin remains tucked toward the chest as the diver straightens the body for a momentary look at the legs. This orients the diver to the position of his legs, thus giving him better judgment for the entry into the water. Next, the diver drops the head back and swiftly extends his arms laterally and downward toward the water until they are squeezed tightly against the head. (Fig. 18-5, *A.*)

Reverse dive—pike. This dive presents one of the most beautiful movements of the body when expertly mastered and controlled. The alternating movement of isolating the trunk from the legs during the lift and just the reverse during the drop is an esthetic achievement which requires a tremendous amount of practice to perform with finesse.

After the reach overhead with the hands held close together, the trunk is held firm, and the legs lift upward toward the hands. The feet

Fig. 18-5. A-K, A series of ideal form for executing various dives from the reverse (gainer) group of dives, body facing the water, from either the 1- or 3-meter springboard. **A,** Reverse dive, tuck.

touch the hands at the peak of the dive. The legs are very near vertical as the touch is made.

The unpike is made by dropping the body away from the legs as they are held just short of the vertical position.

The trunk should be relaxed as it falls away from the stretched legs and the arms are lowered laterally to a position below the head for a vertical entry. (Fig. 18-5, *B*.)

Reverse dive—layout. As the diver jumps from the board, his center of body weight (in the hips) should be directly over the base of support (balls of feet) so that the body is easily projected forward and upward.

The hurdle and take-off should be thoroughly mastered before any of the reverse group of dives are attempted. In learning the dives in this group, the diver should jump out well away from the board until the mechanics and the body control are mastered. Then he may gradually move his dive nearer to the board. It is sometimes helpful for someone to hold a towel up high on the end of a pole, about 5 feet in front of the board so that the diver can aim the feet at it as an aid in moving the body out from the board.

The reverse dive, layout, is one of the most graceful of all the dives. It is, in its essentials, a backward dive from a forward take-off. The diver actually gains distance in a forward direction; thus the name gainer was given to it. It is now called the reverse dive.

Fig. 18-5, cont'd. B, Reverse dive, pike. **C,** Reverse dive, layout.

Fig. 18-5, cont'd. D, Reverse somersault, layout.

The arms lift to a spread position as the diver reaches upward on the take-off. At the peak of the dive, the head and shoulders are levered backward, and the hips and legs are well stretched. The back arches over at the top of the dive as the head tilts back in search of the water. The arms remain in the lateral position until the water is seen and the diver approaches the water. The arms then close, the head is brought between the arms near the water, and the body straightens as it drops into a vertical entry. (Fig. 18-5, *C.*)

Reverse somersault—layout. At the take-off, as the arms swing swiftly overhead, the knees straighten abruptly, and the ankles and toes snap downward onto the board to thrust the hips upward. The legs extend and the back arches as the diver leaves the board. The head pulls back in search of the water. As the body turns into the reverse somersault, the arms extend at right angles from the sides of the body.

As the body completes the three quarter turn, the arms lower to the front of the thighs, and the body is straightened for the vertical entry. (Fig. 18-5, *D.*)

Fig. 18-5, cont'd. E, Reverse somersault, pike.

Reverse somersault—pike. After the reach, the legs are brought upward where the hands grasp the backs of the knees. The hips are forced around the center of rotation by pulling the legs toward the chest. As the pike is made, the head remains in line with the body.

The diver stays in the pike position until over three fourths of a somersault is completed. The legs are then forced downward, and the head and shoulders are pressed backward as the toes reach for the feet-first vertical entry. (Fig. 18-5, *E.*)

Reverse somersault—tuck. After the body is stretched during the take-off, the knees are lifted. The hands are poised above the head preparatory to grasping the shins just before the peak is reached and the knees are pulled sharply into the chest while the head remains in line with the body.

After the body has rotated backward so that the trunk is approaching the horizontal and the eyes are spotting the water, the legs move

Fig. 18-5, cont'd. F, Reverse somersault, tuck. **G,** Flying reverse somersault, tuck.

H

Fig. 18-5, cont'd. H, Reverse one and one half somersault, tuck.

outward toward the tip of the board. The feet stretch toward the water, the head and shoulders are made erect, and the hands slide into position on the front of the thighs as a feet-first vertical entry is made. (Fig. 18-5, *F*.)

Flying reverse somersault—tuck. Perform the movements of the reverse dive, straight, until the body is falling away from the peak. The knees are then brought to the chest, and the hands pull the shins into a close tuck. This shortening of the radius of movement increases the speed of rotation considerably, and the body must untuck immediately so that the legs can be straightened downward and a vertical feet-first entry can be made. (Fig. 18-5, *G*.)

Fig. 18-5, cont'd. I, Reverse one and one half somersault, pike.

Reverse one and one half somersault—tuck. In executing the reach on the take-off, the arms reach shoulder width apart and above the face so that the knees can be lifted up to the hands for the tuck. The knees then lift to the chest, and the tuck is tightened by the pull of the hands just below the knees.

The tuck is held until a one and one quarter somersault is completed, and then the legs are released. The legs kick upward just above the horizontal line, and the arms reach laterally and stretch above the head for the entry. If the opening is made well above the level of the board, the diver will have sufficient time for a good stretch as the body is straightened before the entry. (Fig. 18-5, *H*.)

A common error in executing this dive occurs during the opening. Beginners are likely to hold the legs tucked while opening the arms and trunk. The legs should initiate the opening movement and then be held in place, while the arms and head reach back for the entry.

Reverse one and one half somersault—pike. In the reach, both arms remain straight as they lift directly upward. The muscles of the arms,

Fig. 18-5, cont'd. J, Reverse one and one half somersault, layout.
K, Reverse two and one half somersault, tuck.

shoulders, and body must be tense to make the legs and body lift as a unit with the arm reach. Emphasis is placed on stiffening the knees just as the ankles and toes "snap" down into the board, thrusting the legs upward. The arms hold in the upward reach as the stomach and thigh muscles contract to aid in lifting the legs toward the arms. As the legs rise upward, the hands are clasped just behind the knees. As the reverse somersault turn is completed, the diver takes a glance at the water to orient himself to his position. The body continues to turn until the diver is in a sitting position, with the legs pointing slightly upward. The leg muscles tighten, holding the legs in this position as the stomach muscles relax, allowing the body to push back away from the legs. To help in checking or stopping the body spin as the legs are straightened, the eyes are focused on the legs momentarily. Next, the head is tilted back as the eyes seek the point of entry. The arms reach outward laterally and then close together over the head. (Fig. 18-5, *I*.)

Reverse one and one half somersault—layout. As the diver lands on the board in the hurdle, he sweeps the arms swiftly down past the hips and lifts them upward over the head. The emphasis is on forcefully stiffening the knees, ankles, and toes as they "snap" into the board, thrusting the body upward. The arms lift upward in a fully extended position and make a continual pull backward toward the board. As the legs rise upward, the arms make a sudden change of direction. Instead of pulling away from the legs, they push swiftly to rest against the front of the thighs. This helps the legs turn faster in the reverse somersault direction. There is always a continual backward pull with the head. When the body turns to a horizontal position at the completion of one and one fourth turns, the arms sweep in reach for the water, pulling the body into a vertical entry. (Fig. 18-5, *J*.)

Reverse two and one half somersault—tuck. As the diver leaves the board, the arms are held about shoulder width and lifted directly overhead. The legs are extended forcefully in the jump from the board, and the knees are lifted almost immediately upward toward the hands. The force from thrusting the knees upward and outward carries the diver safely away from the board. The hands move slightly forward at the peak of the lift to clasp high on the shins and quickly draw the knees tightly toward the chest.

As the diver senses the completion of two and one fourth turns, he releases his legs and tilts the head back to sight the water. Then the body snaps to a straight position which helps to stop the rotating action. The legs kick upward at a slight angle as the arms are stretched directly for the water. (Fig. 18-5, *K*.)

Inward dive (cutaway)—tuck. The diver stands on the end of the board, facing inward. He jumps upward away from the board and turns

A

Fig. 18-6. A-H, A series of ideal form for executing the various dives from the inward (cutaway) group of dives, with the body facing the springboard, performed from either the 1- or 3-meter springboard. **A,** Inward dive, tuck.

a one half somersault forward to a head-first entry. In the take-off, jump and push the legs slightly backward as the arms reach above the head and slightly forward. The hips then raise upward, and the legs draw under the body just as the arms are brought forward and downward to the shins. This contact in the tuck position is made at the peak of the dive. The head then tilts down until the eyes focus on the point of entry into the water. This causes enough rotation to put the diver's body in a head-foremost position. The legs then snap straight upward, and the hands slide from the shins to the hips as the body straightens. The arms then reach laterally and continue downward together for the entry. (Fig. 18-6, *A*.)

Inward dive—pike. While the body is poised over the end of the board, the center of weight is over the balls of the feet. During the preliminary arm movements of the take-off, the center of weight remains in this position.

In the lift from the board, the arms raise above the head and in front of the face. Palms are facing forward and slightly depressed.

At the end of the reach, the hips flex and raise upward, the arms are brought forward and downward, and the hands touch the front of the feet at the peak. The hips lift above the head at the peak of the dive. The legs are vertical when the pike is effected. The eyes focus on the water at the peak of the dive.

The body begins to straighten as the diver drops from the peak of the dive.

Fig. 18-6, cont'd. B, Inward dive, pike. **C,** Inward dive, layout.

during the downward arm swing. Then simultaneously as the arms lift up in front of the head, the legs begin pressing down into the board. The toes, ankles, and knees extend, pushing onto the board, and then the hips lift upward and back away from the board. As the hips lift upward, the arms and head drive downward in chase of the legs. The hands grasp the shins and pull the knees close to the chest. As the body spins forward to the sitting position, the legs snap directly down at the same time that the head and shoulders pull up and backward for the vertical entry. (Fig. 18-6, *E*.)

Inward one and one half somersault—pike. In the take-off, the knees and hips flex during the downward arm swing. Then simultaneously as the arms lift up in front of the head, the legs begin pressing down onto the board. The toes, ankles, and knees extend on the board while the hips move upward and back, followed immediately by a whip downward of the hands and the head. The hands clasp behind the knees and help to lift the hips in the direction of the spin. The emphasis is on keeping the head and shoulders erect and over the board in the take-off until the hips begin to lift. The feeling is much like that of a forward one and one half pike, except that the hips and the legs push upward and back from the board. The diver "chases the legs around with the body" until the one and one half turns are completed. The water is then spotted, and the body straightens as the legs lift upward and the arms reach forward in front of the head for the vertical alignment. (Fig. 18-6, *F*.)

Inward one and one half somersault—tuck. In the take-off, the knees and hips flex during the downward arm swing. Then simultaneously as the arms lift up in front of the head, the legs begin pressing down onto the board. The toes, ankles, and knees extend onto the board driving the hips upward and back, with the heels lifting toward the buttocks. Immediately as the hips and legs are lifting from the board, the arms and the head whip downward, with the hands clasping the shins. It is important to keep the head and shoulders erect and over the board in the take-off until the hips begin to lift. The feeling is much the same as for a forward one and one half somersalt, tuck. The emphasis is on a continual tightening of the tuck until the one and one half turns are complete. Upon spotting the water, the legs snap upward simultaneously overhead as the hands stretch for the water.

Common errors in executing this dive from the low board are: (1) lifting the head up during the take-off (this causes loss of balance and control), (2) falling away from the board at the take-off, and (3) pushing the hips away from the board instead of up above the head (the head and shoulders should cut down and under the hips). (Fig. 18-6, *G*.)

Inward two and one half somersault—tuck. This dive must be started with the proper technique in the take-off or it cannot be done. The diver

Fig. 18-6, cont'd. F, Inward one and one half somersault, pike. **G,** Inward one and one half somersault, tuck.

Fig. 18-6, cont'd. H, Inward two and one half somersault, tuck.

must maintain good balance directly over the balls of his feet throughout the arm swing. As the arms circle past the hips and move upward, the knees and hips are flexed. The head is erect, and the eyes are focused forward at the other end of the board. Simultaneously as the legs straighten, thrusting the hips upward, the arms, in an extended position, sweep directly down and forward toward the board. The toes, ankles, and knees snap from the board, upward and outward, and the head and arms continue downward, "chasing" the legs. The hands grasp the shins, and the heels tuck tightly toward the buttocks as the diver begins a continual tightening of the tuck until the two and one half turns are complete. Generally the diver begins looking for the water too soon in the entry. Quite often he will reach his arms into the water first instead of simultaneously snapping his legs straight upward as the arms reach downward. The entry should be completely vertical. (Fig. 18-6, *H*.)

Forward dive, half twist—layout. The arms swing through the take-off

Board

Camera angle

A

B

Fig. 18-7. A-I, A series of ideal form for executing various dives from the twisting group of dives, from either the 1- or 3-meter springboard. **A,** Forward dive, one half twist, layout. **B,** Forward dive, one half twist, pike.

as in a swan dive, but immediately in the lift the arms begin turning the body sideward in a smoothly timed movement. The emphasis is on doing a quarter twist in the lift, with the arms held firmly at right angles to the body. The body should have very little arch. In the twist, one arm and shoulder press under the body, pointing toward the water as the other arm and shoulder turn toward the sky. The diver should have the feeling of doing a swan dive on his side. The eyes focus directly across the pool in the take-off. As the body begins to descend head-first, the eyes are focused on the water. The twist is completed gradually as the diver nears the water. The arm extending upward is moved in a cartwheel motion laterally as it reaches downward toward the water to join with the other arm for the entry. (Fig. 18-7, *A*.)

Forward dive, half twist—pike. The body rises into the pike position at the peak as in the forward (jackknife) dive. When the diver is in the

Fig. 18-7, cont'd. C, Forward dive, one twist, layout. **D,** Reverse dive, one half twist, layout.

inverted V position as he unpikes, the arm on the twisting side is swung around and in front of the legs as the shoulder is depressed. The opposite shoulder is raised, and the arm is borne backward. The hands steer an imaginary large wheel in the direction of the twist, and the legs bear constantly upward.

At the entry, the arms stretch toward the bottom of the pool to align the body straight for the entry. (Fig. 18-7, *B.*)

Forward dive, one twist—layout. The diver rises into the peak in the swan position. If the twist is toward the right, the left arm cuts in across the hip and bears downward. This movement lowers the left shoulder. The right arm is raised and centered above the head and becomes the long axis of rotation. The legs bear upward during the whole movement. A quarter twist is started, and the eyes hold a spot on the point of entry until the twist is far enough to pull the head away. The half twist is made during the ascent to the peak, and the diver is now in a horizontal position. The twist is rapid and continual until completed.

The head is now turned sharply to the right as the right elbow drives backward and the eyes spot the water at the point of entry. The left arm is then extended toward the point of entry, and the right arm joins the left in stretching toward the vertical entry. This stretching action should be emphasized in this dive because it squares the body so that the hips and shoulders are straightened at the entry.

All movements in this dive should center around the longitudinal axis of the diver. Movements of the shoulders must be loose so as to avoid any lateral action caused by strained movements of the arms.

A common error in performing this dive is to drop a shoulder on the take-off causing the body to cast. (Fig. 18-7, *C.*)

Reverse dive (half gainer) with one half twist—layout. The lift from the take-off is made as in the half reverse layout. As the body reaches the near-horizontal level at the peak of the dive with the arms well spread, the right arm is bent, with the elbow pulling behind the back and the arm coming to rest across the chest when the body twists to the right. The head is turned to the right, and the eyes sight the point of entry. The left shoulder is raised as the left arm is stretched upward in line with the longitudinal axis of the body. The legs bear upward throughout. These movements occur simultaneously, and there is no hesitation once they are started.

After slightly more than a one fourth turn has been made, the right arm pushes away from the chest and out to the side as the left arm also pushes out to a position straight from the shoulders. The shoulders and hips square for the vertical head-first entry by stretching the entire body and reaching for the bottom of the pool.

The arm mechanics in executing the twisting movements of this dive deviate from those described in other twisting dives. The deviation from the standard technique is used for the primary purpose of showing another standard method of arm technique in executing a twisting movement. The arm technique described in the preceding conforms to the law of action-reaction. As the arm swings straight across the chest, the body rolls toward the same side but in the opposite direction from that in which the arm is moving. (Fig. 18-7, *D.*)

Forward one and one half somersault, one twist—free. The diver takes off from the board as in a forward one and one half somersault in the open-pike position. As the legs begin to lift from the board, the legs move upward to straighten the body and simultaneously start the twist with both arms. In the twist, one arm is brought across the front of the body while the other arm pulls behind the shoulder and over the head. The joint action initiates a fast pirouette as if the diver were standing vertically on his head in midair. The full twist is completed while the legs are still overhead. Just as the twist is being completed, the dive is "checked" by bending at the waist, pressing the hips downward and

E

Fig. 18-7, cont'd. E, Forward one and one half somersault, one twist, free.

backward, and progressing toward the water head foremost. As the body is piked, the arms extend outward from the body. As the one and one half forward turns are completed, the eyes focus on the water, the body is held stationary, and the legs lift overhead to straighten into a head-first vertical position. (Fig. 18-7, *E*.)

Forward one and one half somersault, double twist—free. Take off from the board as in the forward one and one half somersault in the open-pike position. As the hips begin the lift from the board, the body straightens as the arms set high on the body to begin the twisting action. In twisting to the left, the right arm is started across the front of the body at the same time as the left arm pulls behind the head. Although the arms begin the initial twist while held straight, they quickly bend. The right arm bends firmly against the stomach, and the left arm bends over the head in the longitudinal axis. The fast pirouette is completed just as if

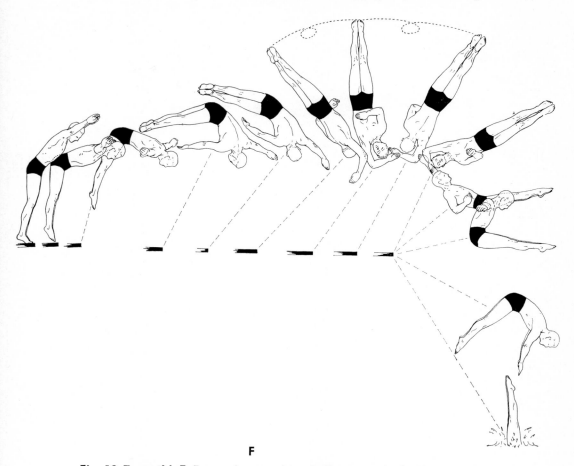

Fig. 18-7, cont'd. F, Forward one and one half somersault, double twist, free.

the diver were standing vertically on his head in midair. As the body completes the second twist, the left arm straightens and pulls out to the side. Almost at the same time, the right arm extends laterally and the hips press downward and backward, progressing the body into a head-foremost position for the entry. (Fig. 18-7, *F*.)

Reverse one and one half somersault, one and one half twist—free. In the successful execution of the one and one half reverse dive, the initial start of the reverse layout must not be too arched. Throughout the take-off of this dive, the muscles of the arms, shoulders, and body must be tense to make the body and arms lift as a unit. In making the lift from the board, the arms lift fully extended, pulling the body upward. There is tremendous emphasis on stiffening the legs as they thrust upward and outward. Hesitate from starting the twist until the legs rise to almost a horizontal position. The head should remain in a straight

Board

Camera angle

G

H

Fig. 18-7, cont'd. G, Reverse one and one half somersault, one and one half twist, free. **H,** Back one and one half somersault, one and one half twist, free.

position with the body as the legs lift upward from the board. Then suddenly the twist is initiated, with the head, arms, and shoulders pulling backward. The twist is started with both arms simultaneously, the one elbow sharply pulling behind the shoulders as the other arm presses stiffly across and over the head and then bending firmly against the stomach. The secret to a fast pirouetting twist is to simultaneously tighten the body and snap into the twist with the arms and hips. It is important to keep the head tilted back slightly throughout the twist.

To check the body at the one and one half twist, the arm is pulled down to a lateral position to create a bend at the hips. The legs press downward and backward simultaneously as the arms press outward and downward. The chest presses down toward the legs, turning the body forward into a head-foremost position. As the one and one half forward turn is completed, the eyes spot the water, and the legs lift upward for the vertical entry. (Fig. 18-7, *G.*)

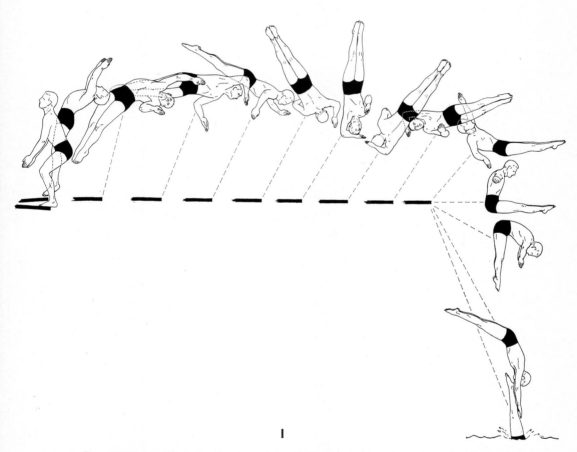

I

Fig. 18-7, cont'd. I, Back one and one half somersault, two and one half twist, free.

Back one and one half somersault, one and one half twist—free. The take-off is begun just as it is for the back one and one half layout. Both arms lift upward above the head and at shoulder width as the diver looks skyward. There is considerable emphasis on initiating a forceful arch of the body in the thrust upward. This is done by overemphasizing the backward swing of the arms when depressing the board on the take-off. The twist is begun immediately as the body arches upward from the board. The legs lift swiftly as the twist with the head, arms, and shoulders is begun. The twist is started by both arms moving simultaneously; the one elbow sharply jerks behind the back as the other arm sweeps across and above the head and then bends firmly down against the chest. The secret of a fast pirouetting twist is to simultaneously tighten the body, removing the arch quickly as the diver snaps into the twist with the arms. It is important to keep the head tilted back throughout the start of the dive and the twist. The diver will have difficulty if he arches the body too far backward and downward in the take-off instead of arching the body almost straight up over the board. To check the twisting action at the one and one half twist, the top arm pulls down causing a bend at the hips, pressing the chest toward the legs. The arms then simultaneously push out laterally to the side. The legs push downward and backward as the somersault progresses head foremost. As the one and one half forward turn is completed, the eyes are fixed on the water, and the legs move upward to allow for a vertical entry. (Fig. 18-7, *H*.)

Back one and one half somersault, two and one half twist—free. Begin the take-off and arm swing as in the back one and one half somersault, layout. Both arms lift upward at shoulder width and the head tilts back. There is considerable emphasis on initiating a forceful arch of the chest in the thrust upward. The twist is begun immediately as the body arches upward from the board. The legs lift swiftly as the twist begins with the head, arms, and shoulders. The twist is started with both arms moving simultaneously. In a twist to the left, the left arm bends as the elbow sharply jerks back while the right arm, remaining straight at first and then bending, sweeps across and above the head. Then a smooth and continuous exchange of arm positions takes place. The right arm bends down across the chest, and the left arm moves to a bent-elbow position above the head.

This latter position is held throughout the remainder of the twist. It is important to constantly pull in the direction of the twist and to keep the head tilted back. As the body turns for the completion of the two and one half twists, the change from the twisting action to the forward somersaulting progression takes place. To initiate the check in the twist, the left arm is snapped briskly downward and outward as the chest and other arm bend downward toward the legs. The hips and legs continue downward and backward as the somersault progresses head foremost. As the one and one half forward turn is completed, the eyes are fixed on the water, and the legs lift upward to allow for a vertical entry. (Fig. 18-7, *I.*)

Chapter 19

Teaching and coaching
tower diving

T INTRODUCTION

Lower diving presents one of the most thrilling and breathtaking experiences found in any sport. Diving from the high platform and floating through the air while executing certain controlled spins and gyrations before entering the water with hardly a splash never ceases to thrill the performer and spectator. Tower diving, like springboard diving, was introduced in the United States by the English at the turn of the century, and soon several springboard divers in America were trying this new sport. When tower diving was added to the 1904 Olympic Games as a new event, G. E. Sheldon won the first gold medal in diving for the United States. Since that time, the Americans have produced more diving champions from the tower than all of the other countries in the world combined. The western part of the United States has produced nearly all of the great male and female tower divers. This has been credited mainly to the longer outdoor practice time provided by ideal weather conditions along with more outdoor tower facilities than are found in any other section of the country.

The present tower diving regulations state that the diver may dive from the 10-meter platform in competition only.*

Diving from a height of 10 meters requires an abundance of courage, self-confidence, strength, body control, agility, desire, and coordination. A poorly executed dive from this height can result in a serious injury to the diver by his landing on the surface of the water. It is highly recommended that the diver first become somewhat proficient on the 3-meter springboard before attempting the dives from a level that is nearly three stories high.

*Amateur Athletic Union of the United States: Official swimming handbook, New York, 1967, Amateur Athletic Union of the United States, p. 71.

TYPES AND CONSTRUCTION OF DIVING TOWERS

Most of the regulation towers built in this country have platforms at 5 and 10 meters. A few of these also have 7½-meter platforms. Today, the ideal tower is one with platforms at levels of 1, 3, 5, 7½, and 10 meters. The diver can learn tower diving with greater confidence and safety by first practicing the lead-up dives and desired dives on the lower platforms before trying them from the 10-meter level. The general size of the platform should be at least 22 feet long and 10 feet wide. Many modern designs are used in the construction of diving towers throughout the world, with Germany having the most modern and greatest variety.* Perhaps the most popular design in America is that with the vertical support being rectangular in shape and rising straight up or slanting toward the pool.

Diving towers are made of one or more of the following materials: cement with reinforced steel, steel tubing, steel beams, wood, or aluminum. Towers made of cement with reinforced steel seem to be the most common type, for they provide very sturdy platforms. Steel tubing and steel beams have also become quite popular in recent years. Wooden tower structures are fast becoming obsolete because they are not as safe or durable as those made of other materials. Several colleges and universities are now building indoor pools with diving towers. Many of these have been made of aluminum with steel or aluminum supports suspended from the ceiling.

The platforms are usually made with steel beam supports and surfaced with cement or wood. The surfaces are then covered with cocoa matting or some other nonskid material. Cocoa matting is most often used, for it provides a soft surface for the diver's feet and prevents him from slipping. It should be noted that, before covering the platform with cocoa matting, the matting should be soaked in water for nearly one half hour and then tacked, nailed, or tied immediately to the platform surface. This will give a smooth running surface for the divers because cocoa matting stretches when it is wet and shrinks as it dries. If the matting is not secured in this manner, it develops folds as it gets wet during use and gives the platform a bumpy running surface. A bumpy surface can easily cause the diver to trip or stumble when attempting a dive, which could result in a painful injury. Aluminum grating has been used as a surface for some new indoor platforms, and it has proved to be quite successful although it is a little rough on the feet.

Outdoor diving towers should be constructed to face north or south. This will prevent the sun from shining directly in the eyes of the diver during the early and late part of the day. The depth of the water for a

*Fabian, Dietrich: Modern swimming pools of the world, Florence, Ala., 1958, National Pool Equipment Company.

10-meter tower should be no less than 15 feet. Whenever possible, the diving towers should be built in an area which is separate from the swimming area. Most modern structures are built with separate diving wells or in pools with L or T shapes so that the diving does not interfere with the swimming.

LEARNING TO TOWER DIVE

The success of the diver in learning to tower dive depends on many different factors: the diver's personal makeup, the kind of tower and the height of the platform levels available, the background and experience of the diver, the experience and competency of the coach, the goal desired by the diver, the experienced tower divers available who can help demonstrate and encourage the learner, the temperature of the air and water, and the length of the diving season.

When first learning to tower dive, the diver should try first to make a mental and physical adjustment to the added height from which he may be diving. The beginner should realize that from 10 meters the body is traveling at approximately 32 miles an hour when it hits the water. He must recognize that the impact on the water when diving from this height is much greater than when diving from a 3-meter springboard. The diver must learn the different tower approaches and take-offs and adjust to the lift from a solid and immobile platform. He must also discipline himself to make every effort to complete a dive that is started regardless of a faulty take-off or poor execution of the dive in the air. Many divers have been hurt as a result of changing their minds in the middle of a dive.

Nearly every tower diver will agree that, when first learning, the difficult part of tower diving is to stand on the 10-meter platform and look down at the water and surrounding area. However, once the diver starts to learn some dives, the tower does not appear nearly so high. Whether the diver is well experienced or a beginner, it is always a challenging and thrilling experience when learning a new dive from the top platform. When executing a dive such as the forward two and one half somersault, the diver finds that the tower does not seem nearly as high as he first believed, for he does not spot the water at the completion of the somersaults until he is around 10 or 15 feet from the water. Actually, the time the diver is in the air when diving from the 10-meter platform is nearly the same as when diving from the 3-meter springboard since the diver goes higher from the point of take-off on the springboard than from the tower.

The actual execution of the dive from the 10-meter platform is basically the same as from the 3-meter springboard with the following exceptions: the take-offs differ because there is no spring in the high platforms, the timing of the dives differs due to the differences in height, and the impact upon the surface of the water differs with height. It must also be understood that some dives that are easy to perform on the springboard are not easy to execute from the high platforms. For example, the front dive with a half twist, layout, is considered a basic dive from the 3-meter springboard, but it is a very tricky dive to execute properly from the tower. Other popular springboard dives that are rarely performed on the tower are: the front dive with a full twist; the back dive with a half twist; the back one and one half somersault, tuck or pike; the inward one and one half somersault, tuck; and the forward two and one half somersault, tuck.

The kind of dives a diver learns on the tower and how well he is able to execute these dives depend almost entirely on the diver's experience on the 3-meter springboard. For instance, a person who can successfully execute a three and one-half somersault on the springboard has little difficulty learning the same dive from the tower because he has learned the motor skills and feeling of spinning three and one half times. On the other hand, a person who has never done more than one and one half somersaults from the springboard will have great difficulty learning any forward somersault dives beyond a one and one half somersault from the high tower.

The diver's personal make up in reference to his courage, strength, desire, ability, etc. has a direct bearing on the diver's progress on the tower. Some divers learn tower diving very quickly because they have control of their fears and they have confidence in their abilities. This type of diver can usually take a lot of punishment when learning new dives and generally learns the dives he desires.

When learning to tower dive, most divers like to try the dive or the lead-up dive from a lower level before trying the dive from the 10-meter platform. This is almost mandatory in learning some dives. However, when the desired lower platform is not available to the diver, he either takes a chance on trying the dive without the desired build up or he postpones the learning of the dive. In the case where the tower does not extend to 10 meters, the diver can learn only those dives which can be executed from the lower platforms. It should then be concluded that the dives learned by the diver have much to do with the height of the diving towers that are available to him.

It is most important that when learning to tower dive the diver should have an experienced coach and/or experienced divers present. The coach is usually aware of the learner's abilities and diving experience so that he can do much in directing and teaching the diver the dives within the range of his abilities. The coach can direct the proper actions in the take-off and execution of the dive and then make corrections once the dive is attempted. If experienced divers are available, they can demonstrate the dives and do much in encouraging the learner to try them. It must be noted that persons who have not developed a sound background in tower diving should not attempt to coach or teach beginners on the tower since their lack of knowledge could easily result in the diver being injured. Also, the beginning tower diver should not try new dives from the high platforms without a competent coach or experienced tower diver present.

It is not uncommon for an experienced 3-meter springboard diver to learn a dozen or more dives from the high platform the first day he attempts tower diving. Quite often a springboard diver will learn a full competitive list of dives on the 10-meter tower the day before or on the day of an important meet. On the other hand, many competent springboard divers have spent years learning a full list of tower dives.

It is very difficult to learn to tower dive when the weather is cold. The muscles of the diver tense up to such a degree that it is difficult for him to function properly. Cold water also provides a harder surface than warm water. Therefore, if the diver wishes to learn a new dive, he should try it when the water is relatively warm. Sometimes the need for learning certain dives for an important meet will inspire the diver to learn or try new dives from the top platform when the weather is very poor and/or the water is very cold. Although poor weather conditions cannot be controlled, the diver can avoid uncomfortable conditions such as these by attempting only those dives he is absolutely sure he can execute safely. The welfare and safety of the diver is much more important than the learning of a new dive. The coach should not, however, let the diver use the weather or the water temperature as an excuse for not practicing.

The length of the outdoor season often has much to do with the learner. It is imperative then that the divers living in the north should carefully plan their practice sessions and try to get in as much tower diving as possible during the warm summer months.

TOWER APPROACHES AND TAKE-OFFS

Because of the solid platform, the tower diver uses several approaches and take-offs that differ from those used on the springboard. Although the diver cannot jump as high from the platform as from the springboard, he finds the platform a much more dependable take-off point than the often unpredictable springboard. In some instances, the diver may use the same type of approach or take-off from the tower as he uses on the springboard. The diver often has more than one choice in the approach or take-off when executing certain dives from the tower. The approach and take-off most desirable is that which will give him the maximum lift and control from the tower and the one which he can perform consistently.

The rules governing the approach and take-off from the platforms are not quite as rigid as those for the springboard, but they do require the diver to make as many smooth and natural actions as possible. It may be safe to say that, if the action on the approach and take-off contributes to the dive's execution, then the action is permissible. The beginner should execute fundamental dives when practicing the different approaches and take-offs from the tower. This will ensure safety to the diver and permit him to concentrate better on the desired actions. The approaches and take-offs most commonly used when diving from the platforms are as follows.

Forward approaches and take-offs. Forward approaches and take-offs in tower diving include the standing take-off, the running approach with either a one- or two-foot take-off, and the running skip approach with a one-foot take-off.

Standing take-off. The diver walks to the edge of the platform and stands near the end, with the feet together and the toes on or curled over the edge. The arms are raised in front of the diver to a position shoulder width apart and at shoulder height. This stance is the same one used when standing backward on the springboard. The diver then takes off from the platform in one of the two following ways:

1. The arms drop to the sides from the stance, then lift overhead and are thrust forward and downward as the hips lift upward. This action is used for standing forward spinning dives. (Fig. 19-1, *A*.)
2. The arms are first dropped to the sides from the stance position. There they lift upward in front of the body above shoulder height and swing behind the body, along the sides, then forward, and upward as when executing the forward take-off from the springboard. This take-off is used for standing reverse dives and front dives. (Fig. 19-1, *B*.)

Running approach with a one-foot take-off. The diver runs easily but forcefully to the end of the platform, placing one foot near the edge as he pushes off the platform with this foot. The arms swing backward, then forward along the sides, and then upward as the diver prepares to lift from the platform. This type of take-off is used when executing swan dives, reverse dives in the layout position, and the front dive with a full twist in layout position (Fig. 19-1, *C*). When the diver wishes to execute reverse somersaults and reverse twisting somersaults, he uses the same approach except that he walks to the end of the tower instead of running. The arm swing is also more forceful when executing the more difficult dives (Fig. 19-1, *D*).

Text continued on p. 300.

A

B

C

Fig. 19-1. A-G, A series of ideal form showing forward approaches and take-offs commonly used in tower diving. **A,** Standing take-off used for forward spinning dives. **B,** Take-off for standing reverse dives and front dives. **C,** Running approach with a one-foot take-off, used when executing swan dives, reverse dives in the layout position, and front dives with a full twist in the layout position.

Fig. 19-1, cont'd. D, Running approach with a one-foot take-off, used when executing reverse twisting somersault dives. **E,** Running approach with a two-foot take-off, used when executing reverse twisting somersault dives, and forward twisting somersault dives. **F,** Running approach with a two-foot take-off, similar to springboard style of approach. **G,** Running skip approach with a one-foot take-off, used in executing reverse somersault dives, reverse twisting somersault dives, and swan dives.

Running approach with a two-foot take-off. The diver takes a run toward the end of the platform. The force of the run depends on the dive that is to be performed. As he nears the end of the platform, the diver raises the arms overhead while taking a low short hop to the end of the platform where he lands on both feet simultaneously (Fig. 19-1, *E*). Another style may be used that is similar to the one used on the springboard. This is where the arms circle behind the body, along the sides, then forward, and upward as the feet land near the edge of the platform (Fig. 19-1, *F*). These two take-offs are used when performing front dives, forward somersault dives, and forward twisting somersault dives.

Running skip approach with a one-foot take-off. The diver walks toward the edge of the platform. As he nears the edge, the back foot is moved up to the heel of the front foot. The weight is then placed on the ball of the back foot, and the front foot takes a short step forward. The weight of the body is then placed on the front foot as the back leg swings forward and upward as when kicking a football. During this kicking action, the arms swing along the sides of the body, then forward and upward to aid in the upward lift of the body from the platform. This type of approach and take-off is used when executing reverse somersault dives, reverse twisting somersault dives, and swan dives (Fig. 19-1, *G*).

Back take-offs. Back take-offs include the springboard take-off and the tower take-off.

Springboard take-off. The diver stands backward on the edge of the platform and uses the same movements as when taking off from the springboard. The flexion of the legs and ankles is not as deep as when springing from the springboard because the platform does not provide for any springing movement. This type of take-off is used for all backward dives (Fig. 19-2, *A*).

Tower take-off. Unlike the springboard backward take-off, the arms raise overhead from the stance position and are then thrust forward and downward in front of the body as the hips lift upward. This type of take-off is used when executing the inward dives (Fig. 19-2, *B*).

Armstand approaches and take-offs. In all armstand dives, the head is in a position where the eyes can sight the water throughout the execution of the armstand. Some divers prefer to place the fingers, up to the first joint, over the edge of the platform when executing the armstand, whereas others prefer to place the whole hand on the surface of the platform near the edge. The armstand must be held for several seconds to exhibit control before the diver can begin the execution of a dive from this position. Once the armstand is assumed, the legs must be straight and together with the feet extended and the toes pointed. The

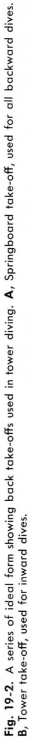

Fig. 19-2. A series of ideal form showing back take-offs used in tower diving. **A,** Springboard take-off, used for all backward dives. **B,** Tower take-off, used for inward dives.

Fig. 19-3. Armstand approaches and take-offs. **A**, One-leg kick-up. **B**, Press up in the tuck position. **C**, Press up in the pike position.

back is slightly arched and the arms are straight and shoulder width apart.

One-leg kick-up. The diver kneels and assumes a "track start" position with one leg tucked in close to the chest while the other leg is extended behind the body. The hands are placed shoulder width apart on or near the end of the platform. The handstand is executed by kicking the back leg overhead as the tucked leg pushes the trunk upward. The tucked leg then extends and comes together with the other leg to form the armstand (Fig. 19-3, *A*).

Press up in the tuck position. The diver squats down near the end of the platform, with the knees together and the hands placed on or near the edge of the platform. The diver leans forward with the shoulders slightly in front of the hands. Then with the arms slightly bent, the diver pushes off with his feet and lifts the hips and tucked legs overhead. The legs extend as they lift overhead, and the arms straighten to form the armstand (Fig. 19-3, *B*).

Press up in the pike position. The diver stands near the end of the platform and bends over with the legs straight and places the hands on or near the edge of the platform. The legs are spread apart as the diver assumes the position for the handstand. When the hands are placed on the platform, the diver leans forward with the shoulders slightly in front of the hands and pushes the legs upward from the tips of his toes. The hips move slightly forward as the legs lift upward. As the straight legs lift overhead, the hips move back slightly to keep the body from falling off the platform. The arms then straighten as in doing the armstand from the tuck position (Fig. 19-3, *C*).

BASIC TOWER DIVES

A beginner on the high platform should learn certain basic dives before attempting some of the more difficult dives. The advantages of the diver learning basic dives first are quite obvious. First of all, he can more easily adjust to the proper take-off from the solid platform by doing dives that are relatively easy. Second, the diver can adjust more easily to the different heights and therefore reduce the chance of injury if he first learns dives which are considered basic. Many of these preliminary dives can be learned by attempting them on the 5-meter platform and then trying them on the high platform. Naturally, learning some of the basic dives on the 10-meter platform is greatly simplified if graduated platforms are available. Some of the basic tower dives are as follows:

1. Running front one and one half somersault—open or closed pike
2. Standing front dive—pike or layout
3. Back somersault—layout

4. Inward dive—pike or layout
5. Armstand, cut through—tuck
6. Flying forward one and one half somersault—pike
7. Reverse somersault—layout
8. Back dive—pike or layout
9. Standing reverse dive—pike or layout
10. Inward one and one half somersault—closed or open pike

The diver should recognize that some of these dives are more difficult to perform when attempted from the lower platforms, that is, some of these dives are actually easier to execute from the 10-meter platform than from the 5-meter level. This is especially true in the armstand dive, the flying forward one and one half somersault, and the reverse somersault.

Running front one and one half somersault—open pike. The diver makes a running approach to the end of the platform, landing near the edge on both feet, and uses one of the two actions shown in Fig. 19-1, *E* and *F*. As the diver jumps from the platform, the hips lift upward, and the body bends at the waist to form a pike position. The arms pull down laterally from overhead and move to a position level with the shoulders to form an open pike position. The downward lateral action of the arms aids in the forward rotation of the body. The diver can sight the water just as he leaves the platform, but, once the pike position is assumed, he sights his legs as he begins to somersault. Remaining in the open pike position, the diver looks for the water as he passes three quarters of a somersault. At this time, the diver begins to reach downward toward the water at an angle slightly short of vertical as his legs continue to rotate. This causes the body to straighten as it drops toward the water. The action of the somersault is controlled by the abdominal and thigh muscles along with proper timing in the reach for the water with the arms. As the diver nears the surface of the water, the arms stretch over the head in line with the body. The body straightens completely as it enters the water slightly short of a vertical position. (Fig. 19-4, *A*.)

Standing front dive—layout. The diver assumes a stance on the edge of the platform similar to that used when executing backward dives except that he stands facing the water. He then drops his arms to his sides momentarily before lifting them laterally and slightly in front of the body. As the arms near shoulder level, they circle back just behind the body and swing down past the hips. The arms bend at the elbow as they pass the hips and lift overhead. The legs are coordinated with the arms as on the take-off from the springboard, except that the legs do not bend as much at the knees and the jumping action is much faster on the platform.

As the diver jumps from the platform, the arms extend quickly and

A

Fig. 19-4. A-J, A series of ideal form showing basic tower dives. **A,** Running front one
and one half somersault, open pike.

firmly to a position at right angles to the body and at shoulder level.
The head remains in line with the body with the eyes looking straight
ahead. The jump from the tower should not be too forceful if control of
the dive is to be retained and assured. There is absolutely no movement
in the body as it drops toward the water except that the eyes sight the
water after the diver has dropped approximately 10 feet. Unlike the
swan dive from the springboard, the legs do not lift upward after the
diver leaves the platform. Instead, the body drops below the legs as the

B

Fig. 19-4, cont'd. B, Standing front dive, layout.

diver moves closer to the water. The body approaches a position slightly short of vertical as the diver nears the water. At this time, the arms extend directly overhead with the eyes sighting the water at the point where the body will enter. The entry is made with the hands clasped and the body stretched as much as possible. (Fig. 19-4, *B*.)

Back somersault—layout. The diver assumes a backward stance and then drops his arms momentarily to his sides. He then lifts the arms laterally and slightly in front of the body before circling them as shown

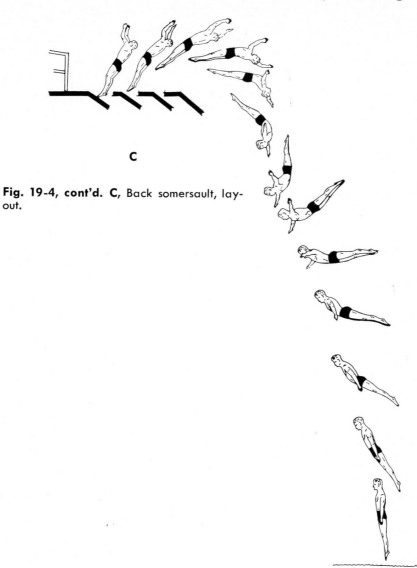

C

Fig. 19-4, cont'd. C, Back somersault, layout.

in Fig. 19-2, *A*. The diver leans back slightly on the take-off and then jumps up as much toward the vertical as possible. The jump is made by extending the legs and lifting the chest and head upward as the arms lift forward and upward over the head. The back arches almost immediately as the chest and head continue to lift upward, and the arms pull laterally to a swan position.

The water comes into view as the diver completes one half of the somersault. When the water is sighted, the diver can then adjust the somersault for the entry by controlling the arch in his back with the use of the stomach and thigh muscles and also by slightly changing the position of the arms. As the diver nears the water, the arms are brought down to the sides at the thighs by passing slightly in front of the body. This prevents the diver from going over on the dive, and it also eliminates most of the arch in the back. The eyes continue to sight the water almost to the time when contact is made with the water. At this last instant, the head lifts to a position directly in line with the body, and the eyes sight the edge of the pool. (Fig. 19-4, *C*.)

Inward dive—pike. The diver drops. the arms momentarily to his sides from the back stance position. The arms are then lifted laterally to a position directly over the head. With the arms remaining overhead, the diver jumps upward and slightly backward from the platform. In this action the hips drive upward, and the arms move straight down in front of the body to form a pike position. The head is lifted very slightly as the pike is made to allow the diver to sight the water and also to permit body control. The hands touch the insteps at the peak of the dive. The diver actually drops 3 or 4 feet in this position before the legs begin to swing backward and the arms start reaching for the water. In reaching downward for the water, the arms spread to a position about shoulder width to provide increased balance. The legs continue to swing back and upward during this action, and the head remains in an unstrained position with the eyes sighting the water directly below. The body straightens as the diver nears the water, with the arms extending over the head and the legs lifting upward. A breath of air is taken after the pike is made to prevent the diver from arching his back as he nears the water. The vertical entry into the water is made after the hands are clasped, and the body stretches as much as possible. (Fig. 19-4, *D*.)

Armstand, cut through—tuck. Once the armstand is assumed, the diver should hold the position for a short time to show that he has complete control of the armstand. The diver begins the dive by leaning the entire body forward away from the platform. This is done by pushing the legs forward slightly, causing the body to lean. The body pivots at the shoulders as it leans over the edge of the platform. This places the arms at an angle with the body while the hands are still in contact with the platform. During the armstand and the leaning of the body, the head remains lifted slightly so that the water can be sighted throughout the entire dive. As the diver continues to lean forward, the hands push away from the platform, and the legs, which bend at the knees, pull down toward the chest. The hands grab high on the shins to form a tuck position for a brief second. The hands then release the legs which extend toward the water, and the arms lift laterally to a swan position. A straight body position with the arms extended at right angles is maintained until

D

Fig. 19-4, cont'd. D, Inward dive, pike.

the diver nearly reaches the water. At the last instant the arms drop slightly in front of the body to the sides for a vertical feet-first entry. (Fig. 19-4, *E.*)

Flying forward one and one half somersault—pike. The take-off is made with the diver landing with both feet near the end of the platform and with the arms raised overhead. As the diver jumps from the platform, the legs push upward, the arms pull down laterally to a swan position, and the head lifts slightly to help create an arch in the back.

E

Fig. 19-4, cont'd. E, Armstand, cut through, tuck.

The eyes sight the water during the flying position. This position is maintained until the body has rotated for approximately one half of a somersault. The body then changes to a pike position as it passes a vertical position. This is accomplished by pulling the head in toward the chest and bending at the waist by contracting the abdominal and hip muscles. The arms remain at right angles during the change in body positions. This helps to control the speed of the somersault as the body

F

Fig. 19-4, cont'd. F, Flying forward one and one half somersault, pike.

changes position. The water can be sighted as the diver completes three quarters of a somersault. At this time, the diver begins to reach for the water as the legs continue to rotate to a position above the head. The arms extend over the head, and the body straightens as it enters the water slightly short of vertical. (Fig. 19-4, *F*.)

Reverse somersault—layout. The diver leaves the platform by kicking one leg upward while lifting the arms, chest, and head. The other leg is then lifted to meet the kicking leg as the arms spread to a swan position, the head continues to pull back, and the back arches. The water is

Fig. 19-4, cont'd. G, Reverse somersault, layout.

sighted as one half of a somersault is completed. The diver continues to arch the back and lift the head as the body continues to rotate. The arms are used to control the speed of the somersault as the diver nears the water. The eyes continue to sight the water in order to make the proper body adjustment for the entry. As the diver nears a complete somersault in the layout position, the arms move slightly in front of the body as they drop to the sides for a vertical feet-first entry. (Fig. 19-4, *G.*)

Back dive—pike. The arms circle around behind thebody and then

H

Fig. 19-4, cont'd. H, Back dive, pike.

reach directly overhead with the head in line with the body as the diver jumps from the platform. The diver leans back slightly before he jumps upward in order to miss the tower. The legs are then lifted upward by contracting the thigh and stomach muscles. As the legs near a vertical position, the arms move forward slightly, and the hands touch the feet at the insteps. The touch is made just as the body begins to drop downward toward the water. The head is in a position which allows the diver

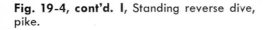

I

Fig. 19-4, cont'd. I, Standing reverse dive, pike.

to watch his hands touch the feet. After the touch, the arms move laterally as they extend over the head. In the same motion, the head tilts back in search of the water, and the back arches slightly. The legs drop a little as the arms extend over the head, but this movement is compensated by the slight arch in the back which pulls the diver around for a vertical entry. (Fig. 19-4, *H.*)

Chapter 20

Teaching skin and scuba diving*

T INTRODUCTION

The underwater world is relatively unexplored and filled with beauty beyond description. It is a world of greater depths than the highest mountain peaks and covers nearly seven tenths of the surface of the earth. It is inhabited by uncountable varieties of animal and plant life. It is a restless, dynamic, changing world possessing rhythm, design, movement, and power. Man is inexplicably drawn to this underwater world. He must, however, proceed with care and skill. This new world can be hostile and sometimes cruel. For these reasons the following information, though brief, is explicit, definite, and important for those who venture below the surface. Learn these lessons well, then enjoy the underwater world with confidence and skill.

HISTORY

The exploration of the land surface dates from the very beginning of man, and the wanderings of man over the surfaces of the world's water masses date from the beginning of recorded history; but the exploration of the underwater world is a relatively recent adventure. Though Aristotle wrote about diving devices as early as 360 B.C., and the great historian Pliny in A.D. 77 described the use of breathing tubes for underwater activity, man's real opportunity for extended underwater movement and investigation did not occur until the introduction of the scuba† regulator in 1943 by Jacques-Yves Cousteau and Emile Gagnan of France.

The forerunners to modern methods of underwater exploration and sport are many. Early Greek and Roman strategists, in an effort to perfect the art of warfare, trained and equipped soldiers of strong swimming ability to approach enemy craft from below the water surface. They were supplied with air through a short length of hollow reed. Soldiers of the fifteenth and sixteenth centuries were fitted with surface-breathing

*From Armbruster, D. A.: Basic skills in sports for men and women, St. Louis, The C. V. Mosby Co.
†Self-contained underwater breathing apparatus.

bags connected to the diver by means of a hose and leather hood arrangement. These divers were held to the shallow depths, which was necessary because of their crude equipment, by weighted shoes. Benjamin Franklin, in his autobiography, described his making of hand and foot fins to facilitate faster swimming. William Forder, in the early 1800's, developed a metal helmet covering one half of the diver's body and supplied with air from the surface by means of a hand-operated bellows. In 1837, Augustus Siebe developed a full, dry diving suit with a rigid helmet. In the latter part of the 1800's the French developed a rubber diving suit and mask, supplied with air from a metal canister carried by the diver. A mechanical regulator was employed to control the flow of air. The American C. J. Lambertsen patented a successful closed circuit—rebreathing unit in 1942. This unit was adopted by the Navy for underwater demolition teams, because with this equipment the diver's expired air did not bubble to the surface to reveal his position as he worked underwater.

In the past two or three years the design of the scuba has been refined and sophisticated, but the basic principle remains the same as the Cousteau-Gagnan design.

DIVING PHYSICS

As the diver goes beneath the water surface, he becomes aware of an increase in the pressure that surrounds him. This pressure has an important effect on parts of the diver's body and the air he breathes.

The air mixture compressed in a scuba tank is atmospheric air, never pure oxygen, and contains the same gas percentages (79% nitrogen, 20.93% oxygen, and 0.04% carbon dioxide). When these gases are breathed under pressure as in scuba diving, there are several basic laws of physics which must be carefully considered.

Boyle's law states that, if temperature is constant, the volume of a gas will vary inversely as the absolute pressure, while the density varies directly as the pressure. If the pressure of a gas is doubled, the volume is decreased by one-half but the density is doubled. This simply means that when a skin diver is descending, the air in his lungs is compressed and as he surfaces it expands. This phenomenon is only important to the skin diver if he dives to exceptional depths. The scuba diver breathing air at the ambient pressure (pressure equal to the surrounding water) must realize that, if he does not exhale and breathe normally when ascending, the volume of air taken into his lungs at depth is going to expand as the pressure of the surrounding water is lessened during his ascent. This gas expansion can cause serious medical problems and might result in a fatal injury.

Henry's law states that the quantity of gas which goes into solution in any liquid is directly proportional to the partial pressure of the gas. This means that if a certain quantity of liquid is capable of absorbing one quart of gas at one atmosphere partial pressure, the same quantity of liquid would absorb two quarts of gas at two atmospheres. An understanding of gas absorption by the blood while diving is important to the diver in appreciating the need for computing a decompression dive.

We live under a constant pressure of 14.7 pounds per square inch, or one atmosphere; but when we dive beneath the surface of the ocean, we add about 0.445 pounds per square inch for every foot depth. When we reach the 33-foot depth, we have added another 14.7 pounds per square inch and are at two atmospheres absolute pressure. For each additional 33 feet we add another atmosphere of pressure. It is the effects of this pressure of water and atmosphere pressure above the water that the diver must understand and appreciate. It is this pressure that causes pain in the diver's ear as he descends, drives gas into solution, and presses his face mask against his face.

Sight and hearing are dramatically affected by the water. Due to the water's refraction and absorption of light, underwater objects appear to be about one-third closer than their actual distance and about one-fourth larger than their actual size. Sound travels much more rapidly in water than in air. When a tank is struck with a hard object such as a knife, the noise can be easily heard for quite a distance; however, it is more difficult to determine the direction from which the sound came in water than it is in the atmosphere. Communicating by voice underwater is very unsatisfactory, so divers must develop a system of hand signals that all divers in the party understand and are able to use.

SKIN DIVING

The term "skin diving" is used to describe diving activity when the diver uses mask, snorkel, and fins and holds his breath while swimming underwater. "Scuba diving" refers to underwater swimming when the diver adds to the basic skin diving items equipment designed to enable him to take his air supply beneath the surface. "Sport diving" is commonly used to include both skin and scuba diving activities.

Prerequisites

The skin and scuba diving student must first possess an advanced swimming ability and be the holder of a lifesaving certificate issued by the American Red Cross, Y.M.C.A., or other recognized agency. A standard first aid card is also desirable.

Swimming test. The following test must not only be the minimum level of swimming competency but should be executed with a high level of skill and with relative ease.

1. Swim 300 yards using overarm, side, and breast strokes.
2. Swim 50 feet underwater without swim aids.
3. Tread water for 5 minutes.
4. Rest on back for 10 minutes with little or no movement.
5. Execute surface dives to 10 feet.

Medical examination. In addition to being a strong swimmer, the student must be in sound medical health. The physician should carefully examine for functional or structural deficiencies in the following organs:

1. Ears—average hearing and drum intact
2. Nose and throat—normal breathing
3. Sinuses—unobstructed
4. Heart and circulatory system—capable of strenuous work loads
5. Respiratory system—clear, normal, and capable of supporting heavy work
6. Eyes—20/30 or better

Chronic symptoms of nervousness, ear infections, sinus irritation, lung disease, and heart ailment should eliminate a person from this sport. No diver can be subject to fainting spells, blackouts, epilepsy, or other neurological disorders. In addition, anyone prone to phobias, fears, and panic should be advised to find interests in other sports.

Equipment

Items essential for skin diving are the mask, snorkel, and fins (Fig. 20-1). When diving in cold water, the diver should wear a neoprene-

Fig. 20-1. Full-footed fins; open-heeled fins; purge-valve mask; equalizing mask; and snorkel. (From Armbruster, D. A.: Basic skills in sports for men and women, St. Louis, The C. V. Mosby Co.)

rubber, wet suit. When a wet suit is worn, a weight belt must also be used to overcome the buoyancy of the suit. Most diving authorities insist that a personal float, such as an inflatable vest or belt, is absolutely essential for safe diving.

Supplementary items of equipment are the surface float, such as a tire tube or paddle board, knife, spear gun, game and collecting bags, diver's flag, compass, depth gauge, watch, and photographic equipment.

Mask. The mask, sometimes called a faceplate, keeps the water from coming in contact with the surface of the eye and eliminates distortion, thereby enabling the diver's vision to be limited only by the light and clarity of the water. It also prevents water from being inhaled through the nose. The mask should fit the face with comfort and provide a watertight seal when the diver is submerged. The lens should be made of safety glass, not plastic, and secured in the mask by a metal retaining ring with a tension screw. The adjustable strap should attach on or near the front of the mask to assure a snug watertight fit. Some models have a one-way purge valve which enables the diver to clear water from the mask without changing the swimming position. Also there are masks with molded depressions that permit the diver to close off his nostrils by pressing with the fingers which facilitates easy clearing of the ears.

Snorkel. The snorkel is a tube that is held in the diver's mouth and entends above the surface of the water. It enables the diver to swim and breathe without lifting his head from the water. A semirigid rubber or plastic tube in the form of the letter J is the most advisable and popular among experienced divers. Those with ping-pong valves and rubber flutter valves are very dangerous and are not recommended for sport diving. A rubber mouthpiece allows the diver to maintain control of the tube and breathe with the head submerged for easy underwater viewing. The snorkel should have a soft rubber mouthpiece that is comfortable to the diver's mouth, permitting extended use without undue mouth fatigue.

Fins. Fins are mainly of two types: open heeled and full footed. Either is satisfactory, depending on the diver's preference, but an adjustable strap model is usually unsatisfactory. The purpose of the fins is to give extra power in swimming, not to increase speed. The fin should fit comfortably to allow circulation and prevent the feet from cramping but be snug enough to be secure when going through the surf. Fins of extra large design can cause undue fatigue, particularly when used by an untrained diver. Beginning divers should use a medium-size fin of medium flexibility.

Exposure dress. Wet suits made of cellular foam neopreme rubber and designed to fit snuggly over the whole body are superior and preferred to the old dry suit model. A small amount of water enters the wet suit, is quickly warmed by the diver's body, and then serves as insulation between his body and the surrounding water. These suits increase the diver's buoyancy significantly, so weights must be worn to enable him to submerge and swim with ease underwater.

Weight belt. This item deserves special attention. Lead weights attached to a web belt are used in varying amounts to overcome buoyancy. Most important is the quick-release buckle, which must be designed to operate effectively with one hand. When the diver finds himself in any questionable situation that could possibly lead to an emergency, he must be able to quickly and surely release his weight belt and allow it to fall away free and clear.

Accessory equipment. Descriptions of, and information concerning, other equipment for skin diving may be found by consulting the references at the end of the chapter. However, let it be understood that no one should dive without some type of personal float, such as an inflatable vest, in addition to a surface float. A good automobile inner tube with attached line makes a very effective and practical surface float for resting. A canvas or burlap bag tied to it serves to carry the diver's equipment.

Skin diving skills

All basic strokes, except breast and side stroke scissors, can and will be used while diving; however, the open, enlarged flutter kick with very loose knee action is the most common source of propelling force. Many divers alternate the dolphin kick with the flutter kick to prevent undue

Fig. 20-2. Skin divers in proper underwater swimming position. (From Armbruster, D. A.: Basic skills in sports for men and women, St. Louis, The C. V. Mosby Co.)

fatigue. A strong kick allows the diver freedom for his hands and arms to carry equipment, shoot fish, take pictures, and pick up interesting objects. Usually the arms are trailed in a comfortable position at the diver's sides when he is swimming and they are not specifically in use. (Fig. 20-2.) This position allows for maximum balance and relaxation. However, when swimming in turbid, murky water with poor visibility, the diver should extend both arms forward at full length to ward off undetected obstructions. When underwater, he should always swim as effortlessly as possible, conserving oxygen and thereby extending the length of "down time."

Diving down. When in open water, the diver should use either the tuck or pike surface dive to submerge. If the dive must be made through kelp or other plant life or into unfamiliar water, a feet-first dive should be executed.

Hyperventilation. Some divers extend their down time by means of rapid and deep breathing with exceptionally full exhalations just before submerging. No other practice in diving is more hazardous. Hyperventilation is the cause of "shallow water blackout" resulting in drowning. Instead, the diver should take two or three deep breaths and then hold a third at about two-thirds capacity just as the dive is started.

Clearing. When the diver submerges, his snorkel will be filled with water, but the air pressure in the diver's mouth prevents the water from entering the mouth and throat. Upon surfacing, the diver can blow the

Fig. 20-3. Clearing mask—head tilted to side; head tilted back. (From Armbruster, D. A.: Basic skills in sports for men and women, St. Louis, The C. V. Mosby Co.)

water in the tube out by a short forceful exhalation while keeping his face submerged.

Sometimes a small amount of water seeps into the face mask during the dive. This water should be evacuated to prevent its being inhaled through the nose. To clear the mask, the diver should roll to one side, press the upper edge of the faceplate inward, and exhale through his nose into the mask. The water pooled in the bottom side of the mask is forced out by the air pressure. Care should be taken to release hand pressure on the mask while still blowing; otherwise water will flood into the mask through the released seal. Another method is for the diver to tilt his head back, press on the top of the mask, and exhale. (Fig. 20-3.)

Equalizing. To provide for comfort and prevent injury, it is essential that pressure inside and outside the eardrum always be equal. When the diver descends, he must equalize the pressure on the eustachian tube side of the drum and that developed by the increasing pressure of water on the outside. Pinching the nose while blowing gently against the closed nostrils seems to work very well for most divers. Other techniques, such as swallowing and moving the jaw from side to side, should also help. The diver must never use ear plugs or place anything in the ears while diving.

Buddy diving. Never dive alone. This is the first and most important rule of safe diving. Diving and staying together takes practice between partners, but it must be done to ensure enjoyable and safe diving. You enter the water with your buddy, you dive together, and you leave the water together.

Entries. Always enter the water from as close to the surface as possible. When hunting, slip, drop, or slide feet first into the water as quietly as possible so as not to frighten game from the diving area. When the entry is from a point well about the surface, such as the side of a boat which is not equipped with a diving platform, the entry should be made with a giant stride, feet-first jump. When executing this entry, cover the face mask with one hand to prevent its being dislodged by the impact of the water. Keep other gear, such as cameras or spear gun, well away from the body. Take a giant stride well away from the take-off point, keeping the body erect and eyes looking forward. After settling in the water, level off and make an approach swim to the diving area.

Ascending. When ascending, always extend one hand and arm overhead, looking up and turning 360 degrees around. This method should always be used to ensure the diver from coming up headfirst under another diver's tank, boat, floating object, or obstruction that could cause him serious injury.

Performance techniques. When beginning a dive, snorkel on the surface, pushing a tube in front with the face submerged until reaching the diving location. Swim easily and relaxed, conserving energy and strength for the dive. The dive should be planned so that both buddies know the intentions of the other. A well-planned dive is the first step toward a safe dive. Surface dives should be made steep to the bottom; then, when underwater, swim slowly. Overall bottom time and total dive time can be increased by limiting the time of each single dive and by making more dives.

SCUBA DIVING

Several types and arrangements of self-contained underwater breathing apparatus enable the diver to take his supply of air below the surface. Scuba has been the greatest advancement in man's effort to explore the underwater world. Such equipment extends diving time to over one hour and at depths of well over 100 feet. Scuba also frees the diver to swim with relatively complete freedom and to roam the depths at will. Though time and depths can be extended dramatically over skin diving limits, the novice scuba diver is cautioned to limit his dive time to 90 percent of tank capacity and to restrict depth for the first 25 or 30 dives to 33 feet. After this, the diver can move to depths of 60 or 70 feet and use up two or three tanks on a given day. (One standard tank provides approximately one hour of diving time.) Not until well after a year of regular sport diving at the depths and times just listed should the diver move into depths approaching 100 feet. These may seem to be unduly restrictive diving limits, but it is interesting to note that many amateur and recreational divers find their most interesting and enjoyable diving in around 35 feet of water. Remaining within this depth limit enables the diver to avoid a decompression dive even though he makes several dives during a 12-hour period.

Equipment

Two general classifications are recognized: the closed circuit or rebreather and the open circuit scuba. Although other equipment is sometimes used, only the open circuit scuba is recommended for sport divers. Open circuit scuba means that all exhaled air is exhausted into the water and none is reused. In closed circuit scuba the breathing gas is recirculated, the carbon dioxide being absorbed by granulated chemicals and the oxygen being added to a breathing bag as needed from a high pressure supply tank. Open circuit scuba uses compressed atmospheric air and never pure oxygen as in closed circuit, because 100% oxygen becomes toxic when breathed under pressure greater than 29 pounds per square inch. This pressure is reached when diving deeper than 33 feet.

Fig. 20-4. Tank with reserve valve (J type) and harness; tank with no reserve (K type) and back-pack harness; two-hose regulator; and single-hose regulator with pressure gauge. (From Armbruster, D. A.: Basic skills in sports for men and women, St. Louis, The C. V. Mosby Co.)

There are three main components of open circuit scuba: the regulator, the tank, and the valve. (Fig. 20-4.)

Regulator. The regulator is the heart of the scuba, as it is responsible for the delivery of the diver's air at exactly the correct pressure and whenever he inhales. For this reason the regulator is often referred to as a *demand* regulator because it permits air to flow into the diver's mouth each time he demands by his slightest inhalation. This inhalation causes a drop in the pressure on one side (dry side) of a rubber diaphragm. The water pressure on the other side (wet side) of the diaphragm is then able to push the diaphragm inward, which in turn activates a liver that opens a valve and allows air to flow through the diver's air hose. When the pressure on both sides of the diaphragm again becomes equal, the valve closes and the air flow is shut off. This pressure balance is regained when the diver discontinues inhaling.

Regulators are designed either with single or double hose. Both types are popular and have their strong points. The student should consult a detailed reference for specifications of each design.

Valves. The valve is located between the tank and the regulator. Basically, there are two types of tank valves: the constant reserve (J type) and the nonreserve (K type). The J valve mechanism is preset to provide air as long as tank pressure remains above 300 pounds per square inch, but below this pressure a spring-actuated piston restricts the diver's air and breathing becomes difficult. This is a signal to the diver that he is low on air and must pull his reserve lever to open the reserve valve and allow the last 300 pounds of air to flow freely. The diver should end his dive at this time by returning to the surface station for another tank or rest period. Never continue diving when on reserve air and always check to make sure the reserve lever is in the up or loaded position before entering the water.

The nonreserve or K type valve has no reserve feature and is simply an on-off valve control. Divers using this valve usually attach an air pressure gauge to their regulators to keep themselves constantly informed as to the air remaining in the tank. Both arrangements are popular among good divers.

Tanks. Air cylinders for diving are available in many sizes and in single, double, and triple units. The size and air pressure of the tank will generally determine the time a diver can remain submerged. However, breathing rate, water temperature, depth, and working rate are also important determinants of underwater time. The tank size usually recommended is the "standard 70." This means the tank contains 70.2 cubic feet of air when filled to 2250 pounds per square inch and will provide air for single dives within the limits of "no decompression" dives.

Harness. A harness, often arranged in combination with a plastic form-fitting back pack and made of canvas webbing, must be fitted with quick-release buckles or safety hitches and must never be put on over the weight belt. The harness must secure the scuba to the diver with comfort and allow freedom of movement in all positions, but it must also be designed to be "ditched" without hesitation or fumbling.

Scuba diving skills

Fundamentally the swimming skills employed in scuba diving are the same as those used in skin diving; however, one point of caution should be noted at this time. No one should attempt scuba diving until he is well skilled and experienced in skin diving.

Entries. When the diver enters and exits through the surf while wearing a scuba, he must remember that though he has a supply of unrestricted air he is also more vulnerable to wave action in the surf and can be easily tumbled and thrown about when attempting to come to a standing position. When exiting through the surf, the diver should remain in an extended swimming position until well up on the beach before attempting to stand, then quickly turn about and shuffle backward until clear of all surge and water action.

When entering from an elevated point, boat dock, or land, the diver should use a feet-first entry but never into unknown water. He should grasp and protect the mask with one hand as in the skin diving entry, and with the other hand hold the tank down to prevent its being forced up and striking his head.

Table 20-1. Diving disorders

DISORDER	CAUSE	SYMPTOMS	TREATMENT
Drowning	Physical exhaustion; running out of air; loss of mask or mouthpiece; flooding of apparatus; entanglement	No respiration; blueness of skin	Immediate artificial respiration, preferably by mouth-to-mouth method; start at once
Air embolism	Failure to breathe normally or holding breath while ascending results in blockage of circulatory system by excessive pressure rupturing lung tissues and allowing air to enter bloodstream	Weakness; dizziness; loss of speech; paralysis of extremities; visual disturbance; staggering; bloody frothy sputum; unconsciousness; death usually within seconds after reaching surface, if not before	Recompress immediately to 74 pounds per square inch (165 feet); medical care; lower head to allow bubbles to go to feet rather than head
Decompression illness (bends or caisson disease)	Bubbles of nitrogen expand in bloodstream and tissues of body from inadequate decompression following exposure to pressure; nitrogen absorption depends on depth, time, and working rate; nitrogen more soluble in fatty tissues	Skin rash; itching; pain deep in joints, muscles, and bones; choking; visual disturbances; dizziness; convulsions; weakness in arms and legs; loss of hearing or speech; paralysis; unconsciousness; death	Recompress by Navy treatment tables; if caught in time, there are usually no serious aftereffects
Nitrogen narcosis	Intoxicating effect of nitrogen when breathed under pressure; no prevention; occurs usually at about 130 feet, though reported at 30 feet	Loss of judgment and skill; feeling of greatness; slowed mental activity; fixation of ideas; similar to alcohol intoxication	Stop work; reduce pressure; effects disappear when ascending; no aftereffects
Oxygen poisoning	Using pure oxygen below 33 feet for longer than 30 minutes; does not apply to all divers, can be less, depends on CO_2 tension and work rate; not probable on compressed air until about 300 feet	Nausea; dizziness; headache; twitching of muscles around mouth and eyes; disturbance of vision (tunnel vision); numbness; unconsciousness	Surface; rest; medical care; never dive below 30 feet on pure oxygen; use only compressed air in tanks
Carbon monoxide poisoning (CO)	Contaminated air supply from internal combustion engines; improperly lubricated compressors; CO combines with blood, causing internal asphyxiation	Same as symptoms for CO_2 poisoning except lips and mouth are bright cherry red; 10% in blood causes headache and nausea; 30% causes shortness of breath; 50% causes helplessness	Surface; artificial respiration if not breathing; oxygen; medical care; may seem to be all right on bottom but lose consciousness on ascent

Table 20-1. Diving disorders—cont'd

DISORDER	CAUSE	SYMPTOMS	TREATMENT
Apnea	Hyperventilation and extended dives in skin diving	No warning symptoms to speak of (perhaps moment of blackness before total unconsciousness)	Fresh air; artificial respiration; do not hyperventilate excessively
Squeeze	Pressure differential over concerned area; middle ear and sinuses usually first place where pain felt; also teeth, face mask, suit, lung (thoracic) squeezes	Usually sharp pain due to stretched or damaged tissues; damage can occur without pain, however	Equalize pressure on affected areas

When entering unknown water, the diver should make a feet-first drop or slide-in entry. This method also reduces the chances of frightening game from the diving area. Other methods, such as forward and backward rolls, are interesting stunts but really have little place in safe sport diving.

Scuba drills. These drills should only be practiced with a partner and with a trained instructor observing.

1. *Submerging and swimming without a mask.* Replace and clear the mask without surfacing. (See skin diving skills for clearing.)
2. *Mouthpiece clearing.* Remove the mouthpiece underwater. Return it to the mouth, give a short sharp exhale to clear it of water, and resume breathing. Always take the first breath slowly after clearing the snorkel or mouthpiece of the regulator.
3. *Buddy breathing.* Two divers share one air supply. The diver with air passes his regulator mouthpiece to his buddy, who receives and clears the mouthpiece and takes two breaths before returning it to his buddy. The diver with the air supply always retains control of the mouthpiece. The second diver uses his hands to help swim and keep the two divers close together.
4. *Free ascent.* Practice this emergency skill to be able to function calmly in an emergency situation resulting in the complete loss of an available air supply while submerged. In this situation the diver looks up, starts his ascent with one arm extended over his head, and exhales continuously for the entire ascent. The student in the class drill of free ascent should remove his mask and then his mouthpiece before starting the free ascent. The diver's buddy and instructor, with air functioning and mask in place, must always accompany the free-ascending diver to the surface.
5. *Buoyancy testing.* This is essential because the addition of a scuba

adds several pounds of negative buoyancy to the skin diver. A slight positive buoyancy is recommended for the start of a scuba dive, as most surface buoyancy is lost at 33 feet of depth. Weights should be added or subtracted to allow the diver to gradually sink after a full exhalation of the surface.

6. *Ditching and recovering.* Do this exercise involving complete mastery of equipment underwater to gain familiarization and proficiency underwater. For details of the drill, consult one of the texts in the reference list.

DIVING MEDICINE

Most diving disorders or medical probems in diving are classified as barotrauma, or a change in normal conditions due to changing pressure. Usually it is an injury resulting from unequal pressure between a space inside the body and the outside water pressure. The cavities of the middle ear and the sinuses are most susceptible to changing pressure, but serious problems can also develop from pressure on the breathing gas. Nitrogen narcosis, oxygen toxicity, and carbon monoxide poisoning are examples of these disorders. Some of these problems and their causes, symptoms, and treatment are given in Table 20-1.

TEN BASIC RULES OF SKIN AND SCUBA DIVING

1. Be in top physical condition and have an annual medical examination.
2. Be a good swimmer.
3. Secure certified training from recognized agency.
4. Never dive alone.
5. Use safe, time-proved equipment.
6. Join a reputable diving club.
7. Be familiar with your diving area *before diving.*
8. Always use a float with surface identification, usually a diver's flag.
9. Heed all pains and strains as warning symptoms.
10. Know basic first aid.

FIVE SUPPLEMENTARY RULES OF SKIN AND SCUBA DIVING

1. Know the basic laws of diving physics and physiology.
2. Practice skin diving frequently *before* scuba diving.
3. Use only time-proved regulators and diving equipment of reputable manufacturer.
4. Secure certified training in the use of scuba from recognized agency.
5. Never hold your breath while scuba diving.

Chapter 21

The swimming pool—
its care and maintenance

Swimming pools, both indoor and outdoor, should be constructed after thorough investigation as to length, width, and depth suitable for instruction, recreation, and competition. Usually there is a strong sentiment expressed by committees that a pool should be built for general swimming only and not for competition. Committees who have been misled by such false sentiment find out later that it is very expensive to make later changes in construction for purposes of holding competitive meets. The modern indoor and outdoor pools should be constructed to combine the several functions.

INDOOR POOL

Because of limited space and cost, sometimes the indoor pool is shortened in length or narrowed in width to distances not conducive to recognized competition. If records of any consequence were established in such odd-length pools, they would probably be rejected by a records committee. Several acceptable pool arrangements are possible. Some people favor two or even three pools in a building, one as a competitive pool and the others in separate rooms to be used for instructional or recreational purposes. Other people favor one large pool with a movable bulkhead so that any length course can be utilized. A larger pool affords greater space for instruction purposes. There are many who favor the indoor long course 50-meter pool with a bulkhead to separate the deep diving board end from the shallow swimming pool end. This latter arrangement makes diving safer and does not interfere with swimmers. This is excellent also for conditioning and training swimmers for outdoor long course meets as well as for the Olympic competition which is always held over the long course.

Length of pool. For indoor swimming pools, 75 feet is the generally accepted length in America. This is called the short-course pool. If a long-course pool is desired, 50 yards or 50 meters (which is approximately

55 yards) are the accepted lengths. A 20-yard course is no longer recommended. A world record cannot be established in such a pool, but an American record can. It has been calculated that from one half to a full second can be gained at each turn. Records for the 20-yard course are thus better than for the 25-yard course.

Width of pool. Usually the width of the swimming pool is governed by the number of lanes the space in the building can provide. Lanes should be 7 feet wide. In league or championship meets, there are six finalists, which would require six 7-foot lanes or a 42-foot width.

Depth of pool. For adult men swimmers, 3½ feet should be the minimum depth at the shallow end of the pool. The somersault turn requires this depth. For high school, 3 feet as a minimum would possibly be satisfactory, but 3½ feet as a minimum is recommended. From this depth a gradual slope should descend to the greatest depth under the springboards. The minimum depth under springboards should be 11 feet. Pool drains should never be located under the diving boards.

Ceiling height. The ceiling should be at least 30 feet high. It should be smooth in construction, free of girders and rafters, and soundproofed.

Pool deck. The ends of the pool should be from 12 to 18 inches in height from the competitive water-level height, which is usually measured from the top lip of the overflow gutter. The sides of the pool may be constructed at any height up to 18 inches. The deck space around the deep end of the pool should be greater than at the shallow end. This deep-end space should be adequate to provide for installation of all diving equipment as well as allowing for free movement of officials and competitors. The sides of the deck should afford adequate space for officials and competitors to move about. This space should be not less than 6 feet. Seating space for both spectators and competitors should be behind this 6-foot space. Spectator interest in competitive swimming is growing steadily, and for this reason ample seating bleachers and balconies should be provided.

Overflow gutters. These gutters can be installed at the sides as well as at the ends. They should be 6 inches in width and at least 6 inches in depth. The back and bottom should curve smoothly to the front side (nearest the pool). The front inside of the gutter should rise vertically to the top lip. This flat vertical trough inside the gutter causes waves to subside there and not spill back into the pool. During all races in a meet, water in the pool should be maintained at a constant gutter-lip level.

Pool markings. Lane lines on the bottom of the pool should be of a dark, distinct color in contrast to the general color of the pool. The lines should be at least 10 inches wide. The distance between lanes should be 7 feet. There should be not less than six lanes for pools holding a championship meet. These lines should be in the center of each lane so that each competitor swims astride a line serving him as a guide from one end of the pool to the other. Just 4 feet from each end of the pool a distinctive cross-lane is placed to serve as a warning to each competitor that the end of the course is near. The swimming lane line should preferably extend from the 4-foot warning cross-lane to the end wall and on up the vertical wall to the lip of the gutter. In some pools the lanes end at the cross-lane marker. The lane numbers should be marked in large distinctive and contrasting colors directly above the lanes and above the water level at each end of the pool. The lanes are numbered from left to right from the starting end of the pool.

Ladders. Ladders in the pool should either be recessed into the sides of the pool or be removable.

Lighting. Lights should be placed over the pool so that they are inside all four walls of the pool. This then will prevent shadows on the pool walls which might cause competitors to misjudge the approach to a turn.

Sunlight through windows creates a glare reflection from the water surface and should be eliminated.

Fig. 21-1. Standard dimensions for diving facilities. (Reprinted by permission of Joint Diving Committee, A.A.U. and N.C.A.A.)

OUTDOOR POOLS

Many designs in outdoor swimming pools are available. Whatever the size and shape, a desirable course for championship competition should be provided. The ideal outdoor competitive dimensions are 55 yards in length (which is the outdoor 50-meter course) and 25 yards in width. This width is desirable for short-course competition. The depth under the 10-meter diving tower should not be less than 15 feet. Many pools today are being constructed so that all diving boards and towers are in a separate pool so as to eliminate danger and interference with swimmers.* Such a plan is most heartily endorsed.

Diving facilities

Standard dimensions for diving facilities. Table 21-1 was compiled by the Joint Men's Diving Committee of the Amateur Athletic Union and the National Collegiate Athletic Association as recommended dimensions for diving facilities. These dimensions are considered to be minimum for safety and economy. When possible or desirable, more extensive plans should be used. There are many lavish pools throughout the world with more elaborate and luxurious designs. Larger diving pool areas increase the flexibility of the pools' use. The most desirable construction is to provide a diving area separate from the swimming area.

Outdoor pool manager

The increase in the number of swimming pools built each year has created a demand for trained personnel to operate and manage them.

The pool manager's main concern is the overall operation of a safe, sanitary, swimming facility. He is responsible for the hiring and supervision of personnel and the administration and maintenance of the outdoor swimming pool complex. He must be thoroughly familiar with the city and state health standards pertaining to the operation of swimming pools. The state department of health will normally provide helpful information in the form of circulars, booklets, or bulletins, if requested. The successful pool manager will improve his knowledge of pool maintenance by attending clinics or short-term schools at the state level.

Selecting personnel. The employees of most outdoor pools can be divided into two groups: (1) assistant manager, head lifeguard, lifeguards, swimming instructors, and pool maintenance crew, and (2) bathhouse personnel, concession operators, and grounds keepers.

---

*See, Swimming pool data and reference annual, ed. 16 and ed. 17, New York, 1948, 1949, Hoffman-Harris, Inc.

Table 21-1. Diving pool dimensions

BOARD SIZE		KEY TO FIGURES	HEIGHT ABOVE WATER LEVEL	A — FROM EDGE OF POOL TO END OF BOARD	B — FROM CENTER OF BOARD TO SIDE OF POOL	C — FROM CENTER OF BOARD TO CENTER OF BOARD	D — FROM END OF BOARD TO WALL AHEAD	E — FROM BOARD TO BEAM OR CEILING ABOVE	F — CLEAR OVERHEAD BEHIND BOARD	G — CLEAR OVERHEAD AHEAD OF BOARD	H — PREFER. / MIN. DEPTH	I — DEPTH IN FRONT	J — DIST. IN FRONT	K — DEPTH	L — DIST. IN BACK	M — DEPTH EACH SIDE	N — DIST. EACH SIDE
LENGTH	WIDTH	KEY (PREFERRED DIM / MIN. SAFE DIM)		(pref / min safe)													
16'	20"	1-Meter springboard	3' 3"	A-1 7' / 5'	B-1 10' / 8'	C-1 8' / 6'	D-1 28' / 25'	E-1 20' / 15'	F-1 6' / 5'	G-1 15' / 12'	H-1 11' / 10'	I-1 9'	J-1 20'	K-1 9'	L-1 3'	M-1 9'	N-1 8'
16'	20"	3-Meter springboard	9' 11"	A-3 7' / 5'	B-3 15' / 12'	C-3 10' / 8'	D-3 33' / 30'	E-3 20' / 15'	F-3 6' / 5'	G-3 15' / 12'	H-3 12' / 11'	I-3 10'	J-3 25'	K-3 9'	L-3 3'	M-3 10'	N-3 10'
18'	7'	5-Meter platform	16' 5"	A-5 7' / 5'	B-5 15' / 12'	C-5 10' / 8'	D-5 43' / 40'	E-5 15' / 15'	F-5 8' / 6'	G-5 15' / 12'	H-5 14' / 13'	I-5 11'	J-5 30'	K-5 9'	L-5 3'	M-5 11'	N-5 10'
24'	8' / 10'	10-Meter platform	32' 10"	A-10 8' / 6'	B-10 20' / 15'	C-10 10' / 8'	D-10 52' / 44'	E-10 15' / 12'	F-10 8' / 6'	G-10 15' / 12'	H-10 16' / 15'	I-10 14'	J-10 40'	K-10 10'	L-10 3'	M-10 14'	N-10 10'

DISTANCES: columns A–H · DEPTHS: columns I–N (IN AREA MEASURED FROM POINT BELOW END OF BOARD)

Lifeguards

The head lifeguard may be designated as the assistant manager and is responsible to the manager. His primary function is the safety of the pool and the supervision of the lifeguards. In the absence of the manager, he assumes full responsibility for the pool operation. He should be mature, experienced, and a leader, capable of following orders as well as giving them.

The lifeguard, like the policeman and fireman, is normally under-paid for the responsibility he accepts in carrying out his job properly. Every effort should be made financially to attract the best lifeguards available.

Qualification standards. The American Red Cross senior lifesaving certificate, the Red Cross water safety instructor's certificate, and the YMCA lifesaving certificate are commonly used as a basis for qualification as a lifeguard. However, many beaches and cities require additional training and testing. It is strongly urged that an additional screening test be given to the applicants to determine their water strength and knowledge. An example of part of such a test could be as follows: The candidate would enter the water using a spread eagle jump, swim a set distance with his head above water, approach the simulated victim with a prescribed approach and carry him to shallow water, then place him in a shallow water carry, move him to a designated point where the candidate would remove the victim from the pool and place him in the proper position for emergency treatment. Timing the procedure will aid the manager in selecting his guards.

The pool manager must determine the number of lifeguards required to safely supervise the pool. Some states have set formulas, such as one lifeguard for every seventy-five swimmers. Where there are neither guide nor regulations to aid the pool manager, he must take into consideration the size, shape, and use of the pool to determine the number of guards.

There should be one guard for each guard station plus one relief guard. It is recommended that the guards rotate so that each would receive a minimum of a ten-minute relief period each hour. A list of substitute guards should be available to be called when needed.

Female lifeguards may be employed to supervise shallow water areas and to teach aquatic art, synchronized swimming, etc.

Duties of a lifeguard:
1. Be aware of his legal and moral responsibility.
2. Stay in top physical condition and practice lifesaving techniques regularly.
3. Avoid accidents by anticipating them and taking action to prevent them.

4. Make a full written report of all accidents.
5. Prevent the abuse and misuse of equipment.
6. Report any faulty equipment to the manager immediately.
7. Enforce all safety rules.

Swimming instructors

A well-rounded aquatic program includes the following: (1) instruction in elementary and advanced swimming and diving, (2) Junior and Senior lifesaving, (3) water ballet, synchronized swimming, or aquatic art, (4) recreation swimming, and (5) competitive swimming and water polo.

The local American National Red Cross may be of great assistance to the pool manager by conducting the swimming lesson program. The Red Cross office should also have the names of qualified water safety instructors.

WATER CONTROL

The person charged with the control of the swimming pool water is vital to the sanitation of the pool operation. He must be thoroughly familiar with the filter plant, its operation, and the treatment of swimming pool water.

Disinfection of water

There are several types of disinfectants for swimming pool use: chlorine, bromine, iodine, ultraviolet, and others. Chlorine and bromine are most commonly used and are generally approved by state health departments.

Pure chlorine gas is liquefied under pressure and is available commercially in steel tanks. At room temperature it appears as a deadly green gas heavier than air. Safety precautions are to be observed in the handling and storage of chlorine tanks. The chlorine is applied to the water by means of a chlorinator. The chlorinator provides for continuous application and control of the amount of chlorine being fed into the water. It is suggested that the point of application be on the filter influent. The use of chlorine as a water disinfectant may also be accomplished by adding chemicals that release chlorine when added to the water. Calcium hypochlorite is available commercially in the form of powder, pellets, and blocks. It is a dry solid and contains 70% available chlorine by weight. When dissolved in water, a heavy precipitate of calcium carbonate is formed. If applied directly to the pool water, this precipitate would tend to make the water cloudy. The calcium hypochlorite should be dissolved in a tank of water. The precipitate is allowed to settle and the clear liquid siphoned off. It is then fed to the pool by means of a hypochlorinator.

rake can be used. When the filter is being backwashed, the rake will easily pass through the expanded sand down to the supporting bed.)

The filter should be backwashed until the backwash water becomes fairly clear. Details of the filter operation such as length in time of filter run, the rate the filter is operated, the rate at which the filter is backwashed, and the length of time of filter backwash, should be recorded.

Types of filters. Most commonly on large pools, gravity sand filtration is used. Many types of material or mixed materials may be used as filter media but the same principal of operation is applicable to all media. The rate of filtration is usually in the range of 2 gallons per minute per square foot of filter area. With proper operation of filters and correct disinfection procedure, the pool water should be clear at all times.

Pressure sand filters may be used and they may be operated at a higher filtering rate. The disadvantages of these units are that the filter media cannot be checked for proper expansion and, when operated at higher rates, turbidity may be pushed through the filter.

The diatomite filters are commonly used on smaller pools and may be used on larger installations. There are two types of these units, that is, a pressure or vacuum type. The pressure type has the disadvantage of not being able to see if the filtering material is being displaced from the septums upon backwashing. On both types, other disadvantages are the cost and operation of the continuous feed of the filtering material and sludge disposal.

Chapter 22

How to conduct dual, championship, and summer age-group meets

The time and care spent in preparation for a swimming meet have their reward in ease and efficiency. The large number of details which require attention must be handled in an orderly manner to avoid confusing oversights. The coaches and managers owe it to the competitors, officials, and spectators to start the meet on time and provide all the information and materials to conduct the events with facility.

The use of checkoff sheets, officials' kits, and duty summaries aid in performing the several tasks. These are presented in detail in order to be of maximum benefit to the novice coach or manager.

SWIMMING MEET CHECKOFF LISTS
Things to do in preparation for swimming season:

1. Arrange for competitive schedule.
2. Arrange for practice schedule, starting date, and time of daily practice periods.
3. Procure team physician and trainer.
4. Call for swimmers, divers, and student managers.
5. Announce to team members to report to equipment room for measurement for suiting.
6. Purchase personal swimming and diving equipment, such as sweat suits or bathrobes; silk, nylon, or rayon swimming trunks; lastex diving trunks; foot sandals; ear plugs; nose clips; foot dusting powder; and castor oil or mineral oil with eyedropper.
7. Procure training room equipment, such as: rubbing tables, oil, alcohol, ultraviolet and infrared lamps, cold and flu shots, and vitamin tablets if recommended by team physician.
8. Secure approval of schedule by director and athletic board.

9. Secure the following training equipment:
   - (a) Kick boards
   - (b) Wheelbarrow tubes
   - (c) Stop watches
   - (d) Whistles
   - (e) .22 caliber gun and shells
   - (f) Finish curtain rope
   - (g) False starting check rope
   - (h) Clip boards and pencils
   - (i) Rule books: N.C.A.A., A.A.U., and F.I.N.A.
   - (j) Textbook
   - (k) Weight chart and scales
   - (l) Diving calculator
   - (m) Diving flash cards
   - (n) Judges' finish cards
   - (o) Timers' finish cards
   - (p) Wall weights and barbells
   - (q) Gymnasium mats
   - (r) Two additional springboards
10. Have coaches' own training devices, such as:
    - (a) Pacing machine
    - (b) Inner tubes and other flotation equipment
    - (c) Harness belt and resistance lines
    - (d) Rubber diving demonstrator
    - (e) Motion picture equipment
    - (f) Movies of swimmers and divers
11. Secure printed material for meets and training:
    - (a) Judges' and timers' cards
    - (b) Scoring forms
    - (c) Divers' individual score sheets
    - (d) Diving announcers' cards
    - (e) Duties of officials
    - (f) National record application blanks
    - (g) Training and conditioning rules
    - (h) Flexibility exercises
    - (i) Pool regulations
    - (j) Folding printed postal cards requesting official services for meets
    - (k) Release forms for parents of minors
    - (l) Printed schedules for distribution
    - (m) Eligibility statements for the conference or league
12. Establish eligibility and system for following athletes' scholastic progress.

13. Prepare a list and contact prospective officials.
14. Arrange for publicity such as news service and photography.
15. Prepare form for preparation of individual achievement record of potential team members for swimming guide and all-American selection.
16. Arrange for pool seating facilities such as chairs, benches, tables, bleachers, etc.
17. Refurbish surface lane markers, diving boards and fulcrums, starting platforms, and backstroke handrail starting blocks.
18. Review home schedules of other sports for possible conflicts to make certain visiting team rooms are available.
19. Draw up contracts with scheduled teams.

Things to do one week before a meet:

1. Notify visiting team coach as to date and hour of meet and to send his entries of eligible men, photos for program and publicity purposes. List hours and days pool will be available for practice.
2. Print program.
3. Mail folding postal cards to prospective officials.
4. Procure eligibility list of own team members from eligibility chairman.
5. Notify equipment manager to have all equipment ready and supply him with a list of eligible competitors for suiting-up purposes.
6. See that equipment manager makes necessary arrangements to have all equipment available for the meet.
7. Conduct time trials.
8. Make the following arrangements if meet is away from home:
   (a) Arrange for hotel and transportation reservations.
   (b) If transportation is by auto, insure cars by semi-school bus clause and insure each member by travelers' insurance.
   (c) If special menus are required, make advance arrangements with hotels and railroad diners.
   (d) Notify coach when pool is desired for practice upon arrival before meet.
   (e) Pass list of team making trip, its itinerary, hotel, time of departure, arrival, and return home.
   (f) Notify faculty the number of days students will be absent on trip.

    (g)   Have each member of team arrange with his instructors for make-up of any work, papers, or tests missed.

9.   Make the following arrangements if meet is at home:

    (a)   Arrange for towels and dressing facilities for visiting team.

    (b)   Assist visiting team in obtaining transportation from depot to hotel and pool, etc.

10.   Notify referee of time of meet.

Things to do the day of the meet:

1.   Check officials' list of all officials who will be available from returned cards.
2.   Arrange tables, chairs, and benches around pool for officials and competitors.
3.   Arrange with visiting coach for his team practice.
4.   Compile kits for all officials and coaches.
5.   Lay out record application blanks.
6.   Arrange for distribution of programs.
7.   Set up and test public address system.
8.   Arrange starting platforms.
9.   Adjust temperature of pool to 75° F.
10.   Close scum gutter drains and fill pool to scum gutter level.
11.   Arrange surface lanes.
12.   Set up the scoreboard.
13.   Test pool lighting and ventilation.
14.   Inspect bleachers for safety.
15.   Check springboard and matting for possible defects.
16.   Lay out catch rope and finish rope.
17.   Procure 100 towels for attendants.
18.   Install comb and mirror for divers.
19.   Notify equipment manager to issue suits, supporters, and sweatsuits to the team, and provide him with list of members to be suited.
20.   Arrange for trainers, rubbers, massage tables, and team physician.
21.   Appoint custodian of equipment (stop watches, gun, clip boards, prizes, rubber bands, paper clips, etc.)
22.   Appoint ticket takers and ushers with programs.
23.   Obtain sharp pencils, extra 3 x 5 inch cards, a ream of scratch paper, rule books, and diving calculator.
24.   Notify press and photographers through publicity department.

OFFICIALS' KITS

The kits listed in Table 22-1 should be made up and presented to each official upon his arrival before the meet. The kits should be collected by a manager at the end of the meet.

Table 22-1. Officials' kits

OFFICIAL	NUMBER OF KITS	ITEMS
Coaches	2 or more	Clip board and pencil; scratch paper; twelve 3 x 5 inch cards; program; list of officials; 2 individual diving score sheets; rule book
Referee (starter)	1	Program; pencil; 2 guns; 2 boxes of cartridges; whistle; rule book; list of officials showing position of judges and timers
Chief finish judge	1	Nine programs; 9 pencils; 100 judges; finish cards; 1 list of officials; 1 whistle
Chief timer	1	Five programs; 16 stop watches, checked and synchronized; 4 pencils; 50 timers' cards; 1 list of officials
Clerk of course	1	Clip board and pencil; 1 program; 1 list of competitors; 1 list of officials; 1 whistle
Scorer	1	Clip board; scratch paper; score sheet; 4 pencils; program; record application blanks; list of officials; rule book
Diving clerk	1	Four pencils; diving scoring table; calculator; rule book
Announcer	1	Clip board and pencil; scratch paper; program; list of officials; information about competitors and records; whistle
Diving judges	3 or 5	Set of flash cards and program
Slap-off judges	4 or 6	Raincoat and towel; program
Inspectors of turns	4 or 6	Program; list of competitors
Scoreboard clerk	1	Program; chalk; eraser
Official scorer of meet	1	Program; score sheet
Student managers	3	Program; handy men to see that equipment is placed at proper time and see that meet runs smoothly

PREPARATIONS FOR A CHAMPIONSHIP MEET

A list of officials and duties of managers and officials is presented. These duty summaries can be copied onto cards for distribution before the meet.

Officials for championship meet*:

1. One swimming referee, one starter, one assistant starter, one diving referee, one announcer, one associate announcer, and one diving announcer
2. One head judge, one assistant head judge, and two judges for each lane
3. One head timer, one assistant head timer, and four timers for each lane, one of which is designated as an alternate in the event that one of the official watches fails to function; one member to serve as take-off judge on relays
4. Five diving judges
5. One clerk of course and one assistant clerk of course
6. Six inspectors of turns, two stroke judges
7. The following officials at the scoring table: chief recorder, record keeper verifier, card recorder, assistant recorders
8. Three computers and recorders at the diving table
9. Score board operator and assistants
10. Two false start rope attendants
11. One flip charts operator for each lane; charts indicate swimmers' time to the spectators
12. Runners to deliver finish cards to scorers' table
13. Meet doctor and trainers

Duties of manager for league championship meet:

1. Send circular letter to all participating coaches announcing conduct of meet arrangements as follows:
    (a) Hotel accommodations and rates
    (b) Dormitory housing if possible and rates
    (c) Best eating accommodations
    (d) Towel and locker arrangements
    (e) Restate deadline for entries to be in
    (f) Request publicity materials—photos, mats, records of teams and individuals
    (g) Request time of arrival by auto, railroad, or bus by visiting team
    (h) Notify coach to bring stop watches, white duck pants, etc.
2. Send out entry forms for all events, receive entries, and collect entry fees.

*See N.C.A.A. and A.A.U. current rule changes.

3. Make arrangements through publicity department for program containing league, national, and world's records as well as interesting pictures of past or defending champions and entries for each event.
4. Make arrangements for adequate locker, towel, training, rubbers, and training room facilities.
5. Check with athletic manager for local schedule conflicts with date of league championships.
6. Erect adequate scoreboard for team totals.
7. Order appropriate league medals and trophies.
8. Arrange for an appropriate room for coaches' meeting.
9. Arrange for a very good public address system and an operator.
10. Arrange for a special dressing room for officials and coaches.
11. Arrange for a lounging room for officials and coaches.
12. Notify press and radio.
13. Scratch box and notification of scratch deadline for each day's events.
    (a) Assist referee and meet committee with drawing up heats, etc.
    (b) Have secretary at meeting to list heats.
    (c) Have pool-bottles with numbers up to 25.
    (d) Get each competitor's selected dives and order of performance from each coach.
    (e) Have scratch paper and pencils available at meeting.
    (f) Have duplicator and operator ready to rush through copies of heats for coaches and all officials.
    (g) Pass out contestants' and officials' pass tickets to meet.
    (h) Make announcements if necessary.
    (i) After final selection of all officials (judges of finish, timers, slap-off judges, referee, starter, inspectors, and diving judges), have copies made for all officials and coaches.
    (j) Have programs available, two for each coach and one for each of his competitors.
    (k) Have original entry lists available at this meeting.
14. Check over all equipment items necessary to conduct meet and have them in readiness.
15. See that meet runs smoothly and efficiently throughout the competition.
16. Have filter operator make a final check on water temperature and see that the pool water is level with overflow gutter.
17. Have several student managers always available to remove and replace equipment whenever needed.

18. After meet have money ready to pay officials.
19. After meet make report of meet, including names of officials, competitors, and institutions, summary of the meet and split times of each event, judges of diving, scores of each dive, and the team total standing.
20. Prepare a financial report showing all guarantees, gross income of meet, receipts of expenditure, etc.

Duties of referee:

1. The referee has full jurisdiction over the meet and sees that all the rules are enforced.
2. He presides at the coaches' drawing and scratch meeting.
3. He examines each entry in the meet for eligibility.
4. He designates time of redrawing of heats and lanes after preliminary heats.
5. He assigns each official and instructs him as to his particular duty.
6. He decides all questions relating to the actual conduct of the meet. He may call on the meet committee to assist him in arriving at a decision.
7. He makes final settlement of any question or problem not covered in the rules.
8. He signals the starter that judges, timers, and inspectors are in position before each start.
9. He disqualifies competitors for any violation of the rules that he personally observes.

Duties of the starter. The starter has full control of the competitors from the time they have been assigned to their proper positions by the clerk of course until after the signal to start has been given. Before starting each heat or race, he first receives a signal from the referee that all other officials are in designated positions. He takes a position where timers can see the gun flash and competitors can hear the report. Before each heat or race he explains the following to each competitor:

1. The signal to be given to start the race
2. The distance to be covered
3. The number of laps
4. At which turn the "gun-lap" will be given (Usually in longer races the gun warning is given two lengths before the race ends.)
5. Where the race will finish

His further duties include:

1. He makes sure he has at least three shells in his gun. (For indoors, a .22 caliber, and for outdoors, a .32 caliber.)
2. He also sees that the two officials are in place with the recall rope placed at 30 feet from starting station.

3. He has jurisdiction over false starts. (See start rule in A.A.U. and N.C.A.A. rule books.)

4. In case the gun is improperly discharged, he calls back all competitors at once by pistol shot, and the recall rope is lowered to the surface of the water.

5. If pistol is properly discharged and any competitor or competitors have obtained an unfair advantage at the start, he recalls all competitors by pistol shot and indicates the competitor or competitors to be charged with the false start.

6. A false start is charged to any or all competitors if they leave their mark before the pistol has been fired or if a competitor is deliberately slow in taking his mark after the signal is given.

7. When a competitor is disqualified by false starts, this counts as an event for the competitor.

Ballot system. The ballot system is the fairest known method of selecting the official finish of a swimming race. Each of the two judges assigned to a lane has one ballot, and the official timer for that lane has another ballot, all three of equal value. The ballots for each lane are recorded and added. The swimmer having the lowest total ballot is designated as the winner of the heat. The second lowest total is second, etc. A tie ballot remains a tie for the given place. In determining the ballot based on official time, the fastest recorded time receives a ballot of one, the second fastest a two, the third fastest a three, etc. The ballot system is described in detail in the N.C.A.A. and A.A.U. swimming guides.

Judges. Two lane place judges are assigned to each lane and are placed on opposite sides of the pool. Each judge determines independently where the contestant in his lanes finishes in the race and records it on the card provided for that purpose. The judge must not record a tie. Each judge must record the highest place his lane contestant actually may have attained. For example, if a lane judge determines that the contestant in his lane has finished in a tie with another contestant for first place, he shall record a first place (1) for his lane, and the same procedure applies to similar situations involving other place positions.

A "runner" is assigned to pick up each lane judge's card immediately after each race and deliver to the scoring table.

Duties of timers. In any race the time is taken by three official timers and an alternate for each lane. They start their watches with the gun flash and stop them at the instant any part of the competitor in that lane touches the finish line. The index finger is used in starting and stopping the watch. The times registered on the three official watches for each lane are written on the card held by the head timer on the lane.

The alternate watch is never used except when one of the official timers' watches has ceased to function. If a record has been made, the watches are shown to the chief timer for inspection. The official time for that race is the one in which two or more watches agree. If all three watches disagree, the intermediate watch is the official time regardless of how much the three watches disagree. The three watches must never be averaged for the official time. If only two watches remain running at the end of a race and they disagree, the watches are averaged to the slowest one tenth of a second.

Duties of the chief timer:

1. He assigns three timers and one alternate to each lane, one of these official timers to serve as head timer of that lane.

2. He supplies each head timer on each lane with cards upon which he records on its face the event, heat number, lane number, and the three official times. Throughout the race, he will also record on the back of this card the lap split times. The alternate watch is normally used for this purpose.

3. He collects all cards from all lane head timers, checks each card for errors, and then gives times to the official scorer.

4. He will designate one member of the timing team to serve as take-off judge on relays for each lane. This judge will determine whether both feet of the second, third, and forth contestants are still in contact with the starting mark when the preceding team-mate touches the end of "the pool." He shall station himself in such a position that he can see the end of the pool and have his little finger in light contact with the little toe of the contestant. An illegal take-off is reported to the referee and results in the disqualification of the relay team.

It will be noted that in championship races timers are placed at every lane, thus eliminating three official timers for the winner of either the heat or the final race of the qualifiers through the heats. The timers are stationed directly over their lane and can accurately judge the hand touch to the finish line, except in races which end in the open water with a pennant curtain held as a finish line. In such cases, the timers stand at the sides of the finish lines. When any part of the swimmer's body strikes the pennant curtain line or passes through this line, the timers stop their watches.

Duties of inspectors. For a six-lane pool, there should be at least one inspector for every two lanes. One or two inspectors placed opposite the finish end of the pool is entirely inadequate and unsatisfactory. It is humanly impossible to observe more than two lanes, especially if competitors happen to turn simultaneously. The inspector observes the rules of the turn and touch of all events, heats, and races and reports any infraction to the referee immediately at the end of the race. He keeps a record of the number of turns and reports which turn was violated.

Duties of clerk of course. The clerk of course should have at least two assistants and is provided with a list of the competitors with heats and lanes already drawn. He notifies each competitor to appear at the starting line and in the proper lane before the start of each race. He controls his assistants and assigns to them such duties as will assist in the prompt dispatch of the meet.

Duties of the scorer. He records the order of finish and the times of each heat in all events as given him by the head judge and head timer. He records disqualifications as given him by the referee. He keeps a running score of the meet. He also acts as clerk of the dives and records their results.

Duties of the announcer. Before the start of each event, he announces the event, the number of heats, and the method of qualifying, and at the start of each heat he announces the lane, the name of each competitor, and school or club affiliation. Immediately after the finish of each heat he announces the results as given him by the scorer. He makes any other announcements as requested by the referee or the management. He should be provided with a public address system. His enunciation should be slow, clear, and distinct.

Duties of the clerk of records. He is cognizant of all times performed in the meet. If any time might equal or break a national or world record, he should have available record application blanks. He should secure in ink the signatures of the referee, three judges, three timers, and the times of each timer opposite his signature and the certification of an engineer of the exact length of the course. The referee shall then give it final approval. This is then sent to either the N.C.A.A. or the A.A.U. chairman of the records committees for final acceptance or rejection.

Duties of the doctor. He is present throughout the championship competition and is prepared to examine any competitors requiring such service. If a competitor becomes ill after the drawing for heats is closed, he must be examined by a physician. Otherwise, if not really ill, the competitor may suffer the consequences of being disqualified from further competition and may lose all honors previously won in the championship.

Duties of the press steward. He obtains the names of all competitors in each event from the scorer and obtains the results of the heats and place winners in the final races. He keeps the press informed of the competition throughout the championships.

Duties of diving officials. The N.C.A.A., the A.A.U., and the F.I.N.A.

Fig. 22-1. A suggested arrangement of personnel and equipment for a championship meet.

A. COMPETITOR'S BENCHES
B. FINISH LINE
C. CHECK ROPE
D. HIGH DIVING BOARD
E. LOW DIVING BOARD
F. TIMERS & JUDGES
G. RUNNERS FOR JUDGES & TIMERS
H. DIVING CLERK
I. OFFICIAL SCORING CLERKS FOR HEAD TIMER & HEAD JUDGE
J. ANNOUNCER
K. PRESS
L. CLERK OF COURSE
M. TROPHIES
N. BLEACHERS
O. PUBLIC ADDRESS SYSTEM

rules are now identical in the rules and regulations governing the conduct of a championship diving contest. Since methods of marking and the duties of the diving referee, the judges, and the diving clerks are specifically and identically described in all three rule books of the above named organizations, no further explanation will be given here.

Pool arrangement. The arrangement of equipment and placement of officials and competitors shown in Fig. 22-1 is recommended for a championship meet. Modifications for a dual meet can be accomplished by making appropriate reductions.

SUMMER AGE-GROUP SWIMMING MEET

The planning and organization for a summer age-group swimming meet is very important to ensure a smooth operation on the day of the contest. A good swimming meet demands that it start on time and finish near the time designated for it to end. For this to happen, the people conducting the meet must be well informed as to their duties. The visiting competitors, coaches, and guests have a right to expect adequate information, correct times, and all material needed to swim the events with ease.

The first procedure to follow in planning an age-group swimming meet is to form a group of persons to do the planning of the meet. This group normally consists of parents of young competitive swimmers who organize and form a local swim club. They should meet several months in advance of the contest and select a meet manager who has had some experience in the swimming world or one who will take time to study what it entails. When considering the date of the meet, it is wise to be sure there is not another meet in the area, because this will cut down on the number of entries. After this meeting the respective members must be aware of the time schedule indicating when different tasks should be done. This group must select the program of events to be contested (Table 22-2). They may consider enlisting the aid of a sponsor for the meet such as the Chamber of Commerce, the local newspaper, or a local service club.

The following committee chairmen should be selected by the meet manager:

1. Officials
2. Supplies
3. General help
4. Awards
5. Publicity
6. Clean-up
7. Food
8. Entries and programs

Task	16 weeks	15 weeks	14 weeks	13 weeks	12 weeks	11 weeks	10 weeks	9 weeks	8 weeks	7 weeks	6 weeks	5 weeks	4 weeks	3 weeks	2 weeks	10 days	5 days	4 days	3 days	2 days	1 day	Meet
Agree on date for the meet	↕																					
Order watches through a jeweler		↕																				
List the events in numerical order				↕	↕																	
Order the awards to allow time for delivery				↕	↕	↕																
Reserve pool						↕																
Write for AAU sanction							↕															
Contact person you want to act as starter							↕	↕														
Contact all members who will be committee heads								↕	↕													
Mail entry blanks and entry cards to be filled out by each coach										↕	↕											
Meeting of committee chairmen											↕	↕										
Make up forms and order supplies											↕		↕									
Get records from AAU records chairman														↕	↕	↕						
Arrange cards by event number													↕	↕								
Type cover for all programs and run copies														↕				↕	↕			
Type preliminary program and run copies																				↕	↕	

AMOUNT OF TIME BEFORE DAY OF MEET

Fig. 22-2. A suggested time chart to assist a summer meet director.

RELAYS — List names on reverse side
Please print — use pencil

Entry card   Event No. _____

Name of event _____

Age   Division   Sex _____

Contestant's name _____

Club affiliation _____

A.A.U. No. _____ Birth date _____

Best time meters/yards _____

Please do not write below.

Heat No.   Lane No.

Timer's name	Min.	Sec.	1/10 Sec.

Ballot

Official time

Judge _____

Judge _____

Place in event   Place in heat

Time _____

Total _____

Fig. 22-3. Suggested time card.

Table 22-2. Suggested schedule of events

1. 7 and 8 100-yard medley relay
2. 9 and 10 200-yard medley relay
3. 11 and 12 200-yard medley relay
4. 13 and 14 200-yard medley relay
5. 15 and 17 200-yard medley relay
6. 7 and 8 25-yard freestyle
7. 9 and 10 50-yard freestyle
8. 11 and 12 50-yard freestyle
9. 13 and 14 50-yard freestyle
10. 15 and 17 50-yard freestyle
11. 11 and 12 200-yard individual medley relay
12. 13 and 14 200-yard individual medley relay
13. 15 and 17 200-yard individual medley relay
14. 7 and 8 25-yard butterfly
15. 9 and 10 50-yard butterfly
16. 11 and 12 50-yard butterfly
17. 13 and 14 100-yard butterfly
18. 15 and 17 100-yard butterfly
19. 11 and 12 100-yard freestyle
20. 13 and 14 100-yard freestyle
21. 15 and 17 100-yard freestyle
22. 7 and 8 25-yard backstroke
23. 9 and 10 50-yard backstroke
24. 11 and 12 50-yard backstroke
25. 13 and 14 100-yard backstroke
26. 15 and 17 100-yard backstroke
27. 7 and 8 25-yard breast stroke
28. 9 and 10 50-yard breast stroke
29. 11 and 12 50-yard breast stroke
30. 13 and 14 100-yard breast stroke
31. 15 and 17 100-yard breast stroke
32. 7 and 8 100-yard freestyle relay
33. 9 and 10 200-yard freestyle relay
34. 11 and 12 200-yard freestyle relay
35. 13 and 14 200-yard freestyle relay
36. 15 and 17 400-yard freestyle relay

Officials

Every effort should be made to obtain experienced personnel to fill the key official assignments: the referee, starter, chief judge, chief timer, clerk of course, head recorder, and announcer (see pages 344 and 349). The official chairman may delegate the responsibility of securing the timers to the chief timer and the judges to the chief judge. The judges and timers should be supplied with a mimeographed, detailed explanation of their duties, the time to report to the pool, and the recommended attire. Provisions should be made for relief timers and judges when a long meet is anticipated.

When there are several hundred entries in the meet, it has proved successful to provide two complete sets of officials, one set at each end of the pool. It is then possible to alternate the start of each heat at one end of the pool and then at the other, resulting in the start of a heat before the other is actually finished.

Clerk of course. The clerk of course and his assistants are responsible for lining up the contestants in their proper heats. The clerk should have one heat on the starting blocks, the next in proximity ready to move to the starting blocks, and the next several heats seated on benches ready to move forward. He must have the cooperation of the announcer who assists him by calling up the contestants at the proper times to keep the meet moving.

Head recorder. The head recorder will need several helpers and will work with the referee. He will keep track of scores and finish places of all contestants.

Announcer. The announcer will announce each event before it starts and tell the name of the contestant, lane number, and the club affiliation. He should also announce the results given him by the recorder.

Supplies

Special supplies are needed for each of the officials and their assistants, according to their individual duties, and are listed as follows:

Referee
1. A rule book that is up-to-date
2. A chair

Starter
1. Two guns
2. Shells
3. Bull-horn
4. Assistant to fill gun

Judges
1. Benches on each side of the pool at the finish line
2. Judges' cards
3. Pencils
4. Cover to put over the judges' benches to keep the sun off

Timers
1. Chair for each timer to rest between events
2. Watch for each timer
3. Pencils
4. Clip boards for each timer or at least for official timer
5. Whistle for head timer
6. Table for head timer
7. If possible, cover for them so that they may keep out of the sun

Clerk of course
1. Table to seat three
2. Three chairs
3. Benches for three groups of contestants
4. Box with entry-time cards in order of events
5. Pencils
6. Towels
7. Cover for other contestants

Recorder
1. Covers for tables
2. Two large tables
3. Twelve chairs
4. Pencils
5. Rubber bands
6. Shoe boxes to put cards in order of events
7. Tissues
8. Ash trays
9. Fly spray
10. Aspirin
11. Four typewriters
12. Stencils and correction fluid
13. Mimeograph machine and ink
14. Stapler and staples
15. Redi-forms
16. Legal-size paper for mineograph
17. Scotch tape for runners to post results
18. Band-aids

Announcer
1. P. A. system
2. Table (near recorder)
3. Chair

Clean-up
1. Truck
2. Garbage cans for each area of swimmers

Food for officials
1. Ice and ice chest
2. Cups and spoons
3. Coffee
4. Tea (instant)
5. Sugar and cream
6. Large coffee pot
7. Rolls, doughnuts, and sandwiches

8. Serving table
9. Chairs for workers

Miscellaneous

1. Lane markers
2. Two chairs for turn judges
3. Plenty of towels for workers
4. Bleachers for spectators
5. Tables for persons selllng patches
6. Table for person disbursing officials' ribbons or pins
7. A rubber mat and a baby swim pool at gate where swimmers enter and leave the pool area

General help

Assistant meet manager
Person to help starter fill gun
A doctor engaged for the day
Runners

1. Two for timers and alternates
2. Two for judges and alternates
3. One to post results
4. One to take results to awards chairman
5. One to do general errands
6. Gatekeepers
7. Persons to hand out programs
8. Persons to sell badges

Awards

The awards chairman will order the awards at least three months in advance of the meet day. He should have an area on the deck of the pool or the office of the pool as his headquarters. The office of the pool is best because the contestants cannot get to him. He will need at least one helper to do an efficient job.

Publicity

The publicity chairman will be responsible to advertise the meet in the newspaper, on the radio and television. He may ask the press to come on the day of the meet to take pictures. He must also turn in the final results to all the news media.

Clean-up

The clean-up committee is very important. If the park and pool area are left cluttered, it will not be easy to get the facilities the next year. It is wise to have about ten persons who will keep picking up during the day. The announcer can help by asking persons not to throw waste around and to pick up before leaving. After the meet, everything should be put in a truck and the area should be left clean.

Food

A group should be selected by the chairman to have food and drink for the workers. If possible, it may be wise for a group to run a concession stand to make money for the club. The number of workers needed will be gauged by the size of operation that the chairman decides to have.

Entries and programs

The coach will send blank entry cards to the invited clubs, and these will be returned with the names, times, and affiliations of the contestants. All these entry cards have to be processed after the deadline, which is about a week before the swim meet. A force of at least ten persons will meet on the Wednesday or Thursday before the meet to put these cards in order according to the times and heats. The cards are then sent to the persons typing the programs who may be the recreation office, chamber of commerce, hired personnel, or volunteer helpers. The night or two before the event, a group will have to staple these programs together. Be sure someone is responsible for getting the programs to the meet and have someone in charge of giving them out or selling them. After the programs have been made up, the event cards (kept in order) are ready for the clerk of course. See that they get to the clerk of course in time for the scratch meeting.

Miscellaneous

Scratch meeting. This meeting is usually held within one hour before the meet. The coaches then have an opportunity to cancel out a contestant and substitute another. After the scratch meeting there can be no more changes.

Public relations. Public relations are a very important part of running an age group swimming meet since the club or team is usually borrowing facilities. Some suggestions are as follows:

1. Send a letter to the park and recreation commission requesting the use of the pool.
2. Consult with the pool manager and tell him the layout of the meet. Ask him for extra help in the locker room on that day.
3. Meet with the manager of the concession stand to inform him about how many persons will be on hand that day and what kind of food the swimmers can eat. Ask for his cooperation.
4. Alert the park administrator and park policemen about the meet and ask them to reserve parking space for the meet manager,

the ambulance (if one is to be on hand), and for several cars that may have to be used on errands.

5. Inform anyone who has anything to do with the facilities; otherwise they feel that the swimming group is trespassing.

Recorder's table

The efficiency of the recorder's table makes a great deal of difference in how fast and how well a swim meet is run. To make it possible to get all the times posted, the information to the announcer, and the places sent to the awards chairman, it is well to have plenty of help at the recorder's table. If possible, the head recorder should not do the actual scoring. He (she) should be available to answer questions from parents and coaches about times, to check on mistakes that are sometimes made by the workers, and to consult with the referee. If there is any difficulty, by being free, the recorder can pull the event, get the referee, and have this straightened out before the announcer or awards chairman gets the results. This prevents an award being given to a child who will later have to return it. All this can be done without stopping the meet.

There are many ways of setting up the scorer's table. Here is a suggested one.

There should be two large tables available for the recorder and his assistants. Seated at the first table, from left to right, in order, they should be as follows:

1. Judge and time card sorter
2. Heat ballot scorer
3. Arranger of all time cards in the event with the fastest time first
4. Announcer who will read the results directly from the cards
5. Typist who will make three copies of the first six places, listing place, name of swimmer, club or affiliation, and official time; typed copies go to the announcer, to be posted for contestants to see, and to the awards chairman.

It is wise for the front side of this table to be left empty.

At the second table, mimeographed results are made so that each coach, the records chairman, registration chairman, and A.A.U. official may have one at the end of the meet. At this table there are two typists to cut stencils of the results of each event. One typist computes the odd number events and the other computes the even number events

There should be a mimeograph machine on the table to run off the stencils. The finished copies of the results can then be put in piles during the meet. At the end of the meet they can be stapled together and handed out.

Index

A

Air embolism in scuba diving, 330
Alkali reserve, 182
American crawl stroke, 5
American Red Cross
  senior lifesaving certificate, 338
  swimming lesson program, 339
Announcer
  in championship meet, 353
  for summer age-group meets, 359
Apnea in scuba diving, 331
Aristotle, 319
Arm and breathing skills, practicing, 34
Armbruster, David A., 7, 9
  all-stroke method for teaching beginning
    swimming, 12-26
Ascent, free, in scuba diving, 331
Attention, swimmer's, at start of race, 52
Australian crawl stroke, 4
Awards for summer age-group meets, 361

B

Back crawl flutter kick, 128
Back crawl stroke
  arm action drill, 140
  arm entry in, 130
  arm press-slide, 130
  arm pull in
    bent, 132
    straight, 131
  arm recovery in, 129
  arm release in, 132
  arm technique and mechanics of, 129-133
  breathing in, 134
  catch, pull, and push drive in, 131
  coaching, 118-141
  head action in, 134
  ideal form for executing, 124
  kick drill for, 140
  Kiefer style of, 126
  land drill for, 138
  leg action in, 128
  origin and development of, 10-11
  position of
    body in, 124-128
    head in, 125

Back crawl stroke—cont'd
  position of—cont'd
    hips and lower spine in, 127
    neck in, 126
    shoulder girdle and upper spine in, 126
  race, finish in, 137
  racing fundamentals in, 138
  start, technique of, 119-123; *see also*
    Start, back crawl stroke
  swimmer, physical qualifications for, 119
  teaching and learning procedure, 138-141
  technique of, 123-138
  timing of arms in, 133
    and legs in, 134
  tumble turn in, 135
  200-yard, split times for various racing
    times in, 139
  water drill for, 139-141
Back dive; *see under* Dive
Back float, 19
Back stroke
  elementary
    arm stroke in, 31
    teaching, 31-32
  resting
    arm stroke in, 29
    kick for, 27-29
    teaching and learning procedures in,
      27, 29-30
  tumble turn, ideal form showing, 136
Ball float, 23
Ballot system in championship meet, 351
Barbell exercises, 188
Barotrauma, 332
Bends in scuba diving, 330
Bobbing, 23
  float, 23
Body building exercises, special, for swim-
  mers, 187-189
Body spin, 20
Boyle's law, 320
Breast stroke, 8
  arm action in, 150
    development of, 156
  arm pull and push in, 150
  arm release and recovery in, 152

Breast stroke—cont'd
    arm thrust in, 152
    arms in glide position in, 153
    coaching methods and techniques for, 155
    development of leg action for, 155
    finish, 158
    head action in breathing for, 154
    ideal form for executing, 146
    kick; *see* Kick, beast stroke
    position of body in, 146
    press-catch with arms and hands in, 150
    start, techniques of, 142-146; *see also*
        Start, breast stroke
    surfacing in, 145
    swimmers, characteristics of, 142
    synchronizing arm and kick action in, 153
    teaching and coaching, 142-160
    techniques of, 146-158
    turn, push-off in, 157
    200-yard, split times for various racing
        times in, 157
    underwater, 144
    water demonstration in, 158
    water drill for, 159-160
Breath control, 17
    and arm stroke, practicing for sprint
        crawl stroke, 96
    in back crawl start, 122
Breathing
    and arm skills, practicing, 34
    for breast stroke, head action in, 154
    in distance crawl stroke, head turning
        for, 112
    explosive method of, 80
    relation between head turning and arm
        and leg cycle, 83-85
    in side stroke, 40
    in sprint crawl stroke, 79-86
    technique, common errors in, 85
    timing of, with arms in dolphin butterfly
        stroke, 167
    two-count system of, 83-84
Brink word-picture system, 16
Buddy breathing in scuba diving, 331
Buddy skin diving, 326
Buoyancy testing in scuba diving, 331

C

Caisson disease in scuba diving, 330
Calcium in diet, 180
Carbohydrates in diet, 177
Carbon monoxide poisoning in scuba
    diving, 330
Cavill, Richard, 3, 4, 10
Cavill, Tum, 3
Center, Dad, 6
Championship period, training in, 209-219;
    see also Swimming meet, champ-
    ionship
Chlorine in diet, 180
Cholesterol in diet, 179
Clean-up for summer age-group meets, 361

Clerk of course
    in championship meet, duties of, 353
    for summer age-group meets, 359
Clerk of records in championship meet,
    duties of, 353
Cold, common, and its prevention, 190
Cole, W., 2
Committee chairmen for summer age-group
    meet, 355
Conditioning, 175-191
    prewater, 15-16
Confidence drills, 16-22
Cousteau, Jacques-Yves, 319
Crabbe, Buster, 6
Crawl stroke
    American, 5
    Australian, 4
    back; *see* Back crawl stroke
    beginning and development of, 3-8
    distance
        arm action in, 110-112
            catch in, 111
            entry in, 110
            glide or support in, 110
            pull, drive, and release in, 111
            reach in, 110
            recovery in, 112
        coaching, 106-117
        common errors in head action in, 113
        drag kick in, 109
        head turning for breathing in, 112
        lateral-spin turn for, 113
        leg action in, 108
            common errors in, 108
        position of
            body in, 108
            head and neck in, 108
            hips in, 108
            legs in, 108
        technique of, 108-116
        timing of arms in, 112
        transition from slow to faster tempo
            in, 109
    European, 6
    500-yard, split times for various racing
        times in, 115
    middle distance
        arm action in, 100
        body position in, 100
        breathing in, 101
        coaching in, 98-105
        coordination of arms and legs in, 100
        finish in, 101
        leg action in, 100
        maintaining rhythm in, 105
        racing fundamentals of, 101-105
        turn in, 101
    100-yard, ideal split times for, 94
    speed, 5
    sprint
        arm action in, 71-78
            catch in, 74

Crawl stroke—cont'd
  sprint—cont'd
    arm action in—cont'd
      common errors in, 72, 74
      pull in, 75
      push in, 76
      recovery in, 77
      release in, 76
      supporting phase of, 73
    arm stroke and breath control practicing for, 96
    breathing technique in, 79-86
    coaching, 61-97
    finish in, 91-92
    flutter kick in, 69
    form for, 64
    kick board drill for, 95
    lateral turn, ideal form showing, 86
    leg action in, 69-71
      common faults in, 71
    position of
      body in, 65-71
      head and neck in, 65
      hips in, 68
      legs in, 68
      shoulder gridle and upper spine in, 67
    technique of, 65-92
    timing of arms and legs in, 78-79
    turn in, 85-91; *see also* Turn
    water drill for, 94, 96
  start, 46; *see also* Start
  teaching and learning procedures of, 94-97
  200-yard, split times for various racing times in, 104
Creeping crawl stroke, 4

D

Daniels, Charles M., 5
Davis, Syd, 3
Decompression illness in scuba diving, 330
Diet
  carbohydrates in, 177
  fats in, 178
  fluids in, 181
  high carbohydrate, 182
  minerals in, 180
  postcontest, 182
  precontest, 182
  proteins in, 179
  for swimmers, regular, 176
  vitamins in, 180
Disinfectants for pool, types of, 339
Distance crawl stroke; *see* Crawl stroke, distance
Distance orientation, 35
  for advanced swimming, 44
Distance race, finish of, 116
Distance swimmers
  characteristics of, 107
  qualifications of, 107

Dive, springboard
  back
    approach in, 236
    ideal form for executing, 255
    layout, 257
    mechanics and technique for take-off for, 236-241
    one and one half somersault
      layout, 259
      one and one half twist, free, 288
      pike, 260
      tuck, 261
      two and one half twist, free, 288
    pike, 256
    pivot step in, 236
    somersault
      layout, 257
      pike, 258
      tuck, 258
    stance in, 236
    take-off mechanics of arms and legs in, 236
    tuck, 255
    two and one half somersault, tuck, 262
  backward jump
    pike, 239
    straight, 239
    tuck, 239
  flying forward one and one half somersault, tuck, 249
  flying reverse somersault, tuck, 270
  forward
    double somersault, tuck, 251
    half twist
      layout, 280
      pike, 281
    jackknife, pike, 243
    layout, 244
    one and one half somersault
      double twist, free, 284
      one twist, free, 283
      pike, 250
      tuck, 250
    one twist, layout, 282
    somersault
      pike, 247
      series of ideal form for executing, 243
      tuck, 248
    three and one half somersault, tuck, 254
    tuck, 242
    two and one half somersault
      pike, 254
      tuck, 254
  front jump
    pike, 238
    straight, 238
    tuck, 238
  inward
    ideal form for executing, 274
    layout, 276

Dive, springboard—cont'd
 inward—cont'd
  one and one half somersault
   pike, 278
   tuck, 278
  pike, 274
  somersault
   pike, 276
   tuck, 276
  tuck, 273
  two and one half somersault, tuck, 278
 jump
  fundamental, 237-241
  ideal form for executing, 241
 reverse
  ideal form for executing, 265
  with half twist, layout, 283
  layout, 265
  one and one half somersault
   layout, 273
   one and one half twist, free, 285
   pike, 271
   tuck, 271
  pike, 264
  somersault
   layout, 267
   pike, 268
   tuck, 268
  tuck, 263
  two and one half somersault, tuck, 273
 twisting, ideal form for executing, 281
Dive, tower
 armstand, cut through, tuck, 308
 back
  pike, 312
  somersault, layout, 306
 basic, 303-316
  ideal form for, 305
 flying forward one and one half somersault, pike, 309
 inward
  one and one half somersault, pike, 316
  pike, 308
 reverse somersault, layout, 311
 running front one and one half somersault, open pike, 304
 standing
  front, layout, 304
  reverse, pike, 315
Diver
 daily workouts for, 223-225
 equipment for, 221
 physical qualifications of, 221
 skin, underwater swimming position in,
   324
 special flexibility exercises for, 186-187
 springboard
  starting position of, 226
  walk, 227
 teaching aids for, 225-226
 tower, personal make-up of, 293

Diver—cont'd
 training and conditioning exercises for,
   221-223
 use of dry land pit by, 225
 use of trampoline by, 225
Diving
 competitive, 242
 facilities, 336
  standard dimensions for, 335
 fundamental techniques of front approach, hurdle, and take-off in,
   226-235
 historical evolution of, 11-13
 officials in championship swimming meet,
   duties of, 353
 physics of, 320-321
 pool dimensions, 337
Diving, scuba, 327-332
 air cylinders for, 329
 disorders, 330
 drills, 331
 entries in, 329
 equipment for, 327
 medicine for, 332
 skills in, 329
 tank for, 328
  harness for, 329
Diving, skin, 321-327
 accessory equipment for, 324
 ascending in, 326
 buddy, 326
 clearing mask in, 325
 clearing snorkel in, 325
 diving down in, 325
 entries in, 326
 equalizing pressure in, 326
 equipment for, 322-324
 exposure dress for, 323
 fins for, 323
 five supplementary rules of, 332
 hyperventilation in, 325
 mask for, 323
 medical examination for, 322
 performance techniques in, 327
 prerequisites for, 321-322
 skills in, 324-327
 snorkel for, 323
 swimming test for, 321
 teaching, 319
 ten basic rules of, 332
 weight belt for, 324
Diving, springboard
 entry in, 235
 height and line of flight in, 234
 hurdle and take-off, 230
 from 1- or 3-meter height, 242-289
 take-off, 232
  ideal form showing various types of,
   229
 teaching and coaching, 220-289

Diving, tower
  approach
    running
      with one-foot take-off, 295
      skip, with a one-foot take-off, 300
      with two-foot take-off, 300
    and take-offs, 294-303
    forward, 295
    ideal form for, 297
  armstand
    approaches and take-offs, 300, 302
    one-leg kick-up, 303
    press up
      in pike position, 303
      in tuck position, 303
  conditioning exercises for, 316-317
  learning, 292-294
  practice sessions for, 317
  safety hints for, 317
  take-offs
    back, 300
    ideal form for, 301
    standing, 295
  teaching and coaching, 290-318
  things to remember for, 318
  types and construction of, 291-292
Diving, underwater, history of, 319-320
Doctor in championship meet, duties of, 353
Dolphin butterfly stroke
  arm action in, 163
    drill for, 170
  arm catch in, 163
  arm entry in, 163
  arm pull in, 163
  arm push in, 164
  arm release and recovery in, 166
  arm support in, 163
  combined arm and leg action drill for, 170
  development of, 161
  finish of, 169
  fishtail, 9
  ideal form for executing, 164
  kick in, 162
    drill for, 169
  land drill for, 169
  origin and development of, 8-10
  start, 167
  teaching and coaching, 161-170
  technique of, 162-169
  timing of arms and legs in, 166
  timing of breathing with arms in, 167
  200-yard, split times for various racing times in, 168
  underwater drill for, 169
  water drill for, 169
Drowning in scuba diving, 330
Dual-meet
  training for, 203-209
  workout plan for week of, 208

E

Elimination, 183

Elongated float, 23
English overarm, 2
Entries and programs for summer age-group meet, 362
European crawl stroke, 6
Exercise, 184-188
  for ankle stretching, 186
  barbell, 188
  conditioning, 184
  crab, 187
  for crotch stretch, 187
  for development of back extensors, 187
  light, 186
  for loosening and stretching shoulder girdle, 187
  for rotating trunk, 186
  special body building, 187-189
  special flexibility, 186-187
  for strengthening abdominals, 187
  for stretching hamstring or leg flexor group, 186
  for stretching shoulder and chest muscles, 186
  for stretching spine, 187
  warm-up, 185
Exposure dress for skin diving, 323

F

Fats in diet, 178
Filter operation for pool, 341
Filters, types of, for pool, 342
F.I.N.A., 9
Finish
  breast stroke, 158
  of distance race, 116
  of dolphin butterfly stroke, 169
  hand touch, 92
  wall, approach to, 91
Fins for skin diving, 323
Float
  back, 19
  ball, 23
  bobbing, 23
  elongated, 23
  front, 19
  jackknife, 19
  jellyfish, 19
Floating position, standing up from horizontal, 19
Fluids in diet, 181
Flutter kick; *see* Kick, flutter
Food for summer age-group meet, 362
Forder, William, 320
Forward dive; *see under* Dive
Franklin, Benjamin, 320
Frazer, Dawn, 7
Front float, 19
Front glide with kick, 20
Furuhashi, 7

G

Gagnan, Emile, 319

Glide, front and rear, with kick, 20
Glucose in diet, 178

H

Handstand balancing and walking, 188
Handy, Jam, 7, 10
Henry's law, 320
Hyperventilation, 51
Hypochlorous acid in pool water, 341

I

Inspectors in championship meet, duties of, 352
Instructors, swimming, 339
International Swimming Federation, 9
Iodine, 180

J

Jackknife dive; *see under* Dive
Jackknife float, 19
Japanese swimming technique, 6
Jellyfish float, 19
Judges in championship meet, 351
Jump dives; *see under* Dive

K

Kahanamoku, Duke, 5
Kick
  in back crawl stroke, drill for, 140
  in breast stroke, 148
    classification of, 146
      narrow, 149
        modified, 149
      narrow knee-spread, timing of, 153
      wide knee-spread, timing of, 153
  dolphin fishtail, 9
  flutter, 4
    back crawl, 128
    crawl stroke, in sprint, 69
    distance, 108
  front glide with, 20
  learning, 34
  rear glide with, 20
  for resting back stroke, 27-29
  scissors, 36
  trudge-crawl, 5
  Trudgeon, 2, 3
  and upper arms in side stroke, 40
Kick board drill
  for back crawl stroke, 140
  for breast stroke, 159
  for dolphin butterfly stroke, 169
  for sprint crawl stroke, 95
    without water drill, 96
Kiefer, Adolph, 10, 118
  style of back crawl, 126

L

Lactose, 178
Lambertsen, C. J., 320
Lane, F. V. C., 2

League championship meet, duties of manager for, 348-350
Lecithin, 179
Leg kick; *see* Kick
Lifeguard, 336, 337-339
  duties of, 338
  qualification standards for, 338
Lipoids, 179

M

Mask
  in scuba diving, submerging and swimming without, 331
  for skin diving, 323
    clearing, 325
Massage, 190
Meet, swimming; *see* Swimming meet
Mental attitude, 15
Middle distance
  crawl stroke; *see* Crawl stroke, middle distance
  race; *see* Race, middle distance
  swimmer, characteristics of, 98-99
  swimming, technique of, 99-101
Minerals in diet, 180
Motivating skills, 21
Mouthpiece, clearing in scuba diving, 331

N

Nicotinic acid in diet, 181
Nitrogen narcosis in scuba diving, 330
Nutrition, essentials of, 177

O

Officials for swimming meet
  championship, 348
  kits for, 347
  summer age-group, 358
Oxygen poisoning in scuba diving, 330

P

Pace training, 202
Pacing machine, 200
Phosphorus in diet, 180
Pliny, 319
Pool
  care and maintenance of, 333
  disinfection of water in, 339
  diving dimensions, 337
  filter operation for, 341
  indoor, 333-335
    deck, 334
    depth of, 334
    ladders for, 335
    length of, 333
    lighting in, 335
    markings, 334
    overflow gutters, 334
    width of, 334
  outdoor, 336-342
    diving facilities, 336
    lifeguard for, 336-339

Pool—cont'd
  outdoor—cont'd
    manager, 336
    personnel for, selecting, 336
    water control for, 339-342
      filter for, 341
    in racing, adjustment to, 101
    types of filters for, 342
    water balance for, 341
    water control for, 339
    water testing and records for, 340
Port-o-pit, 226
Press steward in championship meet, duties of, 353
Proteins in diet, 179
Public relations for summer age-group meet, 362
Publicity for summer age-group meet, 361

R

Race
  distribution of effort in, 200
  middle distance
    maneuvering for position in, 102
    meeting challenge in, 103
    pacing in, 104
    passing an opponent in, 103
    plan for, 116
    speed in early part of, 102
Racing
  adjustment to pool in, 101
  fundamentals
    in back crawl stroke, 138
    in middle distance crawl stroke, 101-105
    in sprint race, 92-94
  relay; *see* Relay racing
Rear glide with kick, 20
Recorder, head, for summer age-group meet, 359
Recorder's table for summer age-group meet, 363
Red Cross water safety instructor's certificate, 338
Referee in championship meet, duties of, 350
Relay racing, 171-174
  team, arrangement of, 172
  technique of take-off in, 173
  types of, 171
Respiratory habits of trained swimmers, 52
Rest, 183
Reverse dive; *see under* Dive

S

Scissors kick, 36
  in side stroke, 40
Scorer in championship meet, duties of, 353
Scratch meeting for summer age-group meet, 362
Scuba diving; *see* Diving, scuba
Sculling, 21

Shipping water, 18
Side stroke
  arm stroke in, 37
  breathing in, 40
  kick, upper and under arm in, 40
  scissors kick in, 40
  teaching, 36-42
  underarm, 2-3
  whole stroke in, 39
Siebe, Augustus, 320
Sieg, Jack, 9
Skin diving; *see* Diving, skin
Sleep, 183
Slow-motion picture camera, 6
Snorkel, skin diving, 323
  clearing, 325
Sodium in diet, 180
Somersault; *see under* Dive; Turn
Speed crawl stroke, 5
Spin, body, 20
Springboard diving; *see* Diving, springboard
Sprint crawl stroke; *see* Crawl stroke, sprint
Sprint race, fundamentals in, 92-94
Sprint swimmer
  anatomic qualifications of, 62
  characteristics of, 62-65
  physiologic qualifications of, 63
Sprint turns; *see* Turn
Squeeze in scuba diving, 331
Starch in diet, 178
Start
  back crawl stroke, 119-123
    breath control in, 122
    entry in, 122
    glide in, 122
    leaving mark in, 121
  breast stroke
    entry in, 143
    glide under water in, 143
    line of flight in, 143
    techniques of, 142-146
  crawl stroke, 46
    ideal form for performing, 47
  dolphin butterfly, 167
  of race
    breathing in, 51
    circular arm action in, 55
    swimmer's attention at, 52
  racing
    coaching, 46-61
    entry in, 58
    flight in, 58
    glide in, 59
    initial strokes in, 59
    knee dip technique in, 56
    knee extension technique in, 56
    leaving mark, 53-55
    position of
      arms in, 50
      feet in, 48
      head and eyes in, 50
      hips in, 50

Start—cont'd
  racing—cont'd
    position of—cont'd
      knees in, 50
      trunk in, 48
    preparatory position, 47
    toe lift technique in, 57
    variations in, 55-58
Starter in championship meet, duties of, 350
Starting position
  assuming, 47
  for back crawl stroke, 120
  ideal form showing, 120
Stroke
  side underarm, 2-3
  Trudgeon, 2, 3
  whole
    learning, 34
    for sprint crawl stroke, practicing, 96
Strokes
  four competitive, comparison of speed
    for, 119
  skilled, teaching higher level, 33-35
Submersion, 22
Sucrose in diet, 178
Sugars in diet, 178
Sulfur in diet, 180
Sullivan, Frank, 5
Swimmers
  daily schedule of living for, 176-185
  regular diet for, 176
  special body building exercises for, 187-
    189
  special flexibility exercises for, 186-187
Swimming
  advanced, 43-45
    distance orientation for, 44
    teaching and learning procedures in, 43
  all-stroke Armbruster method for teach-
    ing beginning, 14-26
  historical evolution, 1-11
  instructors for, 339
Swimming meet
  championship
    arrangement of personnel and equip-
      ment for, 354
    ballot system in, 351
    duties of
      announcer in, 353
      clerk of course in, 353
      clerk of records in, 353
      diving officials in, 353
      doctor in, 353
      inspectors in, 352
      press steward in, 353
      referee in, 350
      scorer in, 353
      starter in, 350
      timers in, 351
    judges in, 351

Swimming meet—cont'd
  championship—cont'd
    league
      duties of manager for, 348-350
      training two weeks before, 209
    officials for, 348
    preparation for, 348-355
    checkoff lists, 343-346
    conducting, 343-363
    officials' kits, 347
    summer age-group, 355-363
      announcer for, 359
      awards for, 361
      clean-up for, 361
      clerk of course for, 359
      committee chairmen for, 355
      director, time chart to assist, 356
      entries and programs for, 362
      food for, 362
      general help for, 361
      head recorder for, 359
      officials for, 358
      public relations for, 362
      publicity for, 361
      recorder's table for, 363
      schedule of events for, 358
      scratch meeting for, 362
      supplies for, 359-361
      things to do day of, 346
      things to do week before, 345
      time card for, 357
Swimming pool; *see* Pool
Swimming season, things to do in prepara-
  tion for, 343-345

T

Take-off in relay racing, technique of, 173
Tank for scuba diving, 328
  regulator for, 328
  valves for, 328
Teaching, successful, professional aid for,
  25-26
Thevenot, M., 1
Thiamine in diet, 181
Time card for summer age-group meets, 357
Time chart to assist summer age-group
  meet director, 356
Timers in championship meet, duties of, 351
Tower diving; *see* Diving, tower, 290
Tower take-off, 300
Training, 192-219
  in championship period, 209-219
  dual-meet period
    first week, 203
    fourth through twelfth week of, 205
    second week, 204
  equipment, checklist of, 344
  interval and repetition, 205
  one length wave in, 212
  postcompetition period, 210
  precompetition period, 194-203
    eighth week of, 203

Training—cont'd
  precompetition period—cont'd
    first through third week of, 195
    fourth through sixth week of, 197-198
    seventh week of, 198-203
  program, 193
  repetition and interval method schedule
      for, 206
  summer period, 210-212
    championship, 219
    practice schedules
      first week of, 213
      second week precompetition, 214
      precompetition, 212-216
      third week, 215
    swim meet period, 216-219
      sample week's workout during, 217
  swimming across pool in, 212
  two-lane weave in, 212
  two weeks before league championship
      meet, 209
  whole pool weave in, 212
Treading water, 24
Trip away from home, 189
Trudge-crawl kick, 5
Trudgeon, J., 2
  era, 2
  kick, 2, 3
  stroke, 2, 3
Tumble turn, 135
Turn
  breast stroke, 156-158
    approach to wall in, 156
    glide and stroke in, 158
    tuck in, 156
  distance, common error in execution of,
      116
  head-out, 88-89
  lateral, 86-91
  lateral-spin, for distance crawl stroke, 113

Turn—cont'd
  no-hand-touch somersault, 91
  somersault, 89-90
  sprint, mechanics of, 86-91
  tumble, back crawl stroke, 135
Twist dives; *see under* Dive

U

Ultraviolet rays, 190

V

Vitamins in diet, 180-181

W

Water
  adjusting to, 18
    by beginner, 16-22
  balance for pool, 341
  deep
    fear of, 22
    jumping from deck into, 24
    orientation, 22-24
  disinfection of, 339
  drill
    for back crawl stroke, 139-141
    for breast stroke, 159-160
    for sprint crawl stroke, 94
      without kick board, 96
  orientation, 16
  shipping, 18
  testing and records for, 340
  treading, 24
Weight belt for skin diving, 324
Weight chart, 189
Weissmuller, Johnny, 5, 6, 8
Whole stroke; *see* Stroke, whole
Wickman, Alec, 3
Wynman, Nicolas, 1

Y

YMCA lifesaving certificate, 338